The Impact of World Recession on Children

Other Titles of Interest

ABDULLAH, T. and ZEIDENSTEIN, S.
Village Women of Bangladesh: Prospects for Change

DAMMANN, E.
The Future in Our Hands

EPSTEIN, T. S. and JACKSON, D.
The Feasibility of Fertility Planning

GILES, H. and SAINT-JACQUES, B.
Language and Ethnic Relations

LOZOYA, J.
The Social and Cultural Issues of the New International Economic Order

MKANGI, G.
The Social Cost of Small Families and Land Reform

SALAS, R.
International Population Assistance: The First Decade

SHAFFER, H. G.
Women in the Two Germanies

Related Journal

World Development*
The multi-disciplinary journal devoted to the study and promotion of world development.
Chairman of the Editorial Board: Paul Streeten, Center for Asian Development
Studies, Boston University, USA

*Free specimen copy available on request

The Impact of World Recession on Children

Edited by

RICHARD JOLLY

and

GIOVANNI ANDREA CORNIA

PERGAMON PRESS

OXFORD · NEW YORK · TORONTO · SYDNEY · PARIS · FRANKFURT

U.K.	Pergamon Press Ltd., Headington Hill Hall, Oxford OX3 0BW, England
U.S.A.	Pergamon Press Inc., Maxwell House, Fairview Park, Elmsford, New York 10523, U.S.A.
CANADA	Pergamon Press Canada Ltd., Suite 104, 150 Consumers Road, Willowdale, Ontario M2J 1P9, Canada
AUSTRALIA	Pergamon Press (Aust.) Pty. Ltd., P.O. Box 544, Potts Point, N.S.W. 2011, Australia
FRANCE	Pergamon Press SARL, 24 rue des Ecoles, 75240 Paris, Cedex 05, France
FEDERAL REPUBLIC OF GERMANY	Pergamon Press GmbH, Hammerweg 6, D-6242 Kronberg-Taunus, Federal Republic of Germany

First edition 1984

Library of Congress Cataloging in Publication Data

Main entry under title:
The impact of world recession on children.
1. Child welfare—Addresses, essays, lectures.
2. Children—Economic conditions—Addresses, essays, lectures. 3. Economic policy—Addresses, essays, lectures. 4. Depressions—Addresses, essays, lectures
I. Jolly, Richard. II. Cornia, Giovanni Andrea.
HV715.I475 1984   362.7′042   84-14694

British Library Cataloguing in Publication Data

The impact of world recession on children.
1. Children—Care and hygiene
2. Economic history—1971-
I. Jolly, Richard II. Cornia, Giovanni Andrea
613′.0432   RJ47
ISBN 0-08-031329-9

Published as a special issue of the journal *World Development,* Volume 12, Number 3, and supplied to subscribers as part of their subscription. Also available to non-subscribers.

Printed in Great Britain by A. Wheaton & Co. Ltd., Exeter

Dedication: To Dudley Seers

Dudley Seers took part in the two-day workshop which launched this study, wrote with colleagues at the Institute of Development Studies at the University of Sussex the methodological note which set its frame and were it not for his death in March 1983, would have participated in the drafting group which prepared the main report. It is appropriate therefore to dedicate this study to his memory.

For other reasons, too, a dedication of this study to Dudley Seers is fitting. Although Dudley had not undertaken previous work for UNICEF, his contributions to ILO, ECA, ECLA and other agencies of the United Nations had over the years been marked by several characteristics: he took on with gusto assignments which enabled him to analyse developments in the real world, contributing his insights and intellectual innovations not in the abstract, but in relation to some actual country situation; he always showed a healthy disrespect for − some would say clear antagonism to − conventional indicators of development, especially growth rates of GNP per capita, but a questing professionalism in exploring alternative measures and concepts; his frame of reference for development studies embraced both developed and developing countries − while warning that any simple division of them into such categories as developed, developing and socialist was misleading; his approach was inter-disciplinary and international − countries, for Dudley, were part of the actual world economy, never existing as separate entities of their own.

Dudley's style and approach to work for the international agencies was also distinctive. He was at his best working with an international team, sharing jokes and comradeship, setting impossible timetables for drafts to be completed − but then by example, organization and support ensuring that they were met. (He would have liked the fact that this report was completed just under a year after the first workshop was held.) His ideal team combined young and old, new and experienced, some from within the UN, some from outside, including if possible one or two persons with sharply contrasting viewpoints or 'positions'. For the ILO employment missions he headed, Dudley introduced the rule that he would only take on the leadership providing, in the final analysis, he alone was responsible for their content − thereby bypassing the bureaucratic caution and excessive sensitivities which he felt too often blurred the message and analysis of many international documents. But Dudley was a realist, not a romantic − and he exercised these responsibilities to produce documents which were innovative but professional, provocative but not embarrassing. And as a point of professional integrity, the contribution of every team member was fully acknowledged.

These are high standards, far from the norms in professional work, international or national.

'Children − Main Victims of Recession' was Dudley's suggested title for this study. This subject matter, and the dearth of earlier writing on this theme, give ample opportunity to follow Dudley's innovative approaches and example. We may not have fully succeeded but our tribute to Dudley is that we have tried.

Contents

List of Figures

List of Tables

List of Contributors

Mr. Oscar Altimir
Chief, Statistics Division,
U.N. Economic Commission for Latin America,
Casilla 179-D, Santiago,
Chile
Tel: 458068

Professor Ugo Colombino
Associate Professor of Statistics,
Via Magenta 50,
Torino, Italy 10100
Tel: (011) 570088

Mr. Giovanni Andrea Cornia
Socio-economic Analyst,
UNICEF,
New York
Tel: (212) 754 8016

Dr. Elizabeth J. Coulter
Professor,
Dept of Biostatics,
School of Public Health,
University of North Carolina,
Chapel Hill, NC 27514
Tel: (919) 966 1107

Mr. José Camarós Fabián
Instituto de Desarrollo de la Salud,
Apartado No. 9082,
Zona 9, Havana,
Cuba
Tel: 44 7261

Mr. Alejandro Foxley
Executive Director,
CIEPLAN,
Av. Colon,
3494 Casilla,
1649 C9, Santiago 8,
Chile
Tel: 2283262

Professor Reginald Herbold Green
Institute of Development Studies,
University of Sussex,
Brighton BN1 9RE,
Sussex, England
Tel: (0273) 606261

Mr. Godfrey Gunatilleke
Marga Institute,
61 Isipathana Mawatha,
Colombo 5, Sri Lanka

Ms. Rachelle Hertenberg
Consultant,
UNICEF,
New York
Tel: (212) 662 8596

Dr. Kumari Jayawardena
c/o UNICEF,
Colombo, Sri Lanka,
Tel: 84610

Dr. Richard Jolly
Deputy Executive Director,
UNICEF,
New York,
Tel: (212) 754 7855

Mr. G. I. O. M. Kurukulasuria
Marga Institute,
61 Isipathana Mawatha,
Colombo 5, Sri Lanka

Mr. Roberto B. M. Macedo
Universidade de São Paulo,
Fac. de Economia,
C. Postal 11498 — AG. Pinheiros,
0100 São Paulo — SP. Brazil
Tel: (11) 212 5471

Mr. José Cobas Manriquez
Instituto de Desarrollo de la Salud,
Apartado No. 9082,
Zona 9, Havana,
Cuba
Tel: 44 7261

Dr. C. Arden Miller
Professor and Chairman,
Dept of Maternal and Child Health,
School of Public Health,
University of North Carolina,
Chapel Hill, NC 27514
Tel: (919) 966 2017

Dr. Sudipto Mundle
Associate Fellow,
Centre for Development Studies,
Trivandrum,
Kerala, India
Tel: 8412 8881 8884

D. José Gutiérrez Múniz
Instituto de Desarrollo de la Salud,
Apartado No. 9082,
Zona 9, Havana,
Cuba
Tel: 44 7261

Professor K. N. Raj
Director,
Centre for Development Studies,
Trivandrum,
Kerala, India
Tel: 8412 8881 8884

Mr. Dagmar Raczynski
Researcher,
CIEPLAN,
Av. Colon,
3494 Casilla,
1649 C9, Santiago 8,
Chile
Tel: 2283262

Professor Hans Singer
Institute of Development Studies,
University of Sussex,
Brighton BN1 9RE,
Sussex, England
Tel: (0273) 606261

Mr. Sang Mok Suh
Senior fellow,
Korean Development Institute,
Seoul, Korea
Tel: 725 2315

Support was also provided by:

Mr. Eduardo Bustelo
Programme and Planning Officer,
UNICEF,
Brasilia, Brazil
Tel: (021) 240 5176

Mr. Jim Himes
Chief,
Americas Section,
UNICEF,
New York
Tel: (212) 754 7988

Mr. Sarup Jha
Word Processing Clerk,
UNICEF,
New York
Tel: (212) 754 4421

Mr. Salim Lone
Editor,
UNICEF,
New York
Tel: (212) 754 3361

Mr. Carlos Massad
ECLA,
Avenida Dag Hammarskjold,
Casilla 169 D
Santiago, Chile

Ms. Sharon Meager
Editor,
UNICEF,
New York
Tel: (212) 754 6812

Miss Josephine Rajasegera
Secretary,
UNICEF,
New York
Tel: (212) 754 8016

Professor G. Solimano
Professor of Public Health and Nutrition,
Center for Population and Family Health,
Columbia University,
60 Haven Avenue,
New York, NY 10032
Tel: (212) 694 5796

Editors' Introduction[*]

RICHARD JOLLY and GIOVANNI ANDREA CORNIA
UNICEF, New York

The world economy is in recession – the deepest, the most sustained and the most widespread since the 1930s. There are glimmers of recovery in the industrial countries, but most serious economic analysts anticipate that rates of growth and levels of economic activity for the rest of the 1980s will remain well below those of the 1960s. As the 1983 World Economic Survey[1] put it, recovery is 'plagued with uncertainties' and the 'outlook for most developing countries is bleak'.

In all that has been written about world recession, the preoccupations have been overwhelmingly and narrowly economic. The analysis has focused on inflation and interest rates, debt and trade deficits, unemployment and declining incomes. Few have investigated the human consequences in more than a superficial manner.[2] Not a single international study has analysed the recession's impact on the most vulnerable half of the world's population – the children.

The need for bringing out clearly the linkages between world economic conditions and child welfare has thus become even more urgent in the last few years. The world scale of current child distress makes it artificial to restrict the analysis of causes to the national level, because of the extent, duration and widespread nature of the world recession and economic setback.

Typically, the relations between child welfare and world economic conditions have not received much attention even from those professionals (medical and social workers, teachers, etc.) who are closely concerned with child survival and welfare. Children's problems are often approached within narrow perspectives which ignore the deeper causes of their unsatisfactory conditions, which attack individual rather than social symptoms and causes. This often leads therefore to inadequate policy analysis and action. Even when a clear emphasis is put on social causes, it is typically within a *national* frame of political, economic and social conditions, rarely linked to the international. Though this neglect of the international may arguably be justified in industrial countries with their higher levels of income, it is hardly justifiable in countries with far more limited resources and where the impact of world recession on these resources may be proportionately much greater.

An international study incorporating such analysis is important as a guide to policy. Children are the generation of the future and the adequacy of the provision made for their health, education and welfare is an important determinant of the future of each country. How is this provision being affected by recession? Rarely has experience in different countries or regions been contrasted to assess the impact of recession or to see how the consequences can be avoided or offset by appropriate national or international action.

1. BACKGROUND TO THIS STUDY

It was this lack of evidence and discussion which prompted UNICEF in 1982 to embark on a study of the impact of world recession on children. The methodological issues and difficulties were first explored in a workshop and subsequently in a paper prepared by Dudley Seers and colleagues at the Institute of Development Studies, University of Sussex, UK. These underlined many of the complexities in tracing through the linkages between world economic changes and the impact on children in particular countries. They identified three major linkages likely to dominate the relationships:

– the impact on household income, via changes in employment, wages and prices;
– the impact on rural peasant incomes, via changes in agricultural incomes and consumer prices;
– the impact on government expenditures, especially on social services.

The methodological discussion also underlined the very great difficulty of separating out the effects of world economic recession from the influences of other economic changes

---

* The views expressed in this paper are those of the authors and not necessarily those of UNICEF.

occurring at the same time. For this reason, it was decided to set the frame of the study as 'the impact on children of the main economic changes since 1970, with particular emphasis on the period since 1978'.

Estimates of GNP and income per capita are available routinely for most economies of the world. But because of lack of comparable statistical attention to the human dimensions of development, there are still wide areas of the world for which there is no reliable information on levels of child mortality, morbidity, nutrition or welfare, let alone up-to-date statistics on how these levels have changed over recent years.

economies' (Brazil and Korea). Three middle-income Latin American countries for which recent and reliable data are available are included, each having followed sharply contrasting economic strategies over the last decade: Chile, which has pursued a strict 'monetarist' and 'free market' strategy; Costa Rica, with its more pragmatic and welfare state approach; and Cuba, following a socialist development path. Case studies on the United States and Italy were also commissioned to explore the results of recession in major industrial countries.

Shortened versions of nine of the case studies (covering 11 countries) are included in this

Table I.1. *Country case studies in relation to income level, dependence on external trade and finance, and infant mortality*

	High dependence on external trade and finance		Less dependence on external trade and finance	
	High infant mortality rate	Low infant mortality rate	High infant mortality rate	Low infant mortality rate
High income		Italy		USA
Middle income	Brazil Nigeria	Chile Costa Rica Korea Cuba		
Low income	Zambia Tanzania	Sri Lanka	India	

In consequence, any study of the impact of a world recession on children has to adopt a partial and more impressionistic approach. The UNICEF approach was to commission a number of country case studies in an attempt to piece together a picture of how recession has affected children in different areas of the world. Twelve countries were selected to give a wide geo-graphical distribution and to represent different socio-economic situations, judged by the country's income per head, its trade and finan-cial dependence on the world economy and its infant mortality rate. A final determining factor was the availability of data.

The countries selected include one least-developed country (Tanzania), two highly contrasting low-income countries (Sri Lanka, small and trade-dependent, and India, very large and insulated with an important industrial sector), a middle-income mineral exporting economy (Zambia), an oil exporter (Nigeria) and two better-off 'newly-industrialized

collection. An additional study by Mahar Mangahas of the Philippines used survey evidence of subjective perceptions of changes in living standards between 1981 and 1982. Although novel and interesting, this study did not provide evidence comparable to the others and was therefore dropped from this collection. A back-ground paper on the impact of adjustment policies was also prepared by Kalyan Vaidya.

In addition to these case studies, the study drew on various international economic reports and sources and on three ILO/JASPA studies on basic needs in Africa: *Tanzania: Basic Needs in Danger* (1982); *Zambia: Basic Needs in an Economy under Pressure* (1981); *Nigeria: First Things First* (1981).

The case studies and the background material were analysed by a UNICEF team in June and July 1983[3] and used to prepare a consolidated study, 'The Impact of World Recession on Children', published as Part II of UNICEF's 1984 Report on the *State of the World's*

Children. This introductory chapter and the article by Cornia providing an overview of the impact largely repeat material in the consolidated study. Apart from this, the other material here presented is original.

2. THE DIFFERENTIATED IMPACT

As the report and case studies document, the burden of recession has not been spread uniformly even amongst the developing countries. There has been an increasing differentiation in the ways different countries, and different regions and social groups within countries, have been affected. Africa seems to have suffered the greatest setbacks, while countries in East and South East Asia seem to have weathered its worst effects with relatively minor dislocations. To a considerable degree, this differentiation has depended upon the strategies countries have chosen to meet the crises, which in turn has determined their adjustments in the social sectors. These adjustments have varied, often sharply, from country to country. Many countries have cut back on social services expenditures; a few have concentrated their resources in one particular area of social welfare at the expense, in part, of other areas, as in Chile; and some, notably South Korea and Cuba from amongst the group of countries studied in this report, have responded by actually accelerating the development of their social service programmes.

Nevertheless, selective evidence from different parts of the world suggests that in most countries significant sections of the nation's children are suffering as one of the consequences of recent economic setbacks. For example, data from Zambia's poorer northern regions indicates that there has been a decline in height-for-age in all four age categories; in Latin America, the number of children treated for severe malnutrition in Costa Rica doubled between 1981 and 1982, while in the state of São Paulo in Brazil, there is a pattern of increasing low-birth-weight babies as well as a significant increase in the number of children given up by their parents because of poverty. Even in the United States, infant mortality rates have increased in 35 cities and some states and areas especially hard hit by recession.

Fortunately, the gravity of the above picture has, to date at least, been moderated by continued improvements in a few areas of child welfare. School enrolments seem generally to have continued to rise, although expenditure **per pupil and** the quality of education appears to be declining. In some countries, attendance rates at health clinics and hospitals have been maintained, sometimes expanded. In most middle-income countries analysed in this study, the gradual, long-term decline in infant mortality as expressed in national averages seems to have continued, until 1982 at least, though usually at a reduced rate.

These points of hope must not be overstated, and in any event they should be balanced by three sobering considerations. First, there is an almost total lack of information about the condition of children in the poorest countries, Africa in particular. This makes it impossible to document the widespread deterioration in nutritional and health status and, possibly, rising infant and child mortality which numerous verbal reports and fragmentary evidence suggest.

Second, there is considerable evidence, explored in the summary article by Cornia, of time lags that may operate between the shock of economic cutback and its consequences for child services and child health. The worst effects of the recession may therefore not yet have been fully felt or recorded. Third, while the level of health understanding and the provision of basic social services has in some countries risen to a point where *temporary* setbacks will not reverse the gains in child mortality rates, the end of the current recession will not, by itself, eliminate the structural problems plaguing the world and national economies which contribute to child and human poverty. The analysis in the article by Raj shows that the major causes underlying the present recession are deep-seated — far deeper in cause than the efficacy of any remedies at present being applied. For children in impoverished families, in other words, the end of the recession by itself will not be enough. Structural changes and restoring momentum to long-term development are vital.

3. LIMITED REACTIONS

Why have these human consequences of recession been so little emphasized so far? A partial answer is that the international *evidence* of the impact so far is limited — and that part of this evidence is an increased *risk* of children dying rather than a demonstrated increase in child mortality. A second clue as to why the human consequences of recession may have been so little emphasized is suggested by a comparison with the 1930s. The existence of social security and welfare systems has greatly moderated the human consequences of unemployment and recession *in the industrialized countries* (notwithstanding the cutbacks in public expenditure and other changes in public policy). The developed-country public has been shielded from many of the personal economic consequences of *their* unemployment and recession — and thus made less sensitive to the impact of recession in developing countries.

In most developing countries, of course, there are few, if any, institutional arrangements to protect people against the consequences of recession and unemployment, let alone of inflation, reduced incomes, low commodity prices, cutbacks in government services and other shortages. Yet these economic difficulties have been occurring in countries many times poorer than the industrialized countries.

This difference may be significant in explaining some of the lack of protest and political response. In industrialized countries, political reaction to rising unemployment has been muted by these social security systems, which have served to shield individuals from some of its consequences. Reaction in developing countries is muted both by limitations on forms and channels of protest and by limited information on those reactions which are taking place. The result internationally is that there has been little protest, let alone presentation, of hard evidence on the human impact of recession. The limited response to long-term demands for international economic reform (such as those presented by the *Brandt Report*) may also have dampened the resolve and effort of some of those wanting to publicize the situation and explore remedial action especially in the present political climate.

4. PRIORITIES FOR ACTION

The main UNICEF report explores priorities for action, emphasizing ways in which the process of economic adjustment can be broadened to avoid the most serious repercussions for children, and at the same time give impetus to long-term development measures which, at relatively low cost, could even *improve* child health and well-being in spite of recession. Both types of action are needed and country experience suggests that when both are combined, the benefits can be very considerable and highly cost-effective.

Within countries, there is both need and opportunity for a wide variety of actions at all levels, from individuals and their families, workers and officials in health services, schools and other community services at local level to officials and leaders, both government and non-government, at regional and national level.

But basic changes in *national and international policy and practice* are also vital because national and international responses to recession, as currently practised, are holding back and often undercutting positive and low-cost remedial action *at lower levels*. Households are less able to cope with the problems of their own children through declining incomes and employment; clinics and schools are less able to respond because their budgets have been cut but overall policy has not been restructured; even productive capacity at local level has commonly been sacrificed, as a by-product of national policy, in spite of widespread evidence of the greater efficiency of small-scale, local-level production in terms of employment creation, capital saving and low levels of important foreign exchange use — the very constraints which are transmitted internationally by recession and which all but the largest or most insulated economies have no choice but to respond to.

5. NEEDED: A BROADER APPROACH TO THE ADJUSTMENT PROCESS

The tendency for governments faced with recession to cut back on child-focused social expenditures arises from many sources, domestic as well as international. But international influence is often critical, especially when linked to the negotiation of an IMF agreement or an international loan. This international influence may be felt in various forms and degrees· as an explicit condition of an agreement, as the technical advice of international experts or as the orthodox wisdom promoted in less formal contacts such as courses on development strategy.

The starting point for change is a broader approach to adjustment policy at both national and international levels. The issue is not whether to adjust but how. In most developing countries, inflationary pressures and rising military expenditures have been an important source of pressure for adjustment — but there have been other sources too, especially declines in export earnings and rising costs of imports. In Africa, the squeeze has been exacerbated by the long-term decline in many economies and in Latin America by the claims of servicing rising debt. But whatever the particular case, government expenditure has been squeezed and, for the reasons given earlier, the squeeze has mostly fallen disproportionately on the social and child-focused sectors. Some adjustment to the squeeze on foreign exchange and government budgets is an unavoidable fact of life for all but the largest and richest countries (where adjustment, when adopted, often reflects domestic choice of policy more than international necessity).

A broader approach to the adjustment process would comprise five elements:

1. First and foremost, a clear recognition of the importance of preserving a minimum level of nutrition, household income (in cash or kind) and basic services for all age groups, as a means towards protecting and maintaining productivity and welfare of the whole population.

2. Second, the maintenance or creation of a network of basic services and support for young children, the most vulnerable section of the population, yet also the one most important for the future of a country and, in most respects, the one least costly to protect.

3. Third, a serious restructuring within the health, education and related social services to achieve maximum cost effectiveness and internal efficiency in the provision of those services. This restructuring should involve a hard-headed review of ways to economize on imported supplies and move efficiently to greater use of local resources in health, education and other services. One also needs to look to the longer-run dimensions of adjustment to ensure a pattern of economic restructuring which can sustain these services from domestic resources.

4. Fourth, more creative reliance on community action and the informal sector, which tend to use more local and low-cost resources and less high-cost and imported supplies. This said, attempts to exploit the benefits of community action too crudely need to be guarded against. If poor communities are left to rely entirely on their own resources for the supply of services when better off communities receive subsidized provision, one can hardly expect an enthusiastic response. In contrast, a combination of community action with public resources has often proved highly effective, as has the use of informal sector production and approaches.

5. Finally, *more* concern with income distribution, *not less* — especially in the sharing of the burden of economic adjustments and cutbacks. The arguments for this are strong, in line with the elementary principles of welfare economics. These are reinforced by the arguments of reducing foreign exchange and increasing employment, since both would be generally encouraged by greater sharing of adjustment.

These five points would add up to more

conscious concern with the longer-run dimensions of adjustment and assisting a pattern of restructuring which can sustain the above services from domestic resources in the longer run.

6. CHILD HEALTH AND SURVIVAL

As a specific example of the above approach, UNICEF is promoting a cluster of low-cost, highly effective actions in the field of child and maternal care which, the evidence suggests, could greatly increase infant and young child survival and development in spite of recession. These include action within the health sector, and beyond it, to attack the main causes of infant and young child mortality:

1. Oral rehydration therapy — a simple and inexpensive method of preventing the dehydration which is induced by diarrhoeal infections and which, with an estimated five million young victims a year, is the leading cause of child death in the modern world.

2. Expanded immunization — using newly improved vaccines to prevent the six major communicable diseases of childhood — measles, tetanus, whooping cough, diphtheria, poliomyelitis and tuberculosis — which kill, it is estimated, an additional five million children a year and disable some five million more.

3. The promotion of breastfeeding and better weaning practices.

4. Growth monitoring — the use of child growth charts as part of community systems for encouraging better health and nutrition through regular weighing of children, with the provision of advice and remedial support for children who are not progressing satisfactorily.

This, of course, is not an exclusive list of needs responses. In each country or community, the basic causes of mortality and morbidity need to be identified and attacked. Nor should one imagine that each cause can be separately isolated. Most child mortality in developing countries is the result of an interaction between poor nutrition and infection or disease, in which multiple causes are involved, often over an extended period. Because action along the above lines, within the context of primary health care, would also be synergistic, it would tackle the main interacting causes of infant and child death — and thus, it is estimated, be able to reduce infant mortality by one-third to one-half in the developing countries over the next decade or so.

The economic point is that priority action is economically feasible because the cost of implementing these priority actions within a system of primary health care is not large in relation to the health budgets of most countries. Vital support is required in information and motivation — but this too need not be costly, if some of the existing capacity of radio and television is turned to such use and the energy and organizing structures of government and non-government organizations (like churches, youth groups, women's organizations, political parties and the school systems) provide support. In spite of recession, therefore, such actions are feasible — and adjustment and restructuring in response to recession needs to ensure that the resources to implement such action are maintained or made available.

NOTES

1. United Nations, *1983 World Economic Survey* (1983), pp. 5 and 8.

2. Among the few, should be noted: UN Centre for Social Development and Humanitarian Affairs, Integration and Welfare Branch, *The Social Impact of Economic Recession on Specific Population Groups during the 1970s and early 1980s* (1983, mimeo); and UN Department of International Economic and Social Affairs, *1982 Report on the World Social Situation* (1982). The *World Development Report 1980* of the World Bank should also be mentioned for its useful focus on 'Poverty and Human Development', though this was essentially concerned with issues and policies of human development in general, not specifically to those related to recession.

3. The team consisted of Eduardo Bustelo, Andrea Cornia, Jim Himes, Richard Jolly, Carlos Massad, Professor K. N. Raj, Professor H. W. Singer, Dr Giorgio Solimano. Josephine Rajasagera, Maria Sarasola and Eileen O'Connor assisted with typing, Salim Lone with editing, and Rachelle Hertenberg with both research assistance and editing.

The Causes and Consequences of World Recession

K. N. RAJ*

Centre for Development Studies, Trivandrum, Kerala, India

Summary. – Diverging trends in productivity since the late 1960s, if not before, between the United States and its competitor countries, lie at the heart of the global slump. Over the 1970s, these trends began to be reflected in large deficits in commodity trade – but the tendency was to resolve them by means other than increased investment: at first devaluation, later restrictive monetary policies and rising unemployment. None of these policies helped significantly to achieve the needed structural adjustments but they did serve to aggravate the position and prospects of the poorer developing countries. By the 1980s, this became a crisis situation of serious proportions. Often drought and war or civil strife have reinforced economic difficulties, compounded further in many countries by rising debt service obligations and declining real commodity prices.

This combination of external and internal difficulties certainly contributed in the poorer countries to the slowdown, since the 1960s, in reducing infant mortality and in tackling basic child survival and development issues. The impressive progress in reducing IMR by an average of 2% or more a year by a number of developing countries, however, shows what can be done. Although rising expenditure is by no means a sufficient condition for child progress, declining expenditures and severe balance-of-payments problems greatly constrain programmes for expanding child services.

1. INTRODUCTION

While there are differences of opinion on the factors responsible for the present world economic crisis, particularly in the relative weightage attached to some of them, it is widely accepted that a major underlying factor has been the emergence of very wide differences in the rates of productivity growth in manufacturing as between the most industrially advanced countries from about the middle of the 1960s. What has lent it special significance from the global point of view is that, as a consequence, the rate of growth of productivity in the 1970s has been lower in the United States, which occupies a pivotal position in the world economy, than in any of its leading industrial competitors. Not only that but the rate of productivity growth in the United States has itself been declining at a very rapid rate during this period, in fact from no less than 3.1% per annum between 1948 and 1967 to 2.3% between 1967 and 1973 and as low as 0.8% between 1973 and 1981.

The reasons for the decline in the rate of growth of productivity in the United States have been the subject of much speculation and controversy and are no doubt numerous and complex. However, as will be evident from the estimates given below, there is little doubt that the success its industrial competitors have had in achieving much higher levels of productivity growth was not unrelated to the very much higher rates of investment they have been able to sustain. (See Table II.1.) This stands to reason, as it is only through fresh investment that successive improvements in technology can be assimilated in the industrial structure, even though increases in productivity can be (and indeed should be) also achieved through improvements in management, in the educational level and health of workers, in their discipline and social commitment, and in various other ways.

Considerations of this nature, highly pertinent to the crisis that was developing, were, however, generally overlooked by policymakers at the political level and even by many economic analysts. Therefore, when these trends in productivity began to be reflected in growing trade imbalances as between the most industrially advanced countries of the world, more particularly in the form of large deficits

---

* The views expressed in this paper are those of the author and not necessarily those of UNICEF. The title suggested by the author for this paper was 'The Causes and Consequences of the Global Slump'.

Table II.1. *Productivity and fixed capital investment in some advanced industrial economies, 1971–80*

	Growth rate of output per hour of manufacturing (%) 1971–80	Investment in fixed capital as percentage of GDP, 1971–80	
		Gross	Net
Japan	7.4	32.9	19.9
Germany	4.9	22.8	11.8
France	4.8	22.9	12.2
United Kingdom	2.9	19.2	8.1
United States	2.5	18.4	6.6

in the balance of commodity trade of the United States, the tendency was to resolve them through other means. Initially, recourse was taken to mere devaluation of the dollar, a process that was greatly helped by throwing away the economic logic and discipline imposed by the international monetary system devised at Bretton Woods in 1944 and launching in its place a new system of free currency floats; the experiment lasted from 1971 to 1979. However, this policy was reversed from 1980 under a new dispensation based on a different political and economic philosophy; instead, severe restrictions were placed on domestic monetary and credit expansion (in the United States as well as in the United Kingdom), and high rates of unemployment have been allowed to develop, presumably in the belief that this would at least help to prevent money wage rates in industrial employment being pushed up at a higher rate than productivity, raise profit margins thereby, and hopefully also induce those in employment to raise their productivity.

For a variety of reasons, some of which we shall briefly touch upon, neither of these policies has so far helped the United States to any significant degree in bringing about the structural adjustments needed for resolving its trade and payment problems on a stable basis. At the same time, precisely because it occupies a strategic position in the world economy through its dominant role in global trade and finance, these policies have vastly aggravated the problems of other countries, particularly of the poorer and less developed among them.

Thus, while devaluation of the dollar did help the United States initially to increase the volume of its exports by no less than 33% between 1971 and 1973, it also had the effect of fuelling inflationary pressures all round. The sharp rise in prices experienced the world over in the immediately following years no doubt occurred partly for other fortuitous reasons

such as the heavy imports of grain by the Soviet Union which raised its price in the international grain markets, and the decision of the OPEC countries at about the same time to raise oil prices precipitously (partly in order to compensate themselves for the secular deterioration in the terms of trade of petroleum relative to manufactures which, for lack of an appropriate corrective mechanism, had been allowed to go on at a rate of no less than 3.4% between 1955 and 1970).

The policies followed by the United States during this period did however substantially add to global inflation and permit it to ignore some of the important structural adjustments within its economy. For instance, the non-convertibility of the dollar and its wide acceptability helped the United States to finance its oil imports at the higher prices without any difficulty, since most of what was paid out in the current account of its balance of payments came back to it in the capital account in the form of dollar deposits. Moreover, the complete removal of controls on capital outflows from the United States in 1974 led to further increase in the supply of dollars for the euro-currency markets; and these markets, not being amenable to control by anyone under any conditions, became also a factor stimulating and supporting waves of speculation in commodity markets all over the world. All this led to loss of confidence in the dollar as a financial asset towards the end of the 1970s, and therefore to flights of capital away from it, as was reflected in the unprecedented rise in the price of gold in world markets to over $800 in 1979.

It was in this context that the policies were changed in a more conservative direction with a strong 'monetarist' orientation. Not only were limits set on monetary and credit expansion within the United States but government expenditures were pruned in almost all spheres, except defence, and more particularly in social services and developmental aid to low-income countries. The dollar has also been allowed to appreciate sharply in response to large inflows of capital (stimulated initially by the high interest rates offered), though this has seriously affected the competitive position of US manufactured products within the country and outside. These measures have therefore an obviously strong contractionist bias, indeed a non-developmental bias except in regard to industries and activities directly or indirectly assisted by the rapidly expanding defence outlays.

High interest rates have no doubt helped to check speculative holdings of commodity stocks and thus lower prices of the commodities so affected. But these have been largely of primary products facing weak demand from the richer countries such as tropical beverages, some agricultural raw materials (like rubber), and food products such as sugar. The prices of most manufactured products, which are usually fixed in relation to costs and therefore often raised in response to increasing under-utilization of capacity, have been continuing to rise, particularly in the cases of machinery, equipment and other capital goods (such as steel) required by the poorer countries of the world for their development. On the price front, therefore, the barter terms of trade have turned against the developing countries in the course of the last two years, unlike in the 1970s when the terms of trade of primary commodities with respect to manufactures did not deteriorate markedly (except for countries heavily dependent on exports of metals and certain other products such as tea).

At the same time the high interest rates in the United States have strongly checked the revival of investment in fixed capital in manufacturing industry. This indirectly accentuated the under-utilization of even the existing installed capacity in capital goods industries (such as in steel) and thereby induced further postponement of the needed upgrading of technology all round. The other advanced market economies in the world have also had to maintain interest rates at relatively high levels, for fear of large outflows of capital to the United States; and since the currencies of these countries do not enjoy the special status that the dollar has in the international financial system, any attempt on their part to reflate their economies independently runs the serious risk of heavy loss of foreign exchange reserves (as France has discovered to its cost). Caught in this bind, contractionary pressures generated by the policies adopted from 1980 have since then led to sharp reductions in rates of growth of output in almost all the developed industrial economies of the world, raised unemployment rates to levels higher than at any time since the Great Depression of the 1930s, and thereby transmitted similar pressures to the poorer developing countries, particularly those closely linked with the advanced industrial economies through the network of international trade and finance.

Consequently, since 1980, the disorder that began to develop in the world economy from the early 1970s and manifested itself in various ways through that decade has taken a very much more serious turn. Though sharp rises in the price of oil and of grain and the generally high rates of inflation had imposed considerable hardships on people in almost all countries in the 1970s, and though there was some deceleration in rates of growth of output in the industrially advanced countries during the first half of this decade (compared to the 1960s), the overall rates of growth of output in both the developed and developing market economies were high enough to prevent decline in per capita output and income. Moreover, some of the poorer developing economies that could export oil (like those of Indonesia and Nigeria) gained significantly from improvement in their terms of trade; and even others adversely affected by the oil price hike could secure loans from various sources (particularly the 'newly industrializing countries' which were able to secure loans on a generous scale from euro-dollar markets through the agency of multinationals) for tiding over their payments problems without excessive adjustment difficulties. All this has changed in the 1980s, and not only have rates of growth of output turned negative in many countries (both developed and developing) but the terms of trade have also moved sharply against most of the developing countries (particularly those dependent on exports of primary products); and those among them that had earlier borrowed heavily are not only burdened now with debt servicing problems on an unprecedented scale (particularly on account of the high interest rates they are required to pay and shorter periods for which the loans are being extended) but by strongly contractionist policies imposed on them by their creditors under the leadership of the International Monetary Fund. What was hitherto only a disorder has thus now turned into a crisis of very serious proportions for developing countries and in fact for the entire world economy. Therefore, we need to pay particular attention to the years since 1980.

2. DIFFERENTIATED IMPACT ON DEVELOPING COUNTRIES

It is in this broad context that we need to consider the different situations in which different groups of countries are placed on account of differences in the levels of income, in the extent of their vulnerability to external pressures transmitted to them through the network of international trade and finance, in the progress they have already made in building up health and educational facilities (particularly for women and children in respect of their vital needs), and thus in the choices that are open, or *not* open, to them in sheltering the younger generation from the economic blizzards now blowing.

It will be seen from Table II.2 that the decline in the rate of growth of output since 1980, though common to both developed and developing economies, has been much sharper in the case of the latter.

developing countries in general were adversely affected by the disorder in the world economy in the 1970s, though no doubt many were (particularly in the African continent) hurt by the hike in oil prices, uncompensated in any other way, as well as by other price movements (such as of metals on the one hand and of machinery on the other). The poorer sections in all countries suffered from the waves of inflationary rise in prices of essentials. The more serious adverse turn took place only from 1980.

This adverse turn itself has evidently not affected the rate of growth of output in South Asia and East Asia so much as in Africa and Latin America (including the Caribbean). This is perhaps explained by (a) the two sub-continental economies of China and India, which have been much less vulnerable to external pressures exerted through international trade and finance and have continued to grow at about the same rate as earlier; and (b) the

Table II.2. *Annual rate of growth of GDP per capita of developed market and developing countries by region (at constant 1980 prices)*

Year	Developed market economies	Latin America	Africa	West Asia	South and East Asia	All developing countries
1972	4.2	4.1	0.4	10.6	3.0	3.6
1973	5.3	5.5	2.3	10.0	6.3	4.9
1974	−0.2	3.5	0.3	6.3	1.4	2.6
1975	−1.1	−0.3	−1.3	−1.1	4.1	0.5
1976	4.1	2.0	4.8	6.6	5.6	4.2
1977	2.9	1.7	5.0	3.3	5.3	3.3
1978	3.0	1.4	2.5	−2.7	4.1	1.3
1979	2.6	2.6	3.5	7.0	0.5	3.1
1980	0.7	2.8	1.0	−10.7	3.1	0.1
1981	0.8	−2.0	−4.6	−8.6	3.7	−1.4
1982	−0.9	−4.1	−4.3	−9.1	1.2	−2.7
1983*	1.2	5.2	−2.0	−4.9	2.8	−2.8

Source: United Nations Department of International Economic and Social Affairs.
*Data for 1983 are based on preliminary estimates for the first eight months. They are, therefore, highly tentative and subject to subsequent revisions.

It is also evident that, while there was some decline in the rate of growth of output in developing countries in the second half of the 1970s, it was much less sharp during this decade than in the developed countries. In fact the rate of growth of output was not perceptibly lower in the 1970s than in the earlier decade except in the case of mineral product and petroleum exporters (who were, however, more than compensated by improvement in the terms of trade in their favour).

It would be inaccurate therefore to say that

greater resilience displayed by some countries in East and South East Asia, presumably on account of the stimulus and support received from their close relations with the dynamic Japanese economy.

The negative rates of growth of output in West Asia have of course a different interpretation, as they reflect in the main the efforts made by OPEC countries to restrict oil output in order to maintain high prices in the face of falling demand.

A country-by-country analysis shows that

the number of countries in which per capita GDP *output* fell from one year to the next increased from 15 in 1979 to 30 in 1980, 42 in 1981 and 51 in 1982. The number whose per capita *income* has fallen must be presumed to have been still larger — as some of them suffered deterioration in terms of trade — and the impact could have been significant in countries that were relatively export-dependent (say, with exports amounting to 15% or more of their GDP in 1980). On the other hand, in the case of some oil exporters, the recorded declines in output (such as in Venezuela) reflect mainly the policy followed to raise and maintain high prices or (as in the case of Iran and Iraq) abnormal conditions created by war and related conflicts; in either case, since the terms of trade were probably improving for these countries, there will have been no corresponding decline in income.

Of the countries (other than oil exporters) whose output has fallen (and income possibly much more) over the last few years, about two-thirds are in Africa and most of them belong to the low-income group. The rest are mainly in Latin America (including the Caribbean) but in this case mostly in countries belonging to the middle-income group. Only a few economies seem to have been affected so far in Asia, but this assessment might change once the relevant data for countries such as Afghanistan, Bangladesh, Bhutan, Laos, Kampuchea, Nepal and Viet Nam (all belonging to the low-income group) becomes available.

This does not mean of course that these are the only countries that have been adversely affected by the deepening of economic disorder in the world over the last few years. There are many who have managed to prevent declines in the rate of growth of output (such as India and the Philippines) but have suffered substantial deterioration in terms of trade (particularly on account of the rise in oil prices and continuing upward movement in the price of machinery and other capital equipment), and have also had to bear rapidly growing debt-service burdens arising from the loans secured to tide over their adjustment problems in the course of the last decade. In fact the high interest rates that have emerged since 1980 have not only checked the revival of investment in the industrially advanced countries but so severely set back the momentum of development in the less advanced countries of all shades (including those that were doing well until then) that the spectre of a world depression that might last several years, possibly the rest

of this decade, cannot be dismissed any longer as a mere figment of imagination.

Where the severity of the pressures exerted by debt service obligations have posed serious dangers to the international financial system some *ad hoc* relief has no doubt been provided (as in Brazil, Mexico and some other countries recently). The corrective measures required of them in this context have however resulted not only in sharp deceleration in growth rates and in the prospect of long stagnation in these countries but in growing unemployment and substantial cuts in various social service programmes that affect seriously the poorest and most vulnerable sections of society. Others face similar prospects, in some respects worse prospects unless the present global trends are reversed by appropriate changes in policy and supporting international action.

It is of course not in the purely economic aspects of the present crisis that we are interested here; our interest is primarily in the social dimensions, particularly in how the direct and indirect (including off-shore) effects of the economic crisis in different countries have already hurt or are likely to hurt the sound and healthy development of children the world over and create more serious problems in the fairly near future. The growing lack of social concern with such vital issues (even when they are demonstrably relevant to raising productivity in the foreseeable future), and the tendency to brush them aside impatiently as if all that matters now are financial adjustments of the kind considered essential to set right economic problems conceived in a much narrower sense, are clearly symptoms of an even graver moral and intellectual crisis that needs to be faced.

We shall therefore try to indicate which are the countries where least progress has been made over the last two decades in providing protection to children through public health and other related measures and which are the ones that have made much more perceptible progress; how the countries belonging to these groups (differentiated according to the progress made hitherto) stand in relation to their economic status (judged with reference to their income levels); and what therefore are the broad considerations we need to keep in mind in proposing, and hopefully helping to carry through, the policies and programmes that countries placed in different situations might be persuaded to accept for safeguarding most effectively the welfare of their children in the reality of the global economic crisis.

For this purpose we adopt the infant mortality rate (IMR) as a first approximation indicator of achieved child protection through public health and other related measures, just as per capita gross domestic product (GDP) is generally used as a rough indicator of achieved levels of productivity and income. It has several limitations, partly on account of deficiencies in the available statistical data relating to IMR and partly for the reason that this index by its nature does not seem to be very sensitive to short-period changes in the economic and social environment except when they are of a very severe nature (as under conditions of famine or political anarchy). Ideally one should therefore be supplementing it with other health indicators such as data relating to morbidity and various anthropometric measures. However, in the absence of such data for most countries, we take the IMR as the most acceptable of the indices now available for a preliminary classification of countries according to their achievement in this particular sphere.

Since a fairly close relationship has been observed in several countries between decline in crude birth rate and decline in infant mortality rate when the latter touches relatively low levels (around 60 per 1000 births), particularly when it is also associated with relatively high rates of female adult literacy, we also present data on these aspects of social development in these countries (where they are available) in Tables II.3 and II.4 relating to low and middle income economies.

It will be seen that, over the two decades 1960–80, middle-income developing economies have generally had perceptibly higher rates of growth of output (i.e. of GDP) than low-income economies (with of course some exceptions such as Jamaica, Senegal and Congo among the former and Pakistan, Malawi and Tanzania among the latter); and that a much higher proportion of these (over 60%) had also succeeded in lowering the infant mortality rates to below 100, compared to only about 1 out of 10 in the case of low-income economies. In fact, approximately 2 out of 3 in the latter group had infant mortality rates higher than 120, and one-half of them rate higher than 150, even in 1980. It is therefore clear that there is a significant difference in the achieved health status of children as between the middle-income and low-income economies when the infant mortality rate is taken as the indicator.

This does not mean, however, that such improvement in the health status of children is dependent largely, or even primarily, on higher income per capita. For, as is well known, a great deal depends on how income is distributed within society and how much priority is given to the development of basic health and educational facilities. This is well illustrated not only by the relatively low infant mortality rates achieved in Sri Lanka, China and Madagascar (all belonging to the low-income group) but the markedly high rates still prevailing in 1980 in countries such as Liberia, Nigeria, Bolivia, Mauritania, Senegal, Congo and Algeria despite their belonging to the middle-income group and despite many of them achieving relatively high rates of economic growth in the two preceding decades. The deplorable state of child welfare in many of these countries is clearly attributable to a large extent to internal policies, and to the underlying social and political structures, and only in part due to the economic pressures exerted by developments outside. This is evident in its starkest form in some of the very high-income oil exporting countries.

The most serious cases as of now are no doubt the countries in which the infant mortality rate was 200 or over in 1960 and has been brought down at rates of less than 1% per annum in the course of the following two decades, namely Malawi, Guinea, Afghanistan, Mali, Upper Volta, Yemen and Angola (of which only the last two belong to the middle-income group). There are also a number of other countries in which infant mortality rates in 1980 were still over 150, such as Benin, Bhutan, Chad, Ethiopia, Somalia and Senegal.

The record of a number of countries, which have been able to bring down infant mortality rates at rates of 1¾ to 2% per annum, shows however how much can be achieved within relatively short periods. To this group belong not only China and Sri Lanka (which are well-known cases) but Togo, Haiti, Burma, Viet Nam, Tanzania and Uganda among the low-income group and Indonesia, Malaysia, Syria, Venezuela, Honduras, El Salvador, Guatemala, Jamaica, Uruguay, Paraguay, Costa Rica, Trinidad and Tobago, Chile, Philippines, Thailand, Kenya and several others belonging to the middle-income group. It will be noticed that in many of them the birth rates have also been falling quite rapidly, particularly where relatively high rates of female adult literacy have been associated with low infant mortality rates.

No doubt much more needs to be done than merely lowering infant mortality rates and birth rates. There may still persist high rates of morbidity which drain the vitality and vigour of growing children, seriously affecting their physical and intellectual development and

Table II.3. *Infant mortality rates and related indices of low-income developing economies*

	Annual average* growth rate of GDP		Infant mortality rate† (per 1000 births)			Female adult literacy	Crude birth rate†		
	1960–70	1970–80	1960	1970	1980	rate‡ 1980 (%)	1960	1970	1980
A. *Low-income economies (export-dependent)*									
Low-income economies other than the least developed									
Zaire	3.4	0.1	154	137	117	37	48	48	46
Sri Lanka	4.6	4.1	76	61	48	82	37	32	28
Togo	8.5	3.4	193	141	115	20	51	49	48
Least developed									
Malawi	4.9	6.3	209	197	179	25	53	52	51
Haiti	−0.2	4.0	194	150	121	24	45	44	42
Guinea	3.5	3.3	213	192	172	14	47	47	46
Niger	2.9	2.7	197	176	151	6	52	51	51
B. *Low-income economies (not-so-export-dependent)*									
Low-income economies other than the least developed									
Burma	2.7	4.6	166	135	107		44	40	39
Kampuchea									
Afghanistan	2.0	4.5	239	217	205	6	50	50	49
Mozambique	4.6	−2.9	166	142	120	23	46	46	45
Benin	2.6	3.3	211	186	160	17	51	50	49
Madagascar	2.9	0.3	114	94	76	55	47	45	45
Burundi	4.4	2.8	153	147	127	15	47	46	45
Pakistan	6.7	4.7	179	146	131	18	47	47	43
China	5.2	5.8	118	75	49		38	32	21
Viet Nam			165	145	106		42	41	40
India	3.4	3.6	173	145	129	29	44	42	35
Least developed									
Laos, PDR			160	148	135	36	43	45	44
Bhutan			200	178	156		47	45	43
Chad	0.5	−0.2	200	179	154	8	46	44	44
Ethiopia	4.4	2.0	180	162	150	5	51	50	50
Nepal	2.5	2.5	200	178	156	6	46	46	44
Somalia			180	162	150	3	47	46	
Mali	3.3	4.9	200	179	160	8	50	49	49
Rwanda	2.7	4.1	151	132	112	39	52	50	50
Upper Volta	3.0	3.5	257	239	219	5	49	48	48
Tanzania	6.0	4.9	159	131	107	23	46	47	46
Haiti	−0.2	4.0	194	150	121	24	46	46	45
Uganda	5.6	−1.7	146	119	101	41	46	44	45
Sudan	1.3	4.4	173	156	131	14	48	46	46
Bangladesh	3.7	3.9	162	150	140	20	50	50	47

Sources. *UN, Projections and Perspectives Studies Branch, DIESA.
†UN, Population Division.
‡UNESCO.

their potential contribution to their societies. The objectives and methods of child welfare promotion must therefore necessarily be broadened as progress is made in blotting out the worst symptoms.

This entire perspective of what can be done for the protection of the future generation and how soon, with such far-reaching possibilities from even the narrow point of view of lowering birth rates and raising productivity in the poorer countries of the world, is in danger of being lost in the midst of the present global economic crisis. Since the richer countries are evidently not going to the roots of the crisis, by raising investment in physical and human capital and thereby reviving growth in productivity where it has slowed down, the period of adjustment involved for revival of economic growth on a stable basis is likely to be much longer than is now being claimed. There may be short phases

Table II.4. *Infant mortality rates and related indices of middle-income developing economies*

	Annual average* growth rate of GDP		Infant mortality rate† (per 1000 births)			Female adult literacy rate‡ 1980 (%)	Crude birth rate†		
	1960–70	1970–80	1960	1970	1980		1960	1970	1980
A. Middle-income economies (export-dependent)									
Middle-income economies moderately or highly dependent on exports (15% of GDP)									
Oil exporters									
Peru	4.9	3.0	173	133	94	73	47	45	39
Algeria	4.3	7.0	170	150	125	24	49	48	47
Indonesia	3.9	7.6	155	130	99	58	47	43	34
Congo	2.7	3.1	176	157	135	44	46	45	45
Nigeria	3.1	6.5	190	164	141	23	52	51	50
Ecuador		8.8	148	115	86	76	47	44	42
Tunisia	4.7	7.5	163	138	107	34	50	44	36
Syria	4.6	10.0	140	107	67	64	47	48	46
Malaysia	6.5	7.8	81	51	33	61	46	39	33
Iran	11.3	2.5	170	143	115	30	47	45	44
Iraq	6.1	12.1	148	111	84	32	49	49	47
Venezuela	6.0	5.0	92	65	45	78	47	41	37
Trinidad and Tobago	4.0	5.1	60	45	35	94	38	28	22
Major exporters of manufactures									
South Korea	8.6	9.5	121	80	59	78	46	32	25
Hong Kong	10.0	9.3	54	23	13	77	36	24	19
Singapore	8.8	8.5	41	24	13	70	42	25	17
Others									
Mauritania		1.7	193	167	149		51	50	50
Zambia	5.0	0.7	159	130	111	58	51	50	49
Bolivia	5.2	4.8	170	158	138	58	46	46	45
Chile	4.5	2.4	117	95	46	91	38	30	25
Ivory Coast	8.0	6.7	179	154	132	24	50	50	48
Kenya	6.0	6.5	145	118	92	35	51	52	54
Senegal	2.5	2.5	186	168	153	14	49	47	48
Angola	4.8	−9.2	215	186	160	19	50	49	48
Liberia	5.1	1.7	199	179	160	18	51	49	49
Honduras	5.3	3.6	153	124	95	62	51	50	47
El Salvador	5.9	4.1	143	112	85	63	49	45	42
Cameroon	3.7	5.6	170	140	115	36	43	42	42
Thailand	8.4	7.2	111	84	59	83	44	42	32
Philippines	5.1	6.3	115	82	51	88	48	41	36
Costa Rica	6.5	5.8	86	66	29	92	48	38	29
Jamaica	4.4	−1.1	71	47	30	93	39	37	28
Guatemala	5.6	5.7	130	102	79	44	49	45	41
B. Middle-income economies (not-so-export-dependent)									
Middle income economies not-so-dependent on exports (15% of GDP)									
Oil exporters									
Mexico	7.2	5.2	96	79	60	80	46	44	38
Major exporters of manufactures									
Brazil	5.4	8.4	125	102	82	73	43	49	33
Argentina	4.2	2.2	62	56	47	94	24	22	21
Others (oil importers)									
Lesotho	5.2	7.9	147	134	120	81	41	40	40
Yemen PDR									
Yemen, Arab Rep.			218	194	170	2	50	49	49
Ghana	2.1	−0.1	149	127	107	37	48	50	48
Panama	7.8	4.0	73	54	36	86	41	38	31
Uruguay	1.2	3.5	53	47	42	95	22	21	20
Colombia	5.1	5.9	102	74	59	84	46	40	32
Paraguay	4.2	8.6	91	67	49	83	44	40	37
North Korea			121	80	59	78	46	32	25

Sources: *UN, Projections and Perspectives Studies Branch, DIESA.
†UN, Population Division.
‡UNECSO.

of economic revival in particular countries, stimulated by factors such as the large budget deficits in the United States, but sustained recovery of the global economy is unlikely until the basic structural adjustments required receive greater attention than they have done so far. During the interim period, the conventional wisdom of policymakers at both the national and the international levels may dictate severe cuts in outlays on health, education and other social welfare programmes of vital importance to the poor and the vulnerable the world over. This is the kind of tragic folly that has now to be faced and combated.

A Survey of Cross-sectional and Time-series Literature on Factors Affecting Child Welfare

GIOVANNI ANDREA CORNIA*

UNICEF, New York

Summary. — This paper reviews the literature on the socio-economic determinants of child welfare. Cross-sectional evidence is first analysed. The relevant literature is subdivided into four groups of studies depending on the main factors influencing child welfare: demographic; related to family circumstances; related to health care and sanitation; and economic. The very few time-series studies on this subject are then examined. While the existing literature does not allow definitive conclusions to be drawn on the predominance or relative importance of these four sets of factors, this paper identifies three related research areas for which particularly severe gaps seem to emerge and for which additional investigation appears necessary. These are: over-time studies, studies for low-income, high-mortality countries of Africa, for middle-income countries and for high-income, high-mortality countries, and studies measuring impact on the basis of indicators of welfare other than infant mortality rates.

1. DEFINING THE SCOPE AND STRUCTURE OF THE SURVEY

Despite the scepticism dominating most of today's literature on child welfare in the Third World, there are few doubts that over the last 30 years infant and child welfare have improved rapidly and substantially in most developing countries. However, the causes of this improvement — or in a few cases the lack of it — are still the subject of lively debate. While the view that medical and health technology was the prime determinant still commands respectable support, it is increasingly accepted that the economic conditions of households — and of a country at large — play a distinct, direct and important role in the welfare of household members, children in particular. A small crop of literature examines the relation between economic fluctuations (whether of internal or external origin) and child status (whether expressed by Infant Mortality Rate or by a 'softer' indicator), but provides no final conclusions. As this area of investigation is still characterized by many not fully understood phenomena and linkages, the need for systematization remains high. Therefore, in view of the complexity and vastness of the subject analysed, a number of points must be made to clarify the structure and scope of this survey of the literature.

(1) The purpose of this research is to examine how the recent *international* economic recession (i.e. external to a country) has affected the well-being of children in a number of countries. However, it was possible in only a few instances to identify clear cause—effect relations between changes in the world economy and the well-being of children in a given nation. One example would be the case of small developing economies (Zambia or Costa Rica, for instance), dependent on trade of a few primary commodities, which have faced sudden, sharp and lasting reversals of their terms of trade. In other cases (for example, some of the poorest countries in Africa), the external recession only deepened the already existing domestic crisis. As it is often methodologically impossible — and illusory — to separate the impact of external changes from domestic economic forces and policies, this survey includes analyses of the effects of all economic reversals (whether due to internal or external factors) on the nutrition,

* The perceptive comments of Richard Jolly on an earlier draft of this paper are gratefully acknowledged. My gratitude goes also to Rachelle Hertenberg and Sharon Meager who skilfully collaborated in the work of bibliographical research and in the editing of this paper and to Josephine Rajasegera and Sarup Jha who patiently reproduced the various drafts. None of these persons bears any responsibility for any remaining error. The views expressed in this paper are those of the author and not necessarily those of UNICEF.

health and overall status of children, the poor and the vulnerable.

(2) This study traces the interrelations between the international environment, the national economy, the creation and use of resources at the household, community and government levels, and the satisfaction of child needs. Perhaps the originality of this study lies in its attempt to examine the net result of *all* these interrelations, as opposed to merely focusing on linkages between two such variables. Some of these linkages have long been analysed and are part of the received theory; in other cases, both intellectual elaboration and empirical evidence are scant. Linkages between international and national economies have been widely explored, for example, in the literature on the *'dependencia'*, on the international transmission of the business cycle, in the studies on the functioning of the international markets for primary commodities and manufactured goods and, more recently, in the works on global interdependence. These linkages have also been the subject of intensive applied research. Large-scale econometric models analyse both the short-term transmission of the business cycle (e.g. the LINK system of models) as well as long-term effects associated with hypothetical changes in the world economy (e.g. Leontief's 'The Future of the World Economy' or the UNITAD system). Although many aspects of the linkages between world and national economies are not fully understood and must be continuously re-examined, there is broad agreement on the nature, direction and intensity of the forces at work. The vast literature on these linkages, therefore, will not be formally surveyed although a few works will be quoted because of their particular relevance to this study.

Because less is known of the relations between economic downturns (whether of external or internal origins), policy adjustments and changes in the conditions of the population — children in particular — the literature on these linkages will be surveyed more comprehensively.

(3) What type of impact of economic recession on children are we trying to measure? Obviously, this impact will vary in intensity and kind according to the situation considered, i.e. whether we are dealing with a very poor and highly vulnerable economy with little or no social infrastructure in which large sections of the population lack mechanisms to resist crisis (savings, food stocks, capacity to borrow, intrafamily solidarity, etc.), or whether we are dealing with a more affluent society with established health services, a widespread social security system and higher levels of personal savings and assets.

In this survey, deterioration in child welfare will be measured both by higher rates of infant and child mortality, morbidity and malnutrition, and by worsening health status, congenital malformations, child abandonment and abuse, reduced access to education, etc. The latter set of measures represents deteriorations less drastic than an increase in deaths (which is the result of a series of deteriorations) but equally indicative of a decline in welfare.

(4) There is substantial — although at times, contradictory — evidence on the relationship between household socio-economic characteristics and child well-being. The overwhelming proportion of this literature, however, consists of *cross-sectional studies* describing how indicators of infant or child mortality, morbidity, nutrition etc. vary at a single point in time in relation to demographic indicators, according to different levels of household income and resources, social expenditure on health and education and other environmental or family circumstances. Studies focusing on changes *over time* in child welfare as a result of economic crises or recession are, conversely, very rare. There are two complementary explanations for this.

First, in most parts of the world, economic growth and social improvement in the period from World War II and continuing up until recently have been historically unprecedented in terms of speed and steadiness, notwithstanding huge variations among regions and over time. Evidence[1] of long-term declines in infant and child mortality in almost all Third World countries has been confirmed by the first results of the recent World Fertility Survey,[2] with the extent and timing of the declines again varying greatly among countries. During this period of progress, there has been a tendency to focus on the *structural* determinants of IMR, CDR and child well-being, rather than on how the latter change in relation to severe economic *fluctuations*.

Second, the lack, even in the more advanced countries, of a permanent and timely system of monitoring the health status and welfare of children poses an almost insurmountable obstacle to any time-series analysis of the fluctuations in child well-being in relation to changing economic conditions. Formulation of public policy therefore can rely only on *ad hoc* cross-sectional surveys.

2. EVIDENCE FROM CROSS-SECTIONAL STUDIES

Although the main focus of this study is the changes *over time* in child status resulting from prolonged economic instability, a substantial, if inconclusive, body of cross-sectional analyses provides highly relevant information for our purposes. Such analyses examine the relations between indicators of child welfare (most often IMR, CDR, health and nutritional status) and a host of socio-economic factors, which are normally subdivided into four major categories: *demographic* (especially maternal fertility factors); *family circumstances* (e.g. the level of parental education); availability and accessibility of *health care and environmental sanitation*; and *economic conditions* of the household. Research on these determinants has continued during the last two to three decades but some major studies have appeared in the last four years which facilitate our work of summarizing the relevant literature.[3] They include the proceedings of the 1979 Mexico City meeting on socio-economic determinants and consequences of mortality, co-sponsored by the United Nations and other international and national development agencies and research institutions,[4] which has been remarkably important in systematizing existing knowledge in this area. In addition, the results of the World Fertility Survey[5] began to become available in 1983. Through this survey, a vast body of fresh information on infant and child mortality has been collected in each of the 29 participating developing countries. This forms a priceless source of updated, standardized and internationally comparable data for testing the influence of several socio-economic determinants on neonatal, infant and child mortality.

(a) *Demographic factors*

These have a general and uncontroversial effect on infant mortality, with tive factors universally singled out as particularly accurate predictors of infant and child survival: birth interval, the sex of the child, the age of the mother at the time of confinement, birth order and the multiplicity of birth.

Results from the World Fertility Survey point to a universal relation between the length of birth interval and infant, and even child, survival: the longer the birth interval, the lower the risk of death. This relation has often been neglected both from the research and, even more important, programmatic points of view.

In many developing countries, the integration of services geared to birth spacing within the context of maternal and child health services may prove an efficient measure in reducing mortality.

With few exceptions, it was found in all countries covered by the World Fertility Survey that infant mortality rates for males exceeded that for females and that the magnitude of the differences ranged as high as 25 deaths per thousand live births, while the mortality differential between males and females was practically nil between the ages of 1 and 5. Similarly, in rural northern Thailand, Frenzen and Hogan (1982) found from 1976–77 survey data that both neonatal and post-neonatal mortality was higher among males.[6] An important exception is Pakistan where female death rates at ages 1 and 2–5 exceeded male rates by 50%, possibly reflecting a pervasive neglect of female children. Similar results were found for India and Egypt.[7] In Egypt, however, the wide mortality differential by sex found in 1966 had almost disappeared 10 years later.[8] In Bangladesh, male mortality was observed to exceed female mortality in the neonatal period, but this differential was reversed in the post-neonatal period. Higher female mortality continued through childhood into adolescence and extended through the reproductive age. The most pronounced differences were observed in the 1–4 age group, where female mortality exceeded male mortality by as much as 50%.[9]

This clear and persistent pattern at the expense of females has been extensively explored and is held to reflect sex-biased health and nutrition-related behaviour, such as preference to sons in parental care, intra-family food distribution, feeding practices and utilization of health services. Firm empirical evidence supports this thesis. A recent study[10] of family food allocation in Bangladesh, for example, found that the nutrient intake of males in the 0–4 age group was regularly higher than for females of the same age, even when adjusting for body weight. In addition, male children under age 5 were brought to the health care centre by their guardians far more frequently than female children.

In countries with reliable vital registration, neonatal and infant mortality are known to vary according to the mother's age at the time of confinement, regardless of the overall level of risk in the community. The relation tends to be J-shaped or U-shaped, with mortality high for the children of teenage mothers, relatively low for those in their twenties, then rising steeply with increasing maternal age.[11] In a few of the countries covered by the recent World Fertility Survey, such as Syria, Sri Lanka and Malaysia, the period of minimal risk occurred between ages 30 and 39.

In most countries for which information is available, birth order — which is obviously correlated with maternal age — proves to be an important predictor of infant mortality. In high mortality countries such as Nepal and Kenya, the first-born children were at greater risk of dying during infancy than their younger siblings, although there is a tendency for risk to increase again at birth orders of seven and above. In countries with lower overall child mortality, the first-born is the most likely to survive while risk of death increases progressively with birth order.

Only 1.8% of the half-million births covered in the 29 World Fertility Surveys had a multiplicity of two or higher. While the deaths of multiple birth children cannot substantially affect overall levels, the mortality rates for this category of children are staggering. Overall, infant mortality rates for multiple births are often found to be between two and a half and six times higher than for single births. This difference persists well into childhood.

(b) Family characteristics

This category covers characteristics of the household and the community in which the child is born and lives, excluding demographic, health and sanitation-related and economic factors. The most important is probably parental education. In virtually all countries for which information is available, all indicators of child welfare show very clear and consistent improvement as the parents' years of schooling increase. Cochrane (1980), summarizing 17 research findings, showed that in two-thirds of the cases infant and child mortality declined unequivocally as the educational level of the mother increased.[12] Perhaps the most rigorous and convincing evidence of the importance of the educational factor is provided by Caldwell (1979), who analysed Nigerian survey data and found that maternal education was the most important single determinant of child mortality.[13] This conclusion held true even when controlling for other variables such as paternal education and occupation, maternal age and occupation, area of residence, type of marriage and access to health facilities.

Analysis of World Fertility Survey data shows that the infant death rates of the lowest educational group can be three times greater than those of the highest, as for instance in Peru and Malaysia.[14] The results provided by a recent article on mortality differentials for Matlab Thana, Bangladesh, are even more shocking: in the age group 1–3 years, the mortality rates were found to be over *five times* higher for children of mothers with no education as compared to those whose mothers had seven or more years of schooling.[15]

While the mother's attainment of primary schooling has been documented to be very important in reducing infant and child mortality, her attainment of secondary schooling seems to be even more critical. A 1982 UNICEF/IBGE study for Brazil clearly documents the differential improvements in child (0–2) mortality according to maternal education between 1970 and 1977, which were years of rapid economic expansion.[16] While child (0–2) mortality fell by only about 2% in cases where mothers had no education or less than one year of it, the same indicator showed a 20 and 30% improvement for children whose mothers had, respectively, 4–7 or 8 and more years of schooling.

Even a cursory survey of the literature leaves, therefore, little doubt as to the overwhelming importance of parental education. Because a high level of parental education is the result of years of investment and effort, it varies very slowly and is unlikely to be affected directly by economic recession. It therefore represents a major protecting factor for child welfare even during periods of economic crisis. A few authors even suggest that the impact of parental education may be greater than income factors and access to health facilities combined.[17]

Another relevant family characteristic affecting the levels of infant and child mortality and — possibly — psychophysical status is the type and stability of union within which the child is born. For instance, Adamchack (1979) found that the risk of death was clearly and positively correlated with instability of unions.[18] Similarly in those World Fertility Survey (mostly Caribbean) countries in which legal marriages were distinguished from consensual unions, children born within the former generally faced lower risks of dying. In addition, children born to women not in a union at the time of confinement also experienced higher than average mortality rates.

The structure of the family unit and the presence (or absence) of a supportive community environment were found to be of importance for child survival by Simmons et al. (1982) who analysed survey data from 2064 couples living in rural areas of two districts of Uttar Pradesh in India.[19] The data analysed refer to children born between 1965 and 1969. This interesting study proves – among other things – that the degree of family support available to the mother plays a relevant role in child survival. Mothers who live in nuclear families without older children to help care for infants are likely to have more difficulties in bringing their children through crisis than mothers who live in an extended joint-family environment. More generally, children born into supportive community environments are more likely to survive.

(c) Health care and environmental sanitation

In the 1960s and 1970s, health care and sanitation were thought to be the key to rapid infant mortality declines. Stolnitz (1965), for example, argued that the evidence of widespread declines in countries at very different levels of development and experiencing different rates of economic growth suggests that the socio-economic setting is of minor significance and that credit should be given to the application of public health technology.[20] A recent paper prepared by the Secretariat of the World Fertility Survey supports this orthodox view, stating '. . . (in the past), mortality reductions were achieved relatively easily and cheaply through the initiation of massive public health programmes that did not require for their success lasting changes in the standard of living of the majority of the population'.[21] However, the same report seems to qualify this strong endorsement by noting that '. . . primary health care services can be expected to contain some of the endemic causes of child death, but it is doubtful that public health measures in themselves can sustain the momentum of mortality decline . . . in the absence of broad social and economic progress'.[22]

Public health measures naturally play an important role in reducing mortality in poorer developing countries, where infectious diseases (microbial and parasitic) which still account for most morbidity and mortality can be treated inexpensively and simply by low-skilled health workers. In a comparative study of mortality between Kerala and West Bengal, Nag (1981) rejects variables such as level of environmental sanitation, nutrition, income and consumption expenditure, income distribution, rate of industrialization and urbanization as possible determinants of the observed mortality differentials and concludes '. . . it seems plausible that greater utilization of medical facilities – both preventive and curative – in Kerala is a major

determinant of the mortality differential between Kerala and West Bengal'.[23] However, he goes on to write '. . . Smaller catchment areas of health centres and better transportation facilities in Kerala may be contributing factors. But a major World Fertility Survey factor appears to be the higher literacy in Kerala, particularly among females. Literacy is likely to increase awareness about the need and the right to use public facilities'.[24]

The importance of health and sanitation is also indicated by some studies based on World Fertility Surveys. In the Philippines, the availability of sanitation (and electricity) proved to be correlates of child mortality even after controlling for other variables.[25] In Panama, the type of water supply and sewage disposal were almost as important as maternal characteristics in determining post-neonatal mortality.[26] A clear relationship between access to toilet facilities and early child survival was seen in Sri Lanka and Mexico.[27]

However, in examining the impact of health and nutrition interventions on infant and child mortality, Gwatkin and Brandel (1981) found that neither cross-national comparisons nor the experience of individual countries permits any clear assessment of whether national health and nutrition programmes are actually contributing enough in terms of reduced morbi-mortality to make their expansion worthwhile.[28] Because there is an almost total lack of programme evaluation at the national level, any argument for primary health care and nutrition interventions must instead be based on project experience. On the basis of micro-experience of 10 specific projects the authors conclude: 'it is possible to speak with considerable conviction about the potential that exists. Potential contribution and actual gain, however, are two different things. . . . The amount of gain . . . is likely to be highly dependent upon the sensitivity, care, and dedication with which national and other large-scale primary care programs are designed and implemented'.[29]

To conclude, it is worth stressing the views of those who take a different position on this matter. In a recent paper analysing mortality trends and differentials in Kenya, Mosley (1983) states '. . . child survival is primarily determined by the social and economic resources in the child's family. Analytically, these family resources may be largely captured by two indicators – maternal education and some index of the economic circumstances of the household'.[30] He later notes '. . . while certain modern technologies like antimalarials seem to have had an impact on mortality . . . for all practical purposes it has been virtually impossible to measure any impact of the existing formal medical system as an independent variable'.[31]

(d) *Economic conditions*

The income of the family (of the mother in particular) appears to be a *necessary* (although not *sufficient*) condition for the satisfaction of child needs, particularly in the areas of nutrition, health care, clothing and housing. Therefore, it would appear that, at least up to a given level, the risk of child death should decrease for increased households with incomes which can provide − *ceteris paribus* − better diet, better housing and sanitation and proper clothing. Cross-tabulations of several child welfare indicators (infant mortality rate, child death rate, health and nutritional status, etc.) with household income levels[32] clearly support this view as do Mosley's findings (1983) on Kenya quoted above.

In comparing the socio-economic determinants of infant mortality for Bogotà, Caracas and Rio de Janeiro, Carvajal and Burgess (1978) successfully tested the hypothesis that, in addition to biological and congenital forces, socio-economic determinants influence foetal and child risk of death.[33] Income was singled out as having a percentage impact on mortality as large as that of maternal education. The authors argue that income varies negatively with foetal mortality by: (1) preventing the occurrence of malnutrition which occurs more often in lower-income brackets; (2) providing sanitation facilities, the lack of which among lower-income earners translates into higher incidence of morbidity; and (3) enabling lower-income mothers to seek adequate medical assistance while pregnant. Similarly, by means of multiple regression analysis, Smith *et al.* (1983) examined the influence of socio-economic, health and education variables on malnutrition of rural Haitian children.[34] Their results show that the amount of food or 'food money available' had the greatest impact on the child's current nutritional health as measured by weight/age. Long-term growth, as measured by height/age, was most affected by education variables. Health variables as a group were the least effective in explaining growth.

One recent interesting result found by various authors is that the mother's income in developing countries is a far better predictor of child nutrition than household income, reflecting the differential behaviour of women in allocating resources for child nutrition and welfare. The

positive income effect is found to be statistically significant even though a negative length of employment is built into it. This is also suggested in the work of Colombino (1981), who found that for two groups of children aged 0−5 and 6−13 in the industrial city of Turin, the probability of being affected by psychosocial disturbances such as insomnia, eating difficulties, enuresis and serious problems at school increases with the number of hours worked by the mother.[35] When the length of maternal employment is controlled, the regression coefficient for maternal wage income almost doubles.[36]

The importance of family income and resources, however, has been reassessed in some recent studies. In the analysis of 1977 family nutritional data for 1167 households in the city of Managua, Wolfe and Behrman (1983)[37] concluded that income is not as critical a determinant of nutrition in all developing countries as previously indicated, particularly by Ward and Sanders (1980).[38] Indeed, the income elasticities of nutrition demand which Wolfe and Behrman found on the basis of their sample were quite small and such as to negate support for a general emphasis on raising incomes to improve nutrition. In the cases analysed, income increments would not have much effect on family and, therefore, child nutrition. In contrast however, price effects appeared significant, implying that market integration and related improvements (resulting in higher real incomes) and an increase in women's knowledge of nutrition would probably pay off in the form of improved nutrition. Finally, the authors suggest that, for similar populations, specific nutrition measures such as direct food distribution and refrigeration are generally more important in improving family nutrition than general income increases.

Similar conclusions were obtained by Bairagi (1980) in studying the incidence of malnutrition among children in the Companiganj Thana of rural Bangladesh during the famine year of 1975.[39] Using weight for age expressed as percentage of the standard Harvard classification, the author used the multiple regression procedure and covariance analysis to examine the importance of variables such as season, family income, maternal education, sex of children and birth order. While showing that the nutritional status of children is related to family income and that an increase in family income is a prerequisite for other attempts to improve the nutritional status, the results indicate that the nutritional status of children in the lowest income group is *not* constrained by income alone. Maternal education, sex of the child and birth order also appear to have a significant influence. An illiterate mother, for instance, with a higher income appears less able than a literate mother to utilize her resources for the child's welfare.

Some evidence of the relation between child welfare indicators and income level can also be found at the macro-economic level. For clarity of exposition it is convenient to distinguish between the effects of national average income levels and income distribution. Behm (1979) refers to de Carvalho who found that life expectancy at birth (and therefore infant and child mortality) of lower-income groups in Brazil in 1970 was 12.1 years less than that of the higher-income groups.[40] Behm also reports on Wood who found that infant mortality rates increased between 1960 and 1970 by 40% in São Paulo and by 68% in Belo Horizonte, two major Brazilian cities. The increase holds true even after errors in registration are corrected. In both cities, a simultaneous decline of the minimum real salary was observed, which the author considers a cause for the increased mortality. The proportion of the population with incomes lower than the minimum salary was estimated at 46% in Belo Horizonte and 43% in São Paulo. Woods — cited by Behm — calls attention to the fact that the rapid development in Brazil between 1960 and 1970 was characterized by a very uneven distribution of income. The same views are also presented in a more recent paper by de Carvalho and Wood (1978).[41]

Gwatkin and Brandel (1981) state that '. . . the pace of economic and social progress is likely to be significant for mortality improvements, even if this progress adheres to a rather traditional growth-oriented path'.[42] On the basis of a simple 'correspondence analysis' they calculate that infant mortality would drop in low-, medium- and upper-income developing countries by 20, 38 and 42% if average per capita income doubled. However speculative these figures might be, they indicate the potential gains in terms of declining mortality that could be inherent to the economic development process, reflected in improved private consumption and standards of nutrition, housing, clothing, transportation, etc.

A few studies are also available on the impact of income distribution on infant mortality. Rodgers (1979), on the basis of an international cross-sectional regression analysis, found that life expectancy may be between 5 to 10 years lower in a relatively inegalitarian country than in a more egalitarian one and concluded that income distribution is consistently and strongly related to mortality.[43] Rodger's results, however, can be questioned since important deter-

minants of infant mortality, such as maternal education, the availability of health services and others were excluded from the regression analysis, possibly leading to an overestimation of the influence of inequality on infant mortality.

In an attempt to overcome some of these shortcomings, Flegg (1982), using data for 47 developing countries, developed a comprehensive regression model including — besides the level of GDP per head and an index of income inequality — the percentage of illiterate women over age 15, the percentage of nurses and physicians per 10,000 persons and a fertility variable (the number of live births per 10,000 women aged 15—44).[44] Interestingly, this comprehensive analysis confirms the importance of income equality as a determinant of infant mortality. For instance, after controlling for all the other variables mentioned above, the reduction of the inequality index from the geometric mean of the 47 countries analysed (i.e. 1.2) to the level (0.7) of more egalitarian countries (e.g. Taiwan and Bangladesh) would reduce infant mortality by 20 deaths for 1000 live births.

3. EVIDENCE FROM TIME-SERIES ANALYSES

(a) *Related research*

To provide an appropriate methodological and historical context for the specific literature on the effects of economic fluctuations on children *over time*, it is necessary to refer to two related research areas: analyses of the seasonal dimension of rural poverty and child deprivation and famine analyses. Both these areas are characterized by a strong variation of welfare over time. Historically, famine analyses were the first studies to pay attention to the relation over time of economic disturbances, loss of welfare and increased death rates. Such studies, in clearly illustrating the conditions and economic and social mechanisms through which famines are generated and propagated, are highly relevant for this survey.

Seasonal studies by definition focus more on cyclical aspects of poverty and child welfare. As cyclical variations can provoke serious long-term aggravations (particularly in societies with a low capacity to resist crises) and can represent the immediate cause of a serious social crisis, they are briefly mentioned here.

(i) *Analyses of seasonality*[45]

The child's physical, social and economic

environment changes radically around the year
and particular seasons of neglect, sickness,
hunger and death can occur. Chambers (1983)
describes one scenario vividly and succinctly:

> Towards the end of the dry season, food gets
> scarcer. Anticipating hard work, some mothers
> take their children off the breast. When the rains
> come, the adults get very busy with urgent agri-
> cultural activities. . . . In this hungry time before
> the next harvest, less and less food is available, and
> it is less varied, less nutritious and less well prepared.
> It is also more often contaminated. . . . Water, too,
> is more likely to carry infections as rains wash
> faeces into water supplies. Diarrhoeas are prevalent.
> The incidence of diseases like malaria, dengue fever,
> guinea worm and skin infections rises. . . . If a child
> is ailing, it is less likely to be noticed or if noticed,
> dealt with. Adults . . . are exhausted, working hard,
> short of time to take the child for treatment and of
> money to pay for it, or sick and weak themselves.[46]

Although this quotation obviously cannot be
generalized, it illustrates how a number of child
problems can grow more acute, leading to higher
seasonal and overall morbi-mortality.

In Matlab, Bangladesh, for instance,
September and October, just before the harvest
of the main *aman* crop, make up the lean period
when there is very little demand for labour.
Agricultural wages are low, food stocks are low,
especially among the landless, and rice prices
are high.[47] In these two months births peak,
reflecting a peak in conceptions during the
often cooler and less stringent period which
follows the main harvest. It is not surprising,
therefore that (a) birth weights decline during
this season when the mother's food intake is
lowest; (b) breastmilk output decreases, indicating a reduced capacity for lactation; (c) nutritional status deteriorates, with most children
either gaining little or losing weight; (d)
morbidity is high and often environment-
specific — diarrhoeas for instance may peak
during the rains; (e) the result is higher infant
mortality, particularly neonatal mortality. In
conclusion, while the seasonal mode of analysis
should not divert attention from more basic
issues, rural poverty is often caused and
deepened by processes which operate seasonally.

(ii) *Famine analyses*

Famine can be viewed as an extreme case of
loss of welfare. Contrary to the evidence
analysed later, i.e. cases in which loss of welfare
necessarily follows some economic dislocation,
famines can occur during periods of economic
stability or even expansion. Most significantly,
famine analysis vividly illustrates that even a
slight impact of an unfavourable exogenous

force (such as a flood or food price increases
in neighbouring countries) may jeopardize the
entire population's chances of survival, particularly in very poor communities. Its most
important analytical contribution consists —
perhaps surprisingly to some — in providing
evidence that even in such extreme circumstances, food availability declines *per se* were
not the prime cause of mass starvation.[48] As
Sen (1981) notes, 'Starvation is the characteristic
of some people not *having* enough food to eat.
It is not the characteristic of there *being* not
enough food to eat. While the latter can be a
cause of the former, it is but one of many
possible causes. Whether and how starvation
relates to food supply is a matter for factual
investigation'.[49] After examining four major
famines (Great Bengal 1943, Bangladesh 1974,
Wollo 1972–73 and Harerghe 1974), the
author finds that in only one case (Harerghe
1974) was there a collapse in food availability.
Paradoxically, the three other famines occurred
in periods of unchanged or even expanding
food availability. For instance, in the 1974
Bangladesh famine, rice output and food availability per head were higher than in any other
year during 1971–75.

One cannot therefore automatically associate
famine either with food availability decline or
even a general economic deterioration. Such
evidence argues clearly for the food entitlement
approach. A famine occurs when there is a
failure in either the *direct* entitlement or in the
exchange entitlement of a given social group.
Attention should be focused on failures of the
direct entitlements (e.g. decline of food output
for small farmers) or exchange entitlements.
Examples of the latter are a decline in the wage
rate or in the occupational opportunities of all
salaried labour or an equivalent rapid rise in the
staple food price, which has occasionally been
determined by a rapid surge of demand following
expansionist policies.

Sen's work also clearly demonstrates that
famines hit with devastating force particular
socio-economic groups, i.e. the landless, the
farmers, the fisherman, the herders, etc., who
have experienced a failure of their entitlement
system. To refer, therefore, to the 'poor' as a
category is not very useful; in his words, 'a small
peasant and a landless labourer may both be
poor, but their fortunes are not tied together'.[50]
We must therefore see such people who are
vulnerable to starvation not as a huge army of
poor people, but as members of particular
occupational groups, with different ownership
endowments and subjected to different entitlements. He also documents that the proportion

of deaths among children aged 0–5 was agonizingly high during the Great Bengal famine although it does not seem to have been higher in percentage terms than in normal periods. These data, however, should be treated cautiously as they are based on current registrations which are affected by a large (although unknown) bias during periods of social crisis like a famine. Furthermore, this finding is contradicted by the observation of death rates by age and sex during the 1974 Bangladesh famine. Colin McCord (1980, see pp. 29–31) notes that the increased deaths there were concentrated among the poor, the very young and the very old.

Finally, evidence points to the existence of *time-lags* between the onset of famine and the manifestation of its worst effects. More than half the deaths attributable to the Bengal famine of 1943 took place *after* 1943, while the mortality did not return to the pre-famine rate for many years.

(b) *Time-series analysis of deterioration in child welfare following economic dislocations*

The observation that economic and social processes clearly affect health status and crude death rate is not new. Eyer and Sterling (1977), for instance, in analysing United States data, point out that the most rapid and sustained death rate declines over the last century all occurred at times of rising unemployment. The authors claim that 'this seemingly paradoxical relationship reflects the fact that heart disease, stroke, cancer, cirrhosis, diabetes, accidents . . . rise during the boom with the lengthening of hours of work, the increase of migration, and its attendant community disintegration. Only suicide and homicide, among death rates, rise and fall with unemployment and its family consequences during depressions. Clearly the social sources of stress which rise during boom outweigh the effects of economic depression on the death rate as a whole'.[51]

The validity of this strong statement could be challenged — at least partially — on methodological grounds. For instance, it would be interesting to run a correlation analysis between unemployment and the crude death rate after a 2–3-year lag. However, Eyer and Sterling's thesis is not necessarily contradictory to findings concerning children since economic crisis wields different impact for adults and children. MacMahon and Yen (1971), also analysing United States data, found increased rates of certain congenital malformations during the 1930s depression.[52] More generally, Brenner, in a classical analysis of foetal, infant and maternal mortality in the United States during periods of economic instability, concluded that '. . . changes in the trends in perinatal, neonatal and post-neonatal and maternal mortality occur regularly in the United States as a result of environmental change . . . economic instability has probably been responsible for the apparent lack of continuity in the decline in infant mortality rates since 1950'.[53]

Brenner uses unemployment as an indicator of economic instability and perinatal, neonatal and infant mortality as dependent variables over the 1915–67 period. Long-term trends were estimated for these variables by the ordinary least-squares methods. Secular trends were then algebraically substracted from the raw data and the residuals were investigated graphically and through regression analysis. In the latter case, alternative specifications with different time-lags for the independent variables were employed. The author has also utilized other statistical techniques (moving differences and spectral analysis) to analyse the fluctuations in child mortality *vis-à-vis* the unemployment rate. His major findings show that there is an inverse relation between economic changes and infant, neonatal and perinatal mortality, which occurs even for the smallest time interval considered (1 year). Increases in foetal mortality rates generally occur within the same year in which the national economic indicator declines. Increases in mortality of 1-day-old infants tend to lag by approximately 1 year while increases in post-neonatal mortality rates tend to lag 3–5 years behind any economic downturn. Some of the above relationships have become increasingly stronger since World War II. For instance, prior to 1929, perinatal mortality could not be associated statistically with unemployment but shows much clearer correlation since then. Brenner also observed some differences by race in sensitivity of mortality to economic changes, non-whites appearing to carry a greater risk of foetal mortality than whites during economic downturns.

Brenner explains the different lags for foetal, perinatal, neonatal and infant mortality by suggesting that the effects of economic crisis are transmitted by different mechanisms, at least for perinatal as opposed to post-neonatal mortality. The causes of post-neonatal mortality, for instance, are typically environment-related and include infectious, respiratory and digestive diseases and accidents. In an industrialized society like the United States where at least some prenatal and postnatal care is generally the rule, substantial and drastic changes in household circumstances or family structure would be required to greatly increase the environment-related risk of death. Such change might not occur within a year of an economic downturn but if unemployment or income decline lasted two or three years, the damage to socio-economic status might be such as to make routine infant care financially or otherwise unfeasible.

On the other hand, changes in mortality of children less than one day old are probably much more closely linked to the mother's condition. Economic fluctuation-related factors increasing perinatal mortality, most likely manifested in increasing rates of congenital malformations and prematurity, would be much more *stress-related*. They might include lack of prenatal care and changes in the mother's physical or emotional health due to diet alterations, smoking, hypertension and the use of alcohol or tranquillizers.

The thesis of Brenner – tested on nationwide data – is supported by Adamchak (1979) who examined the relationship between infant mortality and socio-economic status in Toledo, Ohio, for the years centering around 1950, 1960 and 1970.[54] The starting point of his analysis was the discovery that, while overall infant mortality had declined steadily from 1950 to 1970, post-neonatal mortality for the overall resident population showed a staggering increase between 1960 and 1970 – years characterized in Toledo by adverse economic and social conditions. Post-neonatal mortality is well known to be particularly sensitive to exogenous (or environment-related) rather than to endogenous (or congenital) causes. Using semi-partial correlation coefficients, Adamchak found that the variables most directly correlated with post-neonatal risk of death, particularly in 1960 and 1970, were marital instability, income level and unemployment.

The evidence available for developing countries is – with few exceptions – fragmented and even scarcer. When analysing the long-term trend in infant mortality for Sri Lanka, a country well known for rapid mortality decline, Meegama (1980) found wide fluctuations both in neonatal and post-neonatal mortality, indicating instability in environmental conditions or in food availability.[55] In the early 1970s post-neonatal mortality started climbing again after a long-term decline. In 1974, neonatal mortality continued to decline slowly but post-neonatal mortality increased by an astounding 37% for the country as a whole and by almost 60% in the estate sector. In a single year, 1974, post-neonatal mortality increased by almost

150% in the estate sector. Meegama identifies malnutrition as the main cause of this terrible increase, citing the food shortages Sri Lanka suffered following successive crop failures in 1973 and 1974. Due to high prices, limited food imports (reflecting a worldwide shortage of food after poor harvests in the USSR and India) also led to a general food shortage. As a result the free rice ration was halved in November 1973 and bread prices rose sharply from 35 to over 80 cents. The shortage was severely felt by the poor throughout the country, particularly by the plantation workers, historically the most underprivileged class.[56]

McCord et al. (1980) also provide evidence of increasing infant and overall death rate, for about the same period for the Companiganj Thana, Bangladesh:

In 1974 and 1975 floods in Bangladesh and poor harvests in India led to a general rise in the price of staple foods (rice and wheat) throughout the region. The Bangladesh floods were localized and food aid was considerable, so that food stocks were unaffected, but smuggling to India and hoarding led to sharp price rises. In Companiganj Thana there was no flood, and harvests were better than normal in 1974 and 1975. Nevertheless, the price of rice and wheat more than doubled. The average prices of these foods in 1975 were Tk. 6.60 per seer ($0.46/kg.) for rice and Tk. 5.00 per seer ($0.37/kg.) for wheat flour. The daily wage rate for a labourer never rose above Tk. 10.00 per day, so that it was not possible to meet the minimum calorie needs of a family even if work was available every day of the year, which, of course, it is not.[57]

As a consequence of these factors, crude death rates rose almost immediately by more than 50%, the additional deaths being concentrated among the poor, the very young and the very old and caused mostly by malnutrition, diarrhoea and tuberculosis. McCord et al. also provide evidence of a far higher child (1–4) mortality for the landless than for other families. While child death rates doubled for the latter as compared with 'normal' years, the sharp increase in the price of rice provoked an increase in child mortality among the landless of almost 400%. Surprisingly, however, infant (0–1) mortality increased at a much slower pace during the crisis year of 1975–76, and its variation among social classes remained relatively modest. For instance, infant mortality for families with over three acres of land was almost as high as for the landless because of high risk of death from obstetrical complications and pneumonia.

A shocking discovery of this study is that the number of deaths observed in Companiganj Thana during the 1975–78 period correlates quite closely with the price of rice and that rises in the latter are followed, *with only a two month time lag*,[58] by a corresponding increase in mortality. This reinforces the observation of famine analyses that, through the play of market prices, rapid and generalized increases in mortality can occur in periods of relatively high food production. It also underlines the enormous fragility and vulnerability of a society like that of Companiganj Thana where, clearly, the mechanisms to resist crises must be practically non-existent.

A particular aspect of the Bangladesh 1974–75 crisis is highlighted by Langsten (1981) who argues that – contrary to the normal pattern of higher female mortality in South Asia – males appear to suffer disproportionately during periods of crisis.[59] Langsten observes that for the 15–44 and 45–64 age groups male mortality exceeds female mortality by a wide margin (up to 35%) in periods of crisis (such as 1971–72 or, more clearly, 1975). However, the author provides no conclusive explanation of this phenomenon. What matters the most for the purpose of this study, however, is that the above observation does not hold true at all in the case of infants below 1 year and for the 1–4 age group[60] for which the typical pattern of higher female mortality continues in crisis years.

The United Nations Centre for Social Development has recently published a report on how the deepening of the world economic recession has affected the living conditions of the poor, the children and the vulnerable.[61] However, it is based only on speculative (i.e. not empirical) and dated evidence. Extensive, complete and uncontroversial evidence of social deterioration as a result of externally induced economic crisis, on the other hand, is provided by a recently published work on Costa Rica by Rosero Bixby (1983) which examines the long-term trends in infant and adult mortality over the 1910–81 period.[62] He reckons that the rapid and steady decline in mortality in Costa Rica started in the 1920s with the launching of low-cost and high-efficiency public health programmes, despite the conspicuous absence of substantial economic growth. According to the author:

> Residual insecticides and antibiotics accounted for the most successful decades, the 1940s and 1950s. These advances in health technology broke up in a great degree the determinism that underdevelopment exerted on mortality . . . this does not mean, however, that dependence and underdevelopment are totally negligible factors for the interpretation of the level and tendency of mortality. On the

contrary . . . in periods of foreign trade crisis, the decline of mortality has been smaller and sometimes there have even been fall backs, a dramatic evidence of the impact of economic dependence.[63]

Sanitary progress, in other words, is influenced by socio-economic conditions, which are in turn linked to uncontrollable external factors (prices of exports). To prove his point, the author has computed the annual rate of decline for infant and adult mortality separately for normal and crisis periods, finding that in the years of economic contraction, infant mortality tends to reduce at a slower pace and in a few cases to increase. Although this analysis could be substantially improved from a statistical point of view, the evidence provided unequivocally indicates that in certain crisis-years a rise in infant mortality rates took place. This relation appears even more clearly if a time-lag of one or two years is assumed between economic recession and level of infant mortality since the effect of the crisis takes some time to become manifest.

4. DISCUSSION

Few are the general conclusions that can be drawn after surveying the above literature and it would be pretentious to try to conclude by establishing which factors are most important for the achievement of higher levels of child welfare. Indeed, the lack of a theory pertaining to the socio-economic determinants of mortality is clearly shown in the literature by the lack of agreement on what factors should be included in the analysis. Furthermore, the variety of conditions and values is so great as to discourage the formulation of universal solutions. What matters here is that all determinants quoted above are to a certain degree, or at least in some cases, relevant in explaining the level of child welfare. With the possible exception of maternal education, which is universally recognized to have a major impact on child well-being, the question of whether to give more importance to broad-based socio-economic interventions or to specific medical and public health programmes will have to be decided on a case-by-case basis. It is worth recalling here that while the latter interventions seem to be successful in controlling epidemics and contagious disease-related mortality, improvements in families' education and economic position appear necessary for further progress. Such improvements would make it possible to tackle not only the immediate (clinical) causes of mortality and morbidity but also their underlying causes.

General conclusions about 'instant solutions' are therefore not possible and the debate on these issues will likely continue for some time. However, one may conclude this survey by trying to identify the major gaps in the existing literature. Figure III.1 below provides a first attempt in this direction by plotting the studies quoted in this survey according to the level of GDP per capita and infant mortality rate of the country (or region) considered around 1980. Studies analysing more than one country are quoted separately for each country, while the 15 general and cross-national works reviewed have been omitted. Clearly, only very tentative conclusions can be drawn from Figure III.1 as our survey of the literature, although aiming at a certain representativeness and generality, has certainly not exhausted the extensive literature on this subject, particularly for cross-sectional analyses. The conclusions which follow must therefore be treated cautiously. Still, three points are in order.

First, while there is a relatively large quantity of cross-sectional analyses available, a very limited number of studies investigates the changes *over time* in child welfare resulting from economic fluctuations. The use of cross-

sectional information in a time-series context and for future policy-making is hindered by well-known methodological problems. More efforts may therefore be required in the future for the dynamic analysis of changes in child welfare. This also calls for a major long-term effort at establishing an adequate child monitoring system reporting at regular intervals on the conditions of children.

Second, Figure III.1 seems to reveal a relative wealth of studies for low-income countries with both high (in particular) and low infant mortality. Most of these studies refer almost exclusively to India, Bangladesh and Sri Lanka. A substantial amount of information also exists for the very high-income and low infant mortality countries, among which the United States is certainly the best represented. For the low-middle- and middle-income countries, the studies appear to be less frequent and, in particular, less systematic, with the possible exception of Brazil. As child problems and appropriate solutions vary substantially among groups of countries, more research should be carried out, particularly for the low-income, high infant mortality African countries, for the group of middle-income countries and for the

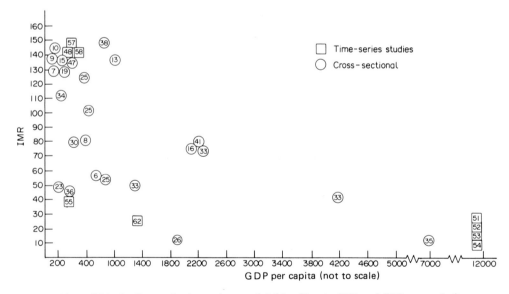

Figure III.1. *Studies on the determinants of child welfare by IMR and GDP per capita**

*Fifteen more studies are quoted with cross-national evidence.
(7) India   (6) Thailand   (15) Bangladesh   (16) Brazil   (30) Kenya   (35) Italy   (41) Brazil   [51] US
[54] US   [58] Bangladesh   (8) Egypt   (10) Bangladesh   (19) India   (25) Phil., Indon., Pak.   (33) Colom.,
Ven., Brazil   (36) Kerala   (47) Bangladesh   [52] US   [55] Sri Lanka   [62] Costa Rica   (9) Bangladesh
(13) Nigeria   (23) Kerala   (26) Panama   (34) Haiti   (38) Ceara, Brazil   [48] Bangladesh   [53] US
[57] Bangladesh.

	IMR (1980)	GDP/capita* (1980)
Thailand	55	447
India	123	154
Egypt	103	501
Bangladesh	136	141
Nigeria	135	689
Brazil	77	1380
Kerala, India	52†	127‡
Philippines	55	423
Indonesia	93	286
Pakistan	126	215
Panama	22	1245
Kenya	87	256
Colombia	56	643
Venezuela	42	2012
Haiti	115	148
Italy	14	4101
USA	13	8084
Sri Lanka	44	354
Costa Rica	24	1148
Ceara, Brazil	155§	320‖

Sources: World Bank, *World Development Report* (1982); and United Nations, Projections and Perspective Studies Branch, DIESA.
* Constant 1975 US $.
† Average 1975–77.
‡ Current 1975–76 prices.
§ Mortality at 2 years of age. Northeast 1977.
‖ Northeast represented 39% of national average income in 1970.

group of high-income high-mortality countries. When all the results of the World Fertility Survey are available, these research gaps will have to be reassessed.

Third, most of the studies surveyed use the infant and, to a lesser extent, child mortality rates as exclusive indicators of child welfare. Fewer focus on the nutritional status of children and almost none focus on their health or more general status as expressed by prevalence of diseases and rate of morbidity, etc. While this situation reflects the relative availability of these different types of information, there is the risk – particularly for countries with very low levels of infant and child mortality – of grossly underestimating losses in child welfare

following economic dislocations because of the narrow and inappropriate choice of the indicators used to measure it. In measuring development, the adoption of the Infant Mortality Rate already represents an improvement over the use of GNP per capita alone. However, the measurement of child welfare can be substantially enhanced by introducing other indicators such as those refering to nutritional status, weight/age, height/age, weight/height, low birth weight, morbidity rates, incidence of infectious and endemic diseases, rates of school achievement etc., and – particularly for the industrialized countries – indicators of children's psycho-social conditions.

NOTES

1. UN Population Division (1982).

2. UN Expert Group on Mortality and Health Policy (1983).

3. Arriaga *et al.* (1980) and Preston (1980).

4. WHO (1979).

5. UN Expert Group on Mortality and Health Policy (1983).

6. Frenzen and Hogan (1982).

7. UNICEF (1981).

8. Darwish (1981), Table 35.

9. D'Souza and Chen (1980).

10. Chen *et al*. (1981).

11. Nortman (1974).

12. Cochrane (1980).

13. Caldwell (1979).

14. UN Expert Group on Mortality and Health Policy (1983), p. 10.

15. D'Souza and Bhuiya (1982).

16. Convenio IBGE/UNICEF (1982).

17. Caldwell and McDonald (1981).

18. Adamchak (1979).

19. Simmons *et al*. (1982).

20. Stolnitz (1965).

21. UN Expert Group on Mortality and Health Policy (1983), p. 19.

22. *Ibid*., p. 20 (emphasis added).

23. Nag (1981), p. 27.

24. *Ibid*., p. 41.

25. Martin *et al*. (forthcoming).

26. Guerra (1981).

27. Hobcraft *et al*. (1982).

28. Gwatkin and Brandel (1981).

29. *Ibid*., p. 48.

30. Mosley (1983), p. 22.

31. *Ibid*.

32. UNICEF (1981).

33. Carvajal and Burgess (1978).

34. Smith *et al*. (1983).

35. Colombino (1981).

36. Kumar (1978), p. 43–46.

37. Wolfe and Behrman (1983).

38. Ward and Sanders (1980).

39. Bairagi (1980).

40. Behm (1979).

41. de Carvalho and Wood (1978).

42. Gwatkin and Brandel (1981).

43. Rodgers (1979).

44. Flegg (1982).

45. Longhurst and Payne (1979) and Chambers (1979).

46. Chambers (1983).

47. Becker and Sardar (1978).

48. Sen (1980 and 1981) and Alamgir (1976).

49. Sen (1981), p. 1.

50. *Ibid*., p. 156.

51. Eyer and Sterling (1977).

52. MacMahon and Yen (1971).

53. Brenner (1973).

54. Adamchak (1979).

55. Meegama (1980).

56. *Ibid*., p. 40.

57. McCord *et al*. (1980) and Alamgir (1976).

58. Other authors have estimated that the major impact occurs within a five-month lag. See Langsten (1980).

59. Langsten (1981).

60. *Ibid*., Table I, p. 84.

61. UN Centre for Social Development and Humanitarian Affairs (1983).

62. Rosero Bixby (1983).

63. *Ibid*., p. 31.

REFERENCES

Adamchak, D., 'Emerging trends in the relationship between infant mortality and socio-economic status', *Social Biology*, Vol. 26, No. 1 (September 1979), pp. 16–29.

Alamgir, M. 'Bangladesh: a case of below poverty level equilibrium trap', mimeo (Dakha: Bangladesh Institute of Development Studies, December 1976).

Arriaga, E. et al., 'La mortalité des enfants dans le monde et dans l'histoire' (Department de Demographie, Université Catholique de Louvain, Ordina Editions, 1980).

Bairagi, R., 'Is income the only constraint on child nutrition in rural Bangladesh?', Bulletin of the World Health Organization, Vol. 58, No. 5 (1980).

Becker and M. Sardar, 'Seasonal patterns of vital events in Matlab Thana, Bangladesh, with specific reference to deaths and socio-economic status', paper presented at the Conference on Seasonal Dimensions to Rural Poverty (3–6 July 1978).

Behm, H., 'Socio-economic determinants of mortality in Latin America', in WHO (1979), pp. 139–164.

Brenner, M., 'Foetal, infant and maternal mortality during periods of economic instability', International Journal of Health Services, Vol. 3, No. 2 (1973).

Caldwell, J., 'Education as a factor in mortality decline: an examination of Nigerian data', Population Studies, Vol. 33 (1979), pp. 395–413.

Caldwell, J. and P. McDonald, 'Influence of maternal education on infant and child mortality: levels and causes', International Population Conference, Manila 1981, Vol. 2 (Liège, Belgium: International Union for the Scientific Study of Population, 1981), pp. 79–96.

Carvajal, M. and P. Burgess, 'Socio-economic determinants of foetal and child deaths in Latin America: a comparative study of Bogota , Caracas and Rio de Janeiro', Social Science Medicine, Vol. 12C (1978).

Chambers, R., 'Health, agriculture and rural poverty: why seasons matter', Discussion Paper No. 149 (Institute of Development Studies at the University of Sussex, UK, December 1979).

Chambers, R., 'Bad times for rural children: countering seasonal deprivation', mimeo (New Delhi: Ford Foundation, June 1983).

Chen, L. et al., 'Sex bias in the family allocation of food and health care in rural Bangladesh', Population and Development Review, Vol. 7, No. 1 (March 1981), pp. 55–70.

Cochrane, S., 'The effects of education on health', World Bank Staff Working Paper No. 405 (Washington, D.C., July 1980).

Colombino, U., 'The economics of the "disturbed" child', Micros, Quarterly Journal of Microeconomics, No. 2 (November 1981).

Convenio IBGE/UNICEF, 'Perfil estatistico de criancas e maes no Brasil' (Rio de Janeiro: IBGE, 1982).

Darwish, M., 'Situation analysis of children and women in Egypt' (Beirut: UNICEF Regional Office, May–June 1981).

de Carvalho, J. and C. Wood, 'Mortality, income distribution, and rural–urban residence in Brazil', Population and Development Review, Vol. 4, No. 3 (September 1978).

D'Souza, S. and A. Bhuiya, 'Socio-economic mortality differentials in a rural area of Bangladesh', Population and Development ⁎ Review, Vol. 8, No. 4 (December 1982).

D'Souza, S. and L. Chen, 'Sex differentials in mortality in rural Bangladesh', Population and Development Review, Vol. 6, No. 2 (June 1980), pp. 257–270.

Eyer and Sterling, 'Stress-related mortality and social organization', Review of Radical Political Economics, Vol. 9, No. 1 (Spring 1977).

Flegg, A., 'Inequality of income, illiteracy and medical care are determinants of infant mortality in underdeveloped countries', Population Studies, Vol. 36, No. 3 (November 1982).

Frenzen, P. and D. Hogan, 'The impact of class education and health care on infant mortality in a developing society: the case of rural Thailand', Demography, Vol. 19, No. 3 (August 1982).

Guerra, F., 'Determinants of infant mortality in Panama', CELADE Series D, No. 99 (1981).

Gwatkin, D. and S. Brandel, 'Reducing infant and child mortality in the developing world, 1980–2000', Overseas Development Council Working Paper, No. 2 (Washington, D.C., April 1981).

Hobcraft et al., 'Socio-economic factors in infant and child mortality: a cross-national summary', paper presented at the Annual Meeting of the Population Association of America (San Diego: 1982).

Kumar, S., 'Role of the household economy in child nutrition at low incomes: a case study in Kerala', Occasional Paper No. 95 (Dept. of Agricultural Economics, Cornell University, December 1978).

Langsten, R., 'Causes of changes in vital rates: the case of Bangladesh', Ph.D. dissertation (University of Michigan, 1980).

Langsten, R., 'The effects of crisis on differential mortality by sex in Bangladesh', The Bangladesh Development Studies, Vol. 9, No. 2 (1981).

Longhurst, R. and P. Payne, 'Seasonal aspects of nutrition: review of evidence and policy implications' Discussion Paper No. 145 (Institute of Development Studies at the University of Sussex, UK, November 1979).

McCord, C. et al., 'Death rate, land and the price of rice 1975–1978', Evaluation Unit Report No. 4, Companiganj Health Project, Noakhali (Christian Commission for Development in Bangladesh, March 1980).

MacMahon, B. and S. Yen, 'Unrecognised epidemic of anencephaly and spina bifida', Lancet (1971), pp. 31–33.

Martin, L. et al., 'Covariates of child mortality in the Philippines, Indonesia and Pakistan: a comparative analysis', Population Studies (forthcoming).

Meegama, S., 'Socio-economic determinants of infant and child mortality in Sri Lanka: an analysis of post-war experience', World Fertility Survey, Scientific Reports, No. 8 (1980).

Mosley, W., 'Will primary health care reduce infant and child mortality? A critique of some current strategies, with reference to Africa and Asia' (Paris: Institut National d'Etudes Demographiques (INED), 1983).

Nag, M., 'Impact of social development and economic development on mortality: a comparative study of

Kerala and West Bengal', Working Paper No. 78 (The Population Council, December 1981).

Nortman, D., 'Parental age as a factor in pregnancy outcome and child development', *Reports on Population/Family Planning*, No. 16 (1974).

Preston, S., 'Causes and consequences of mortality declines in less developed countries during the twentieth century', in R. A. Easterlin (ed.), *Population and Economic Change in Developing Countries* (University of Chicago Press, 1980), pp. 289–341.

Rodgers, G. 'Income and inequality as determinants of mortality: an international cross-section analysis', *Population Studies*, Vol. 33, No. 2 (July 1979), pp. 343–351.

Rosero Bixby, L., 'Social and economic policies and their effects on mortality: the Costa Rican case' (Paris: IUSSP-INED, 28 February–4 March 1983).

Sen, A., 'Famines', *World Development*, Vol. 8, No. 9 (September 1980), pp. 613–621.

Sen, A., *Poverty and Famines: An Essay on Entitlement and Deprivation* (Oxford: Clarendon Press, 1981).

Simmons, G. *et al.*, 'Post-neonatal mortality in rural India: implications of an economic model', *Demography*, Vol. 19, No. 3 (August 1982).

Smith, M. *et al.*, 'Socio-economic education and health factors influencing growth of rural Haitian children', *Ecology of Food and Nutrition*, Vol. 13 (1983), pp. 99–108.

Stolnitz, G., 'Recent mortality trends in Latin America, Asia and Africa: review and interpretation', *Population Studies*, Vol. 19 (1965), pp. 117–138.

UNICEF, 'Analysis of the situation of children in India' (New Delhi: April 1981).

United Nations, Centre for Social Development and Humanitarian Affairs, 'The social impact of economic recession on specific population groups during the 1970s and early 1980s', mimeo (Vienna: 1983).

United Nations, Expert Group on Mortality and Health Policy, 'Findings of the *World Fertility Survey* on trends, differentials and discriminants of mortality in developing countries', paper for the International Conference on Population 1984 (Rome: UN-DIESA, 1983).

United Nations, Population Division, 'Infant Mortality Rates: estimates and projections by country and region, 1970–2000' (New York: March 1982).

Ward, J. and J. Sanders, 'Nutritional determinants and migration in the Brazilian Northeast: a case study of rural and urban Ceará', *Economic Development and Cultural Change*, Vol. 29, No. 1 (October 1980).

Wolfe, B. and J. Behrman, 'Is income overrated in determining adequate nutrition', *Economic Development and Cultural Change*, Vol. 31, No. 3 (April 1983).

World Health Organization, 'Proceedings of the Meeting on Socio-economic Determinants and Consequences of Mortality', held at El Colegio de Mexico, Mexico City, 19–25 June 1979 (New York and Geneva: 1979).

Brazilian Children and the Economic Crisis: Evidence from the State of São Paulo

ROBERTO MACEDO*

Department of Economics, University of São Paulo, Brazil

Summary. — This paper briefly reviews the socio-economic conditions and the situation of children in Brazil during 1960–80, drawing on data for the country as a whole and concentrating on the policies of the 1964–73 years. It also examines more recent developments that led to the current crisis as well as its overall social impact on employment, food consumption and prices, and government social expenditures. The possible effects of the crisis on the welfare of children in the State of São Paulo are examined in detail. Finally, the paper reviews the government policy for protecting the poor and vulnerable in general and children in particular.

1. INTRODUCTION

As the Brazilian economy entered the 1980s, it moved from the unprecedented boom years of the early 1970s to a severe recession that started in 1981 and has not yet ended. Over the period, there was a decay in the annual rate of GDP growth, which averaged 11.4% in 1970–73, 7.1% in 1974–80 and minus 0.3% in 1981–82.[1] During the last two years, with a population still expanding at a rate above 2%, GDP per capita fell for the first time since 1953. Prospects for 1983 and 1984 remain gloomy, with most analyses predicting another fall in GDP per capita.

In Brazil, it is estimated that for employment to keep up with population growth a minimum annual GDP growth rate of 7% is required.[2] However precarious the assumptions may be which support this estimate, it is clear that the country has entered a phase in which employment expansion is being hindered by slow or even negative growth of the economy. Under such conditions, employment is falling in the current recession and one can expect deteriorating rates of unemployment and underemployment in the near future as well.

This occurs in a country which, in spite of a high average rate of growth since World War II relative to the industrialized world and to other developing countries, has not been able to alleviate the serious poverty conditions which still plague a large part of its population. Having arrived at an annual GDP per capita estimated at US $2300 in 1980, Brazil is considered a middle-income country by international standards. However, it is also an often quoted example of a highly unequal socio-economic structure. In terms of the welfare of the Brazilian children, on which this paper will focus, this structure expresses itself as high rates of infant and child mortality and low standards of nutrition, health and education, concentrated in the lower income classes, located in impoverished regions of the country and also in troubled areas of the rich regions.

In the past, when most of the population worked in the agricultural sector and lived in rural areas, the social impact of economic crises was hidden as it was scattered over a large number of small towns or disseminated into the rural areas. In the latter, the possibility of resorting to subsistence agriculture worked as a buffer mechanism that alleviated the impact of a crisis. The small towns had and still have their

*This paper is a summary of a report written at the request of UNICEF and completed on 15 June 1983. The larger version is available from the author, upon request. It acknowledges the help of many people and institutions who provided guidance and data. Special thanks go to Roberto Iunes, a research assistant who made most of the field contacts, to Marcelo Bianconi, for assistance in data processing, and to Dr Alberto Carvalho da Silva, from the Medical School of the University of São Paulo, who at the beginning of the project made helpful suggestions and opened the doors to many persons who gladly received a troubled economist talking about recession and looking for its effects on children. The views expressed in this paper are those of the author and not necessarily those of UNICEF.

own means, however precarious, of coping with crisis. Alms-giving is more common in their tradition as is the support of the St. Vincent de Paul Society and other institutions linked to the Church's network of social care. It should be noted that the population was much less than the 125 million of today (70 million in 1960, 93 million in 1970) and that the proportion of the population in urban areas has increased from 45.2% to 67.7% from 1960 to 1980.[3] Under such conditions, the potential for the surfacing of large-scale social problems was a lot less 50 years ago, or even two or three decades ago, than it is today.

The present worsening economic conditions do not have their social impact hidden or alleviated in the same fashion. In the current economic crisis, this impact has been hardest in the heavily industrialized, densely populated and urbanized regions of the country. These regions grew very rapidly without the concurrent development of means for coping with the social problems as they appear in this different environment. For instance, the lack of income transfers to the affected people (e.g. unemployment compensation) means a further deterioration of the living conditions of the poor when they become unemployed.

The current recession has occurred on top of the persistent poverty and unsatisfactory rates of growth of the late 1970s, making already serious socio-economic problems even worse. In this context, this paper tries to address the following question: is there any evidence that the current recession is having a further impact on the welfare of the Brazilian children, making more severe the unsatisfactory picture which has been diagnosed in the past?

We shall concentrate on evidence drawn from the State of São Paulo. The current economic crisis follows the federal government policy of fighting external indebtedness and balance-of-payments problems by generating a surplus in the trade balance. This is accomplished by curbing domestic demand, the impact on industrial output being noticeably strong given its relatively high income elasticity. Reduced industrial output then leads to diminished employment opportunities in the urban areas. Being the most urbanized and industrialized region of the country, the State of São Paulo has therefore been particularly hard hit by the crisis.

With a population of 25 million of which 13 million are concentrated in the Greater São Paulo area around its capital, as shown by the 1980 census, it is also the most populous and richest of the Brazilian states.[4] However, its demographic structure is still young — the same census shows that 33% of the population was less than 15 years old. Moreover, it is not free of poverty problems as is evident from the many slums that can be found in its urban areas. Containing a large proportion of poor families and their children, being particularly hit by the crisis and being relatively well endowed with data sources, the State of São Paulo thus serves as an appropriate case study on the basis of which we shall attempt to answer the question posed above.

2. MAJOR CHANGES OF THE 1960—80 PERIOD: THE POLICIES OF THE 1964—73 YEARS

This section presents data summarizing important trends and transformations of the Brazilian socio-economic structure from 1960 to 1980. As far as economic growth is concerned, it can be seen from Table IV.1 that these two decades were clearly a period of advancement and modernization by conventional standards. GDP per capita, industrialization and urbanization advanced at fast rates. The new pattern of output also found expression in exports with a higher manufacturing content.

Economic growth, however, did not occur at an even pace. The first two years of the 1960s were at the end of a boom period which started in 1954, itself marked by impressive annual rates of growth, which averaged 7.7% from 1954 to 1961. In 1962 and 1963 the economy lost momentum as the rate of growth plummeted to an average of 3.4% and the country faced a political crisis which culminated in the military takeover of 1964. This led to an authoritarian government that only now is apparently leaning towards a less restricted political system.

Low rates of growth continued until 1968 when the economy entered the 'miracle' years that lasted until 1973. Since then the economy entered a phase of worsening problems which led to the current recession. We shall leave for the next section the review of this last phase, concentrating here on policies followed from 1964 to 1973.

During those years the government followed an economic policy which emphasized new advancements in import substitution, diversification and growth of exports, increase in voluntary and compulsory savings, expansion of public investment and incentives to private capital accumulation. Together with internal political stability and favourable economic conditions from the international point of view,

Table IV.1. *Brazil – population and economic indicators, 1960–80*

Item	1960	1980
Population (million)	70.1	119.1
Average annual rate of growth (%)*	2.9	2.5
Percentage in urban areas	45.2	67.7
Percentage aged 0–15	42.7	37.4
Percentage aged 65+	2.7	4.3
Percentage of labour force		
in the manufacturing sector	8.6	15.7
in agriculture and mining	54.0	29.9
Economic indicators		
GDP (US $billion)	66.8	274.3
per capita (US $/year)	951.9	2302.6
Imports (US $million)	1293	22,955
Exports (US $million)	1269	20,132
Manufactures as percentage of exports	3	39
Average annual rate of inflation (%)*	44.5	42.8

Sources: Fundação Instituto Brasileiro de Geografia e Estatistica (FIBGE) (population); Getulio Vargas Foundation (economic indicators).
*Rates presented refer to 1961–70 and 1971–80, respectively.

this policy created an atmosphere highly favourable to economic growth which reached record rates in the 1968–73 period. To the rulers of the country these rates served to legitimize an era of political oppression and disrespect for human rights.

In addition to the criticism directed to the government's political behaviour, the policies of the 1964–73 years have also been negatively evaluated in their social aspects. There were social achievements, several of which are of recognized merit and are behind some of the figures in Table IV.2. But in my opinion the government social policy was overwhelmed by major handicaps and I shall touch here on four of them, going from an overall evaluation to more specific aspects.

First, there was undoubtedly an excessive emphasis on growth for its own sake. Nowadays only its most earnest defenders do not recognize that the government could have done better had it tempered its growth policy with more concern for the social implications. The worsening of the income distribution, as reflected by the figures in Table IV.2, reveals that the poor persistently lagged behind the rich. Government action in this period was concentrated on promoting economic growth and social policy was neglected to the point that in the current discussion about the role of the State there are more references to an 'Entrepreneurial State' than to a 'Welfare State'.[5] In such conditions, it is difficult to ignore that a lot more could have been done

to improve the living conditions of the poor when the economy was passing through a period of fast growth.

Second, this overall view encounters support when one analyses the distributive aspects of the government's tax and expenditure structures. After 1964, both have been the subject of changes or reforms that could have transformed them into instruments for redistribution of income or of the benefits from government expenditure. However, existing analyses have shown that the structure of taxes and government expenditures in Brazil remains essentially regressive.[6]

Third, the growth of expenditures and programmes in the area of education, social security, health care and welfare emphasized quantity and neglected quality, efficiency, efficacy and equity aspects. For instance, Table IV.2 reveals that growth rates of school enrolment in primary education lagged behind those of higher grades and that expansion was concentrated in college education. It is well known in Brazil that most of this expansion occurred in private colleges where to a larger extent education is considered a profitmaking activity like any other business. To the students it simply means attending classes and answering questions about lectures given by teachers who do not pursue an academic career and survive by lecturing in three or four 'superior schools' in a life that has been called 'taxi-teaching'.

Another example in which quantity accomplishments have their handicaps, this time in

Table IV.2. *Brazil — health-related, education and income distribution indicators, 1960–80*

Item	1960	1980
Health-related indicators		
Life expectancy at birth (years)	55	63
Infant mortality rate (aged 0–1, per 1000)	118	77
Child death rate (aged 1–4, per 1000)	19	7
Population per physician*	2560	1700
Percentage of dwellings with water supply and sanitation facilities[†]		
Piped water	24.5	50.9
Any sanitary device	49.0	75.1
Sewerage network or septic tank	23.8	37.4
Health expenditure as percentage of GNP[‡]:		
1.0 (1949), 2.5 (1975)		4.0
Education		
Number enrolled as percentage of age group[§]		
Primary education	95	89
Secondary education	11	32
Higher education	2	11
Adult literacy rate (15–69)	61	75
Income distribution		
Percentage share of income		
Richest 1%	12	17
Richest 5%	28	38
Poorest 50%	17	13
Average monthly income (Cr $1000 at May 1981 prices)[‖]		
Richest 1%	128.7	403.8
Richest 5%	65.7	187.8
Poorest 60%	4.2	8.8

Sources: World Bank, *World Development Report 1982* (health-related indicators and school enrolment, except water supply and sanitation facilities data and health expenditure as percentage of GNP); FIBGE (adult literacy rate and income distribution raw data; water supply and sanitation facilities data as presented by Knight and Moran (1981), pp. 35–36); Knight and Moran (1981) (health expenditures as percentage of GNP, 1949 and 1975); Oliveira (1982) (health expenditures as percentage of GNP, 1981).
*Second column shows data for 1977.
[†]Second column shows data for 1978 and excludes the rural Frontier as defined by the source.
[‡]Second column shows data for 1981.
[§]Second column shows data which refer to years not more than two years distant from 1979 (see source for additional details).
[‖]Growth of real income of poorest group occurred mostly during the 1970s, figures in the second column overestimate actual growth due to price indices which underestimate inflation.

terms of efficacy and efficiency, is in the area of health care. Here the impressive increase in expenditure share of GNP, as shown in Table IV.2, was accompanied by a radical change in the structural characteristics of the health care provided. The old structure depended on the fiscal budget and concentrated on preventive health care programmes such as the control of infectious diseases. The new system grew under the umbrella of the Social Security, Health Care and Welfare System (SSHCWS). It emphasizes curative medicine and privileged care by private hospitals, leaving public hospitals with excess capacity. Moreover, in both cases high technology curative medicine is provided to a few patients. The belief that the government is already spending too much money on health care hinders the expansion of a preventive system that could have a wider coverage measured in millions of persons who currently either receive inappropriate care or are left completely unattended.

Fourth, since the welfare system is a part of the wider SSHCWS, financed by payroll taxes, many benefits of this system, such as child allowance and lunch subsidies, are given only to urban workers who pay payroll taxes. This condition of eligibility thus excludes from the coverage of these benefits the rural workers, the people who are not wage earners, and those who are but do not have formal employment relationships. Given the structure of the Brazilian economy, this eligibility condition turns out to be regressive from the point of view of income distribution, since in general the characteristics of the poorest coincide with those of the persons excluded from the 'welfare' allowances.

To sum up: the government social policy during the 1964—73 years failed to pursue a growth strategy with more trickle-down effects for the people. This failure is symbolized by the worsening of the income distribution and by living conditions that remain unsatisfactory for a large part of the population. Social achievements could have had a wider scope if quality, efficiency and efficacy and equity considerations were brought into the picture. Now that rapid economic growth has come to a halt, the consequences of the 1964—73 government social policy will be underscored as the emerging additional problems brought about by the crisis will be dealt with by a government social apparatus that is ill-prepared to cope with the new realities of a transformed socio-economic structure.

3. THE CURRENT CRISIS AND ITS ORIGINS: 1974—83

Although it was only in 1981 that a negative rate of GDP growth became a reality in post-war Brazil, the crisis that brought the current recession was already in the making by the end of 1973. It was then that the first oil shock hit the Brazilian economy, then and still today heavily dependent on imported oil. Higher inflation rates and trade deficits immediately surfaced in 1974. Growth, however, was affected only to the extent that in the remainder of the decade the country could not repeat the high rates of the previous six years. Although at lower rates, growth continued until 1980. This was the outcome of the strategy adopted by the Brazilian government when facing the first oil shock.

One option open to the government was to follow the 'adjustment approach', that is, to deflate the economy to generate a trade surplus or at least to reduce the size of the forecasted deficit. At that time, and even today, the idea of tightening the belts was nevertheless very strange to a country coming out of the 'miracle' years. Independently of political beliefs, there is a widespread feeling among Brazilians that ours is the 'country of the future' and that continuing growth must be a basic objective of economic policy. The government was particularly fond of a favourable growth performance since this was considered an important basis for political legitimacy. Moreover, the international money markets found themselves with a lot of petrodollars which had gone to the OPEC countries as a counterpart of the deficits accumulated by the oil-importing nations. There were signs of their willingness to lend this money to Brazil and other nations needing it. Real interest rates in the international money markets were low and attractive.

The result was that the Brazilian authorities preferred to circumvent the crisis instead of taking harsh measures to absorb its impact. The course then followed was based on increased foreign indebtedness, further advancement in import substitution (this time in the area of raw materials and oil and its substitutes), investments in export-oriented projects and a larger debt by the public sector. Inflation was allowed to assume higher levels.

The second oil shock of 1979 further aggravated growth, inflation and balance-of-payments problems, even though the immediate reaction of the government economic authorities was a new attempt to circumvent the problems. External borrowing received new encouragement but this time the country found international bankers less willing to come to the rescue. Brazil then started to pay higher 'spreads' over the international interest rates. Moreover, these interest rates began to increase, posing an additional and important burden on servicing the larger debt.

To complicate further the scenario, the government adopted at the end of 1979 and beginning of 1980 a package of policies that only aggravated problems. The pace of nominal wage readjustments was accelerated by a new wage law, real interest rates were reduced and the exchange rate was left to lose real value after a devaluation undertaken in December 1979. Nineteen-eighty was almost another 'miracle' year: GNP showed a 7.9% gain. However, the trade deficit continued to be large, adding to the problems brought by the higher cost of servicing the debt. At the end of 1980 the country began to attempt adjustment policies; the crisis became evident in 1981.

In 1982, foreign debt management was further complicated by the combined problems of high interest rates, falling prices of commodities, bad export performance in general and the deteriorating confidence of international bankers especially after a group of countries declared their incapacity to service their debt and resorted to various forms of rescheduling or renegotiation. The Brazilian situation became critical after Mexico called for help in September 1982. Since elections were to be held 15 November, the government postponed the negotiations with the IMF and international bankers on the debt problem until December.

Table IV.3 presents data that summarize the events after 1973 and shows the dramatic worsening of Brazilian economic conditions in the past two years: negative rates of change of GDP per capita, inflation close to 100% a year and deteriorating external accounts as reflected by an enormous current account deficit,

aggravated indebtedness and a debt service ratio that reached 0.97 at the end of 1982, practically exhausting all the revenue from exports in amortizations and interest payments.

In its negotiations with the IMF and the international bankers, the major commitment made by Brazil was a planned trade surplus of US $6 billion in 1983 after one of only US $778 million in 1982. To accomplish this, Brazil put into effect a new package of policies to curb further internal demand and generate the surplus. Among the most important were a new devaluation of the cruzeiro, a cut in nominal wage readjustments, credit contention and ceilings on government expenditure.

As of June 1983 the Brazilian authorities were facing additional problems in the management of the external accounts since the IMF was delaying the liberation of one of the instalments of the credits negotiated in February. As a result, the government unveiled on 9 June 1983 a new package of restrictive policies. We shall return to this later in this paper. Among government officials, businessmen, the academic community and the general public, there was widespread pessimism about the course of

Table IV.3. *Brazil – growth, inflation, foreign trade and external debt*, 1973–82

Year	GDP – annual rate of change		Inflation* annual rate (%)	Balance in US $million	
	Total	Per capita		Trade	Current acct.
1973	14.0	11.2	21.2	7	−1688
4	9.5	6.8	32.9	−4690	−7122
5	5.6	3.0	34.5	−3540	−6700
6	9.7	7.0	45.6	−2255	−6017
7	5.4	2.8	42.4	97	−4037
8	4.8	2.3	41.1	−1024	−6990
9	6.7	4.2	56.8	−2840	−10,742
1980	7.9	5.3	94.7	−2823	−12,807
1	−1.9	−4.3	108.7	1202	−11,734
2	1.4	−1.1	95.4	778	−16,279

Year	Debt, reserves, debt service and exports in US $million					Debt service ratio	Gross debt[†]
	Reserves	Amortizations	Interest	Debt service	Exports		
1973	6416	2063	514	2577	6199	0.42	12,572
4	5269	1943	652	2595	7951	0.33	17,166
5	4040	2168	1498	3666·	8670	0.42	21,171
6	6544	3004	1810	4814	10,128	0.48	25,985
7	7256	4123	2103	6226	12,120	0.51	32,037
8	11,895	5426	2696	8122	12,659	0.64	43,511
9	9689	6527	4186	10,713	15,244	0.70	49,904
1980	6913	6689	6311	13,000	20,132	0.65	53,847
1	7507	7496	9161	16,657	23,293	0.72	61,411
2	3994	8179	11,358	19,537	20,175	0.97	69,653

Source: Central Bank of Brazil.
*Measured by national accounts implicit deflator.
[†] Refer only to debt registered at the Central Bank. Unregistered debt as estimated by Central Bank: US $13,636 million at the end of 1982.

events, with practically no one seeing a way out of the recession in the near future.

We now turn to the social impact of the current crisis. Before analysing the indicators of its effect on children, we shall take here a broad look at its impact in terms of unemployment, food prices and consumption and government social expenditures and policies.

No analysis will be made of income and income distribution data. National accounts in Brazil are published only after delay and provide only annual data. The latest figures refer to 1980.[7] Therefore, there is no recent information on aggregates such as disposable income on a short-term basis (e.g. quarterly data), that could show their behaviour since the recession started. Estimates of GDP per capita do exist and have been presented in Table IV.3, which covers the 1973–83 period. It can be seen that there was a reduction in 1981 and 1982.

As to the distributive impact of the crisis we are convinced that on the whole it is regressive. People who lose their jobs are mostly at the lower half of the income distribution. Those who own financial assets are concentrated in the upper half and are benefiting from the high real interest rates that follow the crisis. The burden of food prices, now growing above average prices, as we will report shortly, is also regressive given that the share of family budgets spent on food decreases with the level of income. Poor people are also likely to suffer more from the contraction of the public expenditures on health and education, to be shown later in this section.

(a) Unemployment

Regular unemployment indices on a monthly basis appeared in Brazil only in January 1980. Existing data cover only the six major metropolitan areas: São Paulo and Rio de Janeiro (from January 1980), Belo Horizonte and Porto Alegre (from April 1980) and Salvador and Recife (from June 1980). Analysis of the indices for the period 1980–83 is tricky because around April 1982, FIBGE, the government institute that calculates the indices, adopted a more restricted definition of unemployment, the result being an abrupt fall in the unemployment rate figures at that time. Moreover, FIBGE did not acknowledge the methodological change and the series has been published without mention of it. Another problem is that the seasonal pattern of the series is still unclear and the series is not seasonally adjusted.

To circumvent all these problems we organized the existing unemployment figures in such a way that comparisons between paired years can be made on the basis of compatible definitions of the unemployment rate and of the months to which they refer. The resulting data are presented in Table IV.4, where the dashed lines separate the compatible figures that can be compared in two subsequent years. It can be seen that with only a few exceptions the figures show an increase in unemployment in the 1981–83 years. In the case of São Paulo, on which our attention will be focusing, the increase in the unemployment rates is particularly clear.

Table IV.4. Brazil – comparisons of unemployment rates for metropolitan areas, 1980–83*

Year	Rio de Janeiro	São Paulo	Belo Horizonte	Porto Alegre	Salvador	Recife
1980[†]	7.53	5.67	7.61	4.55	7.09	6.81
1981	8.61	7.25	8.61	5.73	8.47	8.55
1981[‡]	8.34	7.39	9.90	5.91	8.68	8.30
1982	9.33	8.31	8.93	6.35	8.38	9.11
1982[§]	6.77	5.70	6.83	5.32	5.98	7.91
1983	6.47	7.20	7.89	7.10	5.61	8.49

Source: FIBGE.
*Compatible definitions of the unemployed and of the time period to which the rates refer.
[†]Comparisons between 1980 and 1981 are made on the basis of annual averages for Rio and São Paulo, April–December averages, for Belo Horizonte and Porto Alegre, and June–December averages, for Salvador and Recife.
[‡]Comparisons between 1981 and 1982 are based on first quarter averages.
[§]Comparisons between 1982 and 1983 are based on April–June averages.

(b) *Food consumption and prices*

As far as food consumption is concerned, we will first summarize an analysis of the evolution of the agricultural sector in recent years, made by Homem de Mello (1982), a well-known Brazilian agricultural economist. He takes the major components of the typical diet of the population and measures them in terms of their calories and protein content. The final result comprises figures for the total daily per capita calorie and protein content of the domestic availability (domestic production minus export plus imports) of food.

His analysis covers initially the period 1958–79 and shows that both the total calories and the total protein per capita contents remained stagnant since the middle 1960s at, around 2900–3000 calories and around 75–78 grams of proteins daily. For more recent years, Homem de Mello was able to follow only the changes in the calories and protein content of the production of the internal market vegetables group in the period 1977–82. The picture of stagnation again surfaced from the data thus confirming the view that it has lasted since the middle 1960s.

After finding that per capita income increased until 1980 and assuming that the income elasticity of the demand for food is greater than zero, de Mello's hypothesis was that one should expect a demand pull effect on prices. His analysis confirmed this proposition. The relative price of food increased over the years, not only in relation to the general price index but to some regional cost of living indices as well.

After 1981, this picture changed drastically. With falling per capita income, good harvests, high interest rates that discouraged private inventories and a slackened international market, the real price of food went down and exerted a relieving effect on the cost of living figures. This scenario was maintained until the end of 1982 and the beginning of 1983 when excessive rainfall in the South and drought in the Northeast damaged several crops and reduced supply. Table IV.5 shows the changes in various price indices covering two different periods: the year ending in April 1982 and the year ending in April 1983. The different role played by food prices in those two years is evident from the fact that their changes are the lowest in the first year and the highest in the second year.

At the beginning of the rise in the real price of food, the government was able to contain it by using its inventories. At the moment the belief among the experts, including Dr Homem de Mello, is that these inventories are depleted, the same having happened to the private inventories due to high interest rates. Moreover, as we were finishing this report, unusually high rates of rainfall in the autumn caused damage to major crops of basic staples such as rice and beans in the Southern region. It is therefore expected that food prices will continue to rise in the near future above other indices such as those shown in Table IV.5.

As far as manufactured food is concerned, the same table shows that their prices follow approximately the same behaviour of basic staples and agricultural products, especially in the year which ended in April 1983. We looked at the indices of per capita production of food by the Brazilian manufacturing sector in the 1976–82 years and found these indices increasing over the period, with the 1982 index being 108 (1976 = 100), therefore showing a more encouraging picture.[8] However, in this case the data were not corrected for imports and exports (nor inventories) and thus it is a very crude indicator of consumption. Moreover, one

Table IV.5. *Percentage change in various price indices*

Index	Year ended in April 1982	Year ended in April 1983
General Price Index	91.3	117.4
Wholesale Price Index	90.4	119.0
Food (staples)	82.1	138.8
Agric. products	71.8	138.6
Food (manufactured)	95.0	138.6
Cost of living – Rio	94.8	118.3
Food	84.8	133.3
Cost of living – São Paulo	85.6	114.9
Food	75.4	128.9

Sources: 'Conjuntura Econômica' and FIPE-Fundação Instituto de Pesquisas Econômicas.

can expect that the poorest are more limited in their access to manufactured food.

To sum up: except perhaps in the case of manufactured food, the per capita availability of food has not improved in recent years. Up-to-date information reveals that it was reduced in the short-run due to bad crops. This caused higher relative prices of food, a problem that will be made worse by cuts in subsidies to agricultural credit and to specific products such as sugar and wheat, which the government was announcing when we were finishing this report in June 1983. Falling per capita incomes and rising relative prices might further aggravate the availability of food from the standpoint of consumption.

(c) Government social expenditure

We shall present here a brief analysis of the recent trends in government social expenditures in the areas of health and education. We gathered information for the federal, state and city governments by ministry or department. The annual data we obtained are summarized in Table IV.6, which presents government expenditures in health and education as percentage shares of total expenditures and also expressed in indices of real value, in their total and per capita terms.

It can be seen that the only case of a clear increase refers to the expenditures on education by the federal government. Since this sphere of government typically spends mostly in other states the taxes collected in São Paulo, we are convinced that this state did not benefit in a significant way from this increase. Moreover, it is known that this increase was largely the result of an increase in the salaries of the faculty of the federal universities. Therefore, it does not mean an increase in services provided to the poor.

Table IV.6. *Government expenditures on health and education by level of government, 1978–82**

Year	As share of total expenditures		Indices of expenditures at constant prices (1978 = 100)[†]			
	Health	Education	Health		Education	
			Total	per capita	Total	per capita
Federal government [‡] [§] [‖]						
1978	1.9	6.9	100	100	100	100
1979	2.0	7.5	97	95	105	103
1980	1.5	8.0	86	82	127	121
1981	1.6	9.7	80	74	139	130
1982	1.7	10.4	90	82	157	144
State of São Paulo government [¶]						
1978	3.6	15.9	100	100	100	100
1979	3.6	17.8	100	98	111	109
1980	3.3	17.1	87	83	100	96
1981	3.6	16.7	91	85	95	89
1982	3.3	16.8	85	78	98	89
City of São Paulo government [§] [¶]						
1978	4.3	7.9	100	100	100	100
1979	4.8	9.7	106	103	117	114
1980	5.1	9.4	102	97	104	99
1981	6.1	9.8	121	113	106	99
1982	5.5	10.0	108	99	109	100

Sources: Ministry of Planning – National Centre for Human Resources (Federal government data); Department of Finance – State of São Paulo (State government data); Department of Finance – City of São Paulo (City government data).

*As a share of total expenditures and as indices (1978 = 100), total and per capita.

[†] Per capita figures assume a 2.3% annual rate of growth of population.

[‡] Indices are based on data deflated by source.

[§] Includes expenditures on education and culture.

[‖] Health expenditures exclude those made by the medical assistance branch of the social security and welfare system.

[¶] Indices of expenditures after deflation by the General Price Index (Domestic Availability Criterion).

At the state level, expenditures on education have fallen if evaluated in per capita terms while the city government has barely kept them in line with the growth of population. Expenditures on health have decreased at the federal and the state level and only the city has maintained the per capita levels of the past.

Therefore, we are left with an overall picture of falling or, at most, stagnant government expenditures on health and education. From this, however, one cannot jump to the conclusion that this has caused a reduction of the services provided. The largest part of these expenditures are salaries and their stagnation or fall is to a great extent the result of the 'wage squeeze' to which, in general, the salaries of the public servants have been submitted over the years. Of course, sooner or later this wage policy will affect the quality of the services rendered. When we were finishing this report, public servants, from the three levels of government, were engaged in a partial strike against low salaries. Moreover, the services most affected by the strike are those where curtailment causes more problems to the community and therefore enhances the bargaining power of the strikers. On the basis of present and past experiences of strikes of public servants in São Paulo, their action is felt mostly in the case of hospitals, health services in general and child care centres.

4. LOOKING FOR SPECIFIC EXAMPLES OF EFFECTS ON CHILDREN

We follow here the taxonomy suggested by UNICEF for the presentation of indicators. Subsection (a) covers 'outcome' indicators of health conditions such as infant mortality rates (IMR), child death rates (CDR), low birth weight rates (LBW) and several indicators of morbidity. In subsection (b) we present 'process' indicators covering school attendance and coverage of immunization against infectious diseases, 'behaviour' indicators such as child delinquency and abandonment, and 'input' indicators related to government expenditure and availability of housing and public services.

(a) *'Outcome' indicators*

(i) *IMR and CDR*
In the State of São Paulo IMRs have been calculated since the end of the last century. They are defined in the conventional way: number of deaths of children less than one year old per

thousand live births over a period of time. The data is gathered and published by Fundação SEADE, the State's census bureau. The IMR from 1896 to 1982, shows a consistent trend towards lower rates. For the state as a whole they go from around 200 in 1896—1902 to slightly below 50 in 1982. This trend follows improvements in health, education, living conditions and income per capita of the population as well as scientific advancements in the treatment of diseases, including immunization, together with progress in the provision of preventive and curative health care either from government or private sources.

There were, however, deviations from this declining trend. One that attracted attention occurred in the late 1960s and continued until the middle 1970s. After reaching an average of 75.23 in 1960—68, the rates jumped to an average of 85.95 in 1969—75. This rise in IMR, which also coincided with the 'miracle years', can be linked to the increased migration from the rural areas and other Brazilian regions to the heavily urbanized areas of São Paulo State, where deteriorating living conditions (crowded and bad housing, lack of appropriate water supply and sanitation facilities, among others) became widespread. Public investment in infrastructure lagged and there was a decay in the health care provided by the government, particularly in terms of preventive action.

The fall in IMR thereafter is apparently the result of investments made by the government in the area of water supply and sanitation facilities, especially in the 1974—78 years, a reduction of the housing deficit, improved health care and immunization programmes, together with reduced migration and lower birth rates among the poorest groups. When discussing the 'input' indicators we shall return to this question.

This discussion of the long-run trend and of recent fluctuations in the IMR has the purpose of presenting an argument related to the impact of the current crisis. In our opinion the behaviour of IMR is largely the result of factors which work with medium and long-term effects. IMR continued to fall even after the recession started in 1981 but this is probably a result of the continuation of the effects which have brought them down since 1976. As the recession continues, it is not unlikely that IMR will rise again in the future.

Table IV.7 presents IMR for the period 1979—82 covering São Paulo State as a whole, as well as the City of São Paulo, the interior and the 11 administrative regions of the state. We present only the annual rates since 1979.

Table IV.7. *State of São Paulo – infant mortality rates, 1979–82*

Region	1979	1980	1981	1982*
State	59.28	51.75	50.32	48.53
City of São Paulo	62.49	53.63	54.66	51.98
Interior of the State	57.65	50.80	48.11	46.81
Greater São Paulo	64.90	55.86	56.36	53.25
Coast	53.93	57.34	49.49	48.87
Vale Paraiba	52.28	45.34	40.21	37.25
Sorocaba	71.10	67.13	59.55	63.14
Ribeirão Preto	42.88	35.72	36.67	33.45
Bauru	54.04	48.63	53.71	52.57
São José Rio Preto	48.33	40.93	38.78	35.52
Araraquara	44.04	39.05	34.09	32.97
Presidente Prudente	49.61	42.13	41.72	39.69
Marilia	59.14	57.12	52.79	52.56
Campinas	52.37	41.27	37.80	39.72

Source: Fundação SEADE.
*Includes January 1983.

Until the last month for which data were available (January 1983) we found no evidence that the declining trend after 1976 had been broken.

(ii) *CDR*

The relation of the IMR to poverty aggravated by recession is handicapped by the fact that infant mortality is largely the effect of perinatal causes that can be alleviated by specific medical intervention. The literature suggests that CDR are better indicators of socio-economic conditions given that mortality in the age range 1–4 tends to be more affected by malnutrition and exposure to diseases that proliferate in the environment typically faced by the poor: bad housing, contaminated water, lack of sanitation and pollution of all sorts.

We could not find more recent estimates of CDR as they are defined within the age group 1–4. As a proxy for them we took the number of deaths in this age group as a percentage of the total number of deaths. The estimates for the state and the capital covering the period 1975–81 are presented in Table IV.8. As in the case of the IMR, they also show a continuous fall.

As to the major causes of deaths, again we have data only until 1981. Table IV.9 presents information on the causes of deaths within the first year of life and specifically for the age group 28 days–1 year.[9] We present data from 1950 to 1975, at intervals of five years, and annual data from 1979 to 1981 for the state as a whole. Moreover, Table IV.9 contains data for the age group 1–4 for the years 1970, 1975 and 1979–81. The older data serve to show

Table IV.8. *State and City of São Paulo – number of deaths in the age group 1–4 as a percentage of the total number of deaths, 1975–81*

Year	State	Capital
1975	3.45	3.74
1976	3.09	3.39
1977	3.03	3.17
1978	2.73	2.76
1979	2.48	2.52
1980	2.31	2.49
1981	2.11	2.26

Source: Fundação SEADE.

that although in 1981 the health authorities succeeded in reducing the percentage of deaths caused by measles, a disease that can be controlled, the percentage observed for 1981 is still above the lower rates of the 1950s. As we shall see in the following subsection, the recent fall in the percentage of deaths caused by measles can be linked to an increased rate of immunization.

The same table also shows, as compared to the 1950s, that the percentage of deaths by malnutrition is at high levels and that there is an increase in the percentage of deaths caused by respiratory diseases, particularly in the second age group, a result possibly caused by increased pollution. As far as diarrhoea is concerned, it seems that this disease has been attacked effectively only in 1980 and 1981.

Again it is important to look at the age group 1–4. It can be seen that enteritis has been reduced since 1978 but malnutrition continues to take its toll.

Table IV.9. *State of São Paulo – causes of death by age groups as percentage of total within each age group*, 1950–81

Age group and cause of death	1950	1955	1960	1965	1970	1975	1979	1980	1981
Less than 1 year									
Measles	0.30	0.38	0.64	0.74	0.48	0.87	1.20	1.24	0.72
Malnutrition	3.77	3.22	2.48	7.50	3.97	3.88	5.51	5.03	4.65
Diarrhoea	23.29	29.42	21.53	12.11	26.0	31.07	20.43	18.66	17.05
Respiratory diseases	11.90	13.05	16.85	19.03	21.04	18.95	17.09		
28 days–1 year									
Measles	0.46	0.35	0.46	0.49	0.37	0.73	2.30		
Malnutrition	5.04	4.02	3.35	11.92	6.23	5.85	9.62		
Diarrhoea	33.17	41.82	33.42	19.79	39.06	42.73	30.48		
Respiratory diseases	14.62	14.63	20.64	23.52	26.27	23.22	30.56		
1–4 years									
Enteritis					15.06	14.97	9.99	9.21	9.46
Malnutrition					5.07	5.33	4.92	5.08	5.43

Source: Fundação SEADE.

Since the data in Table IV.9 are expressed as percentages, the analysis is handicapped because when one cause loses ground the others increase their shares. In any case we can conclude that although the analysis of mortality shows diminishing IMR and CDR the children continue to die of causes that could be controlled by public action. Although some successes in this respect have been achieved in recent years, there is still a lot to be done. As to the impact of the current recession, one cannot say, for instance, that the higher percentage of deaths due to malnutrition, as shown by Table IV.9, is clearly a result of the crisis. But one is to be concerned that the crisis will cause further hardship to the poor families by making it difficult to increase the public funds directed to the control of the diseases that affect the poor and their children or perhaps even reducing these funds as indicated in the previous section.

(iii) *LBW*

LBW rates were usually measured by taking the percentage of children born alive weighing less than 2.5 kg. We found information from two hospitals that provided the data for 1980–82 shown in Table IV.10. The rates shown are slightly below the international average of 17%, as estimated for 1979 by the World Health Organization.[10] We were informed by doctors that rates above 10% deserve concern. It can be seen that the 1982 figures are above those of 1980, although in 1980 and 1981 there was an up and down movement in the case of the São Paulo Maternity.

Table IV.10. *City of São Paulo – low birth weight data from two hospitals*, 1980–82

Hospital	Percentage of children born alive weighing less than 2.5 kg		
	1980	1981	1982
São Paulo Hospital	14.51	15.02	15.36
São Paulo Maternity	14.83	16.12	15.41

Sources: São Paulo Hospital and São Paulo Maternity.

Aggregate data from Fundação SEADE confirms a worsening picture. It records LBW rates from infant mortality data (children less than one year old), both as percentage of the total cases of infant mortality and as percentage of the cases where weight at birth was known by the person who provided the information. The rates for the State of São Paulo, the capital and the Greater São Paulo area are presented in Table IV.11, which covers 1979–81. There is a consistent pattern of increasing LBW rates over this period.

Again it would be over-hasty to attribute these findings to the current recession. But here we have found another indicator of health conditions that should be monitored by the public health authorities. At the moment it is showing signs of a deteriorating picture that requires closer inspection. However, in the absence of monitoring by those authorities, there will be no knowledge of the information, nor inspection and no action taken if it turns out to be a real problem.

Table IV.11. *Children who weigh less than 2.5 kg at birth who die before first birthday as a percentage of all children who die before first birthday and as a percentage of those whose weight at birth is known. State capital and Greater São Paulo Region, 1979–81*

Year and region	Percentage of known and unknown weight at birth	Percentage of known weight at birth
State of São Paulo		
1979	17.1	67.9
1980	18.2	68.2
1981	19.9	73.3
Greater São Paulo		
1979	19.3	69.3
1980	21.6	69.6
1981	22.0	72.3
City of São Paulo		
1979	19.7	73.8
1980	22.2	73.7
1981	23.1	74.3

Source: Fundação SEADE.

(iv) *Morbidity: the FAISA data*

A major difficulty of the data thus far presented in this section is that they refer to aggregate information and do not cover 1982, the second year of the recession. For the analysis of morbidity we found more detailed and up-to-date information which better suits the purpose of this paper.

This information comes from Santo André, one of the most important cities of the state, with a population of 550,000 in 1981. It is located in the most industrialized region of the state, the so-called ABC region, comprising the cities of Santo André, São Bernardo and São Caetano. Being an industrial city, it was particularly hard hit by the current recession. Moreover, we found there an institution which provides health care to the city's children and which keeps good records on its patients and services. This institution is FAISA (Foundation for the Assistance to the Children of Santo André).

Founded in 1966, FAISA is supported mainly by the city's budget. It has a network of units composed of a hospital, 20 health care centres scattered in the city and two centres for emergency cases, open daily on a 24-hour schedule. We have been told that it is not 'supply constrained', that is, if required it could increase the services provided. This is an important analytical point since what we are looking for are signs of an increased demand for these services as a result of the crisis.

In addition to this overall structure, our attention was attracted by the amount of detailed information collected by FAISA from the children and their families and by the fact that this information is assembled in readily available monthly reports. We made extensive use of this information by constructing various monthly indicators of morbidity and other phenomena revealed by the FAISA data, collected for the period 1980–82.

We shall present here only a few examples of the nature of the data available and a summary of what they show. Monthly averages of total attendance of outpatients in FAISA's network showed the following figures: 16,267 (1980), 16,089 (1981) and 17,556 (1982). Therefore, there was a sharp increase in 1982. This rise is consistent with what one would expect from the down-and-up movement of the crisis. Since 1980 was a good year, its effect might have continued in 1981, with the impact of the crisis thereafter felt in 1982.

The 1982 increase was stronger in the emergency services. Data gathered from the diagnosis of the children attended by these services are presented in Table IV.12. Attendance is presented by age group, together with the percentage of the diagnosis of several diseases which are considered indicators of poverty and hardship conditions. The percentages by themselves show a mixed picture and the down-and-up pattern is again present in the largest aggregate of diseases listed in the Table IV.12

Table IV.12. *City of Santo André – FAISA emergency services diagnosis of diseases, 1980–82 (monthly averages)*

Information	1980	1981	1982
Number of outpatients	7170	7443	8578
Percentage by age group:			
less than 1 month	2.64	2.08	1.84
between 1 and 12 months	26.68	27.68	26.82
between 1 and 4 years	44.34	46.68	46.25
Percentage of cases of:			
1. Gastroenterocolitis	10.15	10.44	9.68
2. Measles	0.52	0.28	0.36
3. Malnutrition	0.07	0.07	0.10
4. Kwashiorkor	0.001	0.004	0.004
5. Anaemia	0.21	0.26	0.30
6. Bronchopneumonia	3.22	2.53	3.22
7. Pneumonia	0.45	0.28	0.25
8. Marasmus+1+2+3+4+5	10.96	11.05	10.44
9. 8+6	14.17	13.57	13.66
10. Behaviour disturbance and school deficiency	0.04	0.08	0.08

Source: FAISA.

(line number 9). However, the large increase in attendance means that the absolute number increased in all cases in 1982. In addition to this, concern emerges from the higher proportion of the 1–4 year group in 1981–82, as well as with the cases where an increasing trend is clearer (malnutrition and anaemia).

It would be interesting to check if the income status of the additional families that looked to FAISA in 1982 was different from the families usually treated, with an effect on the percentages shown in Table IV.12. FAISA gathers data on the income status of the families but they refer only to families who register their children in the health care centres. The number of families reached 229 (1980), 233 (1981) and 222 (1982). On the basis of the cost of a basic diet which takes into account the family needs given its age structure, FAISA separates cases of income surplus from income shortage. The ratio of the former to the latter reached 0.34, 0.24 and 0.26 in these three years, respectively. Thus there was a reduction of the proportion of cases of income surplus from 1980 to 1981 but no important change thereafter, when the largest increase in attendance occurred. Another indicator of increasing economic hardship is that shortage cases ranked by their importance show an increasing proportion of complete shortage of income.

FAISA also evaluates the nutritional level of the children up to three months old who are registered in its health care centres for regular attendance. Data for 1981 and 1982 show 943 and 915 registrations respectively. There were only slight changes in the results of the diagnosis between the two years. The percentage of first degree malnutrition changed from 15.5 to 15.8, second degree from 5.1 to 4.9 and third degree from 0.7 to 0.8.

Therefore, the analysis of the information gathered from FAISA shows signs of increasing economic hardship that is reflected in the higher demand for the services it provides. It was not possible to check if this higher demand means that FAISA services are taken as substitutes for other services or if it was caused directly by the crisis in the sense of a larger attendance due to increasing need, regardless of substitution effects.

In any case, the increase raises concern, as do the signs of aggravation of morbidity cases. Although the impact of the crisis is not yet clear, there are already signs that should come to the attention of the public authorities. Another lesson learned from the FAISA data is that they certainly constitute valuable information if one is to follow the impact of the crisis. Being up to date, comprehensive and detailed, they are particularly suited for this type of analysis.

(b) *Other indicators*

(i) *'Process indicators'*

In this case, the indicators refer to school attendance and behaviour and coverage of immunization against infectious diseases. We first looked at figures of schooling rate by age (enrolment as percentage of age group) and rates of failure (drop-out plus lack of achievement rates) in the public (state) school system. The available data do not go beyond 1981. Schooling rates from 1970 to 1981, taken from FIBGE's household surveys, show an increasing trend for all age groups except the 7–9 group. Even in this group there is growth between 1977 and 1981, recovering from a previous fall. The same pattern occurs both for the Greater São Paulo region and the State as a whole.

The rates of failure, provided by the State's Department of Education, cover the first eight grades and were analysed for 1978–81. They show an increase over the years, caused mainly by the increase in the lack of achievement rate. Since the worsening of the rate of failure appears from the beginning of the period, it cannot be linked with the current recession. However, if the slackening of growth since 1974 has translated itself into higher unemployment rates before 1981, these might have affected school behaviour. This could occur, for instance, if larger enrolment consists of children with poor educational background who are taken into the school system either to get free lunches or to allow their parents to work or to look for a job. Lack of money for educational materials and other effects of economic hardship at home might also have affected their behaviour.

The worsening of the rates of failure probably also reflects supply problems. It is well known in São Paulo that, in general, the public school system offers poor quality education. The private system is preferred by those families who can afford it. The state system suffers, among other problems, from poor administration, low salary teachers who have no incentives to work efficiently, lack of money for material expenses and size (it has around 200,000 teachers).

Although we found no signs of a specific effect of the crisis in 1981, it is likely that, in view of the demand for schooling, the current crisis will further aggravate the low achievement rates and, to a lesser extent, the drop-out rates. Nevertheless, looking at the current situation from the side of supply, it is clear that any attempt to improve the public system will require huge sums of money. Given the shortage of money in the public budgets of the State and cities, which are the major source of support for primary and secondary education, one cannot help being pessimistic in this respect.

Immunization coverage. This is an area where clear improvements have been accomplished in recent years. We examined figures provided by Fundação SEADE on the number of doses of various vaccines applied from 1975 and 1981 in the State of São Paulo. There were sharp increases, clearly above population growth and particularly in 1980–81, in the number of vaccines of various types (Sabin, measles, D.P.T. and D.T.). The decreases were found in the cases of vaccines against smallpox, which has been practically eradicated, and tuberculosis, now apparently under control.

This expanded immunization coverage is probably one of the reasons for the fall in infant mortality examined in the previous subsection. In the case of deaths caused by measles, it seems that the extended immunization was in response to aggravated needs. Lags in the monitoring system and/or in corrective action have occurred in this and other cases. The challenge for the future is to enhance the role of immunization as a preventive measure and, if a problem emerges, to have rapid knowledge of it and to reduce the lag between knowledge and action. The analysis re-emphasizes the need for a good monitoring system and the importance of directing resources to preventive medicine. Again we find an area where shortage of public funds can have serious consequences for the children.

(ii) *'Behaviour' indicators*

'Behaviour' indicators were obtained from FEBEM (The State of São Paulo Foundation for Children's Welfare) and from the social service units (SSUs) of the State of São Paulo Department of Social Welfare which are attached to some police districts in the city of São Paulo. Additional data were provided by the State's Special Court for Minors.

FEBEM data for the years 1979–82 showed a slight reduction in the number of assisted children from 1980 to 1982. A clear increasing trend was found in the percentage and absolute number of children given up by parents and delivered by them to FEBEM, most commonly for economic reasons. At the same time there was a reduction in the corresponding figures of children found abandoned and then taken up by FEBEM. This change of behaviour on the part of the families might reflect an increased willingness on the part of FEBEM to accept children. It was not possible to certify the influence of demand behaviour or supply constraints.

Similarly, no clear picture emerges from SSU data. Occurrence of social cases (child abandonment and migrants without money, among others) increased in some police districts and fell in others. Creation of new units made the analysis very difficult: do new units reflect additional demand or supply or do they substitute for units already in existence? The system is still new and has only a few units. In most cases, however, they show an increasing proportion of cases of unemployment and economic hardship.

Data from the State's Special Court for Minors did not show an increase in the number of cases involving major or petty crimes in the City of São Paulo. However, it is known that cases that go to the Court are only a minor part of the cases that actually occur. These are also underrepresented in the police records since victims rarely fill in complaint forms.

(iii) 'Input' indicators

Here we will report on information on the availability of services and government expenditures that can be considered 'inputs' to children's welfare. As far as government expenditures are concerned, the information presented here is more specific than the data discussed in Section 3.

A study undertaken jointly by UNICEF and FIBGE in Brazil shows, for the State of São Paulo, a considerable improvement in the home use of water supply and sanitation facilities linked to public networks. Coverage of water supply from this source increased from 58.6% in 1970 to 74% in 1977; in the same period, coverage of the public sewerage network rose from 22.2 to 49.3%.[11] The information is not up-to-date but it is important since it reveals improvements that can also be associated with the falling mortality rates presented in the previous subsection. It is also relevant if one bears in mind the impact of the current crisis on the expansion of water supply and sanitation facilities, as government budgets become increasingly tight.

Data from FIBGE's household surveys also reveal an improvement from 1978 to 1981 of the housing conditions of the population in the State of São Paulo, since they show an increase in the average number of rooms per house, practically across the entire range of the size distribution of houses.[12] This we attribute to the effect of the housing programme established by the government in the middle 1960s, which is financed by savings accounts in the banking system and by compulsory savings accruing from payrolls. The latter constitute a fund also used for severance pay to workers who leave their jobs and is therefore suffering from the depression both in terms of inflow and outflow of resources. From this compulsory saving scheme also comes the money that finances most of the public investment by states and cities in the area of water and sanitation facilities. The savings account deposits in the

banking system are also losing ground in the recession and are adversely affected by the competition of other financial assets as well as foreign exchange and gold. Thus the outlook for the housing programme is also gloomy and one can expect an unfavourable impact on housing conditions as the crisis develops, which will compound the lack of resources for water supply and sanitation facilities.

For the city of São Paulo, Department of Education data show a considerable expansion of the nutrition programmes in its primary school system and day-care centres, from 1979 to 1982, both in quantity and real value terms. Therefore, it seems that the city government is responding to the deficiencies of nutritional status diagnosed in the past and to the increasing needs brought by the recession. However, as we talked to local authorities we found cause for concern in the fact that the 1983 budget will need additional resources if the levels of programme attendance are to be maintained. Increasing food prices also add to the problem. It is likely that the Department of Finance will provide additional resources but further expansion of the programme is now very much in doubt.

5. EFFORTS AND POLICIES TO PROTECT CHILDREN AND THE VULNERABLE, 1979–83

As the crisis worsened and unemployment figures reached the headlines, spokesmen for public opinion and the government authorities began to discuss how to cope with the crisis. Since there is no unemployment compensation, the unemployed are clearly vulnerable. The widespread concern that the crisis might lead to social unrest and political problems became stronger after riots and looting occurred in São Paulo early in April 1983.

It is the federal government which holds the key to concrete action. It manages most of the public resources and controls most of the areas that could be influenced by legislation, particularly in terms of new taxes, credit, money and welfare protection. Thus far the federal government has rejected the idea of establishing a system of unemployment compensation. Government authorities continue to say that they prefer an 'employment policy' but this idea has not yet advanced beyond lip service.

But it would be unfair to say that the federal government has no social concern in the face of the crisis. A couple of months after the second oil shock, in 1979, the government changed the indexation of wages in the private sector and public enterprises from annual to semi-annual. Moreover, it decided that for wages up to three times the minimum wage the workers would receive an additional 10% bonus calculated on the basis of the rate of indexation itself. On the whole, the new scale of indexation established that the higher the wage the lower the rate of readjustment.

When the semi-annual wage indexation system was adopted, inflation was around 50% a year. Now it is close to 130%. Therefore, the idea of the new policy was frustrated by increasing rates of inflation. More recently, the government eliminated the 10% bonus over the rate of indexation, following the policy of curbing domestic demand. Now lower wages continue to receive higher readjustments than higher wages but the erosion of their purchasing power proceeds.

When we were finishing this report, the word in the headlines was 'de-indexation'. It seems that the government is altogether dissatisfied with the role of indexation in perpetuating inflation and internalizing external price shocks. Therefore, it wants to phase out a part of the existing system. De-indexation is a process in which some social groups might lose more than others, and a few might even gain, depending on the timing and extent to which their incomes will be disconnected from the indexation mechanisms and on their reaction to it. The best hope one could have is that it would be conducted on the basis of equity principles and that the poor would not be hurt in the process. At the moment they are being hurt by unemployment and the rising real cost of food. A second-best hope is that de-indexation will not compound their plight.

Another action that reflects social concern on the part of the federal government was the creation of the FINSOCIAL (Fund for Social Investment) in May 1982. Following the tradition of the Brazilian tax system, it is funded by indirect taxation. Assuming that its incidence falls on consumers, the FINSOCIAL is a regressive tax. Again, this is no novelty in Brazil. However, this evaluation could lose force if the expenditure side of the scheme was clearly progressive.

The expenditure side of FINSOCIAL is not, however, clearly defined. The decree-law that introduced it says that its funds are for programmes in the areas of food and nutrition, housing for the poor, health, education and support of poor farmers. In the first year of the programme, revenues of Cr $132 billion, or roughly US $300 million, were collected

and not immediately spent by the agency in charge of the FINSOCIAL, the BNDES (National Bank for Social and Economic Development). For 1983 it is expected that the fund will raise Cr $500 billion or approximately US $1 billion.

The first allocation, at the end of 1982, comprised only Cr $60.8 billion, of which Cr $11.9 billion went to nutrition programmes, Cr $14.4 billion to school lunch for first grade students, Cr $14.5 billion to facilitate location of families in the frontier regions and Cr $20 billion to housing for poor families.[13] Thus far there has been no analysis of the impact of these expenditures although it is clear that the lag between revenue and expenditure is one of the major handicaps of FINSOCIAL.

In retrospect, we think that the expansion of the nutrition programmes by the Department of Education of the city of São Paulo is also a case that reveals concern by public authorities with regard to those affected by the crisis.

On the whole, however, the lack of a consistent effort to cope with the effects of the crisis as it affects people in general and children in particular, overwhelms these few instances in which some action has been taken. The scope of the problems that are emerging is clearly beyond the impact of the measures thus far undertaken. Moreover, there is no evidence that the federal authorities, who actually hold the power to introduce major changes, are yet in the process of changing their minds. This change by itself, would be a good start.

6. CONCLUSIONS AND LESSONS TO BE LEARNED

As we were finishing this paper in June 1983, the IMF had suspended the second instalment of the loan it had promised to Brazil in February, arguing that the government had failed in applying the stabilization programme negotiated with the Fund. Major failures occurred in the control of public debt and credit limits from the financial sector.

Reacting to this suspension, the government decreed a new package of restrictive measures, raising taxes and cutting expenditures, just as an IMF mission was arriving for new negotiations. Thus far there is no news of cuts in social expenditures of the type analysed in Section 3. However, the government decided to cut subsidies of wheat prices as well as of oil, a major input in mechanized agriculture. This sector is also going to suffer from cuts in subsidized credit to producers.

As we argued in this paper, food prices have

been increasing more than most of the price indices. The cut in subsidies will aggravate this situation. On top of all this, an unusual rainy season in the past three weeks has destroyed a considerable portion of the basic staple crops such as rice and beans.

On the whole, inflation is expected to rise as a result of the phasing out of subsidies. The existing system of staggered indexation, on a semi-annual basis, is insufficient to maintain the purchasing power of wages even in the cases where full indexation is applied. Moreover, starting this month the government curtailed from 11.5 to 7 times the minimum wage the range of wages where full indexation applies. Therefore, the picture ahead is truly bleak. Falling real incomes and further unemployment caused by a stabilization programme applied with renewed emphasis will compound the distressing situation of the poor families, particularly acute in the case of food.

In Section 4 of this paper, we concentrated on the analysis of the possible effects of the current recession on the welfare of the Brazilian children by developing a case study of the State of São Paulo. When assembling the data for this purpose, our concern was to widen the coverage of the data as much as possible. This was because the purpose was to look for evidence of the impact of the recession on the basis of various indicators. It was not within the scope of the analysis to investigate in detail the factors operating behind each indicator, although we have raised some hypotheses for a few cases. Nor was its intent to make detailed statistical analysis of the time-series assembled from the various sources.

The overall picture we obtained is one in which there are thus far no clear indications that the crisis has brought serious additional problems to children, in the sense of clearly causing a general and substantial worsening of the indicators of undesirable effects. However, there is already reason to be concerned about specific pieces of evidence gathered through the end of 1982. Worthy of special attention are the data that reveal the still high incidence of infectious diseases as causes of IMR and CDR, the worsening of the indicators of LBW, the aggravation of a few indicators of morbidity, the increased abandonment of children to public authorities and the gloomy outlook for food prices and government expenditures in general and, in particular, in the areas of health, education, water and sanitation, together with government induced investments in housing.

In addition to this concern over existing problems, there is now a widespread feeling in Brazil that the real challenge lies ahead. This is because the recession is becoming more serious and it seems, as suggested by the analysis presented in this paper, that its effects will come with a lag.

In this paper we covered various indicators. More difficult than the actual writing of the paper was the task of discovering these indicators, contacting people and friends to facilitate the access to data, and finding them after various attempts, including some unsuccessful ones. We are surprised not only by the large number of indicators that can be found scattered here and there but also by the fact that they remain largely ignored by those who ought to be concerned about them.

Therefore, an effort should be made to assemble all these indicators into an integrated and comprehensive system for monitoring the impact of the crisis as it affects people in general and children in particular. Such a system is badly needed first to arouse concern within the appropriate agencies of government, and second, but even more important, to induce these agencies to take corrective and preventive action.

NOTES

1. See Tables IV.1 and IV.2 for additional information on GDP rates of growth as well as the source of the data.

2. Furtado (1982) suggests a rate of 7%. Bonnelli's (1983) estimate is even higher: 7.7%.

3. Population data are from Fundação Instituto Brasileiro de Geografia e Estatistica (FIBGE). Table IV.2 contains other data on population.

4. FIBGE is the Brazilian census bureau.

5. See, for instance, Von Doellinger (1983).

6. The tax structure was analysed by Eris et al. (1983) and the expenditure side by Oliveira et al. (1979).

7. There are some estimates of family income on the basis of household surveys undertaken by FIBGE. The last one refers to 1981. However, these surveys have problems of comparability from one year to another. Moreover, the income data are published in such a way that the highest income bracket is open-

ended, thus making difficult the estimation of average incomes.

8. Monthly and annual indices of production in the manufacturing sector, at the two-digit level of industrial classification, are available from FIBGE. We assumed a 2.3 annual rate of population growth to obtain the per capita indices.

9. The disease cases that appear in the table have

been selected in consultation with experts in the analysis of the relation between health and poverty.

10. World Health Organization (1981).

11. FIBGE–UNICEF (1982).

12. FIBGE (1980 and 1983).

13. BNDES (1983).

REFERENCES

BNDES, *BNDES Report, 1982* (Rio de Janeiro: 1983).

Bonelli, Regis, Investimento e emprego face a desequilibrios internos e externos, in Persio Arida (ed.), *Divida Externa na Recessão e Ajuste Estrutural* (Rio de Janeiro: Paz e Terra, 1983).

Eris, Ibrahin, C. C. C. Eris, D. K. Kadota and N. R. Zagha, *A Distribuicão de Renda e o Sistema Tributário no Brasil* (São Paulo: Pioneira, 1983).

FIBGE, *National Household Surveys, 1978 and 1981* (Rio de Janeiro: 1980 and 1983 respectively).

FIBGE–UNICEF, *Perfil Estatistico de Criancas e Mães no Brasil* (Caracteristicas Socío-Demográficas – 1970–77) (Rio de Janeiro: 1982).

Furtado, Celso, *A Nova Dependência* (Rio de Janeiro: Paz e Terra, 1982).

Homem de Mello and Fernando Bento, *Conjuntura Agricola e Necessidade de Instrumentos de Estabilizacao da Renda*, research report (São Paulo: Fundação Instituto de Pesquisas Economicas, 1982).

Oliveira, José Teófilo, C. N. Porto, M. A. S. Vasconcellos and Nessim Zagha, *Efeitos Distributivos dos Gastos Públicos*, research report (São Paulo; Fundação Instituto de Pesquisas Economicas, 1979).

Von Doellinger, Carlos, As disfuncões sociais do estado, *Conjuntura Econõmica*, Vol. 37, No. 4 (April 1980), pp. 97–104.

World Health Organization, *Preparacion de Indicadores para Vigilar los Progresos Realizados en el Logro de la Salud para Todos en el Año 2000* (Geneva: 1981).

Vulnerable Groups in Recessionary Situations: The Case of Children and the Young in Chile

ALEJANDRO FOXLEY and DAGMAR RACZYNSKI*
CIEPLAN, Santiago, Chile

Summary. – This study analyses the impact which recessionary conditions have had in Chile on a particularly vulnerable age group: children and the young. In addition to the external crisis, Chile experienced serious imbalances in the form of inflation and balance-of-payments deficits in the early 1970s. Social development experts have long recommended the application of selective policies to 'target groups' whose situation is especially vulnerable to economic fluctuations. During the early 1970s, Chile implemented policies specifically designed to improve the situation of children, especially in terms of mother and child care, and programmes were undertaken to combat infant undernutrition. This paper evaluates the success of these programmes in counteracting the negative effects of the recession and the recessionary adjustment policies.

1. CHILEAN RECESSIONS: EXTERNAL AND INTERNAL FACTORS

The Chilean economy over the last decade provides an interesting case study of the impact of recessions on the most vulnerable population groups, particularly children and the young.[1]

From 1974 to 1982, the growth of GDP per capita in Chile was nil, as can be seen from Table V.1. The stagnation of the economy is also reflected in the low levels of investment during the period, as is also apparent from the figures in Table V.1. The average ratio of investment to GDP for the period 1974–82 was 15.2% which compares unfavourably with an average rate of 20.2% in 1970.

Table V.1. *Chile – macroeconomic indicators, 1974–82*

	GDP per capita		Investment rate	Real wages Index 1970 = 100	Real pensions	Unemployment rate		Social expenditure per capita P000 of 1978	Inflation rate
	P000	Annual				Open	Including MEP*		
1970	30.3		20.2†	100.0	100.0	5.7	5.7	4.853	36.1
1974	28.9	−0.6	17.4	65.0	59.3	9.2	9.2	5.345	369.2
1975	24.8	−14.4	15.4	62.9	52.0	14.5	16.8	4.004	343.3
1976	25.2	1.8	12.7	64.7	56.3	14.4	19.4	3.885	197.9
1977	27.2	8.0	9.9	71.4	60.9	12.7	18.5	4.317	84.2
1978	29.0	6.4	14.5	76.0	67.0	13.6	17.9	4.205	37.2
1979	30.8	6.5	15.6	82.3	75.9	13.8	17.6	4.247	38.9
1980	32.7	6.0	17.6	89.4	82.8	12.0	17.3	3.779	31.2
1981	34.0	3.9	19.5	97.7	n.d.	10.8	15.6	4.024	9.5
1982	28.7	−15.5	14.1	97.2	n.d.	20.5	26.3	4.268	20.7

Sources: Central Bank, *Cuentas Nacionales de Chile*, 1960–1980, INE; Cortázar (1980); Marshall (1981); Cortázar (1982); Ministry of Finance, *Exposición sobre el Estado de la Hacienda Pública* (Office of the Controller-General of the Republic).

*This column includes among the unemployed, persons employed under the Minimum Employment Programme (MEP), an emergency programme under which workers receive less than $30 per month.

†Average for the period 1960–70.

---

* The views expressed in this paper are those of the authors and not necessarily those of UNICEF.

The economic sluggishness of the last decade was due to the recurrence of two recessions in the Chilean economy: the first from 1975 to 1976 and the second beginning in 1981 and continuing at full strength up to the time of writing, June 1983 (see Table V.2). Between the two recessions there was a period of economic recovery, characterized by high growth rates of GDP.[2] As in other countries, intense discussions have been held on the origins of these recessions and, in particular, on the relative importance of the external factor, i.e. the general recessionary conditions prevailing in the international economy during a good part of the 1970s and the 1980s up to the present time.

Table V.2. *Chile – cycles within the recessionary period*, 1974–82

Years	Average growth rates of GDP
1960–70	4.2
1970–73	0.5
1974–76	−3.1
1977–80	8.5
1981–82	−4.7

Source: Central Bank, *Cuentas Nacionales de Chile*, 1960–1980.

In this connection it is interesting to compare the performance of the Chilean economy with that of other Latin American economies during the period in question. ECLA figures show that the performance of the Chilean economy has been below average since the 1970s, but the differences are more noticeable from 1974. It is also clear that the fluctuations in the growth of GDP per capita are much greater in Chile than in the rest of Latin America.[3]

The downward trends of GDP in the years in which external recessionary conditions prevail are much more striking in the case of Chile. Thus, for example, in 1975 GDP per capita fell by 14.4%, whereas for Latin America as a whole it rose by 1.1%. Only one other country, Argentina, showed negative growth for that year, but its rate was −2.2%, almost one-seventh of the drop for Chile. Something similar happened in 1982 when Chile again registered the greatest economic contraction, −15.5% as compared with −3.3% for the region as a whole. Moreover, in years of recovery, from 1977 to 1980, the Chilean economy showed higher rates than the others, partly owing to the previous larger fall.

An exhaustive analysis of the factors explaining these differences is not the purpose of this study, but the main explanations derive from two sources. The first is that the probable impact of the external crisis on Chile was different from that felt by other countries. This hypothesis would imply that the rise in import prices, including, of course, oil, and the drop in export prices affected Chile more severely than they affected other countries.

There is certainly some evidence of a deterioration in terms of trade in Chile both in 1975 and in 1982. The phenomenon was particularly severe in 1975 owing to the very favourable price conditions that had prevailed in the immediately previous year when the price of copper soared to extremely high levels while import prices did not yet show the impact of the rise in the cost of oil and other raw materials (we refer to 1974). The gains of 1974 were lost in 1975 when the terms of trade took a turn for the worse in Chile.

The fall in the terms of trade during 1975 is nil if compared with 1977, and 3–4% of GDP if the basis of comparison is the prices of 1965 (former National Accounts). If we assume that during the expansion of 1974 no countercyclical action was taken, such as building up reserves to offset future declines in the terms of trade, as actually occurred the following year, this would mean that the adjustment required was an amount equivalent to somewhere between 8 and 5% of GDP (combination of the gain of 1974, which disappeared the following year, plus the loss of 1975).

A sound economic policy would have enabled this adjustment to be spread over several years. Actually the terms of trade showed a recovery as early as 1976, so that part of the adjustment, had it been postponed, would have been avoidable.[4] Under existing economic policy, however, the whole adjustment was carried out in 1975 by means of a 'shock treatment'. The result was a much greater drop in GDP per capita, equivalent to −14.4%, as indicated in Table V.1. A similar reaction to the deterioration in the terms of trade took place in Chile in 1982. A 2% drop in terms of trade was accompanied by a 15.5% contraction in GDP per capita.[5] Once again this contraction was far greater than in other Latin American countries.

Is Chile's external sector structurally more vulnerable to fluctuations in external prices than that of other Latin American economies? Figures indicate that the terms of trade fell 40% for Chile in the recession of 1974–75, but for other countries of the region, such as Uruguay and Argentina, the impact was of the same order of magnitude (somewhat stronger in Uruguay and somewhat weaker in Argentina, if the impact accumulated in 1974 and 1975 is taken into account). Nevertheless, the performance of the latter two countries in terms of growth was less negative than in Chile: Uruguay grew by 4.5% in 1975 and Argentina by −2.2%, whereas Chile's rate was −14.4%.[6]

In light of the foregoing, the following conclusion may be drawn: the external factor was important in the recession which has beset the Chilean economy in recent years, but the reason for a good part of this recessionary phenomenon was strictly internal, namely, the nature of the policies chosen in Chile for carrying out the adjustment to adverse external prices. This conclusion is 'justified by a comparison of this case with the performance of other Latin American countries facing similar conditions.

2. THE RECESSION AND THE ADJUSTMENT POLICY CHOSEN: RESULTS

(a) *Distributive effects*

Since a large part of the Chilean economy's poor performance in the last decade (as illustrated in Table V.1), particularly its ineffective adjustment to negative external conditions, was due to the nature of the economic policies carried out, it is worth while to dwell briefly on a review of these policies.

Following a military coup in late 1973, Chile adopted an adjustment policy of a strictly monetarist nature to tackle these imbalances. It carried out these policies with a zeal and devotion which were made possible by the coming to power of an authoritarian regime which, over a period of 10 years, pledged full support for these policies. Thus, we have a case which is close to being a 'pure case' of monetarism in practice. In the view of its formulators this policy appeared to be the most suitable approach for dealing with these acute imbalances besetting the economy from the early 1970s, high inflation and a balance-of-payments deficit.

To achieve these objectives, a policy of cutting down aggregate demand was followed for a period of almost 10 years. For this purpose public expenditures, real wages and the incomes of the non-active population (pensioners) were drastically reduced. A contractionary monetary policy was implemented, but not always with successful results. At the same time, efforts were made to transfer to the private sector many of the functions previously exercised by the government, including the provision of basic social services in education, health, housing and social welfare. The economy was at the same time abruptly opened up to the outside world.[7]

As a result of the drastic monetarist experiment applied in Chile, the inflation rate was successfully reduced as indicated in Table V.1, but the economy stagnated: per capita growth was nil from 1974 to 1982. The rate of investment fell and the living conditions of wage-earners and lower-income groups deteriorated drastically. Real wages and pensions shrank by 40% as compared with a normal year (1970). On the average, unemployment (including the Minimum Employment Programme) continued at a level above 17% of the labour force, a rate more than three times higher than that of the 1960s. Per capita expenditure in the social sectors fell significantly, as indicated in Table V.1 (by 20% from 1974 to 1982). Moreover, consumption of the lower-income groups also fell off, unlike that of the high-income groups, as is apparent from Table V.3.

Table V.3. *Chile − consumption by income bracket**

Household	1969	1978
20% poorest	5953	4112
20% lower-middle	9243	7354
20% middle	12,219	10,754
20% upper-middle	16,058	16,527
20% richest	34,857	40,328
Average	15,666	15,815

Source: Cortázar (1980), Table 2.
*Monthly average per household in December 1979 pesos.

The defenders of the present monetarist approach have repeatedly maintained that the negative effect of some of the macroeconomic variables on the income levels of the poorest groups has been offset by an increase in expenditures in the so-called social sectors, and that a better 'safety net' has been created for those who suffer a drop in income or a deterioration in their employment conditions during the recession. Before evaluating that argument, it may be useful to outline briefly the historical background to the role played by the state in Chile in providing basic social services.

(b) *Social policies: historical context*

Chile has long experience in the implementaion of social policies.[8] Since the 1920s the state was given the responsibility of organizing the coverage of elementary needs in respect of education, health, nutrition, housing and social security. From the mid-1960s a further impetus was given to the social policies designed to incorporate the rural and marginal urban sectors. Thus social public expenditure expanded and policies of agrarian reform, rural trade union formation, neighbourhood organization in the urban popular sectors and redistribution of assets from the more concentrated private area to the state and social areas were promoted.

A study of the late 1960s reveals that public expenditures were distinctly progressive in that period. Social expenditures benefited the poorer half of the country in a proportion considerably higher than this group's share of the national income. Although this study shows that much leeway remained for making social expenditures even more progressive, these expenditures basically fulfilled the original purpose of redistributing income and property in favour of the poorer groups (Foxley *et al.*, 1979).

From 1974, with the military government and the implementation of monetarist policies as described above, for the first time since the 1920s a substantial decline occurred in per capita social expenditures, as will be discussed later. This was the result of stabilization policies that sought to cut back demand by reducing money supply and public expenditures.

According to the orthodox approach prevailing in Chile, the improvement in the lower-income sectors was expected to come mainly from economic growth rather than from income-distribution policies. Nevertheless, it was recognized that social programmes had a role to play in remedying inequities in the distribution of the national income.

The social programmes after 1973 were highly selective. They were often carried out in a context of overall reduction of expenditure in the sector concerned. Some of these programmes were certainly not new, they constituted an extension, with some changes, of programmes that had been in operation in the country for many years. The changes were designed to make selective some programmes that had previously been all-embracing and to enhance the benefits of the programmes in the case of high-risk or highly vulnerable groups. We will illustrate this in following sections.

Passing on now to institutional aspects, some radical reforms were undertaken. For example, efforts were made to let the market operate in the social sectors. For that purpose reforms aimed at encouraging the participation of the private sector in these activities were introduced and put into effect. With regard to social security, for example, in 1980 there was a transition from a distribution system administered by public bodies to a private system of capital formation in which pension funds were in the hands of private financial companies, the AFP (Arellano, 1980, 1981). In housing, the system of state-subsidized housing was reduced in size. The private sector was supposed to increase participation in the processes of financing, producing and marketing the housing intended for those entitled to the state contribution (Arellano, 1982, Tagle, 1982).

In education, management of the primary and intermediate school establishments was transferred to the municipalities in order to decentralize decision-making. At the university level, the registration fee for students was raised substantially. The system of state financing of the universities was changed so that the universities now compete for state funds by trying to attract the most promising students, for whom each university received a grant (Echeverría and Hevia, 1980; Nunez, 1982).

Reforms in the health sector were slower to appear than in the other sectors and were limited in relation to those originally proposed. From 1978 efforts were made to ensure that the allocation of funds among the public assistance units was related increasingly to the delivery of services. A proportion of the resources was allocated against submission of an invoice for care actually provided, for which purpose administrative prices were laid down for the various health services rendered. From the mid-1980s, as a pilot project, primary health care units began to be transferred to the municipalities. Furthermore, in late 1980 authorization was given for wage-earners' mandatory contributions to the health system to be used to contract for health care with private agencies (ISAPRES) which were to provide care equivalent to that of the public institutions with these contributions (Raczynski, 1982).

(c) *Pattern of social expenditures in the period* 1974–82

As mentioned earlier, the defenders of the present monetarist approach have argued that there was an increase in expenditures during the period, which allegedly offset the drop in the income levels of the poorest groups. In order to evaluate this, we updated a study by Marshall (1981), the results of which are presented in Tables V.4 and V.5. Table V.4 is self-explanatory in showing substantial cuts in social expenditures: the total per capita fell by 20% from 1974 to 1982. Moreover, per capita expenditures on education declined by 7%, and those on health by 8%. Public expenditures on housing shrank by 75% from 1974 to 1982. Only the expenditures on 'labour' showed a large increase, reflecting the cost of unemployment subsidies and the Minimum Employment Programme. Nevertheless, unemployment insurance coverage continued to be insignificant during this period. Only 15% of the unemployed were entitled to this benefit,[9] in stark contrast to the situation in the industrialized countries.

An examination of the figures for public investment in the social sectors shows the situation to be even more distressing. The relevant information appears in Table V.5. Investment in the social sectors fell by 80% from 1974 to 1982, as is apparent from a comparison of investment levels reached in each of these years. By 1982 investment in health and education was almost non-existent and in housing amounted to only 20% of the 1974 level.

3. THE IMPACT ON CHILDREN AND THE YOUNG

The above-mentioned economic conditions certainly had a negative effect on broad sectors of the population. The figures suggest that the impact was more detrimental for lower-income families. How did they affect the most vulnerable family members: the children and the young? That is the subject of the following sections of this study.

A warning should be given at this juncture. Owing to the nature of the information available which is either very condensed or too specific, it is not possible to obtain a complete picture of the impact on children and the young of the recessionary conditions prevailing in Chile over the last 10 years. This being so, attention should be drawn to the following two aspects. First, it is obvious that anything that has a negative effect on the welfare of families has a similar repercussion on children and the young. The conclusions of the previous section are therefore also applicable to children and the young. Second, the differential impact which recessive conditions can have on children and the young, as compared with other population

groups, will be influenced by several factors, in particular, the impact which specific policies designed for children and the young may have in worsening or improving the situation of these groups *vis-à-vis* the rest of the population.

As will be seen from the following pages, the present case under study is one in which, despite negative macroeconomic policies, the government implemented some specific policies designed for children, especially those of pre-school age, the outcome of which may be considered a success. The analysis will cover mainly indicators relating to health, feeding, education and labour, as relevant to three specific age groups: pre-school children (under 6 years); children aged 6—14; and the young, aged 14—24.

(a) *Situation of the pre-school population*

(i) *Infant and child mortality*
Traditionally infant and child mortality rates have been regarded as indicators reflecting the quality of life of a population. Thus, in the case of Chile, several studies in the past have revealed a close link between economic factors and the risks of infant mortality. Behm (1962) and Legarreta (1976) provide evidence to show that a child's risk of death decreases as the socio-economic level of the family rises. Again, Behm *et al.* (1970) and Boccardo and Corey (1976) detect a strong negative link between the gross domestic product (GDP) per capita and the infant mortality rate (IMR). These authors attribute the halt in the downward trend of the IMR in the 1950s to Chile's economic stagnation in those years.

In the light of the findings mentioned in the previous paragraph, the steep decline of GDP on two occasions between 1974 and 1982, which was accompanied by reductions in wages and in employment and consumption levels, would seem to presage a levelling off in the historic downward trend of the IMR, but the statistics indicate that the opposite was the case. As shown in Figure V.1, the decline in the IMR has been continuous and steady from 1964 to the present day. This decline occurs in the two components into which this rate is usually subdivided: the neonatal and the post-neonatal, and it is not concentrated in specific geographical zones but occurs in all regions of the country at a similar pace (Raczynski and Oyarzo, 1981; Oyarzo, 1983). Moreover, taking the mother's level of formal education as representing the socio-economic stratum, it will be noted that the IMR decreases at each of the three levels which the infor-

Table V.4. Chile – social public expenditure*

Year	Education		Health		Labour		Housing		Other		Total	
	Total	per capita	Total	per capita	Total	per capita	Total	per capita	Total	per capita	Total	per capita
1969	16,581	1803	11,303	1229	180	20	13,102	1424	385	42	41,551	4517
1970	18,586	1990	13,016	1394	168	18	12,972	1389	588	63	45,330	4853
1974	21,344	2129	13,511	1348	146	15	18,197	1815	394	39	53,592	5345
1975	16,722	1640	10,805	1060	1824	179	11,061	1085	418	41	40,830	4004
1976	16,972	1636	9674	933	4734	456	8057	777	856	83	40,293	3885
1977	18,434	1747	11,250	1066	4272	405	10,244	971	1348	128	45,548	4317
1978	19,721	1837	12,979	1209	3350	312	7929	739	1158	108	45,137	4205
1979	20,479	1876	13,032	1194	3055	280	8219	753	1586	145	46,371	4247
1980	18,595	1675	11,207	1009	3286	296	7358	663	1522	137	41,968	3779
1981	21,120	1870	13,317	1179	2510	222	6215	550	2285	202	45,447	4024
1982	22,782	1983	14,207	1237	5177	451	4811	419	2054	179	49,031	4268

Sources: Marshall (1981); Office of the Controller-General of the Republic, *Estado de Ejecución Presupuestaria del Sector Público*; INE, *Proyección de Problación total del país por sexo, según edades 1970–2000* (July 1980).
*Millions of 1978 pesos.

Table V.5. *Chile – public investment, social sectors**

	1969	1970	1974	1975	1976	1977	1978	1979	1980	1981	1982
Total public investment	26,082.4	27,830.0	40,198.0	20,838.0	15,390.7	17,189.0	14,097.9	17,349.1	15,174.6	15,187.1	11,128.1
Investment											
– social sector	13,610.3	12,929.2	19,220.2	10,381.5	7105.9	8999.4	5955.8	7397.9	7147.9	5062.9	3663.3
– education	2477.6	2016.0	1419.3	1059.0	595.5	891.5	824.3	872.9	460.6	384.5	124.6
– health	1166.5	1193.2	1490.4	661.4	445.9	215.4	275.6	362.5	245.9	383.5	365.6
– labour	21.3	14.3	0.2	0.2	1.2	3.6	1.1	12.0	8.5	1.1	3.4
– housing	9920.8	9662.2	16,296.9	8657.0	6057.4	7822.0	4835.6	6130.6	6432.3	4289.6	3167.8
– other	24.4	43.5	12.4	3.9	5.9	66.9	19.2	19.8	0.6	4.2	1.9

Sources: Marshall (1981); Office of the Controller-General of the Republic, *Estado de Ejecución Presupuestaria del Sector Público*.
*Millions of 1978 pesos.

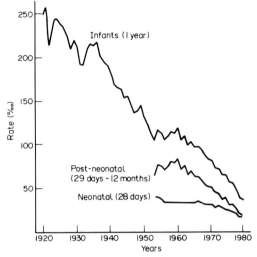

Figure V.1. *Chile – infant mortality rate, 1920–81.*
(Per thousand live births.)
Sources: 1920–35: National Statistics Service; *Demografia* (1953); 1936–52: Behm (1961); 1952–79: National Statistics Institute; *Demografia* (1972–73) and (1979).

mation enables us to identify. The drop is somewhat smaller in the case of mothers with no education, but in 1980 they accounted for only 3% of all child-bearing women (see Table V.6). The IMR differential per socio-economic stratum was maintained. Something similar

occurred with the regional differentials (Oyarzo, 1983).

The child (1–4 years) mortality rate fell at a pace similar to that of the IMR, at about 60% between the first and last years of the period 1974–81, a percentage substantially higher than that observed for the mortality rate of the other age groups.

(b) *Causes of death in the pre-school population*[10]

As may be seen from Table V.7, in the early 1970s Chile found itself in a situation where the main causes of infant deaths were connected with enteric, respiratory and malnutrition diseases and with parturition and perinatal problems. Causes of this nature became relatively fewer throughout the period, whereas there was an increase in causes connected with congenital anomalies and anoxic and hypoxic ailments. The last-mentioned are caused by a lack of oxygen during childbirth and are avoidable provided that suitable technology is available. They can result in the child's death or irreparable injury. Accidents are also a major cause of death in this age group. Throughout the period almost 5% of the deaths of infants under 1 year were caused by an accident, violence or poisoning.

In the group aged 1–4 years, transmissible enteric and respiratory infections and mal-

Table V.6. *Chile – infant mortality rate by educational level of mother**

| Years | IMR‡ (under 1 year) | CMR§ (1–4 years) | Education of mother† | | | |
			None	Primary	Intermediate and higher	All
1970	82.2	3.444	164.8	86.7	41.9	82.2
1971	73.9	2.972	155.5	76.6	41.5	73.9
1972	72.7	2.874	153.9	76.8	41.3	72.7
1973	65.8	2.380	144.6	70.1	38.2	65.8
1974	65.2	2.614	157.3	68.0	38.5	65.2
1975	57.6	2.215	133.5	60.7	37.4	57.6
1976	56.6	2.103	136.5	60.3	38.1	56.6
1977	50.1	1.695	133.2	54.3	32.6	50.1
1978	40.1	1.605	97.4	43.6	28.2	40.1
1979	37.9	1.489	107.9	41.7	26.2	37.9
1980	33.0	1.240	95.2	36.8	23.8	33.0
1981	27.0	1.131	75.3	24.8	16.8	27.0

Source: INE, *Anuario de Demografia* of each year.
*Rate for 1000 live births. Births at each level of education of the mother were adjusted by the registry omission factor determined by INE, namely, 5%. For 1970–80 births and deaths for which the mother's education level was unknown were distributed according to the known data, for 1981 they had to be included in the 'no education' category.
†In 1970, 8.9% of the mothers who gave birth had no formal education, 66.9% had one or more years of intermediate or higher education. In 1980, these respective percentages were 2.7, 56.0 and 41.3.
‡Per 1000 live births.
§Provisional figures per 1000 inhabitants 1–4 years of age.

Table V.7. *Chile — principal causes of mortality in the population under one year of age**

Cause of death†	1972–73	1975–76	1977–78	1979–80
Enteritis and other diarrhoeic diseases		10.9	10.7	6.9
Other bacterial diseases	5.2	7.5	6.7	6.2
Avitaminosis and other nutritional deficiencies	4.1	4.6	3.9	2.4
Meningitis	2.0	2.2	1.6	1.2
Other pneumonias	25.7	20.5	16.8	16.3
Congenital heart anomalies	1.9	2.4	3.4	4.9
Other congenital anomalies	2.6	3.8	4.2	6.3
Birth lesions and distoxic deliveries	4.3	4.0	3.4	2.9
Anoxic and hypoxic ailments	11.3	13.3	17.5	21.8
Other causes of perinatal morbidity and mortality	16.4	12.6	7.8	7.4
Indeterminate symptoms or conditions	2.1	7.2	14.4	12.4
External causes: accidents and violence	4.8	2.9	3.5	4.9
Other causes	5.9	8.1	6.2	6.4
Total deaths of infants under 1 year	18,628	14,045	10,332	8528

Source: INE, *Anuario de Demografia*, of each year.
*Percentage of total deaths of infants of less than 1 year in each biennium.
†International classification, intermediate list of 150 causes. All causes were identified in which, during one or more bienniums, deaths of infants under 12 months exceeded 2%.

nutrition were a major cause of death, together with accidents, violence and poisoning. Throughout the period the former became less frequent and the latter relatively more frequent to the point of representing close to 32% of all deaths for this group in 1979–80 (see Table V.8).

This is, however, a partial view of the problem. Actually it is a known fact that in situations where the risk of death has diminished significantly and where, in addition, there is a health recovery system covering majority percentages of the population, mortality rates cease to be a suitable indicator of the population's state of health and susceptibility to disease. In fact, they only reflect the ultimate risk, that of dying. In other words, in order to make a proper evaluation of the state of health of Chile's pre-school population, it would be necessary to have a wider knowledge which would include the tendency of surviving children to contract diseases. An examination must therefore be made of the pattern of morbidity in the pre-school group.

(c) *Morbidity of the pre-school population*

Ascertaining the incidence of the diseases affecting a population is not an easy task. The morbidity surveys in Chile are not continuous

in time or coverage, and not mutually comparable. Existing statistics make it possible to establish indicators that cover only the following aspects of child morbidity: state of nutrition, reasons for paediatric consultation, incidence of notifiable diseases and hospital morbidity.

(i) *State of nutrition*

The official statistics indicate a drop in the undernutrition indices for the population under 6 years of age for the period stretching from 1975, the first year for which information is available, to 1982 (see Table V.9). The information is compiled for all children of less than 6 years under control in the Ministry of Health establishments. Their number exceeds one million in every year of the period and represents approximately 70–75% of the population under 6 years in the country.[11]

The data in Table V.9 reveal an increase in undernutrition in 1976, as compared with 1975, which steadily decreases in the following years.[12] This decrease, as will be seen later, is the result of a highly selective nutrition programme aimed at early detection of children suffering from any degree of undernutrition.

(ii) *Morbidity indicators: notifiable diseases*

In Chile, transmissible infectious diseases

Table V.8. *Chile – principal causes of mortality in the population aged 1–4 years**

Cause of death[†]	1972–73	1975–76	1977–78	1979–80
Enteritis and other diarrhoeic diseases	8.3	5.9	6.2	4.7
Other bacterial diseases	1.6	2.6	2.2	2.1
Measles	1.6	2.2	0.7	1.8
Avitaminosis and other nutritional deficiencies	3.3	4.3	3.5	2.8
Meningitis	3.5	3.7	4.5	3.4
Other diseases of the nervous and sensory systems	2.0	2.0	1.2	2.2
Other forms of heart diseases	1.5	1.8	2.4	2.4
Acute respiratory infections	2.2	1.9	2.1	2.1
Other pneumonias	26.4	19.8	14.0	12.9
Indeterminate morbid symptoms and conditions	7.9	13.0	14.7	13.8
External causes: accidents and violence	21.7	22.0	27.6	31.8
Other causes	20.0	20.8	20.9	20.0
	100.0	100.0	100.0	100.0
Total deaths in population aged 1–4 years	2594	2165	1644	1347

Source: INE, *Anuario de Demografía*, of each year.
*Percentage of total deaths in this age group for each biennium.
[†]International classification, intermediate list of 150 causes. All causes were identified in which, during one or more bienniums, deaths in the population group aged 1–4 years exceeded 2%.

Table V.9. *Chile – nutritional state of children (under 6 years) under surveillance in Ministry of Health establishments**

Years	Number of cases examined (thousands)	Total	Percentage of undernourished		
			Slight	Moderate	Advanced
1975	1015	15.5	12.1	2.7	0.7
1976	1048	15.9	12.1	3.0	0.8
1977	1071	14.9	11.9	2.5	0.5
1978	1048	13.0	10.8	1.8	0.3
1979	1023	12.2	10.4	1.6	0.2
1980	1048	11.5	10.0	1.4	0.1
1981	1063	9.9	8.7	1.1	0.1
1982[†]	1161	8.8	7.8	0.9	0.1

Source: Ministry of Health, *Recursos y Atenciones* (each year).
*Information available only from 1975.
[†]Provisional figure, Department of Statistics, Ministry of Health.

(typhoid and paratyphoid fever, scarlet fever, diphtheria, whooping cough, poliomyelitis, measles, meningitis, carbuncle, typhus) must be reported. Hence there is an information-gathering system which is useful for detecting trends in these diseases.

These diseases were registered for the entire population regardless of age. Nevertheless, some of them affected mainly children under 15 years of age, particularly those aged 2–12, thus including pre-school children. The diseases in question were basically diseases such as measles, whooping cough, diphtheria and polio-myelitis which are preventable through vac-cination. The morbidity due to these diseases varied considerably each year. This was reflected in successive outbreaks in response to which vaccination campaigns were launched. Thus immunizations for children under 15 years increased substantially from 1974 to 1976, then decreased and started to climb again in 1982. There is therefore no discernible trend in this indicator.[13] This conclusion should, however, be viewed with caution because it gives a partial and incomplete picture of the situation. As will be seen later, there were notifiable diseases which actually showed a steep rise during the period, namely, those indicative of a deterioration in basic sanitation and in the quality of feeding, such as typhoid and hepatitis. These diseases also affected pre-school children but much less frequently than adolescent students and adults.

(iii) *Morbidity involving hospitalization*

Unfortunately, hospital statistics in Chile are far from up to date. The last yearbook of discharges from hospitals is for 1975. Subsequent figures cover only the number of beds and the percentage of beds occupied. A comparison of the hospitalization of children under 5 years in 1975 with the figures for 1970 shows a 35% increase in the rate of hospitalization, namely, from 101 per 1000 children under 5 years in 1970 to 136 in 1975.[14]

It is important to emphasize that the hospitalization rate rose and that the reasons for hospitalization followed patterns different from those of the causes of death. Indeed the previously observed drop in mortality for respiratory and perinatal diseases was not accompanied by an equivalent drop in morbidity involving hospitalization for these diseases.

(iv) *Paediatric consultations*

In Chilean health statistics paediatric consultations are classified as consultations for children under 15 years of age. It is not possible to separate those intended for the pre-school population, but the information available shows that paediatric medical consultations for morbidity increased by 40% between 1974 and 1982.[15] Unfortunately, the reasons for consultation are unknown. An increase in the number of consultations may be due as much to a greater incidence of diseases among the population as to a greater supply of services.

The supply does not, however, appear to have increased. The number of consultation hours remained constant, as will be seen later. Demand rose substantially and was covered in the same number of medical consultation hours. This increase in demand occurred especially in respect of morbidity. The information is consistent with the hypothesis that there was an increase in the incidence of diseases in this stratum of the population in the period 1974–82.[16]

To sum up, the statistics suggest that in the period 1974–82 there was a continuous and steady drop in infant and child mortality in spite of the economic deterioration and low living levels. The various morbidity indicators for this population suggest a deterioration, to counter which, palliative or control measures were apparently taken (e.g. care for the under-nourished and immunizations).

(d) *Why did the infant mortality rate fall in Chile?*[17]

Chile's birth rate fell markedly between the first and last years of the period. In 1975, 1976 and 1977 the number of births decreased in absolute terms.[18] From 1978 there was a slight recovery, which was particularly strong for the years 1979–81, after which the rate levelled off (slight decrease). During the period under review, there seems to have been a close relationship between the economic cycle and the fertility pattern of the population in Chile.

The drop in the number of births had at least a two-fold effect on the population's risks of death: (i) it facilitated professional care before, during and after birth by alleviating the pressure on the obstetric and paediatric resources of the health system, and (ii) the drop in the number of births and in the birth rate was linked with changes in the pattern of births in the sense that births were concentrated to an increasing extent in demographic and social strata with a lower death risk.

The first of these points will be dealt with in the section on the health resources and services delivered to the pre-school population. As regards the second, it may be observed that, concomitantly with the drop in the number of births, there was a concentration of births among mothers between 20 and 34 years of age, in lower birth orders (large number of first-born and second-born children) and among mothers with intermediate and/or higher education. Each of these strata implies, for biological and/or cultural reasons, a lower death risk for the newborn.

Estimates of the impact of these changes in birth distribution on the decrease in the Chilean IMR during the period are consistent in concluding that approximately 25% of the drop is attributable to these changes, those related to the mother's educational level being the most influential (Raczynski and Oyarzo, 1981; Taucher, 1982). The changes in birth distribution also contributed to the drop in the IMR in the years preceding the period under review. Hence this was not a new factor. What is specific to the period 1974–82 is the influence of the recession on births. As already pointed out, the number of births proved sensitive to the recessionary cycles by decreasing more sharply during such periods.

We calculated this impact both for the first recessionary cycle of the economy (1975–76) and for the recovery period immediately following (1977–80). Our findings show that the impact of the changes in the birth pattern on the IMR was indeed stronger in the recessionary cycle. Education would explain 24% of the drop in the IMR between 1974 and 1977 and only 21% between 1977 and 1980. The birth order, for its part, would explain 9% in the first subperiod and 3% in the second.[19]

Another factor influential in the reduction of IMR is related to the role of the state. The strong impetus given to state intervention in the social sectors that existed in Chile since the beginning of the century led, in the health sector, to the creation of a system of care based on the National Health Services (NHS), a public body, with establishments of varying complexity ranging from the rural post to the specialized hospital with sophisticated technology. This ensured wide health-care coverage of the population, especially the development of mother and child health-care programmes with obvious advances on this front and in tackling the problems of nutrition and enteric and respiratory diseases.

While it is acknowledged that the system suffered from certain inefficiencies, it is generally agreed that it contributed significantly to improve the health situation of the population, especially in respect to mother and child health-care. It is also generally accepted that it particularly benefited the lower-income groups.[20] This public health system, organized at the national level, was a cornerstone which made it possible to reduce the death risks of the pre-school population in the period 1974–82, as we shall see later.

(i) *Resources of the public health sector*

As pointed out in Section 2, the severe economic recession of 1975–76 was accompanied by a drastic retrenchment of public expenditure in each of the social sectors.

Table V.10 shows the evolution of public expenditure on health. Only in 1981 did it reach the level of 1974. As regards the country's total ·population, even in 1982 public expenditure on health was below the 1974 level. The drop was exceptionally steep in 1975–76. Thereafter there was a recovery, followed by a further drop in 1980 which is the year in which the act drastically changing the structure of the system entered into force, terminating the National Health Service and establishing 27 regionally decentralized health services.

Table V.10 also shows changes in the allocation of public expenditure on health. In 1974, 39% was for personnel, 27% for operational expenses connected with the purchase of supplies and 11% for investment. In 1975, the figures were 41, 21 and 6%, respectively. In other words, during the first recessionary

Table V.10. *Chile – public expenditure on health, amounts and purposes**

| Years | Total[†] | Operational | | Real investment |
		Personnel	Supplies	
1969	11,302	4778	2931	1666
1970	13,016	4878	3063	1193
1974	13,511	5302	3635	1490
1975	10,805	4428	2255	661
1976	9674	4318	2135	445
1977	11,250	4677	2373	215
1978	12,979	5166	3091	276
1979	13,032	5046	2839	362
1980	11,207	4164	3357	246
1981	13,317	4477	2663	383
1982	14,207	4185	3654	366

Sources: 1969–79: Marshall (1981); 1980–82: Office of the Controller General of the Republic, *Estado de Ejecución Presupuestaria del Sector Público.*
*Millions of 1978 pesos.
[†]Including operational, investment and transfer costs.

cycle there was a substantial cut in the public expenditures of the health sector for investment and in expenditures on the purchase of essential supplies for the system's operation.

Furthermore, investment never recovered in any year subsequent to those considered in this study. On the contrary, it continued to fall until it levelled off at 3% of public expenditure in health as from 1979. This figure of about 350 million pesos (at 1978 prices) was barely 25% of the amount invested in the first years of the decade. Expenditures on personnel also fell in the first recessionary cycle, recovered and fell again with fluctuations after 1980. The pattern of expenditures for purchasing supplies was similar: in no year of the period did they again reach the level of 1974.

The shortage of investment in the sector and the cut in expenditures for the purchase of supplies very probably led to a deterioration in the health sector's infrastructure and equipment and consequently in the quality of care. This was corroborated by the frequent complaints expressed on this matter during the entire period by doctors and other officials in the sector (Raczynski, 1982).

Because of a decrease in the investment in health of the magnitude indicated it was possible to maintain the level of health services over the short term at the expense of the programmes of equipment, maintenance and expansion of installed capacity. The cut in the real wages of personnel employed in the sector also helped in this connection. It should be noted that in the health sector about 40% of the total expenditure is traditionally used to pay the wages of personnel.

(ii) *Priorities in health policy*

The health policy during this period shows, as from 1975–76, a very heavy concentration on primary care for mothers and newborn infants. Top priority was given to expanding programmes for monitoring the health of children and pregnant women and to programmes of nutrition intervention.[21] The public health plan was, therefore, highly selective.

The available background information on the implementation of this policy indicates that there was in fact a concentration of resources on the care of mothers and newborn infants. Thus, during the whole period obstetric medical consultations and midwifery consultations for newborn infants were expanded on a continuous and steady basis. The percentage of births with professional care at the time of delivery and the supply of beds in midwifery clinics increased.[22]

The situation with respect to paediatric medical resources and services differed from that of mothers and newborn infants. The information suggests that there was a falling off in the number of medical hours allotted to paediatrics. Moreover, the number of hospital beds in this special field remained almost constant.[23]

Accordingly, the supply of resources for child care seems to have remained relatively stable, whereas medical consultations increased steadily from 1976 after a drop of 7% in 1975 compared with 1974. Between 1975 and 1981 they grew by 22%. As stated previously, the medical consultations showing the largest increase were those concerned with morbidity.

The findings of a survey conducted on a representative sample of homes in Greater Santiago in 1978 suggest that the available paediatric medical resources benefited the pre-school population particularly. The findings of this survey indicate that a lack of medical care was the exception in the case of unweaned infants and pre-school children, even of those at a low socio-economic level who had a greater annual incidence of disease (Kaempffer and Medina, 1980).

(iii) *Nutrition and feeding programmes*

Several nutrition and feeding programmes were implemented. Some of these have been in operation since the 1950s in Chile.

National Supplementary Feeding Programme (PNAC). From 1971 to 1974 this programme distributed milk to all children under 15 years and to pregnant women and wet-nurses. From 1975, children from 6 to 14 years of age were excluded. In addition, the quality (protein content) of the foodstuffs delivered was changed[24] and the tonnage of milk and/or protein mixtures rose. For pregnant women the increase was continued until 1982, levelled off from 1979 for nursing mothers and wet-nurses and fell off for children aged 2–5 years from 1977.[25]

Covarrubias and Torche (1980) undertook an economic evaluation of PNAC and concluded that the programme contributed to an improvement in the nutritional state of the recipients belonging to homes at the lowest socio-economic levels (the lowest 40% of the population). This is borne out by the fact that it had a favourable effect on the weight of children at birth and on the probability of survival after the first year of life.

Since the food provided by PNAC was distributed mainly in the assistance centres of the public health sector and since, in order to obtain it, it was compulsory to undergo a health check by nurses, midwives and/or medical aides, the programme was also of help in the early detection of diseases.

Programme for monitoring nutritionally deficient children (OFASA programme). This programme, launched in 1976, provided additional food and nutrition education to families under the surveillance of the National Health Service whose members actually included undernourished children below 6 years of age (degrees 1, 2 or 3). For a period of 6 months these children were given milk and/or milk substitutes which, according to existing studies, were designed to increase the PNAC food contribution by 50% in the case of infants under 1 year and by 100% in the case of those over 1 year (Inual, 1977). The volume of food distributed under this programme increased considerably in 1977 over that of 1976, fell off in 1978 and rose steadily from 1978 to 1982.[26]

A study evaluating the impact of this programme on the nutritional state of children shows a rehabilitation percentage varying from 30 to 40% in the case of the slightly undernourished and from 60 to 70% in that of the moderately or seriously undernourished (degrees 2 and 3). In the great majority of cases rehabilitation occurred during the first quarter of the programme and, as might be expected, was less marked and slower in the case of the chronically undernourished than in that of the recently undernourished.[27]

Programme of Closed Nutritional Rehabilitation (CONIN). This programme was launched as a pilot project from August 1975 to late 1975. Its purpose was to eliminate undernutrition (degrees 2 and 3) which apparently affected a small number of children but was a very costly item for the health care services. According to a diagnostic study carried out for 1975, the seriously undernourished (degree 3) children in Chile numbered approximately 8200,[28] all of whom were under 2 years and 73% under 6 months. Most of them had been in different hospital centres with diagnoses of acute diarrhoea, loss of liquids and bronchopneumonia.

For the rehabilitation of children suffering from serious undernutrition and for those with moderate undernutrition and a high risk of declining into a state of serious undernutrition,

the Corporation for Infant Nutrition (CONIN) was established. It set up a system of rehabilitation centres for the undernourished in which children remained until total recovery. The evaluation of the pilot project from 1975 to 1977 shows positive results in terms of nutritional and psychomotor rehabilitation, mortality and the incidence of infectious morbidity. It also indicates that the rehabilitation levels of children treated in the centres were maintained after a 7-month observation period.

The programme was implemented at the national level in 1977. In 1982 there were 28 centres throughout the country with an approximate capacity of 1200 beds. Between 1978 and 1982 a total of 12,424 children up to 2 years of age had attended these centres, of whom 49% had entered with a diagnosis of serious undernutrition and the rest with moderate (degree 2) undernutrition. The family history of these children showed that they belonged to the country's poorest sectors: 54% had illiterate mothers, the fathers of 92% of the children were unemployed or temporary workers or self-employed, and 92% were living in inadequate housing conditions (Monckeberg and Riumalló, 1981; Monckeberg, no date). Mortality among the children of the programme was barely 3%; 77% were discharged fully recovered (Table V.11). About 78% of the children discharged continued with their surveillance programmes and maintained a normal state of nutrition. Only about 18% experienced a slight relapse (Monckeberg and Riumalló, 1981).

It appears from the foregoing that each of these three programmes of selective nutrition intervention was relatively successful. One interesting characteristic of the programmes is the fact that they complemented each other. PNAC helped to increase the supply of calories and proteins for children under 6 years, the OFASA programme meant an additional increase for children actually suffering from undernutrition, and lastly, the CONIN programme collected and ensured the rehabilitation of children who, in spite of the previous programmes, continued to suffer from a deficiency.

In December 1982 a new programme was formulated to replace PNAC. The new programme, called Feeding Programme for the Control of Infant Undernutrition (PRACODIN), was designed to distribute milk and other food products to children under 6 years and to pregnant women according to their vulnerability and risk of undernutrition. The caloric– protein input was to increase with the degree

Table V.11. *Chile – number of rehabilitation centres and population served by CONIN*

	1977	1978	1979	1980	1981	1982
Number of centres	11	18	25	27	28	28
Intake		1468	2468	2715	2741	3032
– seriously undernourished		938	1330	1366	1264	1152
– moderately undernourished		530	1138	1349	1477	1880
Total discharged	411	1068	2071	2676	2680	2995
– rehabilitated		903	1704	2255	2262	2460
– deaths		37	83	61	65	76
– other reasons*		128	232	360	353	459

Source: Information provided by CONIN.
*Cases of secondary undernourishment of children taken out prematurely by their parents.

of vulnerability and risk. In January 1983 the launching of this programme was postponed and PNAC with its recipient population was continued, but the monthly delivery of food to the pre-school population was reduced.[29]

To sum up, it may be concluded that the health programmes aimed primarily at the mother and child constituted a positive experiment. They probably slowed down the rise in the death risks of the pre-school population which might have resulted from the recessionary policies that tended to impoverish the poorest sectors still further. The other factor which helped to lessen the impact of the recession on children was the drop in the birth rate and the above-mentioned changes in the birth pattern. These changes involved a heavier concentration of births in socio-demographic strata less prone to infant mortality.

(e) *Quality of life of the pre-school population*

The quality of life of pre-school children, once the threshold of survival has been passed, depends basically on the constitution and stability of the nuclear family, on the care and time (psychosocial and cognitive stimuli) that their parents can provide, on the economic condition of the household, on housing and basic sanitation conditions, etc.

The relevant information is scarce. All the evidence presented in Section 2 on the distributive impact of the economic policies being applied (wage cuts, high unemployment rates, drop in consumer expenditures) indicates a deterioration in the quality of life. To this we may now add information on the quality of housing and basic sanitation.

(i) *Housing and sanitation situation*

Chile has always had a large housing deficit.

In the past it was covered in part by state grants which enabled 'state operations' to be carried out, community housing to be built by the government for the poor groups and subsidized credit to be granted by public agencies for the purchase of housing.

From 1974 the housing policy implied fewer public-sector resources for housing and urbanization programmes and a smaller supply of credit for housing, as described in Section 2. As part of this policy, the intervention of the state in housing and urbanization was reduced. Regulations on the use of urban land were eliminated. The sale of publicly owned land was accelerated and the functions of project preparation, land acquisition, construction, financing and marketing of housing were transferred to the private sector.

The effect of these policies, combined with less public expenditure on housing, could only be negative. Thus, for example, estimates of the increase in the housing deficit coincide in affirming that it showed an upward trend as the years went on (Arellano, 1982). On the other hand, studies by Tagle (1982) and Arellano (1982) evaluate the distributive effect of the state's housing activities. They conclude that the programmes are inadequate and unselective and tend to worsen the living conditions of the poorest sectors.

This situation would explain the enormous increase in the number of 'relatives' living in just one house, that has been observed in recent years in the popular sectors with all the resultant overcrowding problems. By way of illustration, Parker et al. (1981) place on record for 1978–79 an average of 5.7 persons per housing unit in neighbourhoods of Pudahuel; Aylwin (1979) reports an average of 6.6 persons per unit in a sample of the very poor. These figures far exceed the national average which, according to preliminary data from the 1982 population and housing census, amounted to 4.5 persons per unit.[30]

To this should be added inadequate drinking water supply, electric light, water quality and sewage disposal. Although the water and lighting systems were relatively extensive, light and water were cut off when households failed to pay within the proper time. This occurred more frequently in the most recessionary years. Information provided by the Metropolitan Sanitary Works Enterprise (ENOS) indicates that, during the first months of 1983, 26% of its customers were one or more months in arrears on their water bills. Obviously the users falling behind in their payments belonged to the poorest strata of the population. Apparently some 130,000 poor families in the metropolitan area had this vital service cut off.[31]

There is also some evidence of a deterioration in the treatment of sewage. The easiest and cheapest method was followed, namely direct discharging without prior treatment into watercourses, lakes, etc., with the consequent pollution of the water for irrigating vegetables. This is one of the factors explaining the steady rise in reported cases of diseases such as typhoid and hepatitis.

(ii) *Lack of protection for children*

The deterioration in the quality of life extended beyond the physical and health environment. The worsening of the economic situation obliged adult household members to seek ways of earning more income, which led to a rise at low socio-economic levels in the female participation rate in the labour force during the most critical cycles of the economy (Rosales, 1979).

This situation probably contributed to a greater lack of protection for the children in such households, since there were no institutions for looking after children in the absence of their mothers. Studies carried out in marginal communities, while using different methodologies, samples and times confirm this hypothesis.[32]

Part of the adverse effect of higher female participation rates in the labour force in the absence of child-care infrastructure was lessened by the temporary increase in enrolment in pre-primary education. According to sources in the Ministry of Education, enrolment in this type of education followed a pattern similar to that of the economic cycles, relative stagnation in 1974–75, expansion between 1976 and 1979, and abrupt decline in 1980–81. In 1975–76 no more than 7% of the population under

6 years had access to pre-school education. From 1976 to 1979 this percentage climbed to 11% and fell to 8% in 1980–81.[33]

(f) *Situations of children of school age (6–14 years)*

The housing and basic sanitation situation and the working conditions for mothers described above obviously affected both pre-school and school age children. In some ways they affected the latter group more severely.

(i) *Health situation of children aged 6 to 14 years*

The mortality rates for these children declined, but at a distinctly slower pace than that of mortality in the pre-school group, partly because the initial levels were low.[34]

At the same time, there was a significant increase in the notifiable diseases indicative of basic sanitation, the quality of food and the presence of vectors transmitted mainly via the digestive system or inoculation. Typhoid and hepatitis showed the greatest increase in absolute terms and relative to the population (Table V.12). The first showed a marked rise from 1975 to 1978, the number of reported cases shot up by 182% and the rate by 165%. Between 1978 and 1981 the rate fell by 21% and rose by 16% in 1982. The hepatitis rate rose by more than 200% in 1974–77, fell by over 50% from 1977 to 1980 and rose by almost 80% in 1981 and 1982. It is thus obvious that the incidence of these diseases was sensitive to the economic cycles.[35]

(ii) *Food situation*

There is no national information on the nutritional state of schoolchildren. The Supplementary Feeding Programme (PNAC) covered all children under 15 years until 1975. Subsequently, it covered only the pre-school population (under 6 years).

In addition, the traditional school feeding programme (breakfasts, lunches) was severely cut during the period.[36]

Table V.13 shows that the breakfast/snack rations distributed in 1982 were 46% smaller than those of 1974. The rations shrank by 44% between 1974 and 1976, increased by 37% from 1976 to 1978, decreased by 38% in 1979 and then levelled off. The dinner/lunch rations shrank by 55% between 1974 and 1977 and remained more or less at this level until 1982. This information suggests a worsening of the nutritional situation of schoolchildren, as is

Table V.12. *Chile – notifications of transmissible infectious diseases**

Years	Total†	Typhoid	Hepatitis
1970	88	57	14
1971	96	50	30
1972	86	47	25
1973	97	37	45
1974	88	46	27
1975	126	60	44
1976	124	60	47
1977	211	109	86
1978	192	122	56
1979	165	99	57
1980	144	98	39
1981	191	96	86
1982‡	n.d.	111	70

Sources: Ministry of Health, *Anuarios de Enfermedades de Notificación Obligatoria*, (each year); INE, *Proyección de Población, total pais, por sexo según edades* (July 1981).
*Rates per 100,000 inhabitants.
†The diseases included are those deriving from basic sanitation, food quality, presence of vectors, etc., and which are transmitted and spread mainly via the digestive system or by inoculation, viz.: typhoid fever and paratyphoid, bacterian dysentery, infectious hepatitis, intestinal amoebiasis, brucellosis, hydatidosis, trichinosis, human rabies, carbuncle and tetanus.
‡Provisional figures.

Table V.13. *Chile – school feeding programme, meals distributed**

Years	Breakfasts/ snacks	Lunches/ dinners
1970	1301.2	619.2
1971	1408.4	653.6
1972	1536.6	715.9
1973	1445.6	674.3
1974	1338.5	663.2
1975	745.7	593.6
1976	769.8	361.0
1977	1055.2	296.3
1978	1054.6	307.6
1979	759.4	294.5
1980	759.9	295.0
1981	759.1	295.1
1982	759.0	295.3

Sources: Latorre (1981); JNAEB, *Anuarios Estadistico* (1982), Tables 1 and 2; Presidential Message, 11 September 1982.
*In thousands.

borne out by a study showing that school-children from marginal districts had a higher undernutrition rate than pre-school children with the same social characteristics. The respective percentages were 36 and 29% undernutrition.[37]

(iii) *Situation in the school system*
Primary education in Chile lasts 8 years.

In the first years almost 100% of the population is covered. Public expenditure on primary education fell by 16% from 1974 to 1975 but later recovered and reached the 1974 level again in 1978. Investment in primary education fell off from 1975 to virtually zero from 1977 to 1982 (Table V.14).

Enrolment in primary education declined in almost all the years of the period. Between the

Table V.14. *Chile – public expenditure on primary education, primary-school enrolment and primary-school drop-out rate*

Year	Public expenditure (millions of 1978 pesos)		Enrolment (regular and special education) (thousands)	Drop-out (state schools)
	Total	Investment		
1970	5927	79.1	2045	5.0
1971			2202	4.0
1972			2265	6.0
1973			2325	6.0
1974	7147	39	2346	6.9
1975	5967	30	2314	6.2
1976	6414	9	2260	7.7
1977	6568	2	2265	7.1
1978	7443	0	2250	6.4
1979	7768	0	2252	6.5
1980	6276	0	2207	n.d.
1981	*	2	2159	n.d.
1982	*	1	2086	n.d.

Sources: Marshall (1981); Office of the Controller-General of the Republic, *Estado de Ejecución Presupuestaria del Sector Público*; Ministry of Education, Office of Statistical Planning and Data Processing, *Boetines Anuales de Matricula.*
*In 1981, the transfer of education to the municipalities began. The basic information for these years does not make it possible to differentiate, in the public expenditure allocated to municipal educational establishments, between the amount earmarked for primary education and the earmarkings for intermediate education.

first and last years there was a decrease of 11%. Part of this decline was due to demographic factors since the population of school age shrank by 3% in the same space of time. The remaining percentage probably dropped out of the system. The percentage of drop-outs from primary school grew from 1974 to 1977 and was higher than that of 1970–73 throughout the entire period.[38]

To sum up, the background information collected concerning the situation of the primary-school population suggests a decline in the levels of nutrition and a rise in morbidity due to infectious diseases, all of which are correlated with a falling off, although not a very marked one, in primary-school enrolment and a rise in the drop-out index. In both of these indicators the deterioration was more serious in the first recessionary cycle of the Chilean economy (1975–76).

(g) *Living conditions of the young: education and employment*

Obviously the young were subjected to the same environmental conditions as other age groups and therefore what has been said about the general deterioration in living conditions during the recessionary period starting in 1975 also applies to them. But one characteristic of the people in this age group is the fact that

they were faced with the option of continuing their education by enrolling in the intermediate level or of entering the labour force. The prevailing economic conditions and the opportunities offered by the educational system, in terms of vacancies and the cost of education in relation to family incomes, had a bearing on their choice. The figures for the participation of these age groups in the labour force show that one out of every five of those aged 14–19 opted for entering the labour force, while two out of three in the 20–25 bracket did likewise.[39] Presumably the remainder chose to continue their education.

What was the situation in terms of educational opportunities for the young in the period 1974–82? Although the subject is rather complex, we shall give two indicators, the enrolment pattern and the cost of education. Enrolment in intermediate education rose by 16% during the period, a rate higher than the growth rate of 10% for the population aged 14–18. The slight increase in intermediate-level enrolment was consistent with the downward trend in the rate of participation in the labour force of those aged 14–19, unlike the next-higher age bracket (20–24 years) for which this rate remained steady. The school enrolment ratio (number enrolled out of the population of the 14–18 years age level) rose from 52 to 54%. The opposite occurred in the case of enrolment in higher education which fell by 29% from 1974 to 1981 (Table V.15). When the recession became more severe (in 1975 and 1982) enrolment tended to fall off, especially at the intermediate level.

The increase in intermediate-level enrolment and the marked decrease in higher education were accompanied by an upswing in the cost of education. Taking into account the 'clothing', 'school equipment' and 'registration' components of the consumer price index (CPI), we

have calculated a cost-of-education index (see column 4 of Table V.16). By way of comparison, in column 5 we give the value of the general price index. It will be seen that the CPI for education, except in 1979, was always higher than the general CPI. In 1982, the cost of education was 207 times higher than in 1974, whereas the CPI was only 124 times higher and nominal wages 184 times.

As regards the situation of young people

Table V.15. *Chile – enrolment in intermediate and higher education*

Years	Intermediate education*		Higher education	
	Enrolment (thousands)	% of population 14–18 years	Enrolment (thousands)	% of population 19–24 years
1970	308.1	41.3	77.0	7.6
1971	373.3	48.3	99.6	9.7
1972	415.4	51.4	126 0	12.1
1973	445.9	52.7	140.0	13.2
1974	455.5	51.7	144.0	13.3
1975	448.9	49.3	147.0	13.2
1976	465.9	50.0	134.1	11.6
1977	487.3	51.2	130.7	10.9
1978	510.5	52.9	130.2	10.4
1979	536.4	55.0	126.4	9.7
1980	541.6	55.2	119.0	8.8
1981	554.7	56.6	102.8	7.5
1982	528.5	54.4	n.d.	

Sources: Central Bank, Directorate of Financial Policy, *Indicadores Económicos y Sociales 1960–82* (April 1983); INE, *Proyección de población, total país por sexo, según edad* (July 1981).
*Enrolment in scientific–humanistic and technical–professional education. Enrolled students over 18 years of age, who are defined in statistics as enrolled in adult education, are excluded.

Table V.16. *Chile – annual growth rate of the average cost of education, of the Consumer Price Index (CPI) and of nominal wages, 1976–82*

Year	Cost of education				CPI	Nominal wages
	Clothing	Equipment	Registration	Total		
1974*	6873.1	10,948.2	427.9	5468.7	9238.0	6031.0
1975	268.6	441.5	1537.1	453.4	379.2	360.1
1976	301.6	228.6	804.0	311.9	232.8	246.5
1977	161.5	126.8	119.2	129.3	113.8	132.8
1978	56.2	58.8	65.2	60.1	50.0	59.7
1979	25.1	29.0	29.7	28.6	36.6	47.8
1980	31.6	47.6	35.2	41.8	35.1	46.9
1981	25.8	14.6	41.0	23.1	19.7	30.3
1982	15.1	6.9	14.3	10.3	9.9	9.7
1974 price	144.0	149.7	1514.6	207.3	124.2	183.8

Sources: INE, *Listado de precios base para cálculo del IPC*; Cortázar and Marshall (1980).
*Cumulative growth rate, 1970–74.

entering the labour force, the average wage for those in the 14–19 years age group who found work was approximately one-third of the average wage for the population as a whole. This percentage became 50% for those in the 20–40 years bracket (Table V.17).[40] These differentials partly reflect different levels of training and experience, but also a precarious situation at the income levels of this population sector.

The most worrying indicator, however, which shows a serious worsening of the economic situation of the young, is that given by the unemployment percentage for this sector. Unemployment in the 14–19 years bracket rose from 16.8% in 1970 to 41.6% in 1975.

Average unemployment in this stratum remained at 33% from 1975 to 1982. Unemployment soared as the recession worsened. It climbed from 23.6% in 1981 to 38.1% in 1982 (Table V.18).

The situation was also highly precarious for the young aged 20–24, for whom the average rate of unemployment for the period 1975–82 was 22.5% as compared with 11.3% for a normal year (1970). Steep rises also occurred in periods of acute recession: the rate increased to 23.4% in 1975 and to 35.3% in 1982 (see Table V.18).

It is important to stress that young people under age 25 constituted 40–45% of the total unemployed in Chile during this period, a fact

Table V.17. *Greater Santiago – average hourly wage by age group* *

Years	14–19 years		20–24 years		Total	
	Males	Females	Males	Females	Males	Females
1969	15.1	15.1	29.7	25.1	52.2	33.0
1974	12.4	13.4	21.0	19.1	28.3	22.3
1975	10.0	13.8	14.7	16.9	25.1	19.4
1976	11.0	13.4	18.0	20.5	35.9	23.7
1977	14.0	14.8	21.8	22.4	39.0	31.4
1978	13.2	16.0	22.0	23.2	45.0	30.7
1979	17.5	17.8	24.7	28.7	48.4	36.7
1980	14.0	16.2	23.7	26.5	45.6	32.9
1981	21.2	16.3	29.1	32.7	56.8	44.515
1982	15.0	21.0	32.0	33.9	56.7	47.4

Sources: Data obtained from the Employment and Unemployment Surveys in Greater Santiago of the Economics Department, University of Chile, for June of each year; Cortázar and Marshall (1980).
*December 1978 pesos. The information does not include domestic servants.

Table V.18. *Greater Santiago – average hourly wage by age group* *

	14–19 years	20–24 years	25 years and over
1970	16.8	11.3	3.7
1974	n.d.	n.d.	n.d.
1975	41.6	23.4	12.8
1976	43.8	26.1	14.2
1977	31.2	19.9	7.9
1978	28.5	19.8	8.7
1979	28.1	20.4	7.9
1980	26.5	20.5	6.7
1981	23.6	14.6	5.4
1982	38.1	35.3	13.1

Source: R. de Bonnafos (1983), based on data from the Employment and Unemployment Surveys in Greater Santiago of the Economics Department, University of Chile, for June of each year.
*Percentages. The information does not include domestic servants.

that is indicative of the unequally distributed cost which fell so heavily on the young as a result of the recessionary adjustment of the economy throughout the period 1974–82. The relevant figures are given in Table V.19.

Lastly, it is interesting to note that the unemployed in this age bracket do not necessarily belong to the less educated group of young people. Seventy-five per cent of the unemployed aged 15–19 and 80% of the unemployed between 20 to 24 had from 7 to 12 years of education, i.e. some secondary education.[41] The figure is only 37% for the rest of the population in which 48% of the unemployed have only 1–6 years of education.

Although the foregoing information is still insufficient for arriving at definitive conclusions, the indicators provided, except those for the increase in secondary-school enrolment, point categorically in the direction of a serious deterioration in the situation of the young during the recessionary period.

Table V.19. *Greater Santiago – share of unemployed under 25 years of age in total unemployment**

Years	Total
1969	48.8
1974	50.8
1975	45.5
1976	43.2
1977	36.4
1978	41.8
1979	44.5
1980	44.2
1981	44.0
1982	38.1

Source: Data obtained from the Surveys of Employment and Unemployment in Greater Santiago of the Economics Department, University of Chile, for June of each year.
*Percentages. The information does not include domestic servants.

NOTES

1. See UNICEF (1979), CEPAL-ILPES-UNICEF (1979), Molina and Pinera (1979), Prealc (1980), CEPAL-UNICEF (1981).

2. For a detailed description of these phases see Foxley (1982 and 1983).

3. See ECLA, *Economic Survey of Latin America*, for the period 1973–81.

4. Terms of trade figures can be found in Central Bank of Chile, *Cuentas Nacionales de Chile 1960–1980* (Santiago: 1982).

5. Other negative factors came into play in 1982, such as the sudden decrease in the abundant flow of external credits available for the Chilean economy in previous years.

6. Figures from ECLA, *Economic Survey of Latin America*, for the period 1973–81, and from ECLA, *Balance Preliminar de la Economia Latinoamericana en 1982, Notas sobre la Economía y el desarrollo de America Latina* No. 373, January 1983.

7. See Foxley (1982).

8. See Arellano (1982).

9. See Cortázar (1982).

10. It is difficult to classify the causes of death. This is reflected in the percentage of deaths in the 'indeterminate morbid symptoms and conditions' category.

11. According to a study made by a consultancy office, in 1978 the National Health Service in Chile covered 80% of the children under 6 years in towns over 100,000 inhabitants, approximately 84% in the other towns and almost 97% in rural areas. These percentages were achieved regardless of the remoteness and accessibility of health centres (Inual, 1978).

12. The figure for 1982 is provisional. This fact coincides with unofficial figures that cannot be verified, to the effect that the progress in this indicator is being reversed.

13. See Ministry of Health, *Anuario de Enfermedades de Notificación Obligatoria*, for years 1970 to 1982.

14. Chile, Ministry of Health, *Anuario de Egresos Hospitaliarios 1975*.

15. Ministry of Health, *Anuario de Recursos y Atenciones*, years 1970–82.

16. As an alternative hypothesis, the incidence of diseases could be equivalent, but a larger percentage of them would receive medical attention through paediatric consultations. It is not clear why this behavioural change in the population could have taken place, especially since strict control was exercised during the period under study over those entitled to free care and those not so entitled. In several instances there were accusations in the media claiming that people entitled to free care had been charged for medical services (Raczynski, 1982).

17. This section draws heavily on Raczynski and Oyarzo (1981).

18. This also happened in the past (between 1965 and 1970) as a result of the implementation of an extensive family-planning programme. For birth rate statistics, see INE, *Anuario de Demografia*, published every year.

19. For the methodology see Raczynski and Oyarzo (1981).

20. Various studies deal with this matter. See, *inter alia*, the studies of Medina (1977) and Kaempffer (1977), Romero *et al*. (1976), Jiménez *et al*. (1977), Arellano (1976) and Foxley *et al*. (1979) in the *Revista Médica de Chile*.

21. Various documents emanating from the Government, the Ministry of Health and ODEPLAN set this priority. See, *inter alia*, Ministry of Health (1977), the various social reports of ODEPLAN and CONPAN-INTA (1978).

22. See Ministry of Health, *Anuario de Recursos y Atenciones*, available for each year.

23. Ministry of Health, *op. cit.*

24. The PNAC's caloric contribution although better than in the past, was still below the level recommended by FAO/WHO. It apparently amounted to 75% of the norm for children under 6 years, 33% for infants of 6–23 months, to 15% for pre-school children and to 78% for pregnant women. The protein contribution, expressed in the same way, showed excessive coverage of the group of children under 2 years (223% of those under 6 months, 105% for those between 6 to 23 months) and reached 34% for pre-school children and somewhat over 50% for pregnant women and wet nurses. See González *et al*. (1980). It should be noted that other studies arrive at rather different figures as regards the PNAC caloric and protein contribution (Inual, 1977, Table 2; Covarrubias and Torche, 1981, Table 1).

25. Ministry of Health, *op. cit.*

26. Ministry of Health, *op. cit.*

27. Inual (1977). This study also detects significant variations from one clinic to another in the percentage of rehabilitation of undernourished children and in drop-outs from the programme. Apparently there was a relationship between the frequency of diseases and the nutritional state of children that was characteristic of the health team and its relations with the community. The relationship between the nutritional state of children and the duration of diseases was, however, negative. Lastly, the study shows that different foodstuffs with the same caloric/protein composition have different effects on the nutritional state of children, thus revealing that the presentation and texture of foodstuffs are important factors as regards their acceptance and actual consumption by children.

28. According to the National Health Service statistics, there were 7105 seriously undernourished (degree 3) children under 6 years in 1975 (Table V.5).

29. According to press reports, overall budgetary problems were impeding the implementation of the new programme. Moreover, while the official figures on nutrition have become confidential and are unknown, unconfirmed information suggests a levelling off in the undernutrition indices of the population for the first months of 1983. If this is the case, it would be a natural consequence of the economic contraction that became more acute with the 1982 economic crisis in Chile and severely affected all the public programmes, including nutrition programmes, as from early 1983.

30. See also McDonald (1982) and Puga (1979).

31. Quoted in 'Codo a Codo', Year II, No. 14 (April 1983), of the body called Neighbourhood and Community Action (AVEC) of the Archbishopric of Santiago.

32. See the studies of Aylwin (1979), Covarrubias and Muños (undated), Parker *et al*. (1981), Dahse (1982), Vives (1983).

33. Ministry of Education, *Boletines Anuales de Matriculas* (yearly).

34. From 1974 to 1982 the mortality rate for this group fell by approximately 28%: in 1974 the rate was 7.2 and in 1982 5.2 per 100,000 children aged 5–14 (INE, *Anuario de Demografia* for each year).

35. Kaempffer (1981) quotes information from a clinic in north Santiago which shows that the main reasons for consultations concerning children aged 10–14 in 1975 were: respiratory ailments (23%), skin diseases, mainly impetigo (11%), infections and parasitic diseases (10%), intestinal infections (7%) and nervous and sensory disorders (7%). The main reasons can thus be seen to be related to the quality of environmental sanitation and to respiratory ailments.

36. This programme was designed to provide schoolchildren with nutrition additional to that received at home. It was aimed principally at children in primary, state and free private schools. It consisted mainly of providing breakfasts/lunches or snacks/dinners for seriously socio-economically deprived children, and lasted 10 months each year.

37. The sample in each case consisted of 1501 children eating in refectories. See Chateau (1981).

38. In a sample of 1501 children aged 6–14 in marginal districts of Greater Santiago in 1979, a drop-

out rate of 18% was reported for this social stratum (Chateau, 1981).

39. See R. de Bonnafos (1983).

40. These figures should be viewed with caution

because the data on incomes come from an employment survey and this introduces distortions difficult to evaluate in measuring incomes. See Cortázar (1980).

41. INE, *Encuesta Nacional de Empleo* (1981).

REFERENCES

Arellano, J. P., 'Gasto público en salud y distribución del ingreso', in M. Livingstone and D. Raczynski (eds.), *Salud Pública y Bienestar Social* (CEPLAN, Universidad Católica de Chile, 1976).

Arellano, J. P., 'Sistemas alternativos de seguridad social: un análisis de la experiencia chilena', *Colección Estudios CIEPLAN*, No. 4 (Santiago, Chile: November 1980).

Arellano, J. P., 'Elementos para el análisis de la reforma provisional', *CIEPLAN Notas técnicas*, No. 4 (July 1981).

Arellano, J. P., 'Politicas de vivienda popular: lecciones de la experiencia chilena', *Colección Estudios CIEPLAN*, No. 9 (Santiago, Chile: December 1982).

Aylwin, N., 'El costo social del actual modelo de desarrollo en un sector urbano en extrema pobreza', Documento de Trabajo, Escuela de Trabajo Social, Pontifica Universidad Católica de Chile (January 1979).

Behm, H., *Mortalidad infantil y nivel de vida* (Universidad de Chile, 1962).

Behm, H. *et al.*, 'Mortalidad infantil en Chile: tendencias recientes', *Cuadernos Médico Sociales,* Vol. 11, No. 3 (Santiago, Chile: 1970).

Boccardo, H. and G. Corey, 'Medio ambiente: efectos sobre la salud', in M. Livingstone and D. Raczynski (eds.), *Salud Pública y Bienestar Social* (CEPLAN, Universidad Católica de Chile, 1976).

de Bonnafos, R., 'Influencia de los cambios demográficos y de la participación sobre la tasa de desempleo en Chile', mimeo (Santiago: Department of Economics, University of Chile, 1983).

CEPAL-ILPES-UNICEF, *Pobreza, necesidades básicas y desarrollo en América Latina*, 3 vols., mimeo (Santiago, Chile: 1980).

CEPAL-UNICEF, *Pobreza critica en la niñez. América Latina y el Caribe*, Fernando Galofré (compiler) (Santiago, Chile. 1981).

Chateau, J., 'Algunos antecedentes sobre la situación de los pobladores en el Gran Santiago', Working Paper No. 115 (Santiago, Chile: Programme FLACSO, June, 1981).

CONPAN-INTA, *Antecedentes y acciones para una politica nacional de alimentación y nutrición de Chile* (Chile: Editora Nacional Gabriela Mistral Ltda., 1976).

Cortázar, R., 'Distribución del ingreso, empleo y remuneraciones reales en Chile, 1970–78', *Colección Estudios Cieplan*, No. 3 (Santiago, Chile: June 1980).

Cortázar, R., 'Chile: Distributive results 1973–1982', mimeo (CIEPLAN, November 1982).

Covarrubias, R. and M. Muñoz, 'La familia de los trabajadores del PEM y sus estrategias de subsistencia', Working Paper No. 43 (Instituto de Sociologia, Pontifica Universidad Católica de Chile, n.d.).

Covarrubias, P. and A. Torche, 'Evaluación de un programa de nutrición: El case del PNAC', documento presentado al Encuentro Anual de Economistas 1980, Punta de Tralca, Chile, 11–13 December 1980, 11/80/150/1/D-21.

Dahse, F., *Situación del niño de la familia pobre. El caso de Chile* (UNICEF, 1982).

Echeverría, R. and R. Hevia, 'La politica educacional del régimen militar', mimeo (Programa Interdisciplinario de Investigaciones en Educación, PIIE, Academia de Humanismo Cristiano, Santiago, Chile, 1980).

Foxley, A., 'Hacia una economia de libre mercado: Chile 1974–79', en *Colección Estudios CIEPLAN*, No. 4 (Santiago, Chile: November 1980).

Foxley, A., 'Experimentos neoliberales en América Latina', número especial, *Colección Estudios CIEPLAN*, No. 7 (Santiago, Chile: March 1982).

Foxley, A., 'Enfoques ortodoxos para el ajuste económico de corto plazo: lecciones de la experiencia y temas de investigación', Documento de Trabajo (Santiago; Chile: Programa Regional del Empleo para América Latina y el Caribe (PREALC), 1983).

Foxley, A., E. Aninat and J. P. Arellano, *Redistributive Effects of Government Programmes* (Oxford: Pergamon Press, 1979).

Ffrench-Davis, R., 'Indice de precios externos para calcular el valor real del comercio internacional de Chile: 1952–80', CIEPLAN, *Notas Técnicas* 52 (Santiago, Chile: June 1981).

González, N., A. Infante and F. Mardones, 'Análisis del impacto de la atención primaria de salud sobre los indicadores de salud y nutrición. Chile 1969–78', *Revista Pediatria* (Hospital Roberto del Rio), Vol. 23 (Chile: 1980).

Gutierrez, H., 'La integridad del registro de nacidos vivos en Chile: 1953–66' (Departamento de Bioestadisticas, Facultad de Medicina, Universidad de Chile, 1968).

INUAL, 'Final report on the program against infant malnutrition. Program SAWS/OFASA' (Santiago, Chile: January 1977).

INUAL, 'Informe final' Proyecto: sistema de información continua sobre estado nutricional de la población chilena', tomo I, Bases de Diseño (Santiago, Chile: June 1978).

Jimenez, J., 'Desnutrición en Chile. Análisis de algunas experiencias de solución', in H. Lavados (ed.),

Desarrollo social y salud en Chile, (Santiago, Chile: Corporación de Promoción Universitaria (CPU), 1979).

Jimenez, J. *et al., Medicina social en Chile* (Chile: Editorial Aconcagua, 1977).

Juricic, D., 'El abastecimiento de agua potable y el saneamiento en los últimos 10 años en Chile', *Cuadernos Médico Sociales* (Colegio Médico de Chile), Vol. XXIII, No. 2 (June 1982).

Kaempffer, A. M., 'Evolución de la salud materno-infantil en Chile, 1952–1977', *Revista Médica de Chile*, Vol. 105, No. 10 (Chile: October 1977).

Kaempffer, A. M., 'Adolescencia y salud pública: aspectos socio demográficos', in E. Bobadilla and R. Florenzano (eds.), *El adolescente en Chile. Caracteristicas y problemas* (Santiago, Chile: Corporación de Promoción Universitaria (CPU), 1981).

Kaempffer, A. M. and E. Medina, 'Morbilidad y atención médica infantil en el Gran Santiago', *Revista Chilena de Pediatria*, Vol. 51 (Chile: 1980).

Latorre, C. L., 'Asistencialidad estudiantil en el periodo 1964–81', Documento de Trabajo (Santiago, Chile: Programa Interdisciplinario de Investigaciones en Educación (PIIE), Academia de Humanismo Cristiano, December 1981).

Legarreta, A., 'Factores condicionantes de la mortalidad en la niñez', in M. Livingstone and D. Raczynski (eds.), *Salud Pública y Bienestar Social* (CEPLAN, Universidad Católica de Chile, 1976).

Livingstone, M. and D. Raczynski, 'Distribución geográfica de la salud del preescolar', in M. Livingstone and D. Raczynski (eds.), *Salud Pública y Bienestar Social* (CEPLAN, Universidad Católica de Chile, 1976).

McDonald, J., '25 años de vivienda social. La perspectiva del habitante', Documento de Trabajo (Santiago, Chile: Corporación de Promoción Universitaria, (CPU), 1982).

Marshall, J., 'Gasto público en Chile 1969–79, metodologia y resultados', *CIEPLAN Notas Técnicas*, No. 33 (Santiago, Chile: July 1981).

Medina, E., 'Evolución de la salud pública en Chile en los últimos 25 años', *Revista Médica de Chile*, Vol. 105, No. 10 (October 1977).

Medina, E., 'Evolución de los indicadores de salud en el periodo 1960–77', in H. Lavados (ed.), *(Desarrollo social y salud en Chile* (Santiago, Chile: Corporación de Promoción Universitaria 1979).

Medina, E. and A. Kaempffer, 'Morbilidad y atención médica en el Gran Santiago', in H. Lavados (ed.), *Desarrollo social y salud en Chile* (Santiago, Chile: Corporación de Promoción Universitaria, 1979).

Ministry of Health, *Politica de salud* (Chile: 1977).

Molina, S. and S. Pinera, *La pobreza en América Latina: situación, evolución y orientaciones de politicas*, Proyecto Pobreza Critica en América Latina (United Nations, CEPAL, PNUD, E/CEPAL/PROY. 1/1, June 1979).

Monckeberg, F., 'Centros de recuperación nutricional: La experiencia Chilena', mimeo (CONIN, n.d.).

Monckeberg, F. and J. A. Riumallo, 'El programa de centros cerrados de recuperación nutricional en Chile: una experiencia con la marginalidad', in CEPAL-UNICEF, *op. cit.* (1981).

Nunez, I., 'Evolución de la politica educacional del régimen militar', Documento de Trabajo (Santiago, Chile: Programa Interdisciplinario de Investigaciones en Educación, PIIE, Academia de Humanismo Cristiano, June 1982).

ODEPLAN, *Informe social* (Chile: various years).

Oyarzo, C., 'Desigualdades en el campo de la salud: Chile, 1970–79', *CIEPLAN Notas Técnicas*, No. 53 (Santiago, Chile: February 1983).

Parker, C. *et al., Rasgos de cultura popular en poblaciones de Pudahuel* (Chile: Vicaria Zona Oeste, Archbishopric of Santiago, 1981).

PREALC, *Necesidades esenciales y politicas de empleo en América Latina* (Geneva, Switzerland: ILO, 1980).

Puga, J., 'Consecuencias sociales del déficit habitacional', Documento de Trabajo No. 176 (Santiago, Chile: Corporación de promoción Universitaria, 1979).

Raczynski, D. and C. Oyarzo, 'Por qué cae la tasa de mortalidad infantil en Chile?', *Colección Estudios CIEPLAN*, No. 6 (Santiago, Chile: December 1981).

Romero, M. *et al.*, 'Nivel de salud y atención pediátrica preventiva', *Cuadernos Médico Sociales,* Vol. XVII (Santiago, Chile: June–December 1976).

Rosales, O., *La mujer chilena en la fuerza de trabajo: Participación, empleo y desempleo (1957–1977)*, Memoria de prueba para optar el Grado de magister en Ciencias con mención en Economia (ESCOLA-TINA, Facultad de Ciencias Económicas y Administrativas, Universidad de Chile, July 1979).

Tagle, J., 'Subsidio habitacional y politica de vivienda', *Notas Técnicas*, No. 51 (CIEPLAN, March 1982).

Taucher, E., 'La mortalidad on Chile desde 1955 a 1975. Tendencias y causas', *Notas de Población*, Vol. VI, No. 18 (CELADE, December 1978).

Taucher, E., 'Effects of declining fertility on infant mortality levels: A study based on data from five Latin American countries', mimeo, Report to the Ford Foundation and the Rockefeller Foundation, (Santiago, Chile: CELADE, 82-2-222, 1982).

UNICEF, *Situación de la infancia en América Latina y el Caribe*, Regional Office for the Americas, Juan Pablo Terra, Co-ordinator (1979).

Vives, C., *Crisis en la familia popular, y su visión de futuro* (Departamento de Investigaciones Sociológicas, Centro Bellarmino, January 1983).

The Recent Worldwide Economic Crisis and the Welfare of Children: The Case of Cuba*

JOSÉ GUTIERREZ MUNIZ, JOSE CAMARÓS FABIÁN and
JOSÉ COBAS MANRIQUEZ
Instituto de Desarrollo de la Salud, Havana, Cuba

and

RACHELLE HERTENBERG
Columbia University, New York

Summary. — As a consequence of the deeply interdependent nature of today's world, Cuba has been affected by the world recession and by the critical roles of international trade and finance. However, the Cuban government has maintained a constant commitment to the protection of the poor and the children through increasing allocations of resources to education and health and through the promotion of increased levels of popular participation. This paper describes the improvements in the areas of nutrition, health and education and the persistent problems in the area of housing. It shows that the improvements observed have reached the majority of the population, eliminating great disparities.

1. INTRODUCTION

The Cuban Revolution of 1959 inherited a highly specialized agricultural sector, a rather backward industrial structure heavily dependent on imported materials and an economy lacking many crucial resources. Agriculture was clearly extensive as reflected in a low investment in irrigation and in the scarce utilization of improved seeding. In 1959, one-third of the arable land remained idle and 60% of the cultivated land was devoted to sugarcane.[1]

Cuba did not share in the general wave of industrialization that occurred in most of Latin America during the 1930s and 1940s. After 1959, the dependent industrial structure underwent a drastic change in supply sources for materials, spare parts and technology. The introduction of Soviet embodied technology resulted in severe problems of adaptation that initially reduced efficiency. This coincided with a substantial 'brain drain', owing to the emigration of more than 500,000 persons during the first decade of the Revolution.

The investments required for recapitalizing the Cuban economy and for its structural transformation were considerable and their import component was high. The scarcity of natural, human and capital resources, as well as the small economic size of the country's market placed serious constraints on the possibility of undertaking industrialization programmes. It was necessary to rely on the maximization of its comparative advantage in order to expand the output that would generate the hard currency needed for industrial modernization and diversification.

During the second half of the 1970s, developing countries responded to the world economic situation by implementing structural adjustment measures. These measures were mainly designed to increase the volume of exports at a faster pace than imports, and to adjust their productive structure to the new set of relative prices in the international market. However, in the past few years, shifts in the terms of trade and increases in interest rates have considerably weakened the financial position of the Third World

---

* This is a summary version of two larger papers: 'La Crisis Economica Mundial y el Nino: La Situacion de Cuba' prepared by Dr José A. Gutierrez Muniz, Lic., José Camarós Fabián, Lic. and José Cobas Manriquez and 'Cuba's Economic Strategy and Effects of Recent Trends in the World Economy: Implications for Social Development' by Rachelle Hertenberg. The views expressed in this paper are those of the authors and not necessarily those of the United Nations.

countries and have imposed different adjustments leading to the restriction of imports and
to a deceleration in overall growth.[2]

Recession in the developed market economies
has been transmitted to developing countries
through international trade and financial
markets. The high interest rate policy of the
developed market economies has imposed a
significant economic cost on all the capital-
importing developing countries. The increases
in interest rates since 1979 have been the major
determinant of the rise in interest payments on
debt capital, which in turn has been almost the
principal source of increase in overall total
payments.

The difference between the current recession
and the 1973—76 crisis is that during the earlier
period real interest rates (defined as nominal
rates deflated by the export prices of developing
countries) remained low. In the present situation,
the real interest rates have risen sharply and are
likely to remain high, although nominal rates
are easing somewhat, they are still above the
rate of increase in the prices of developing
countries' exports.[3]

The impact of the decline in prices of primary
commodities on the balance of payments of the
non-oil developing countries has been severe.
Their external terms of trade, which had
deteriorated by some 10% during 1978—80, in
the wake of the sharp increase in oil prices, fell
by a further 7% in 1981—82 in spite of the
substantial stabilization of oil prices. These
price movements and the decline in the volume
of exports of non-oil developing countries led
to a higher current account deficit, amounting
to $108 billion in 1981 and to $87 billion in
1982, about twice the average annual level
during 1977—80.[4]

As a consequence of the deeply interdependent nature of today's world, Cuba has
been affected by the world recession and by the
critical roles of international trade and finance.
Nevertheless, Cuba can be differentiated from
other developing countries because of its
centrally planned economy geared towards
egalitarian goals and its participation in the
CMEA. However, like many other Third World
countries, Cuba is simultaneously facing structural constraints and external pressures, both
interacting and influencing the direction of
domestic economic and social policies.

2. EFFECTS OF THE RECESSION ON THE CUBAN ECONOMY

During the period 1971—75 the global social
product (GSP) increased at an average annual
rate of 7.5%. Between 1976 and 1980 this rate
became 4%. In 1982, the rate of growth was
still 3.9% despite the crisis. As detailed later in
this report, the rate of growth was accompanied
by increased productivity and important changes
in economic policies.

Nevertheless, the worldwide economic crisis
of 1979—82 posed severe difficulties for Cuba's
economic strategy because of the situation of
international relative prices (lower prices for
primary commodities, while those of manufactured goods have increased rapidly). The
impact on Cuba can be seen through the
evolution of the prices of its main export
commodity (sugar) *vis-à-vis* prices of some key
imported goods. In 1960, the earnings from the
sale of 1 ton of sugar could buy 6.3 tons of oil;
in 1982 it purchased only 0.7 tons. In 1959,
one 60-HP tractor could be acquired with the
earnings from the sale of 24 tons of sugar, but
by the end of 1982, 115 tons of sugar were
required to purchase the same tractor.[5]

The change in sugar prices attests to changes
in the underlying supply conditions. The price
of this key component of Cuban exports had
soared in 1980, but fell by almost 70% between
October 1980 and December 1981. It has held
below the most pessimistic predictions and has
even plunged below the minimum price established in the International Sugar Agreement
(that is, below US $.13 per pound). Cuba has
lost approximately US $500 million over the
last years due to these prices.[6]

The rest of the export commodities, which
represented 17% of the total in 1980, showed
diverse performances. The foreign sales of
nickel, frozen fish, citrus fruit, rum and canned
fruits increased, while those of chrome and
seafood declined slightly. Sharp depressions in
the sales of tobacco and cocoa also affected
Cuban export income. The price of the latter
fell as a result of several years of overproduction.
The price of nickel held up well during the first
years of the current world economic recession,
but began to drop during the last quarter of
1981 and continued to fall during the first
quarter of 1982, before stabilizing at a level
7% lower than average levels in 1981. Thus,
the market prospects for Cuba's key export
commodities have not been very encouraging.

Cuba has curtailed its imports in hard
currency as part of the adjustment measures
adopted by the government. However, machinery
imports, the major Cuban import from industrialized capitalist countries, will still represent
a pressure for the country's deficit situation, as
manufacturers entering international trade may

very well continue to increase prices since it is unlikely that the inflation in developed market economies will dramatically decelerate. This has led to the search for international financing both to cover balance-of-payments deficits and to continue existing programmes and projects. In the early 1970s, the Soviet Union financed Cuban trade deficits and also provided the necessary guarantees to make Cuba credit-worthy to capitalist lending agencies. Credits from capitalist countries have been available from two sources: governments and private banks. Cuba has also borrowed from inter-national financial markets. Foreign affiliates of US banks are prohibited from extending any-thing but short-term credit to Cuba, but European banks have provided the National Bank of Cuba with medium-term Eurocurrency loans.

However, access to international financial markets has become more complicated in recent years because of the increasing interest rates in developed countries and because of uncertainties related to the payment possibilities of the heavily indebted Third World countries. Each increase of one percentage point in interest rates in Eurocurrency markets represents about 20 million pesos of interest costs of the Cuban foreign debt. (Until 1971 the Cuban peso was exchanged par with the dollar. In 1981 the official exchange rate fluctuated between US $.73 and US $.83 for one Cuban peso.) Thus such interest costs during 1982 were about 80 million pesos higher than they would have been at the interest rate prevailing in 1978.[7]

Cuba has prudently managed its debt. Cuban planners reduced imports in 1978 and 1979, following the fall in sugar prices, and were able to finance higher import levels in 1980 and 1981 without net borrowing, thanks to the temporary improvement in world sugar prices in those years. Yet Cuba experienced a large and sudden reduction in short-term credit facilities, which began in the fourth quarter of 1981 but was concentrated in the first half of 1982. Many other Third World countries have faced a reduction in their access to foreign finance throughout the recession. However, percentage reduction in Cuba's outstanding debt was particularly steep — 25% — three times the average of the group of Third World countries experiencing reductions in the same period.[8]

Cuba has recently renegotiated one-third of its debt. In September 1982, Cuba went to the governments and banks of its creditor countries in order to renegotiate approximately US $ 1.3 billion, which represents the medium- and long-term debt, with assurances that the payment of interest due on this amount would continue. Satisfactory agreements were reached in March 1983. Guidelines have been adopted by the National Bank of Cuba for the future debt management, which include having a total disbursed debt not exceeding 3.5 billion pesos and a debt service/export ratio under 45%.[9]

Cuba's ties to the USSR and its participation in the CMEA softened the effects of the current recession on Cuban trade and on its financial position. Cuba entered the CMEA in 1972, but has had intense bilateral ties with all the CMEA members since the early 1960s and has enjoyed all CMEA membership benefits except formal integration. These early ties with socialist countries as well as present economic relationships with them have been decisive for the prospects of the Cuban economy. Without access to socialist markets and supplies, the Cuban Revolution would have quite possibly failed.

The long-term trade agreements give Cuba stability in terms of sales of its products and guaranteed prices, which allow for better planning and forecasting. Nevertheless, these agreements have been flexible enough to allow Cuba to redirect its trade flows towards developed countries' markets when prices have been favourable in order to obtain more hard currency. Cuba's oil supplies have been included in the pricing agreement with the USSR which has partially sheltered Cuba from the infla-tionary effects of the oil price increases.

Cuba's economic links with socialist countries also include financial activity and technological assistance. Substantial financial assistance was received from the Soviet Union through low interest credits with privileged repayment conditions. These credits have been extended for construction of factories, oil exploration, modernization and expansion of the nickel plants and the mechanization and modernization of the sugar industry among other projects. In 1972, a new long term Cuba—Soviet Union agreement was signed, according to which the repayment of the debt accumulated up to 1973 would be deferred until 1986. After that, the debts are to be repaid in interest-free instal-ments over 25 years. Since then, Cuba has received new low interest credits to finance balance-of-payments deficits, with interest-free repayment also beginning in 1986.[10]

3. DOMESTIC POLICY ADJUSTMENTS

The Cuban government has responded to the

repercussions of the world crisis by taking austerity measures at the economic level and by giving more flexibility to its planning structure, as well as to its socio-political organization. The most important change regarding the planning structure and the regulation of domestic markets was a more formal approach to implementing economic planning by adopting fully articulated development planning with subordinated lower level plans, accepting tools such as cost analysis and by introducing, in most cases, a new method of economic accounting ('calculo economico'). This method is meant to ensure the self-financing and profitability of individual firms by requiring each unit to account for a margin of profit after having covered its own expenses with the income it generated. By 1980, 95% of the firms were operating under such a system.[11]

The introduction of a 'parallel market' and a wage reform have also been key features of the recent adjustments to both the new international economic environment and domestic socio-political conditions. Today there are three different domestic markets operating simultaneously: the market of rationed basic goods at low and fixed prices; the parallel market for complementary goods and industrial products at higher prices, which represents 10% of total retail value of sales in the country; and the markets of the peasants, artisans and workers where prices are determined by supply and demand.[12] The state contributes to this last market by providing the necessary physical infrastructure and services.

In 1981, a new wage reform, the first since 1963, introduced a wage rate based on the complexity and qualifications required by the job as well as a system of additional payments for surpassing 'normal' production levels. Payments for 'special working conditions' were established in order to achieve a better geographical and sectoral distribution of labour. In the agricultural sector, characterized by lower incomes, the minimum wage was increased by 27%. Special wages were determined for the personnel of activities such as public health and education.[13]

In 1980, the national monthly average income was 148 pesos. In 1982, it was 176 pesos, an increase of 19% in two years. In the same period, the minimum wage increased 14%. For the period 1976–80, the increase in wages was about 10%. Only after these income rises took effect was the retail price reform enacted. Prices had remained constant since 1965; in 1981, after 16 years, prices of 1500 of the more than 150,000 products sold through the

retail distribution network rose by 10 to 12% on the average.[14] (Note: for the period 1965–81, therefore, figures in current prices can actually be considered equivalent to those in constant prices.) In addition, a policy of guaranteed employment plus the rises in minimum wage levels have assured the poorest segments of Cuba's population a minimum family income.

Despite the repercussions of the world crisis, the Social Security Law was introduced, an important policy step which included security in terms of both pensions and social care. The law increased the number of people protected and granted protection to all the elderly. It broadened the scope of protection in the case of partial incapacitation, sickness and work related accidents, increasing the subsidy rates by 19%. Also, the law included pension increases for those remaining on the job after retirement age.[15]

In terms of policies related to the external economic situation, the government's austerity programme has constrained consumption by reducing the imports of the intermediate and capital goods required for the production of consumer goods, and by utilizing hard currency to increase production for exports and to reduce the import requirements. During the first years of the crisis (1979–80) Cuba made an effort to decrease further the importance of the capitalist market as a source of its imports in favour of purchases from the CMEA. In 1982 the total quantity of imports decreased about 2%, mainly reflecting the reduction in such operations with the capitalist market, while those involving socialist countries increased by 6%.[16] The government's policy regarding foreign debt has been basically one of renegotiation without requesting new loans. Presently, Cuba's total foreign debt amounts to approximately US $3 billion.[17]

The austerity programme also resulted in more carefully chosen investments in terms of the utilization of existing capacity and in relation to import requirements. Thus, investments in electric energy were directed to increase efficiency levels and decrease the oil consumption of the thermo-electric plants (which produce 99% of the energy in Cuba) by modernizing equipment and introducing generators from the USSR, Czechoslovakia and Japan. In the intermediate goods industry, the most significant growth occurred in textiles, a result of more intense utilization of the industry's installed capacity. Although building materials did not show a very dynamic performance, they benefited from the expanded cement production.

The modernization of the sugar industry has continued and eight new sugar mills will be built during the next five years, as well as an auxiliary infrastructure for the shipment of sugar. In the construction of the new sugar mills, the domestic component has been approximately 60%; the rest is imported from socialist countries, Western Europe and Japan.

Investments in the nickel industry are expected to continue increasing. However, a most important obstacle for this industry is the level of energy consumption involved in the treatment of nickel.

The investment efforts of the last years seem to have taken place at the expense of personal consumption. Nevertheless, the weight of 'services provided to the population' and consumption of 'collective goods and services' in the Global Social Product slightly increased, which is one indication that the basic needs of the population were met. (See Tables VI.1 and VI.2.) Furthermore, none of the components

Table VI.1. *Utilization of the Global Social Product*, 1975–81*

	1978		1979		1980		1981	
	Level	Share	Level	Share	Level	Share	Level	Share
Intermediate consumption	6968	42.8	7416	43.9	7900	44.9	10554	47.5
Final consumption	7476	45.9	7970	47.2	8268	47.0	9436	42.5
of which:								
– personal consumption	6106	37.5	6430	38.1	6646	37.8	7510	33.8
– services provided to the population	780	4.8	892	5.3	1015	5.8	1105	5.0
– collective goods and services	590	3.6	649	3.8	607	3.5	821	3.7
Net capital formation	2200	13.5	1906	11.3	2039	11.6	3063	13.8
– fixed investment	1505	9.2	1422	8.4	1462	8.3	234	10.6
– inventory accumulation	695	4.3	484	2.9	577	3.3	712	3.2
Losses	17	0.1	17	0.1	20	0.1	50	0.2
Exports minus imports‡	−140	0.9	−179	1.1	−518	2.9	−778	3.5
Statistical discrepancy	−239	1.4	−232	1.4	−118	0.7	−124	0.5
Global social products	1622	100.0	16898	100.0	17590	100.0	22203	100.0

Memo items: gross investment	1975		1978		1979		1980		1981	†
Productive sectors	1782	12.8	2055	12.6	2042	12.1	2213	12.6	2671	12.0
Non-productive sectors	522	3.8					530	3.0	500	2.3
Total	2304	16.6					2743	15.6	3171	14.5

Source: Republic of Cuba, State Statistical Committee, *Cuba en Cifras* (1981). From: UNCTAD, *Cuba: Recent Economic Development and Future Prospects, Report to the Government of Cuba* (November 1982).
*Figures in millions of pesos; shares in GSP in per cent.
†Preliminary.
‡Of goods and productive services.

Table VI.2. *Employment, Productivity and Wages, 1979–82*

Years	Productivity (pesos)	No. of workers (thousands)	Month average wages (pesos)
1979	7251	2768.2	143
1980	6568	2733.8	148
1981	7413*	2824.4	170
1982	7487*	2881.7	176

Sources: *Anuario Estadistico de Cuba* (1980 and 1981).
*Estimated.

of the austerity programme (reduction in imports, curtailment of personal consumption, price increases, wage reform, debt renegotiation) have jeopardized the satisfaction of the basic needs of the population nor have they set back achievements in the areas of nutrition, education and health. This is demonstrated by the increasing budget allocations for education and health, and by the performance of the social sectors, as described below.

4. PERFORMANCE OF THE SOCIAL SECTORS AND THE WELFARE OF CHILDREN

Aside from its humanitarian aspects, the protection of children through education and health care represents a long-term investment in social infrastructure and human capital which is an essential condition for the success of strategies committed to the transformation and development of Third World countries.

Before the Revolution of 1959, most health services and infrastructure were centralized in the capital and urban areas. The infant mortality rate was estimated to be about 60 per 1000 live births, infectious diseases had a high incidence and non-institutional deliveries were very frequent. The government spent around US $3 per capita on health care.[18] According to a survey of agricultural workers done by the Catholic University Association in 1957, 14% had contracted tuberculosis, 13% typhoid fever, 36% intestinal parasitism and 43% were illiterate.[19]

(a) *Demographic profile*

Perhaps the most outstanding demographic characteristic of Cuba in recent years has been the drastically low rate of natural increase of the population (births and deaths), which is approximately 0.9% per year. Cuba, with a population of almost 10 million people, had a birth rate of 14.8 per 1000 population in 1979, and the density of the island was 88 inhabitants per square km in 1981.[20]

In post-revolutionary Cuba, the early baby boom which peaked in 1963–64 was followed by persistent and gradual declines in birth rates until 1973, and sharper declines thereafter. Between 1973 and 1981, the crude birth rate declined 44%, while the general fertility rate declined from 122 births per 100 women aged 15–44 to 60 births. A large part of the fertility decline can be attributed to the increased use of fertility regulation and, to a lesser extent, to the low marriage rates during the 1970s when the government made efforts to increase the female participation in the labour force. The housing shortage, which has affected the marriage rate, has also had an impact on this decline.[21]

The fertility decline has been uninterrupted and steeper in rural areas and in provinces with a large proportion of rural population, although the differential among urban and rural fertility rates had been reduced by the end of the 1970s (the highest differential being 2.6 in Oriente and 1.9 in Havana for 1977).[22]

Such declines in fertility have occurred while mortality levels were remaining at the low levels of 5.6–5.8 deaths per 1000 population, which resulted in declining crude rates of natural increase from 19 per 1000 in 1973 to 8 per 1000 by 1980.[23]

The population growth rates have also been affected by the huge numbers of emigrants from Cuba over the past 25 years. There have been successive waves of emigration; the first one reached a peak before the missile crisis of 1962, while the latest one involved approximately 125,000 Cubans who left in the so-called 'Mariel sealift' of 1980.[24]

Cuba's pre-revolution demographic profile was very advanced. By 1958, life expectancy at birth was more than 60 years and the birth rate had declined to the mid-twenties per 1000 population. Today, the life expectancy at birth is 72 years which is approximately the average for developed countries and far higher than that of developing ones.

(b) *Nutrition*

If measured only in terms of per capita caloric availability, the nutritional status of the population today is approximately the same as before 1959. In 1958, the average caloric availability was 2730 per day, while today the daily caloric intake is 2800 on the average.[25] The pre-revolution figures, however, disguise the fact that 'in the 1950s no rich man ever suffered from food shortage, but the poor were extremely lucky to escape it'.[26] In addition, the current average caloric intake and the average protein intake (presently 73 grams per day) are not merely national averages but a minimum that virtually all Cubans are guaranteed regardless of income. Rationed foods alone currently provide a daily average of 2100 calories per capita, and even the lowest paid household can afford to buy their full ration book (*libreta*) allowance.[27]

Given this figure and the FAO definition of hunger as the consumption of fewer than 1500 calories per day, we can conclude that Cuba has virtually eradicated this problem. This is an important achievement if we consider that in 1956 the proportion of the Cuban population receiving fewer than the requisite daily number of calories was nearly 40%.[28] According to official surveys of 1979, an average Cuban was consuming more than the desired level of cereals (104%), nearly the target level of fats (85.5%), black beans (85.8%) and eggs (83.5%). The consumption of other products was below desirable levels: milk and dairy products (70.6%), meat (56.8%), fish (56.7%), root crops (63%), fruit (49.8%) and vegetables (36%).[29] These levels of consumption are not exclusively a result of availability or shortage of such foods, but are also related to consumer tastes.

The data show that the average diet in Cuba contains heavy doses of starches and insufficient amounts of fruits and vegetables, pointing to the need for better nutrition education. Although it is known that changes in food preference are very hard to achieve, Cuba seems to have a better chance in terms of education because it has already built channels for popular mobilization and for educational campaigns.

Rationing was initially part of a response to the agricultural problems of 1962. The post-revolution shortages that necessitated rationing also reflected a large increase in consumer demand, owing to the greater purchasing power of the lower classes. As production of some items increased, they were removed from the ration books. Thus, in terms of availability of different types of food, there have been changes during this past decade. In 1980, eggs, fish, yogurt and certain types of sausages were unrationed. Rice, bread, milk, meat and poultry, dry beans, cooking oil, butter and coffee were rationed. Vegetables, tubers and fruits were sold in unlimited quantities as long as they were not in short supply.[30]

In addition to the consumption of food through the marketplace, a considerable part of the population (one-fourth of the total population according to calculations made by Leyva for 1969) received subsidized meals in the form of low-cost luncheons in cafeterias near their workplace or through free school lunches. In 1980, the majority of secondary school students were attending rural boarding schools where all their nutritional needs were met.[31]

One of the changes in domestic policy was the introduction of free peasant markets co-existing with the rationed and parallel market. As a result, more food was brought into the cities. However, this additional flow of food in the urban areas is probably directed towards the middle-income consumer rather than the lowest income segment of the urban population.

Concern about the nutritional situation of the population and especially of children and child-bearing women has been a constant feature of government programmes. In 1976 a Nutrition Institute was created and in 1979 30 professional M.D.s were getting postgraduate degrees in this discipline. In the same year, a National Nutritional Programme was initiated with the collaboration of UNICEF and the PAHO/WHO which was mainly concerned with nutrition education.[32]

There is a network of services directed towards the early detection and periodical control of child malnutrition. During the first years of the revolution, homes for nutritional recuperation were created. Today, they have disappeared because they are no longer required, and also because of the introduction of community medicine in 1974.[33]

(c) *Health care for children: a high priority*

The early achievements in health care as well as the more recent improvements in standards are related not only to the high priority given to public health in economic planning in terms of investment and resource allocation, but also to the emphasis on preventive medicine, the response to the most compelling needs of the population in terms of most common diseases, and to the importance given to health education and to popular participation.

During the first decade of the revolution, diseases such as diphtheria, polio and tetanus neonatorum were eradicated. The main cause of infant mortality, acute diarrhoeal disease, was reduced by two-thirds. However, infant mortality rates slightly increased during some years of that decade: to 41.7 per 1000 in 1962 and to 46.7 per 1000 in 1969.

In 1970 a new maternal–child care programme was introduced with the goal of halving infant mortality over a 10-year period. This programme covered preventive aspects of maternal and child care and was integrated into the established national health system.

During the last 10 years, infant mortality has been significantly reduced (see Table VI.3) and by 1982 a rate of 17.3 per 1000 live births was reached, child mortality (from 1 to 4 years) was 1.0 per 1000 inhabitants and acute diarrhoeal diseases became the last of the five main causes of death in children younger than one year of age.[34] During 1979–82 the infant mortality rate continued to drop and by the latter year it reached 17.3 per 1000 live births, a level that corresponds to the usual status of infant mortality in developed countries.[35] In 1982 the child mortality rate reached 0.9 per 1000 which is an indirect indicator of a good nutritional standard.[36] This is a result of the priority given to maternal and child care in Cuba (see Tables

VI.4 and VI.5 for data on the causes of infant and child mortality over the period 1969–81).

The following have been some important factors in the achievement of these reductions:[37]
— improvement in the nutritional status of the child due to the availability of food and access to it through equitable distribution;
— improvement of the population's general level of education as well as health education;
— elimination of unemployment;
— eradication of urban squatter areas;
— improvements in housing conditions;
— improvements in environmental hygiene and food hygiene;
— creation of a health care network with total and free coverage in all the territories;
— immunization of all infants;
— increase in the material and human resources for maternal and child care;
— perfecting obstetric hospitals and services for newborn babies;
— introduction of national norms for paediatric and obstetric care;
— creation of 'maternal homes' in isolated areas to guarantee institutional deliveries and prenatal care.

Currently, Cuba is investing 60.42 pesos per citizen on public health services. This represents a significant improvement over the 25.0 pesos spent in 1970 or even the 41.98 pesos spent in 1979 (see Table VI.6), and certainly contrasts with the 3 pesos spent for this purpose in pre-revolution Cuba.

The increase in the budget allocation for public health from 409.2 million pesos in 1979 to 594.7 million pesos in 1982 resulted in additional improvements in the infrastructure and services provided. The office visit rate per

Table VI.3. *Birthrate, general mortality, childhood mortality and infant mortality, 1971–82*

Year	Per 1000 inhabitants			Per 1000 live births
	Birthrate	General mortality	Childhood mortality	Infant mortality
1971	29.5	6.2	1.0	37.4
1972	28.0	5.5	1.0	27.4
1973	25.1	5.7	1.2	28.9
1974	22.2	5.7	1.2	29.0
1975	20.8	5.4	1.1	27.3
1976	19.9	5.6	1.0	22.9
1977	17.7	5.9	1.1	24.8
1978	15.4	5.7	1.1	22.2
1979	14.8	5.7	1.0	19.3
1980	14.1	5.7	1.0	19.6
1981	14.0	6.0	1.1	18.5
1982	16.3	5.8	0.9	17.3

Sources: *Anuario Estadistico de Cuba* (1975 and 1981) and *Cuba en Cifras* (1982).

Table VI.4. *Main causes of infant mortality*, 1969, 1976–81

Causes	1969	1976	1977	1978	1979	1980	1981
Causes of mortality (B-44)	2097	596	307	235	267	236	269
Main perinatal complaints (B-43)	1456	1304	1403	1198	1088	1055	960
Influenza and pneumonia (B-31, B-32)	2105	487	627	459	218	221	181
Enteritis and other diarrhoeal diseases (B-4)	1640	397	435	235	140	144	141
Congenital disorders (B-42)	934	742	614	556	554	536	516
Accidents (B-47, B-48)	128	119	110	109	71	86	63
Sepsis	1654	295	273	202	151	102	85

Sources: *Statistical Yearbook of Cuba* (1975 and 1981); State Committee of Statistics.

Table VI.5. *Main causes of child mortality*, 1969, 1976–81

Causes	1969	1976	1977	1978	1979	1980	1981
Influenza and pneumonia (B-31, B-32)	354	170	160	151	94	84	65
Accidents (B-47, B-48)	231	180	196	180	140	142	128
Congenital disorders (B-42)	164	106	95	82	89	63	64
Enteritis and other diarrhoeal diseases (B-4)	128	44	55	45	29	15	13
Malignant tumours	92	83	74	60	73	59	49
Meningitis (B-24)	89	44	40	37	12	16	24

Sources: *Statistical Yearbook of Cuba* (1975 and 1981); State Committee of Statistics.

Table VI.6. *Budget allocations for education and health*, 1973–82*

Year	Education and health (million pesos)	Education (million pesos)	(per capita)	Health (million pesos)	(per capita)
1973	889.1	648.5	72.06	240.6	26.48
1974	1010.1	728.8	80.09	281.3	30.50
1975	1112.6	808.5	87.88	304.1	32.50
1976	1302.3	978.5	104.10	323.8	34.13
1977	1370.0	1047.9	110.31	322.1	33.57
1978	1547.6	1156.8	120.50	390.8	40.37
1979	1681.4	1272.2	131.15	409.2	41.98
1980	1781.0	1340.8	138.23	440.2	45.44
1981	1908.0	1349.1	139.08	558.9	57.34
1982	2040.3†	1445.6‡	147.51	594.7	60.42

Source: Ministerios de Educación y Salud Publica.
*Million pesos and per capita.
† *Ley de presupuesto del estado.*
‡Estimated.

delivery increased from 7 in 1970 and 11 in 1979 to 11.4 in 1982, while those related to general paediatrics have doubled since 1970 (from 1.4 to 2.8 per inhabitant). In terms of numbers of children under 15 years per hospital bed and per professional operating in paediatrics, the evolution has been as follows: in 1979 there were 341 children per bed while in 1982 there were 296; in 1979 the number of children per paediatrician was 1658 and in 1982 it dropped to 1410. During the same period, 31 new intensive care units were built and equipped in children's hospitals and paediatrics services around the country.[38] See Table VI.7 for more figures on the provision of health services.

The proportion of children with low birth weight is an important indicator of the nutritional status of children. In 1979, 10.2% of babies weighed less than 2500 grams at birth. This was reduced to 8.2% by 1982.[40] Production and import of drugs and medical equipment are handled through a public enterprise managed by the Ministry of Public Health, which has allowed more efficient utilization of the Ministry's budget. Finally, a most important aspect of Cuba's ability to keep improving its standards of health care during periods of economic hardship has been the cumulative nature of previous achievements in this area and the continuous high priority given to health care.

Table VI.7. *Health resources*, 1970, 1979, 1982

	1970	1979	1982
Hospitals:	225	265	267
– children's hospitals	18	21	26
– other hospitals	207	244	241
Maternal homes	22	65	81
Hospitals for handicapped children	6	9	16
– health centres	308	377	397
– hospital beds	43,562	42,051	44,224
Outpatient visits (millions)	29.3	43.1	49.4
– per capita paediatric visits	1.4	2.2	2.8

Sources: *Anuario Estadistico de Cuba* (1975 and 1981); *Cuba en Cifras* (1982); *Salud Publica – Cuba* (1982).

The national norms of child growth and development which are applied in paediatric office visits and in national evaluations are the result of research undertaken in 1972 at a national level among the 0–19-year-old population. This research, the Growth and Development Study and the Perinatal Mortality Study, is now being updated.[39]

Cuba has taken an innovative approach to the promotion of public health services. A good example of this is the creation of 'maternal homes' which are houses managed by health personnel where pregnant women from isolated areas of the country can spend the last weeks of their pregnancy. At delivery time they are sent to a nearby maternity hospital. Today there are 81 of these homes with more than 1500 beds. This has contributed to the improvement in the percentage of institutional births which reached 98.9% in 1982.

(d) *Education*

It is estimated that one million inhabitants out of a total of more than 6 million people were illiterate[41] in pre-revolution Cuba. The creation of more than 10,000 schools, the introduction of a National Education System and a literacy campaign resulted in a drop of the illiteracy rate to 3.9%. In 1970, 96.1% of the population in the 6–12-year range had received schooling as had 63.8% of the population between 13 and 16 years of age.[42] The budget for education has increased 4.5 times and in 1970 represented an investment of 147.5 pesos per capita. During the latest years this budget has continuously increased, in 1979 it amounted to 1272.2 million pesos and increased in 1980 to 1445.6 million pesos (see Table VI.4).

Day-care centres were created for the preschool age children of working mothers. By

1970, 475 centres were completed and in 1982 there were 839 centres serving 91,830 children.

According to Mesa-Lago (1981), there are discrepancies in the results of the literacy campaigns. In 1961, the government reported a reduction of illiteracy to 3.9%, but the 1970 Census shows an annual average rate of illiteracy reduction of 0.68% (in 1943–58 it had been 0.51%).

The reduction between rural and urban illiteracy was more significant; the gap was cut from 12 and 42% in 1953 to 7 and 22% in 1970.[43] The most important achievements of recent years have been related to improvements in the quality of education, as indicated by the reductions in the pupil–teacher ratios to 19.5 at the primary level and to 13.1 at the secondary level in 1982, and by the recent upgrading of all primary school teachers.

It should be pointed out that one of the guiding principles of Cuba's education system has been the combination of study and work. This system which seeks to provide formal education as well as developing working habits, has significantly contributed to the country's economy. The first experiences in this area took place in 1962 and 1966 when the plan called 'School in the Field' (Escuela en el Campo) was introduced with thousands of pupils and teachers working in the fields of Camaguey.[44] During the 1970s this type of experience was generalized into a network of 'schools in the field' combining study and work. Secondary-level students work 45 days per year in these schools; they have 3-hour long working sessions which are combined during the day with the studying sessions. Each of these boarding schools has 500 pupils and is built according to a model of modern construction which includes housing facilities for teachers. The schools grow different types of crops in adjacent fields. By 1982, 573 such schools were opened at the pre-university and secondary level.

Current trends of declining enrolments are due to earlier successes in expanding primary school education to cover virtually the entire school age population, and due to the decline in the population growth rate. (See Table VI.8.) However, the enrolment at the technical and professional levels has been very dynamic in the last years, increasing from 94,000 students in 1974–75 to 264,000 in 1981–82.[45]

Finally, although there are differences of opinion as to the quality of the education received, as MacEwan points out, the schools' role in establishing new social relations as well as the fact that a greater number of people passed through them are of major importance.

(e) Housing

In 1960, the government introduced a Law of Urban Reform which turned all rental housing over to the state and forbade private rental. The law also prohibited the possession of more than one house per family and set rents for tenants at a level equivalent to no more than 10% of their income. Although this law guarantees the universal right to proper housing, it has been an unfulfilled promise so far.[46]

Two main problems affected the construction of new dwellings during the revolutionary years: the shortage of construction materials and the insufficient number of specialized workers. During the early 1960s, part of the housing shortage problem was alleviated by the reallocation of the dwellings left behind by the waves of emigrants.

The government had acknowledged a deficit of more than one million units by 1970.[47] The

Table VI.8. *Main indicators of education, 1970–71, 1979–80, 1981–82*

Items	1970–71	1979–80	1981–82
Number of schools			
– primary level	15,190	12,675	11,771
– secondary level	410	1318	1364
Teaching personnel			
– primary level	60,592	77,063	72,045
– secondary level	15,273	60,553	62,903
Enrolment			
– primary level	1,654,634	1,550,523	1,409,765
– secondary level	186,667	825,852	826,477

Source: *Anuario Estadistico de Cuba* (1981).

actions taken to improve the situation include: the promotion of the dynamic growth of the cement industry and additional investments in new plants for the production of construction materials. On the other hand, workers from certain plants are encouraged to increase productivity as a way to free 'microbrigades' of 30–35 workers each, who undertake the construction of new dwellings close to the plant. Some 37,500 units were built through this system between 1971 and 1975.[48]

These measures have proved inadequate to meeting the housing needs. By 1980, the deficit has been estimated to be at a level of approximately 1.5 million units, and the goals for the construction of 100,000 housing units per year by 1980 were far from being reached – in that year only 15,000 units were finished.[49] Despite this huge deficit, significant progress has been made in terms of distribution of housing and the elimination of income discrimination in this area.[50] Considerable improvements in the quality of housing in rural areas as well as a better utilization of territory has also been achieved.

Special priority was given to the construction of housing and creation of new communities in areas with low density populations. All these new communities are linked to specific productive activities; among them, the majority are linked to sugar (122 new towns), cattle (88), rice (21), citrus (20) and industrial plants (15). Each settlement, with an average population of 150,000 was provided with basic housing (apartment buildings with four floors and 20 units), a supermarket, a primary school and day-care centre.[51]

Rural sanitation and the provision of piped water and utilities have been improved, although the precise number of upgraded houses is not available. In 1980, the construction of sewage infrastructure increased significantly (21.7%).[52]

5. SOME LESSONS FROM THE CUBAN EXPERIENCE

Cuba was and still is a country with scarce resources. Despite its relatively substantial pace of economic growth during a good part of the 1970s, it is still a developing country vulnerable to fluctuation in international markets. Additionally, Cuba faces political constraints that affect its development strategy. First, the Cuban Revolution has always had to tie up a considerable part of its scarce resources in military investments, in order to deal with threats of invasion and to fulfil its political commitments in Africa and Latin America.

Second, there has been a persistent economic blockade of a different nature than that of the early stage of the revolution. Cuba has been sheltered from the effects of the present recession, only to the extent that it has mechanisms which are inherent to the nature of its planned economic system and to the privileged relations with the CMEA allowing the island to diversify and redirect its foreign sector when times are difficult in the international capitalist market.

At the same time, Cuba's achievements in terms of the improvements in the quality of life of the majority of the population and the elimination of great disparities have been impressive. They have been possible due to a consistent commitment of the Cuban government to the protection of the poor and the children, as reflected in its decision to maintain its expenditures on education and health in 1982 while the public sector budget was being reduced by more than 10%. A great deal of credit for these achievements should be given also to the high levels of popular participation, which have been responsible for the flexibility and corrections in the design of social service systems.

A good example of this is the changes which occurred in the public health system as a result of initiatives and demands of the participants. Such levels of participation have been possible due to early redistributive and egalitarian measures: 'In all societies, a more educated and informed population carries the prospect of more versatile and more diversified forms of participation in public affairs'.[53] And in the case of Cuba, participation has been facilitated by the nature and orientation of the educational system which was perceived from the beginning as a system integrated into the real life conditions and needs of the population, and was attuned to the structural changes that were taking place. The work-study system has been very instrumental for the purpose of preparing the Cuban youth for its role in building the new society, and has also made the educational system – which takes up so many of the country's scarce resources – an immediate contributor to the productive sphere. Therefore, we can safely say that the successes in education will be a long-lasting and cumulative asset for Cuban society.

Another important feature of the Cuban experience is that the austerity measures which necessarily imply a slow down in the levels of economic growth have been accompanied by responses from the population in terms of efficiency and productivity which attenuate to a certain extent the effects of the crisis.

In addition to the participation of the population in the distribution of wealth and to the sustained efforts in education, we should point out the aforementioned impressive results in the area of health care, in which Cuba has surpassed the majority of Third World countries. These have been accomplished — in our opinion — through a combination of imagination, adaptation of the health services to the concrete conditions of the country, the conception of public health as a preventive rather than only a relief system, and the satisfactory co-ordination and integration in the monitoring of health, education, nutrition and other social services.

Last, but certainly not least, we should remember that the foundation for all these socio-political efforts and achievements lies in the conscious commitment to eliminate traditional class barriers to the access to social services.

NOTES

1. MacEwan (1981).

2. UN, Department of International Economic and Social Affairs (1982).

3. *Ibid.*

4. IMF (1983).

5. Castro Ruz (1983).

6. *Prisma* (April 1983).

7. UNCTAD (November 1982).

8. *Ibid.*

9. *Ibid.*

10. *Ibid.*

11. CEPAL (January (1982).

12. *Prisma* (April 1983).

13. CEPAL (January 1982).

14. *Prisma* (April 1983).

15. *Cuba Update* (1980).

16. Comite Estatal de Estadisticas (1982).

17. *Prisma* (April 1983).

18. Torras, *Economia Y Desarrollo*, No. 13.

19. *Economia y Desarrollo*, No. 12.

20. Comite Estatal de Estadisticas (1981).

21. Guttmacher and Danielson (1977).

22. Diaz Briquets and Perez, in *PRB Bulletin.*

23. The 1979 National Demographic Survey showed that 28.9% of the total labour force was female and 31.9% of women of age 14 and above were economically active during the week prior to the survey, which is the highest rate in Latin America according to the International Labour Office.

24. Guttmacher and Danielson (1977).

25. *Cuba Update* (1980).

26. Leyva (1972).

27. *Cuba Update* (1980).

28. *Ibid.*

29. Foster and Handelman (1982).

30. *Ibid.*

31. *Prisma* (April 1983).

32. Foster and Handelman (1982).

33. Cordova Vargas and Amador (1977).

34. Ministerio de Salud Publica (1979).

35. *Ibid.*

36. Ministerio de Salud Publica (1982).

37. Ministerio de Salud Publica (1975).

38. Ministerio de Salud Publica (1979–82).

39. Rojas Uchoa (1981).

40. Ministerio de Salud Publica (1979–82).

41. Castro Ruz (1975).

42. Ministerio de Educacion (1981a).

43. Mesa-Lago (1981).

44. Ministerio de Educacion (1981b).

45. *Cuba en Cifras* (1982).

46. Barkin (1979).

47. Diaz Briquets and Perez in *Population and Development Review.*

48. Barkin (1979).

49. Diaz Briquets and Perez in *Population and Development Review.*

50. Barkin (1979).

51. CEPAL (January 1982).

52. Dominquez (1978).

53. UN, Department of International Economic and Social Affairs (1982).

REFERENCES

Barkin, D., 'La transformacion del espacio en Cuba post-revolucionaria', *Boletin de Estudios Latino-americanos y del Caribe*, No. 27 (1979).

Castro Ruz, F., *Informe del Comite Central de PCC al ler Congreso* (Havana: 1975).

Castro Ruz, F., *La Crisis Economica y Social del Mundo* (Havana: Oficina de Publicaciones del Consejo de Estado, 1983).

Cordova Vargas, L. and M. Amador, *Prevencion de la Mala Nutricion en Cuba* (1977).

Cuba, Comite Estatal de Estadisticas, *La Economia Cubana 1982.*

Cuba en Cifras (1982).

Cuba, Ministerio de Educacion, *Cuba: Organizacion de la Educacion 1978–80*, prepared for the XXXVIII International Education Conference, Geneva (1981a).

Cuba, Ministerio de Educacion, *Resumen del Trabajo Anual del MINED, Ano Escolar 1980–81* (Havana: 1981b).

Cuba, Ministerio de Salud Publica, *Cuba: La Salud en la Revolucion* (Havana: Editorial Orbe Instituto Cubano del Libro, 1975).

Cuba, Ministerio de Salud Publica, *Informe Anual* (Havana: various years).

Cuba Update, 'The Cuban economy: answers to some questions', Vol. 1, No. 5 (New York: Center for Cuban Studies, 1980).

Diaz Briquets, S. and L. Perez, 'Cuba: the demography of a revolution', *PRB Bulletin*, Vol. 36, No. 1.

Diaz Briquets, S. and L. Perez, 'Fertility decline in Cuba: a socio-economic interpretation', *Population and Development Review*, Vol. 8, No. 3.

Dominguez, J., *Cuba: Order and Revolution* (Harvard University Press, 1978).

Economia y Desarrollo, 'Encuesta de los trabajadores rurales, 1956–57', No. 12 (Havana).

Foster, N. and H. Handelman, 'Government policy and nutrition in revolutionary Cuba: rationing and redistribution', *UFS Reports*, No. 19 (1982).

Guttmacher, S. and R. Danielson, 'Changes in Cuban health care: an argument against technological pessimism', *International Journal for Health Services*, Vol. 7, No. 3 (1977).

International Monetary Fund, *World Economic Outlook, 1983* (Washington: 1983).

Leyva, R., *Health and Revolution in Cuba* (New York: Anchor, 1972).

MacEwan, A., *Revolution and Economic Development in Cuba* (New York: St. Martin's Press, 1981).

Mesa-Lago, C., *The Economy of Socialist Cuba* (University of Mexico Press, 1981).

Prisma, Latin American Focus No. 1, 'Interview with H. Perez' (April 1983).

Rojas Uchoa, F., *Investigacion Perinatal* (Havana: Editorial Cientifico-Tecnica, 1981).

Torras, J., 'Los factores economicos en la crisis medica', *Economia y Desarrollo*, No. 13 (Havana).

UN, CEPAL, 'Cuba: Evolucion reciente de su economia', *Revista Comercio Exterior*, Vol. 32, No. 1 (Mexico: January 1982).

UNCTAD, *Cuba: Recent Economic Development and Future Prospects*, report to the Government of Cuba (November 1982).

UN, Department of International Economic and Social Affairs, *World Economic Survey, 1981–82* (1982).

Poverty, Income Distribution and Child Welfare in Latin America:
A Comparison of Pre- and Post-recession Data

OSCAR ALTIMIR*

United Nations Economic Commission for Latin America,
Santiago, Chile

Summary. – The traditional and external dependency of most Latin American economies and their recent pattern of growth has made them particularly vulnerable to the unexpected and severe changes of the world economy that began in 1979–80. Even those countries with less open economies have been forced to seek adjustments to the new world situation that are, both in nature and consequences, essentially different from those of the interdependent industrial economies.

This paper attempts to evaluate the impact of these recent economic changes on the living conditions of the populations of Chile, Colombia, Costa Rica, Panama and Venezuela. It is based on household data and is limited to those aspects of household living conditions that can be observed through the variables included in labour surveys. It analyses changes in overall income distribution, the movement of different socio-economic groups within the income pyramid and changes in these groups' livelihood strategies.

1. LATIN AMERICA'S DEVELOPMENT CRISIS

The characteristics of the present world recession have been widely analysed (see, for example, World Bank, 1983). Its impact on the Latin American region has been aggravated and extended, becoming further complicated in many countries by the deterioration of processes and mechanisms that characterized their recent growth patterns.

Regional per capita product, which was growing at an average of 2.9% yearly during 1975–79 (with only a couple of countries showing steady reductions), continued to rise in 1980 in the region as a whole, but a greater number of countries began to suffer deteriorations. Real per capita product for the whole of Latin America dropped some 1% in 1981 and 3.2% in 1982. Within the regional aggregate, 10 of the 20 Latin American countries were already experiencing the fall of their real per capita product in 1981 and in 1982 goods and services available had declined in all countries except Cuba and Panama.

As shown in Table VII.1, the decline of Latin American exports became visible in 1981, affecting both the oil exporting countries and the rest. This was aggravated by the deterioration of terms of trade, which non oil exporting countries had been experiencing since 1978. The severe contraction of imports in 1982 did not, as a rule, narrow the external gap caused by the reduction in export volume, the fall of the terms of trade and the giddy rise of interest payments. The current account deficit of the region as a whole, which had averaged US $15 billion a year in 1975–79, climbed to US $28 billion in 1980 and US $39 billion in 1981, then declined marginally to US $36 billion in 1982. Interest payments, which in 1979 represented 17% of the value of exports (on a gross global debt of around US $200 billion), reached 24% of exports in 1980 and 35% in 1982 (on a debt exceeding US $260 billion).

In the present situation of credit rationing and balance-of-payments problems, most Latin American countries are trapped in a rather Kafkian predicament. On the one hand, the

*The effective and unfailing assistance of Marilú Avendaño, Mabel Bullemore, Juan Carlos Feres and Pedro Tejo in preparing the data base and analysing the tabulations is gratefully acknowledged. The views expressed in this paper are those of the author and not necessarily those of the UNICEF.

Table VII.1. *Latin America: main economic indicators*

Indicator	1975–78	1979	1980	1981	1982
Annual average rates (%)					
Gross domestic product	5.1	6.5	5.9	1.5	−0.9
Gross domestic product per capita	2.5	3.9	3.4	−0.9	−3.2
Real gross domestic income	5.0	7.2	6.6	0.8	−1.5
Terms of trade of goods and services	−0.7	4.8	4.8	−5.5	−6.2
Current value of exports of goods and services	14.3	33.7	28.7	8.0	−9.0
Current value of imports of goods and services	12.0	26.4	31.1	8.9	18.2
Billions of dollars					
Balance on current account	−13.8	−19.5	−28.1	−38.8	−36.3
Total reserves (minus gold)	23.7	38.5	35.4	34.1	23.1
Gross global external debt*		166.6	204.3	242.5	262.9
Percentages of exports of goods and services					
Balance on current account	−26.8	−23.7	−26.5	−34.0	−35.0
Net payments of profits and interest	14.9	16.5	16.9	24.0	35.2

Source: ECLA.
*Does not include supplier credits without official guarantee.

renegotiation of their foreign debt would imply a type of adjustment that would aggravate their internal recession beyond socially endurable levels, while their weakened participation in uncertain external markets does not seem to allow them to generate enough resources to face an unprecedented financial burden. On the other hand, the very failure to comply with such commitments and to generate the necessary resources to pay the full amount of interest due on the external debt conspire against obtaining new additional financing needed to design feasible, long-run solutions.

The present world recession has unveiled the structural limitations of the dependent development prevailing in Latin America, which had been temporarily masked by two decades of expanding external markets, price increases of many of the region's basic products and low international interest rates joined, in the mid-1970s, by the sudden enhancement of private financing following the recycling of petro-dollars. Structural internal and external disequilibria reappear: the persistence of inflationary pressures despite severe adjustment policies; the chronic discrepancy between resources, their allocation and the expectations promoted by the very style of development; and the difficulties of deepening industrialization while overcoming technological lags.

It is therefore dubious that the reaction of the Latin American countries to international recovery will be symmetric to the recessive impact and that the multiplicative effects of

the downswing will operate in reverse with the same intensity of Latin American GNP, even disregarding the bigger welfare losses (Singer, 1983) involved for the whole of the Latin American population.

At the same time, it is difficult to disentangle the impact of world recession on the population's levels of living from the effects produced by the exhaustion of expansion mechanisms previously at work or from the effects of adjustment policies which had been put in practice under previous external conditions and which highlighted the crisis of the development model before world recession did.

2. THE APPROACH AND THE DATA

The lasting consequences of the Latin American crisis have been predetermined by its structural character which underlines the need for continuously monitoring changes in living conditions. At present, this can be aided by drawing relevant indicators from the information provided by recurrent household surveys, comparable over time, even though their coverage, definitions and survey techniques are not the most adequate to assess living conditions and their change (Altimir and Sourrouille, 1980). It is hoped that these limitations for observing possible damage in delicate social tissues may prompt decision-makers and producers of statistics to plan for and invest in more appropriate tools for measuring and analysing levels of living.

The analytical approach followed in this paper had to be adapted to the availability of information. The data base selected is made up of household surveys on employment, comparable over time, whose data were incorporated in the ECLA Data Bank and could, therefore, be readily processed.[1] The countries covered are Chile, Colombia, Costa Rica, Panama and Venezuela. The characteristics of the surveys are included in Table VII. 2.

The coverage of available surveys limits the scope of the analysis. Those of Colombia, Chile and Panama cover only main urban areas. On the other hand, the national coverage of the Venezuelan sample allowed the analysis to focus both on the metropolitan area of the capital city and on one of the regions. The data for Costa Rica are also of national coverage. In the case of Costa Rica and Panama, income data covered only wages and salaries thus restricting analysis to employees' households.

As a consequence of these data limitations,

Table VII.2. *Household surveys utilized*

| Country | Survey denominations | Executing agency | Rounds used | | Geographical coverage |
			For base period	For 1982	
Chile	Employment and unemployment survey	University of Chile	June 1982	June	Greater Santiago
Colombia	National household survey	DANE	September 1979	September	Seven main cities
Costa Rica	National household survey	DGEC	July 1979	July	National
Panama	Manpower survey	DEC	August 1979	March	(a) Metropolitan area
Venezuela	Household sample survey	DGECN	2nd semester 1980	1st semester	(b) Los Andes region

Labour surveys do not provide the best information for analysing living conditions, but are the only type of surveys carried out in many Latin American countries on a recurrent and comparable basis (CEPAL, 1983). They do not provide 'output' measures in terms of needs satisfaction. Even in terms of the 'input' measures, household surveys do not provide data illustrating the whole picture; data on social services, such as those analysed by Foxley and Raczynski (1983), do illuminate the likely effect of the crisis on those components of the levels of living that depend on access to basic public services or assistance for education, health, housing or work. However, updated and comparable data of this kind are not always readily available or decipherable.

The selection of countries was thus determined by the availability of household survey data. Although the set is not totally representative of all national reactions to the crisis, it is sufficiently differentiated to allow insights as to the direction, magnitude and characteristics of the socio-economic impact of crisis in various economic, political and policy contexts.

the assessment of the impact of the crisis is primarily concentrated on urban households. Rural conditions are, of course, likely to have been also affected. International prices of most agricultural exports of the region fell between 1979 and 1982. In addition, although agricultural product in 1982 was higher in real terms than in 1972, relative prices have shifted against agriculture. However, as these negative developments have mainly affected commercial agriculture, their effects on the poorer segments of the rural population may presumably have been softened.

For each of the five countries, the results of surveys for a period immediately prior to the crisis are compared with those from the latest available and usable surveys.

The time span covered by the analysis cannot capture all, or even most, of the impacts of the present economic recession. On the one hand, the initial and quite significant effects of internal adjustment policies, which had been implemented well before the outburst of the external crisis (as happened in Chile), had already taken place. On the other hand, as has already been pointed out, the crisis in Latin America is still in progress. Besides, there are a series of lags, differing from country to country, between deterioration of the external situation and the implementation of ensuing adjustment policies, between changes in economic conditions and households' adjustment of livelihood strategies, between these changes in living conditions and their effects on individuals as welfare subjects and as social actors.

In this paper, changes in overall income distribution and poverty levels are first analysed. Next, changes in the relative position of different socio-economic groups in the income pyramid are assessed while changes in livelihood strategies are also considered.

3. EXTERNAL CONDITIONS AND INTERNAL ADJUSTMENTS

The external crisis has hit the Chilean economy hard and its welfare effects have been amplified by particular conditions and adjustment policies at the national level. As shown in Table VII.3, GDP per capita in 1980 had just surpassed the 1970 level, while the vulnerability of the external sector had increased. A temporary boom culminated in 1981, with gains in per capita GDP (particularly in per capita consumption) and in real wages, accompanied by a drop in the unemployment rate. However, terms of trade continued to deteriorate and the fall of exports in the face of strongly expanding imports put the balance-of-payments deficit at almost the entire value of exports. The internal boom was clearly being financed by a growing external debt. The termination of this growth pattern brought a deep recession, with 1982 per capita GDP and private consumption falling 15.5 and 19.1%, with a drastic fall in real wages and with open unemployment rising to 20% of the labour force.[3]

Colombia has undergone a mild recession. The first problems in its external sector appeared in 1979, when a fall of the terms of trade eroded the gains made since 1975. Growth began to decelerate in 1980 and GDP per capita suffered a slight fall in 1982. The deterioration of export performance and terms of trade in 1981 put the balance-of-payments deficit in current account at around US $2 billion, a gap representing almost 50% of the value of exports. Because of continuing increases in imports, this gap persisted in 1982, despite the partial recovery of exports and terms of trade. As can be seen from Table VII. 3, in 1982

per capita GDP has not yet fallen to 1979 levels and real wages had resumed their rise.

The Costa Rican economy has suffered a severe external impact. In 1978, the existing external disequilibrium began to deepen, with growing indebtedness financing the gap between increasing imports, weakened exports and dwindling terms of trade. In 1981 a profound contraction of imports started but the fall of exports and terms of trade in 1982 nevertheless put the current account deficit at 38% of the value of exports, with interest and profits absorbing even more than that portion of external resources. As can be seen in Table VII.3, real GDP per capita declined by 17% between 1979 and 1982; real wages fell by 34% in the face of an accelerated inflation while the unemployment rate doubled from 5 to 10% in 1982.

Panama has been almost exempt from the wave of international recession. Although terms of trade have steadily deteriorated, the expansion of exports kept the external gap at around 40% of their value, less than half of it corresponding to interest payments on a manageable external debt. Nevertheless, GDP continued to grow at around historical rates, with per capita GDP increasing by 4.5% between 1979 and 1982 and private consumption per capita by somewhat more.

The Venezuelan oil exporting economy ran into trouble as early as 1978, mainly for internal reasons. A restrictive economic policy was enforced in 1979—80. The corresponding stagnation of GDP, as can be seen from Table VII.3, anticipated the external impact of 1982, when the significant fall in the value of exports and the mounting interest payments on a considerable external debt brought about for the first time a current account deficit in the balance of payments amounting to a fifth of exports. As a consequence of the stagnation of economic activity, per capita GDP fell steadily, at a rate of 12.7% between 1978 and 1982.

4. INCOME DISTRIBUTION AND POVERTY

Table VII. 4 presents the distribution of per capita household income by decile groups in the countries and areas indicated, both for a period previous to the recession and for 1982. These data should not be taken as depicting the overall inequalities in the countries concerned. Beyond the limitations already pointed out regarding income concepts, area coverage and socio-economic segments (and indicated

Table VII.3. *Relevant economic indicators of the countries selected*

Countries and periods	Internal economy						External sector				
	GDP	GDP per capita	Private consumption per capita	Consumer prices	Real wages	Urban unemployment (% of labour force)	Value of exports	Value of imports	Terms of trade	Balance on current account	Profit and interest payments
		(Annual average rates, %)					(Annual average rates, %)		(%)	(% of exports)	(% of exports)
Chile											
1970–76	−1.3	−2.9	−4.9	208.7	−5.7	9.1	11.6	9.5	−8.3	−15.1	12.8
1976–80	8.5	6.7	5.4	48.4	10.3	13.7	25.4	37.2	−3.4	−25.7	15.0
81	5.7	3.9	11.3	19.7	11.7	9.0	−7.7	26.3	−13.7	−88.4	25.9
82	−14.1	−15.5	−19.1	9.9	−2.9	20.0	−8.7	−39.7	−10.7	−48.6	40.8
Colombia											
1975–79	5.7	3.4	3.3	22.1	4.0	9.7	20.1	17.9	7.7	7.8	8.4
80	4.1	1.9	2.2	28.0	0.2	9.7	17.4	39.2	9.8	−12.8	5.2
81	2.1	−0.1	−0.2	29.5	−0.2	8.2	−19.3	10.4	−15.2	−46.8	7.9
82	1.2	−1.0	−0.6	15.2	3.9	9.3	5.1	6.9	9.2	−50.8	12.9
Costa Rica											
1975–79	6.4	3.3	3.1	5.7	7.7	5.4	16.5	19.0	4.7	−35.9	10.6
80	0.8	−2.1	−6.0	18.1	−1.5	6.0	9.2	9.1	−6.6	−54.9	18.0
81	−4.6	−7.2	−8.3	37.1	−12.8	9.1	1.8	−20.6	25.7	−30.4	24.6
82	−6.3	−8.8	−5.2	90.1	−23.4	9.9	−11.1	−19.2	−7.4	−38.0	42.3
Panama											
1975–79	4.2	1.7	3.9	5.2	−2.6*	9.7	7.6	8.4	−5.4	−25.4	6.1
80	5.3	1.1	4.5	13.8	3.9*	9.8	48.4	14.6	−6.2	−24.1	9.7
81	3.8	1.5	−1.0	7.3	...	11.8	4.0	9.6	0.6	−43.2	23.3
82	4.0	1.8	2.1	4.3	...	...	−3.4	1.7	−2.6	−35.7	17.5
Venezuela											
1975–78	6.0	2.4	5.6	7.5	2.3	6.4	1.6	28.7	−3.7	−16.1	−1.1
79	0.9	−2.5	2.4	12.3	3.9	5.8	52.6	−6.4	29.9	2.5	0.0
80	−1.8	−5.1	0.0	23.1	−1.0	6.6	33.5	6.5	25.7	23.8	−1.6
81	0.4	−3.0	−5.0	14.6	−3.8	6.8	3.7	13.0	2.9	19.5	−3.9
82	0.6	−2.7	−1.0	10.0	−1.0	8.2	−16.7	6.4	−0.7	−19.8	11.1

*Corresponds to minimum wages.

Table VII.4. Aggregate income distributions*

Percentile groups of household by per capita income	Chile Greater Santiago		Colombia 7 main cities		Costa Rica National†		Panama Metropolitan area†		Venezuela Metropolitan area		Los Andes region	
	1981	1982	1979	1982	1979	1982	1979	1982	1978	1982	1978	1982
1–10	1.7	1.5	0.8	0.8	2.2	2.6	3.2	3.0	3.5	3.3	2.6	2.9
11–20	2.9	2.7	1.4	2.1	4.0	4.3	4.1	4.8	5.4	5.4	4.1	4.3
21–30	3.6	3.5	3.7	3.2	4.9	5.4	4.8	5.2	6.7	6.6	5.1	5.7
31–40	4.6	4.5	4.7	4.0	6.0	6.7	6.9	6.5	7.7	7.5	6.1	6.7
41–50	5.2	5.6	5.5	5.4	7.3	7.7	8.2	7.8	8.6	8.4	7.5	8.1
51–60	6.7	6.6	6.0	6.9	8.3	8.9	8.5	8.9	9.4	9.9	8.5	9.1
61–70	7.5	8.3	9.0	8.9	9.5	9.8	11.3	9.4	11.0	10.9	10.5	10.5
71–80	9.7	11.0	11.7	11.8	12.1	11.1	12.8	12.7	12.4	12.4	12.3	13.0
81–90	15.1	17.4	16.7	16.9	17.3	15.3	15.6	15.1	14.9	15.6	16.8	15.5
91–100	43.9	38.9	39.9	40.0	28.4	28.2	24.6	27.3	20.1	20.0	26.5	24.2
Gini coefficients	0.498	0.489	0.513	0.516	0.376	0.346	0.327	0.335	0.257	0.262	0.354	0.319
Log variance	0.139	0.153	0.223	0.211	0.092	0.076	0.071	0.067	0.044	0.047	0.081	0.067
Mean household income‡	27,406	25,531	13,609	15,640	3146	1906	478	450	4225	3420	1795	
Incidence of poverty (% households)	12.0	16.0	48.7	44.8	17.3	29.4	18.8	14.8	2.3	3.2	31.2	26.8
Income concepts	Primary incomes in cash		Primary incomes in cash		Wages and salaries in cash		Wages and salaries in cash		Primary incomes in cash			
Reference periods for incomes	May		August		June		August	March	October	April	October	April

*Percentage shares of total income.
†Households headed by employees.
‡Monthly incomes at base period prices.

in Table VII. 4 for each distribution), a general caveat is necessary as unadjusted survey data are presumed to underestimate income concentration (Altimir, 1983). However, as far as both the coverage and the biases of each survey are comparable over time, the analysis of differences in survey results can be taken as indicative of *changes* in the relative overall distribution of income.

According to these statistics, shifts in aggregate income distribution do not appear to have been of great significance in most of the countries considered despite considerable changes in real and monetary incomes. Therefore, the analysis should go beyond the aggregate picture, as these changes may have significantly modified the relative position of different socio-economic groups which could not be reflected by aggregate indicators.

To give a view of the main shifts that have taken place in the relative position of different socio-economic groups, Table VII.5 includes two coefficients, (R) and (B), that respectively indicate the percentages of households of each socio-economic group that have shifted below the second income quintile and below the third income quintile. Thus, R indicates net shifts out of (negative) or into (positive) the bottom 40% of households, which in Latin America broadly corresponds to a notion of relative poverty. Likewise, B broadly indicates shifts above (negative) or below (positive) average income of all households in the distribution.

From another viewpoint, the tendency towards the lessening of absolute poverty through general economic growth has suffered a setback in the countries hit by the recession. In order to assess changes in the incidence of absolute poverty due to the present recession in each country, the corresponding distributions of households by per capita household income were cut off by relevant poverty lines. The latter were calculated extrapolating the minimum consumption standards estimated for 1970 (Altimir, 1982). In this extrapolation it was assumed that expectations promoted by the very style of development prevailing in Latin America would determine an upward movement of absolute poverty lines in line with general economic growth. An elasticity of 0.25 with respect to per capita GNP was therefore assumed for extrapolating the 1970 poverty lines to the end of the 1970s, prior to the crisis period.[4] Poverty lines were maintained invariant in real terms during our comparison periods, as a reflection of the fact that expectations ingrained in the value system and collective

behaviour over the long-run may be further frustrated but never eroded when incomes fall and opportunities shrink.

In general, cutting the distribution of households according to their per capita income as measured by labour surveys using poverty lines that correspond to minimum consumption standards tends to overestimate the incidence of poverty.[5] Nevertheless, the comparison over time of such biased estimates of the percentage of households in poverty, under the assumption that biases have the same direction and similar degree in both years, may provide a sufficiently accurate idea of the *changes* in the incidence of poverty. It is for this purpose only that such biased measures of poverty are included in Table VII. 4 and the corresponding measures of the incidence of poverty by socio-economic groups are included in Table VII. 5.

(a) *Chile*

Income distribution in Chile has undoubtedly suffered, reflecting recent economic fluctuations. Average income of urban households has decreased in real terms (around 8% in Santiago, according to the surveys). A clear drop in the share of total income accruing to households in the upper decile is evident: from 43 to 39%. Apparently the relative shift has been in favour of upper-middle strata between the 60th and 90th percentile of distribution, whose real incomes might have been maintained despite widespread recession. Statistics show only a slight drop in the share of the bottom 40% of households, their average income falling around 10% in real terms.

Table VII. 5 shows clearly that the fall in real incomes in Chile had most impact on blue-collar households, those of transport workers (both employees and own-account workers) and those of merchants and salesmen. Households headed by professionals and managers (whether employees or self-employed) and by administrative workers or armed forces personnel improved their relative position.

The fall of household incomes in Chile brought about a significant increase in the incidence of poverty. The estimates for Greater Santiago indicate that perhaps 4% more households fell into the poverty category, increasing the incidence of poverty by a third. Although not included in Table VII.5, survey data show that poverty increased most (by around 60%) among households headed by own-account workers and white-collar employees.

Table VII.5. *Incidence of poverty and shifts in the relative position of socio-economic groups in income distribution**

Socio-economic groups	House-holds in each group (%)	Base year			1982			Differences		
		P	R	B	P	R	B	ΔP	ΔR	ΔB
I. Chile										
Professional, technical and related workers	10.5		7.3	17.6		7.2	14.3		−0.1	−3.3
Managerial workers	1.9		−	−		−	−		−	−
Administrative and clerical workers	12.0		21.9	42.4		20.2	39.7		−1.7	−2.7
Sales workers	14.4		36.1	55.4		39.0	57.5		2.9	2.1
Other workers	9.9		57.3	78.7		57.9	79.4		0.6	0.7
Transport equipment operators and labourers	7.3		44.0	70.7		43.8	74.0		−0.2	3.3
Production workers	30.8		52.0	74.8		56.8	78.8		4.8	4.0
Armed forces	1.0		22.0	66.7		−	36.8		−22.2	−29.9
Other workers n.i.e.	12.1		53.3	71.4		49.3	72.2		−4.0	0.8
Total	100.0	12.0	40.0	60.0	16.0	40.0	60.0	4.0	0.0	0.0
II. Colombia										
Employees outside agriculture										
− managers, professionals and technicians	9.9	10.1	7.5	17.7	14.0	12.1	23.6	−3.9	4.6	5.9
− clerical and sales workers	12.8	36.3	28.1	46.9	31.9	27.7	48.5	4.4	−0.4	1.6
− manual and services workers	45.6	36.7	53.4	76.2	56.0	51.3	71.4	−19.3	−2.1	−4.8
Own-account workers outside agriculture										
− professionals and technicians	2.0	17.0	15.0	24.3	19.9	16.3	31.4	−2.9	1.3	7.1
− merchants and transport equipment operators	9.1	50.1	38.3	63.6	38.7	33.4	55.4	11.4	−4.9	−8.2
− manual and other service activities	12.6	54.8	44.1	67.8	45.8	40.5	63.4	9.0	−3.6	−4.4
Employers outside agriculture	6.4	25.3	19.3	31.1	26.6	23.7	38.5	−1.3	4.4	7.4
Total	98.4	48.7	39.8	60.0	44.8	40.3	60.0	−3.9	0.5	0.0
III. Costa Rica										
Employees in agriculture	27.0	34.0	66.8	84.4	53.4	64.1	80.7	19.4	−2.7	−3.7
Employees outside agriculture										
− managers, professionals and technicians	14.2	1.2	5.7	15.3	0.5	2.5	10.6	−0.7	−3.2	−4.7
− clerical and sales workers	11.7	6.7	22.7	38.8	8.8	17.7	36.6	2.1	−5.0	−2.2
− manual and services workers	47.1	15.2	40.7	65.8	26.8	39.7	64.8	11.6	−1.0	−1.0
Total	100.0	17.3	40.7	60.5	29.4	40.0	60.0	12.1	−0.7	−0.5
IV. Panama										
Employees in agriculture	3.6	44.3	65.4	81.7	43.7	67.7	81.7	−0.6	2.3	0.0
Employees outside agriculture										
− managers, professionals and technicians	21.4	4.8	13.2	28.1	2.9	15.0	29.4	−1.9	1.8	1.3
− clerical and sales workers	18.5	8.9	26.2	47.7	8.9	31.6	53.4	0.0	5.4	5.7
− manual and services workers	56.5	25.8	54.7	75.3	19.2	49.6	72.4	−6.0	−5.1	−2.9
Total	100.0	18.8	40.9	60.3	14.8	39.6	60.1	−4.0	−1.3	−0.2

(continued)

Table VII.5. *(continued)*

Socio-economic groups	House-holds in each group (%)	Base year			1982			Differences		
		P	R	B	P	R	B	ΔP	ΔR	ΔB
VI. *Venezuela – Los Andes region*										
Employees in agriculture culture										
– managers, professionals and technicians	18.9	0.5	14.3	30.3	0.2	12.8	26.7	–0.3	–1.5	–3.6
– clerical and sales workers	13.0	1.6	39.0	61.2	3.2	40.9	62.2	1.6	1.9	1.0
– manual and services workers	37.7	3.4	55.6	77.1	4.2	54.0	76.0	0.8	–1.6	–1.1
Own-account workers outside agriculture										
– professionals and technicians	3.1	–	20.4	40.2	–	9.1	21.6	–	–11.3	–18.6
– merchants and transport equipment operators	8.7	1.4	46.0	68.8	3.9	43.6	66.8	2.5	–2.4	–2.0
– manual and other services activities	5.1	5.1	51.2	74.3	2.4	40.9	67.1	–2.7	–10.3	–7.2
Employers outside agriculture	8.6	0.7	17.2	34.0	0.3	11.7	28.5	–0.4	–5.5	–5.5
Inactive	4.5	4.8	57.9	76.3	9.0	57.5	79.2	4.2	–0.4	2.9
Total	99.6‡	2.3	40.1	60.3	3.2	39.0	60.1	0.9	–1.1	–0.2
VI. *Venezuela: Los Andes region*										
Employees in agriculture	9.4	58.7	64.8	85.2	51.9	64.2	77.1	–6.8	–0.6	–5.4
Employees outside agriculture										
– managers, professionals and technicians	7.1	4.4	7.8	18.0	4.8	8.9	19.9	0.4	1.1	1.9
– clerical and sales workers	4.2	13.5	23.8	47.9	13.1	24.4	46.7	–0.4	0.6	–1.2
– manual and services workers	23.4	27.9	38.7	63.8	21.6	38.1	63.6	–6.3	–0.6	–0.2
Farmers	24.9	44.0	57.8	74.7	35.7	51.6	71.2	–8.3	–6.2	–3.5
Own-account workers outside agriculture										
– professionals and technicians	1.6	6.4	13.5	25.3	4.9	18.8	30.5	–1.5	5.3	5.2
– merchants and transport equipment operators	10.3	18.8	29.0	51.0	17.4	28.3	50.6	–1.4	–0.7	–0.4
– manual and other service activities	4.4	39.8	48.9	68.3	33.6	48.1	64.8	–6.2	–0.8	–3.5
Employers outside agriculture	6.4	5.5	6.7	18.3	3.6	8.1	26.8	–1.9	1.4	8.5
Inactive	8.3	37.8	50.0	70.2	36.5	50.2	69.3	–1.3	0.2	–0.9
Total	100.0	31.2	41.0	60.2	26.8	40.2	60.3	–4.4	–0.8	0.1

*Percentages of households in each socio-economic group.

P: percentage of households below the poverty line.

R: percentage of households below the 40th income percentile of the distribution of all households.

B: percentage of households below the 60th income percentile of the distribution of all households.

†Excludes agricultural activities and domestic service.

‡Excludes agricultural activities.

(b) *Colombia*

The Colombian sample only reveals a slight drop in the share of the bottom 40% of households between 1979 and 1982, and little change in the relative position of other strata, with a real rise of almost 15% in average household income.[6] Behind the stability of aggregate income distribution, however, significant changes have occurred in the relative position of socio-economic groups. Blue-collar households and those of own-account workers in services and manufacturing have improved their position. On the other hand, employers, professional employees and managers and self-employed professionals have descended somewhat in the income pyramid, while households headed by white-collar employees more or less maintained their relative position in the overall distribution.

The significant increase of household incomes and the stability of the overall distribution of income brought about a further reduction in the incidence of poverty in Colombia, by about 8% of the percentage attained in 1979, according to the normative criteria used in this exercise. However, not all socio-economic groups have fared well. As can be seen from Table VII.5, while the incidence of poverty significantly decreased among the mostly manual own-account workers in manufacturing and service activities and among households headed by white-collar employees, poverty more than doubled among households of blue-collar employees and almost doubled among the heterogeneous group of more skilled (professional, technical, etc.) employees.

(c) *Costa Rica*

Income data for Costa Rica only cover, as already indicated, wages and salaries. Therefore, the corresponding distributions in Table VII.4 have been restricted to households headed by employees. Average real household income of this broad population group has fallen 37% in real terms between the 1979 and 1982 surveys, while average incomes of all households may have decreased at a rate of something around 20% in the same period, judging by the fall in aggregate private consumption per capita (Table VII.3). In the context of this generalized drop in wages, income distribution among employees' households has flattened somewhat, the high-income households losing relatively more than those in the middle, with the bottom 40% improving its share. However, the exclusion of households headed by own-

account workers, among them those engaged in informal activities and subsistence farmers concentrated at the bottom of the income pyramid, may distort this picture.

The dramatic fall in employees' incomes hit all groups. But, as can be inferred from Table VII.5,[7] it affected mostly the relative position of the households of manual workers, while that of agricultural workers and white-collar workers improved slightly and the households headed by professionals, managers and technicians suffered less, significantly improving their relative position *vis-à-vis* the rest of employees' households, despite the drastic real fall in their average income.

The fall in real wages between the two periods observed dramatically increased the incidence of poverty among the households of wage and salary earners; at the national level, it may have increased by more than two-thirds. Most of this increase consisted of households of agricultural workers and manual workers in non-agricultural activities.

(d) *Panama*

The distributions of income included for Panama in Table VII.4 also cover households headed by employees recording their per capita income of wages and salaries. During the period, average incomes of employees' households suffered a moderate fall. During the crisis, households of high-income employees have improved their share, while those in the middle strata have reduced theirs and the bottom 40% of employees' households have more or less maintained their share of total wages and salaries, but with those in the bottom 20% registering improvement. Beyond this aggregate picture, however, manual workers improved their relative position while households headed by white-collar workers shifted downwards in the relative picture, as can be seen in Table VII.5.

The improvement at the bottom of the distribution, though slight, brought about a decrease of around one-fifth in the incidence of poverty, which was shared by most groups of employees' households.

(e) *Venezuela*

The Venezuelan data allow for assessing changes in the distribution of income not only in urban Caracas, but also in the rich agricultural economy of the Los Andes region.

The real fall of 15% in average household incomes in Caracas was accompanied by only a minor shift in the relative structure of overall income distribution: the comparison reveals only a slight gain in the share of the top quintile group and a minor loss in the share of the bottom 40%. Conversely, real household incomes in the Los Andes region suffered only a moderate average fall and the comparison reveals a considerable improvement in income inequalities: households in the upper quintile lost 3.6% of total income, in favour of the middle-income strata and particularly of the bottom 40%, which gained 1.7% of aggregate incomes.

The fall in real incomes involved a slight retrogression in the process by which absolute poverty had been gradually diminishing in Caracas where the incidence of poverty had been reduced to a small proportion of households. Although poverty increased in most socio-economic groups, the rise in poverty was concentrated among households of clerical employees and salesmen, among those headed by small traders and transport operators (mostly informal) and among the inactive.

This uneven resurgence of poverty corresponds to the changes that took place in the relative position of each socio-economic group. As can be seen from Table VII.5, the relative position of the three groups indicated deteriorated in the overall income distribution, while other groups of households (such as those headed by self-employed professionals and technicians, by employers in all activities, or by employed managers and professionals) significantly improved their relative position in the downswing.

The improvement of income distribution in Los Andes brought about a moderate decrease in the incidence of poverty but involved a number of shifts in the relative position of socio-economic groups. As indicated in Table VII.5, agricultural households (both producers and employees) significantly improved their relative positions in the region's aggregate income distribution. The same can be said of households headed by own-account workers in service activities and, to a lesser extent, of those of white-collar employees. On the other hand, both professional and technical employees and self-employed professionals shifted significantly downwards, while employers in non-agricultural activities suffered the severest drop in relative position.

The decrease in the proportion of poor households involved almost all socio-economic groups, although it was only marginal in some of them. According to the proxy measure included in Table VII.5, poverty alleviation

during the period would have acquired remarkable dimensions among agricultural workers and peasant households and among non-agricultural manual employees and own-account workers in service activities.

5. ADJUSTMENTS IN LIVELIHOOD STRATEGIES

Households adjust their livelihood strategies in response to changes in economic conditions and opportunities in order to maximize welfare. Such micro-level adjustments characteristically take place in the medium-term, when economic conditions tend to improve and opportunities tend to be enhanced. However, when both economic conditions and the opportunity of access to institutionalized systems rapidly deteriorate, one may expect to find significant short-term changes in households' livelihood strategies. Labour survey data provide the means to look at changes in livelihood strategies associated with working opportunities and decisions to participate in the labour force or in education.

Table VII.6 summarizes these changes in terms of percentages of total households or heads of households and of other household members of active age 'shifting' from one situation to another between the initial period and 1982, for all households, for poor households and for households in each quintile group.[8,9]

(a) Chile

In Chile, 8% of household heads were no longer employed, a small number (1.5%) falling into inactivity and the rest becoming unemployed. Among all household members of active age, 6% were no longer employed, mostly to be unemployed. The shift out of employment affected all economic strata, but acquired dramatic dimensions among households in the bottom quintile group (most of them poor): more than 20% of household heads moved into unemployment. Seven per cent of all household members lost employment, while an additional 4% of them were willing to participate in economic activities. As a result those unemployed or seeking work for the first time increased by 11%. Low- and middle-income strata were also affected by the loss of employment in degrees decreasing with income: 8.2% among members of households in the second quintile group, 5.6% in the third quintile and 3.8% in the fourth quintile. A por-

Table VII.6. *Changes in the situation of households and their members by groups of per capita income**

Characteristics	All households	Poor households	Percentile groups of per capita household income				
			1–20	21–40	41–60	61–80	81–100
I. Chile							
(a) *Heads of households*							
Participating in labour force	−1.5	—	−0.1	−2.0	−3.9	−0.5	−0.9
Unemployed	6.5	—	20.4	3.8	4.6	2.5	1.2
Working or with employment	−8.0	—	−20.5	−5.8	−8.5	−3.0	−2.1
Female	0.7	—	2.4	−0.2	2.3	−2.8	1.7
(b) *All members of active age*							
Participating in the labour force	0.5	—	4.1	−3.2	−1.2	−0.9	0.0
Unemployed or seeking work for the first time	5.4	—	11.2	5.0	4.4	2.9	2.0
Working or with employment	−5.9	—	−7.1	−8.2	−5.6	−3.8	−2.0
II. Colombia							
(a) *Households*							
Number of unemployed in the household							
0	−1.3	−0.7	−1.5	1.6	−2.7	−2.3	−0.8
1	0.2	−1.3	−0.9	−2.7	1.0	1.4	1.7
2 or more	1.1	2.0	2.4	1.1	1.7	0.9	−0.9
(b) *Heads of households*							
Participating in the labour force	−1.9	−2.2	−1.8	−2.6	0.0	−1.4	−3.4
Unemployed or seeking work for the first time	0.1	−0.4	−0.4	−0.2	−0.4	0.6	1.0
Working or with employment	−2.0	−1.8	−1.4	−2.4	0.4	−2.0	−4.4
Female	1.3	1.8	0.7	2.0	1.4	1.3	1.3
(c) *Other members of active age*							
Participating in the labour force	0.8	2.7	4.1	1.5	3.1	−2.8	−2.7
Unemployed or seeking work for the first time	0.6	0.6	0.4	0.4	1.3	0.5	−0.1
Working or with employment	0.2	2.1	3.7	1.4	1.8	−3.3	−2.6
Inactive	−0.8	−2.7	−4.1	−1.5	−3.1	2.8	2.7
Housewives	0.5	−0.1	−1.3	1.8	−1.8	2.3	1.7
Students	−0.5	−1.4	−0.9	−2.1	−0.9	1.3	0.8
Disabled	−0.2	−1.3	−0.4	−0.3	−0.3	—	0.3
Other	−0.6	−0.9	−1.5	−0.9	−0.1	−0.8	−0.1
III. Costa Rica							
(a) *Households of employees*							
Number of unemployed in the household							
0	−3.0	−3.0	−3.8	−1.2	−4.5	−4.7	−0.7
1	2.3	2.7	3.0	−0.1	3.8	4.6	0.3
2 or more	0.7	0.3	0.8	1.3	0.7	0.1	0.4
(b) *Heads of households*							
Participating in the labour force	0.4	0.9	0.9	1.0	0.3	0.2	−0.5
Unemployed	1.2	2.0	1.5	0.8	0.8	1.1	1.4
Working or with employment	−0.8	−1.1	−0.6	0.2	−0.5	−0.9	−1.9
Female	1.6	−1.6	0.7	3.4	1.1	−0.3	3.5
(c) *Other members of active age*							
Participating in the labour force	3.6	12.4	12.5	1.8	1.2	0.9	5.4

(continued)

Table VII.6 *continued*

Characteristics	All households	Poor households	Percentile groups of per capita household income				
			1–20	21–40	41–60	61–80	81–100
Unemployed or seeking work							
for the first time	2.0	3.1	3.9	1.2	2.8	0.6	0.2
Working or with employment	1.6	9.3	8.6	0.6	1.6	0.3	0.5
IV. *Panama*							
(a) *Households of employees*							
Number of unemployed in							
the household							
0	3.2	6.4	6.7	7.8	−2.7	2.1	1.6
1	−1.9	0.5	−	−6.9	1.7	−2.0	−1.8
2 or more	−1.3	−6.9	−6.7	−0.9	1.0	−0.1	0.2
(b) *Heads of households*							
Participating in the labour							
force	−0.1	−0.1	−0.3	0.0	0.3	0.0	0.0
Unemployed	−0.1	−1.5	−2.1	−0.4	1.0	0.3	0.3
Working or with							
employment	0.0	1.4	1.8	0.4	−0.7	−0.3	−0.3
Female	0.9	−5.8	−7.5	4.1	0.2	3.3	4.5
V. *Venezuela – metropolitan area*							
(a) *Households*							
Number of unemployed in							
the household							
0	−4.1	−6.0	−5.7	−5.5	−4.2	−2.8	−2.6
1	3.3	5.7	4.7	4.2	3.1	2.0	2.4
2 or more	0.8	0.3	1.0	1.3	1.1	0.8	0.2
(b) *Heads of household*							
Participating in the							
labour force	−0.2	0.7	−0.6	−1.2	−1.1	1.9	−1.0
Unemployed	2.2	0.8	2.8	2.5	2.7	1.4	1.1
Working or with							
employment	−2.4	−0.1	−2.2	−3.7	−3.8	0.5	−2.1
Female	0.2	−9.3	−3.4	0.8	2.2	−	1.6
(c) *Other members of active age*							
Participating in the labour							
force	−3.1	0.5	−3.9	−6.0	−0.8	−3.9	1.0
Unemployed	1.3	2.3	1.3	1.7	1.5	1.1	0.8
Seeking work for the							
first time	0.4	1.1	0.9	0.2	0.2	0.1	0.4
Working or with							
employment	−4.8	−2.9	−6.1	−7.9	−2.5	−5.1	−0.2
Inactive	3.1	−0.5	3.9	6.0	0.8	3.9	−1.0
Housewives	2.4	9.9	6.3	5.2	1.0	1.3	−4.0
Students	1.3	−10.5	−2.0	1.5	1.5	2.5	3.2
Disabled	−0.4	−0.8	−0.7	−0.1	−0.8	−0.3	−0.1
Others	−0.2	0.9	0.3	−0.6	−0.9	0.4	−0.1
VI. *Venezuela – Andes region*							
(a) *Households*							
Number of unemployed in							
the household							
0	−1.3	−0.8	−1.2	−1.9	−0.2	−3.5	−0.7
1	1.1	0.6	0.9	1.1	0.4	3.0	0.4
2 or more	0.2	0.2	0.3	0.8	−0.6	0.5	0.3
(b) *Heads of households*							
Participating in the labour							
force	−1.8	−1.5	0.0	−0.5	1.3	−2.1	−2.0
Unemployed	0.1	0.7	0.6	0.0	−0.5	1.5	−0.9

(*continued*)

Table VII.6 *continued*

Characteristics	All households	Poor households	Percentile groups of per capita household income				
			1–20	21–40	41–60	61–80	81–100
Working or with employment	−1.9	−2.2	−0.6	−0.5	1.8	−3.6	−1.1
Female	0.2	2.5	2.1	−0.1	−2.6	0.5	1.3
(c) *Other members of active age*							
Participating in the labour force	−0.4	−2.0	−0.8	−1.5	−1.1	3.1	0.5
Unemployed	0.7	0.2	0.3	0.8	0.0	1.5	1.2
Seeking work for the first time	0.1	−0.2	−0.1	0.3	−0.1	0.2	0.0
Working or with employment	−1.2	−2.0	−1.0	−2.6	−1.0	1.4	−0.7
Inactive	0.4	2.0	0.8	1.5	1.1	−3.1	−0.5
Housewives	−0.6	−1.1	−2.0	−1.7	−0.5	−1.8	1.2
Students	1.2	2.5	2.7	2.8	2.1	−0.3	−1.9
Disabled	−0.3	0.3	−0.1	−0.3	−0.3	−1.0	0.2
Other	0.1	0.3	0.2	0.7	−0.2	0.0	0.0

*Differences between percentages of each population in the base year and in 1982.

tion of these new unemployed shifted into inactivity, while between 3 and 5% of all members of active age became unemployed. Among household heads in these strata, the shifts have been more or less similar to those among the other members, except in the middle quintile group, where 8.5% went out of employment, including 3.9% into inactivity.

(b) *Colombia*

Unemployment in Colombia remained at roughly 9% of the labour force, but the general rise of income during the period brought about only marginal changes in the willingness to participate in the labour force. However, as can be seen from Table VII.6, there has been a significant change in households' strategies, since heads of households losing work (averaging 2% for all groups, including the poor) and becoming inactive were replaced by other members moving from inactivity into employment, at least in the middle and lower groups. Among the poorer households (the bottom 20%) in particular, 4.1% of other members entered the labour force, 3.7% of them into employment. Likewise, the small changes among the unemployed involved not so much unemployed household heads (moving into inactivity) but rather unemployed non-heads of households. Most of the increase in labour force participation among non-heads of the households was attained at the expense of education.

Households headed by females tended to increase at all levels of the distribution.

(c) *Costa Rica*

The rise of unemployment in Costa Rica affected mostly supplementary earners in households headed by employees. Around 1% of household heads in all quintiles went out of work into unemployment. Among poor households, in addition to this shift, an equal proportion of household heads came out of inactivity so that the number of the unemployed increased by 2%.

A remarkable adjustment of livelihood strategies of employees' households has been the incorporation of 3.6% of other members of active age into the labour force, 2% into unemployment or seeking work and 1.6% into employment. But this movement has acquired sweeping dimensions among poor households: more than 12% more members of active age were incorporated into the supply of labour, 3% went into unemployment but around 9% found themselves work of one kind or another. Thus, in the environment of opportunities prevailing in Costa Rica, the fall in real incomes of poor households provoked profound changes in their livelihood strategies, significantly raising the participation rate of the poor, both of heads and of other members, by pushing them out of inactivity and, for the most part into employment.

(d) *Panama*

At the aggregate level, there seem to have been relatively small changes in livelihood strategies, in the context of a stable income picture. However, as Table VII.6 reveals, the proportion of household heads shifting out of unemployment and into work reached 1.4 and 1.8% among the poor households and those at the bottom quintile respectively.

(e) *Venezuela*

The rise in unemployment in Caracas hit mostly low- and middle-income households. At the bottom quintile, there was an increase of 5.7% of households which had at least one member unemployed in 1982. The corresponding increase was 4.2% for households at the middle and 2.6% for households at the top.

In the bottom quintile group (in which poor households are included), 2.2% of household heads went out of work, but 2.8% more were unemployed, since their rate of participation rose somewhat. Likewise, among other household members of active age in the same stratum, 6.1% lost employment, but two-thirds became inactive. This and the 2% decrease in the number of students may explain the 6% increase in housewives among members of active age. At the same time, the number of female household heads decreased significantly.

As can be seen from Table VII.6, 3.7 and 3.8% of household heads in the next two quintile groups went out of employment. Almost a third of them went into inactivity, the rest remaining unemployed. Among the other household members of active age, 7.9 and 2.5%, respectively, went out of work, 1.7% remained unemployed and the rest became inactive. These increased the number of housewives and those studying. Conversely, in the fourth quintile group the proportion of household heads willing to participate in economic activity increased, largely to become unemployed. Among the other members of active age, there was a shift out of work, mainly to become inactive as housewives or, for the most part, as students.

The economy of the Los Andes region suffered a lesser impact of unemployment and a more moderate fall in real incomes in face of which livelihood strategies of households underwent smaller changes. As can be seen from Table VII.6, the loss of jobs hit the poor households harder: 2.2% fewer household heads and 2% fewer non-household heads had jobs, mainly to increase inactivity. Household heads in the fourth quintile group also suffered a lack of jobs but this was partially compensated for by more participation of other members. Shifts into inactivity of 1–2% of non-household heads members in the low- and middle-income groups increased the numbers studying.

6. THE IMPACT OF THE CRISIS ON CHILDHOOD

The adjustments in household livelihood strategies comprise both the changes in household members' participation in the labour force and changes in their consumption patterns in face of changes in real incomes. Unfortunately, no relevant data are available for assessing this second pattern. Adjustments of livelihood strategies also take place in the decisions regarding education of children and adolescents; however, the surveys do not provide enough information for analysis in this area.

The data base which has been used here to assess the impact of economic conditions in levels of living allows us to view changes in the situation of children from at least two perspectives.

Table VII.7 shows changes in the incidence of poverty and relative shifts in the distribution of income among households of different characteristics which are relevant to the situation of children within those households.

Households headed by females — usually representing between 15 and 20% in urban areas and systematically more affected by poverty — fared worse than those headed by males in Santiago, Chile, but were somewhat more shielded from economic impact in Costa Rica and Caracas. On the other hand, in areas which experienced a slow reduction of poverty, such as Colombia and the Los Andes region, households headed by females lagged somewhat behind in the gains. In Panama, however, exactly the opposite happened: the incidence of poverty was significantly reduced among female-headed households and their relative position has improved so that their situation is now similar on both counts to that of male-headed households.

In those countries where poverty increased in the period under review, households with a larger number of children suffered more. In Costa Rica, the incidence of poverty increased among households of all sizes in terms of number of children in the households, as can also be seen from Table VII.7. Although poverty incidence broadly doubled among households with three children or less, the situation among

Table VII.7. *Changes in the incidence of poverty and shifts in the relative position of households of different characteristics*

Groups of households	Households in each group (%)	Base year P	Base year R	1982 P	1982 R	Differences ΔP	Differences ΔR
I. Chile							
Sex of head							
Male	83.0		40.1		40.0		−0.1
Female	17.0		38.9		39.9		1.0
II. Colombia							
Sex of head							
Male	82.0	48.4	39.3	44.2	39.2	−4.2	−0.1
Female	18.0	50.4	41.9	47.2	41.7	−3.2	−0.2
No. of children in the household							
0	33.3	32.5	25.1	31.8	27.4	−0.7	2.3
1	24.9	44.3	34.9	42.5	36.8	−1.8	1.9
2	22.1	55.2	43.3	49.2	43.7	−6.0	0.4
3	11.2	68.5	59.0	60.4	54.9	−8.1	−4.1
4	5.6	79.0	72.3	68.7	64.3	−10.3	−8.0
5 and more	2.9	88.0	83.8	80.2	78.1	−7.8	−5.7
III. Costa Rica							
Sex of head							
Male	89.3	16.9	41.4	29.8	40.7	12.9	−0.7
Female	10.7	20.4	34.4	26.3	34.9	5.9	0.5
No. of children in the household							
0	27.6	4.9	17.3	12.7	20.0	7.8	2.7
1	25.0	9.2	31.8	19.2	31.4	10.0	−0.4
2	22.5	16.7	45.0	29.8	42.3	13.1	−2.7
3	13.3	29.5	65.0	45.8	57.9	16.3	−7.1
4	6.5	40.2	71.8	63.9	74.5	23.7	2.7
5	2.9	58.8	80.5	79.9	85.8	21.1	5.3
6 or more	2.2	71.0	94.4	93.1	96.0	22.1	1.6
IV. Panama: Metropolitan area							
Sex of head							
Male	82.7	16.7	39.3	14.3	39.4	−2.4	0.1
Female	17.3	29.0	48.5	16.9	40.7	−12.1	−7.8
No. of children in the household							
0	27.2	4.6	13.0	−	−	−	−
1	18.7	7.3	27.7	6.1	34.9	−1.2	7.2
2	20.4	14.1	41.5	17.3	57.6	3.2	16.1
3	17.2	25.0	60.0	24.0	68.8	−1.0	8.8
4 or more	16.5	55.0	81.6	−	−	−	−
V. Venezuela: Metropolitan area							
Sex of head							
Male	80.4	1.7	38.2	2.8	37.9	1.1	−0.3
Female	19.6	4.6	48.2	4.9	43.6	0.3	−4.6
No. of children in the household							
0	30.6	0.8	15.2	0.6	16.2	−0.2	1.0
1	21.8	1.0	30.7	1.1	29.5	0.1	−1.2
2	22.4	1.7	45.3	2.0	46.0	0.3	0.7
3	12.7	1.7	62.1	5.9	64.4	4.2	2.3
4	6.6	4.7	79.6	11.5	82.7	6.8	−1.2
5 or more	5.9	15.1	93.8	21.7	91.2	6.6	−2.6

(continued)

Table VII.7 *continued*

Groups of households	Households in each group (%)	Base year		1982		Differences	
		P	R	P	R	ΔP	ΔR
VI. *Venezuela: Los Andes Region*							
Sex of head							
Male	84.4	30.2	40.0	25.3	38.8	−4.9	−1.2
Female	15.6	36.2	46.5	34.9	47.6	−1.3	1.1
No. of children in the household							
0	19.2	10.6	16.9	7.8	17.4	−2.8	0.5
1	17.6	17,3	26.8	13.4	25.0	−3.9	−1.8
2	17.3	24.5	35.3	21.5	34.9	−3.0	−0.4
3	14.0	31.4	40.8	27.2	43.4	−4.2	2.6
4	12.9	44.7	58.2	41.0	58.0	−3.7	−0.2
5	8.2	53.4	66.4	56.4	72.2	3.0	5.8
6 or more	11.0	67.1	76.5	70.4	84.2	3.3	7.7

P: Percentage of households below the poverty line.
R: Percentage of households below the 40th income percentile of the distribution of all households.
*Percentages of households in each group.

those with four or more appears to have worsened to dismal proportions.

In Caracas, poverty alleviation also retrogressed; this occurred almost exclusively among households with three or more children. In those households with three and four children, among which poverty had been reduced to minor proportions, it flared up to three times the previous levels. Among those with five or more children, around 15% of which were already in poverty, it increased by one-half.

In Colombia, poverty alleviation progressed apace despite the economic pressures of this period. This process involved households of all sizes, but was relatively more intense among those with three or more children. These households previously suffered a larger incidence of poverty. In contrast, in the Los Andes region of Venezuela and, up to a point, in Panama, the incidence of poverty diminished among households with four children or less (and proportionately more among the smaller households) but it increased among households with five or more children.

Table VII.8 indicates changes in the proportions of children belonging to different types of households in absolute poverty or below the relative poverty norm of the fourth income quintile.

As can be seen by comparing the incidence of poverty among children in Table VII.8 and the incidence of poverty among households in Table VII.4, the proportions of small children

and school-age children in poverty are significantly higher than those of households in all the countries considered. This is a consequence of the larger number of children among poor households. The data also show that the incidence of poverty is far greater among children belonging to the 10−15% of households headed by females. Likewise, when the relevant data are available they show that the incidence of poverty among children belonging to households where the head is illiterate or has only primary education is well above the average incidence for all households.

Chile is no exception to this pattern. The increase in the incidence of poverty between 1981 and 1982 aggravated the situation of children, bringing about a similar rise in the proportions of children in poverty.

In Caracas, the increase in the incidence of poverty affected small children and school-age children of almost all types of households. In contrast, in the Los Andes region, small children benefited from the reduction in poverty.

Alleviation of poverty advanced in Colombia during the period, improving the lot of both small and school-age children in all types of households, but affecting those most disadvantaged more significantly: i.e. children in households where household heads had a low level of education.

A similar pattern emerges in the case of Panama, where children in households headed by females or by adults with primary education

Table VII.8. *Incidence of absolute and relative poverty among children of different types of households*
(percentages of children in each group)

Type of households	Children in each group (%)	Small children* Base Year P	R	1982 P	R	Differences ΔP	ΔR	Children in each group (%)	Primary school-age children† Base Year P	R	1982 P	R	Differences ΔP	ΔR
I. Chile														
All children by sex of the head	100.0	18.6	—	20.8	—	2.2	—	100.0	21.5	—	25.2	—	3.7	—
Male	91.4	17.2	—	19.3	—	2.1	—	89.4	20.8	—	24.9	—	4.1	—
Female	8.6	32.6	—	33.9	—	1.3	—	10.6	27.4	—	27.3	—	−0.1	—
II. Colombia														
All children by sex of the head	100.0	62.0	52.6	55.8	51.3	−6.2	−1.3	100.0	66.6	57.7	57.3	52.5	−9.3	−5.2
Male	89.3	60.5	50.8	54.3	49.7	−6.2	−1.1	86.2	64.7	56.3	55.6	50.9	−9.1	−5.4
Female	10.7	75.2	67.4	65.3	60.7	−9.9	−6.7	13.8	78.2	67.3	66.2	61.4	−12.0	−5.9
Education of the head														
Illiterate	4.8	84.4	77.3	76.5	72.5	−7.9	−4.8	5.7	86.1	75.2	75.1	71.8	−11.0	−3.4
Primary	49.2	79.6	69.3	67.8	63.0	−11.8	−6.3	55.4	81.6	73.1	67.7	62.6	−13.9	−10.5
Secondary	33.4	50.7	40.5	47.4	42.2	−3.3	1.7	29.3	49.6	39.6	45.6	40.4	−4.0	−0.8
Higher	12.6	15.1	10.2	17.0	14.3	1.9	4.1	9.6	20.2	13.6	15.8	13.4	−4.4	−0.2
III. Panama‡														
All children by sex of the head								100.0	34.0	62.2	27.5	69.8	−6.5	7.6
Male								85.6	30.2	59.4	25.7	69.5	−4.5	10.1
Female								14.4	56.7	78.7	38.1	71.7	−18.6	−7.0
Education of the head														
No education								2.1	46.9	100.0	68.3	100.0	21.4	—
Primary								47.1	48.2	82.6	40.2	86.8	−8.0	4.2
Secondary								38.0	26.4	51.2	19.9	65.0	−6.5	13.8
University								12.3	0.5	10.2	—	18.3	−0.5	8.1
IV. Venezuela: Metropolitan area														
All children by sex of the head	100.0	5.0	60.9	6.9	60.3	1.9	−0.6	100.0	6.0	64.8	9.3	63.8	3.3	−1.0
Male	83.6	3.7	58.2	6.0	57.0	2.3	−1.2	81.9	4.6	61.7	7.5	61.8	2.9	0.1
Female	16.4	11.6	74.0	11.1	76.6	−0.5	2.6	18.1	12.3	79.1	17.5	73.1	5.2	−6.0
Education of the head^δ														
Illiterate	6.4	15.3	80.2	16.0	83.5	0.7	3.3	5.6	18.5	86.7	18.1	82.0	−0.4	−4.7

Table VII.8. (continued)

Type of households	Small children*							Primary school-age children†						
	Children in each group (%)	Base Year		1982		Differences		Children in each group (%)	Base Year		1982		Differences	
		P	R	P	R	ΔP	ΔR		P	R	P	R	ΔP	ΔR
Primary	52.4	6.4	73.1	8.3	73.4	1.9	0.3	54.9	7.8	76.5	11.3	75.3	3.5	-1.2
Secondary	27.0	1.9	47.9	5.1	50.3	3.2	2.4	24.5	1.9	49.5	6.5	58.8	4.6	9.3
Higher	10.2	1.0	11.1	0.6	11.8	-0.4	0.7	10.4	0.9	19.0	1.9	13.2	1.0	-5.8
V. Venezuela: Los Andes Region														
All children by sex of the head	100.0	46.5	56.1	40.8	55.7	-5.7	-0.4	100.0	46.1	57.9	46.1	60.1	—	2.2
Male	87.6	45.2	55.1	39.3	54.8	-5.9	-0.3	83.8	43.9	56.1	41.9	56.6	-2.0	0.5
Female	12.4	55.6	63.1	49.3	61.2	-6.3	-1.9	16.2	57.6	67.4	64.9	75.6	7.3	8.2
Education of the head δ														
Illiterate	27.6	71.0	81.0	60.3	74.4	-10.7	-6.6	31.4	66.0	78.5	64.9	77.9	-1.1	-0.6
Primary	53.4	42.2	51.8	40.5	57.3	-1.7	5.5	52.6	40.4	52.9	42.7	57.5	2.3	4.6
Secondary	11.9	13.5	21.8	9.8	20.9	-3.7	-0.9	8.7	13.3	19.5	16.2	31.4	2.9	11.9
Higher	2.3	5.9	8.0	2.5	6.2	-3.4	-1.8	1.7	2.8	6.4	—	0.9	-2.8	-5.5

P: percentage of children below the poverty line.
R: percentage of children below the 40th income percentile of the distribution of all households.
*Chile: 0–5 years; Colombia: 0–6 years; Venezuela: 0–6 years.
†Chile: 6–13 years; Colombia: 7–13 years; Venezuela: 7–11 years.
‡Panama: 0–14 years.
δNot included unknown education.

experienced larger advances in their escape from poverty.

7. CONCLUSION

(a) The Latin American crisis appears to have had, up to the present, a more generalized impact on the living conditions of urban populations. Rural populations in areas depending on export crops undoubtedly suffered a more severe impact when external market or production conditions for these crops have deteriorated. But some rural populations in relatively prosperous and diversified agricultural areas may have fared better during the recession than urban populations, as indicated by the data for the Los Andes region in Venezuela.

(b) The poor and the bottom strata of the social pyramid have been harshly hit in those countries where the recession has been severe. But middle strata have also suffered.

(c) In the absence of a significant reshaping of income distribution, the rise or fall of real household incomes in the short run involves the decrease or increase in the incidence of absolute poverty. Thus, the fall of household incomes in Santiago, Caracas and Costa Rica brought about a significant rise in the proportion of households in poverty. In contrast, despite stagnating activity in Colombia increased household incomes allowed for a further step in the alleviation of poverty. But among Panamanian employees' households and in Los Andes households, the moderate fall in real incomes was more than offset by improvements at the bottom of the income pyramid. As a consequence, the process of poverty alleviation was not reversed.

(d) Aggregate distribution of household income by size does not appear to be a sensitive measure of changes taking place in the relative position of different household groups. In some instances (Colombia and Panama) in which real household incomes continued to increase or fell only moderately, the pattern of the aggregate distribution of urban incomes was revealed to be relatively stable. In contrast, the general fall in real incomes in Chile appears to have been accompanied by a swift erosion of the upper groups' positions attained in the previous boom; however, the pattern of the 1982 distribution is similar to that prevailing in 1980. On the other hand, in Costa Rica the relative improvement generally concentrated among employees might well have been offset by a change in the distribution of the self-employed, within the general context of relative stability in overall distribution, despite

rapidly falling real incomes. In Costa Rica, as in the Los Andes region of Venezuela, improvements in the aggregate urban–rural distribution are partly due to the relatively better performance of agricultural households. This also underlines the possibility that aggregate distribution of urban incomes might be more stable in its pattern than currently presumed.

(e) Considerable contrast exists between national situations but the question of which socio-economic groups fared worse and which fared better is apparently more associated with the institutional setting and opportunities and with the social orientation of economic policy than with the direction and degree of the recession's immediate impact. In Colombia, where incomes rose, as well as in Panama and Venezuela, where real income fell, households headed by blue-collar workers and even by manual own-account workers (including those in informal activities) improved their relative position in the overall distribution of income; white-collar employees' households more or less maintained theirs; the better-off groups (employers, self-employed professionals and even professional, technical and managerial employees) retrogressed relatively in the overall distribution. On the other hand, the opposite happened in Chile and Costa Rica: these latter groups improved their relative positions in a context of generally deteriorating incomes. The contrast between the changes which occurred in these two countries and those that took place in Caracas, where there was also a considerable fall in real incomes, is revealing in this regard.

(f) The comparative analysis undertaken suggests that when welfare concerns are paramount in economic and social policy orientation and when representative participation and institutionalized opportunities exist, households as a whole and those relatively disadvantaged in particular are more effectively protected from immediate economic impacts. Consideration of the situation in Colombia, Panama and Venezuela during the critical period highlights the possibility at each stage of 'cushioning' the successive impacts that multiply from external shocks at the level of internal economic activity, household incomes, the popular strata and the poor. On the other hand, the Costa Rican case exemplifies those instances in which the depth of the crisis wipes out such safeguards for the sake of severe adjustment policies.

(g) Livelihood strategies do not appear to change drastically in the immediate term. Perhaps the dimensions of the changes in livelihood strategies of Chilean and Costa Rican households dramatically restricted the magnitude of their short-term adjustment strategies.

(h) In general, falling real incomes and rising unemployment have involved, on the one hand, the shift of household heads from employment to unemployment but also, in some instances, to inactivity. On the other hand, this pattern has been supplemented, in Chile and Costa Rica, by rises in the participation rates of other household members, even resulting in an increase in the number of unemployed. Conversely, in Venezuela the main shifts have been from employment to inactivity, lowering participation rates both for heads of household and for other household members. In the Colombian situation of rising household incomes, adjustments have also been seen in a decrease in the participation of household heads in economic activity, but in this case, countered by a rise in the participation rates of other members, mostly into unemployment.

(i) Adjustments in the livelihood strategies of the urban poor in each country regarding their participation in the labour force and shifts to unemployment roughly correspond to the general patterns outlined above, differing from middle strata households only in the proportions involved.

(j) In the face of rising unemployment, entry into education appears to be a valid alternative for household members of active age in middle and upper-middle strata, if the opportunities provided by the institutional setting makes it a feasible strategy, as is the case in Venezuela. This, however, appears not to be an alternative for the urban poor.

(k) The aggravation of poverty had affected households with a larger number of children more severely, among which the incidence of

poverty was greater to start with. On the other hand, in Colombia, where poverty declined, these disadvantaged groups of households have been the most protected. The situation of households with a large number of children appears to have worsened in Panama and Los Andes as well, in the context of reductions in the general incidence of poverty. This suggests the hypothesis that these types of households may constitute a particularly hard 'core' of poverty, where the situation may be more difficult to alleviate than that of other types of households.

(l) The proportion of small children and school-age children in poverty is always larger than the proportion of poor households; there are also more children in poverty among those belonging to households whose heads are female or who have little education. In those instances in which poverty has increased, children of all ages and belonging to all types of households appear to have been affected. However, there is ground for suspecting that in such situations small children might have suffered more than indicated by the proportions involved: in some of those more disadvantaged households, when faced with a still more astringent economic situation and the need to drastically adjust livelihood strategies, there might be a tendency both for childcare to deteriorate and for increased discrimination against small children in the internal allocation of resources. Conversely, in those instances in which poverty alleviation progressed, as in Colombia, Panama and Los Andes, the proportions of small children in poverty decreased relatively more than did the proportions of poor households, illustrating how crucial the reduction of poverty is for the fate of children.

NOTES

1. The ECLA Data Bank of Economic and Social Statistics (BADESTAL) includes a data bank of household surveys (BADEHOG) which aims to make available for research microdata from the main household surveys carried out for different purposes in Latin American countries by national statistical institutes. The special effort to incorporate the latest available household surveys for analysing the impact of the crisis was made with the co-operation of UNICEF and the active collaboration of most national statistical institutes to which the request for data was addressed. Besides those of the countries covered in this analysis, delays and technical difficulties have hindered the timely analysis of the data provided by national institutes of Argentina, Bolivia, Mexico and Peru.

2. For detailed descriptions of these policies, see Foxley (1982) and Ffrench-Davis (1983).

3. Total unemployment has been estimated at 26% of the labour force, if account is taken of a relief employment programme which grants monthly income of less than US $30.

4. Poverty lines estimated by Altimir (1982) for the corresponding area (metropolitan, urban or national) in each country for 1970 were extrapolated in real terms applying a 0.25 elasticity to the average rate of growth of GDP per capita – calculated by regression, to take into account only the medium-term growth trend – from 1970 to the first year of

the present comparison. These lines at 1970 prices were further repriced using consumer prices indices for all items.

5. First, measured income covers at best only primary incomes received in cash by households. Secondly, at the bottom of the distribution households usually consume more than their income. Thirdly, the short reference periods used in labour surveys may result in more low-income situations, including those that are only temporary. Lastly, pervasive underreporting shifts the whole distribution downwards (for a detailed discussion, see Altimir, 1982).

6. This increase in average household income between the two surveys, in the face of an increase of around 1% in per capita GDP and in aggregate private consumption per capita is likely to actually reflect a more favourable short-term evolution of household incomes than of those incomes appropriated by the other institutional sectors, and a better performance of urban incomes than rural incomes since the alternative explanation of an improvement in the quality of survey data *vis-à-vis* national accounts estimates appears rather far-fetched.

7. Although differences in *R* and in *B* are negative

for all groups, this is due to considerable shifts in the composition of employees by groups, between the two periods.

8. When interpreting these 'shifts', it should be taken into account that this is not a cohort analysis, so changes in the relative income position of households between the two periods may shift households to a quintile group different from where they were located in the initial period. More important, when considering poor households in the two periods, these 'shifts' are mere differences in the composition of the poor by the characteristic considered and hence in the behaviour of the groups of households that were poor in 1982, that may be significantly bigger or smaller than the groups that were poor in the previous period.

9. It should be noted that changes summarized by means of 'shifts' of household heads and other members may be affected by non-random changes in the identification of the heads, involving changes in the proportion of housewives or paterfamilies (irrespective of their income) considered as heads, particularly when the households' livelihood strategies are being adjusted to the immediate situation.

REFERENCES

Altimir, Oscar, 'The extent of poverty in Latin America', World Bank Staff Working Papers No. 522 (Washington, D.C.: The World Bank, March 1982).

Altimir, Oscar, 'Income distribution statistics in Latin America and their reliability', paper presented to the IARIW 18th General Conference, Luxembourg, 21–27 August 1983 (June 1983).

Altimir, Oscar and Juan Sourrouille, 'Measuring levels of living in Latin America: an overview of main problems', *Living Standards Measurement Study*, Working Paper No. 3 (Washington, D.C.: The World Bank, October 1980).

CEPAL, 'Las encuestas de hogares en América Latina', *Cuadernos de la CEPAL*, No. 44 (Santiago, Chile: 1983).

Ffrench-Davis, Ricardo, 'El experimento monetarista en Chile: una síntesis crítica', in *Desarrollo Econó-*

mico [Buenos Aires, Instituto de Desarrollo Económico y Social (IDES)], No. 99, Vol. 23 (July–September 1983); published in English as 'The monetarist experiment in Chile', *World Development*, Vol. 11, No. 11 (November 1983).

Foxley, A., 'Experimentos neo-liberales en América Latina', *Colección CIEPLAN* (7 March 1982). (English version by the University of California Press).

Foxley, Alejandro and Dagmar Raczynski, *Grupos Vulnerables en Situaciones Recesivas: El Caso de los Niños y Jóvenes en Chile* (Santiago, Chile: Corporación de Investigaciones Económicas para Latinoamérica (CIEPLAN), 1983).

Singer, Hans W., 'North–South multipliers', *World Development*, Vol. 11, No. 5 (May 1983).

World Bank, *World Development Report 1983* (New York: Oxford University Press, July 1983).

Sub-Saharan Africa in Depression:
The Impact on the Welfare of Children

REGINALD HERBOLD GREEN and HANS SINGER*
Institute of Development Studies
at the University of Sussex, Brighton, UK

Summary. — This paper analyses the impact of the economic crisis on the welfare of children in Sub-Saharan Africa, an area which includes most of the least developed and most severely affected countries. These countries are characterized by: low levels of skilled personpower, dependency on their primary product exports, small industrial sectors, a lagging food production growth, a high proportion of rural population and a child dependency ratio that is virtually 1 to 1. The situations of Nigeria, Zambia and Tanzania are examined in detail. In Zambia where there is substantial evidence of worsening of the condition of children in the 1970s, the most urgent requirement is additional resources, particularly foreign exchange. Such is also the case with Tanzania, while Nigeria does have the resources to develop a more coherent economy and finance basic services adequately.

> We too often forget that even today the depth of human
> suffering is immense. Every two seconds of this year
> a child will die of hunger or disease. And no statistic
> can express what it is to see even one child die . . . .
>
> Willy Brandt
> *Common Crisis* (1982)

> After the first death,
> there is no other
>
> Dylan Thomas
> *A Refusal to Mourn the Death,*
> *by Fire, of a Child*

1. A CONTINENT IN DEEPENING CRISIS

Sub-Saharan Africa is poorer than any other region. Except for 1977—79 its growth rates have been lower than the average for least developed countries. In the 1960s this meant slow per capita growth (under 1.5% a year), in the 1970s near stagnation (under 1% a year), and since 1979, absolute decline.[1] The *World Development Report 1983*'s rather optimistic median 1985—95 projections for low-income Africa show 0.2% per capita GDP growth (3.3% gross) even assuming net capital inflow of 7% of GDP annually.[2]

The same combination of a very poor starting position and relatively slow improvement applies to social indicators. In 1981 for Sub-Saharan countries with populations over one million, the average Infant Mortality Rate was 130. Only three countries (Madagascar, Kenya, Zimbabwe) had IMRs significantly below 100 while in five more the IMR approximated 100 (Uganda, Tanzania, Ghana, Zambia, Cameroon). The average child death rate was 27.5 with three countries (Madagascar, Kenya, Zimbabwe) having CDRs significantly below 20 and six more with CDRs near 20 (Uganda, Tanzania, Ghana, Lesotho, Zambia, Cameroon). Average life expectancy was 47.5 years and exceeded

---

* The views expressed in this paper are those of the authors and not necessarily those of UNICEF.

Table VIII.1 *Life and health indicators*

	Nigeria	Zambia	Tanzania	Lower-middle-income countries	Low-income countries
GDP per capita 1981	870	600	280	850	270 (240)*
IMR 1960	183	151	152	145	165 (163)
1981	133	104	102	95	99 (124)
CDR 1960	42	33	33	27	27 (30)
1981	28	20	19	14	14 (21)
Life expectancy					
1960	39	40	42	46	41 (41)
1981	49	51	52	57	58 (50)
Population per doctor					
1960	73,710	9540	18,220	27,807	12,222 (37,737)
1980	12,550	7670	17,560	7751	5785 (15,846)
Population per nurse					
1960	4040	9920	11,890	4925	7217 (9707)
1980	3010	1730	2980	2261	4668 (8953)
Average calorie supply (% of requirements)†					
1980	91	93	83	106	97 (92)

Source: World Bank, *World Development Report 1983.*
*( ) Data exclude China and India.
†Subject to significant unreliability. Do not necessarily correspond to best national data available, especially in case of Tanzania.

50 years in only seven countries (Tanzania, Ghana, Kenya, Liberia, Lesotho, Zambia and Zimbabwe).[3]

The gap between Sub-Saharan Africa and all least developed countries (LDCs) has grown.[4] Child mortality in Sub-Saharan Africa was between 50 and 60% above all LDCs in 1950. Over 1950–80 it fell by slightly over 40% as opposed to an all-LDC reduction of over 50%, making it almost twice as high as the latter's. The fall in IMRs over the same period was about 30% as opposed to 40%. Although over 1975–80 Sub-Saharan Africa's rate of decline slightly exceeded the LDC average, IMR for the region was still 127% of the LDC average. Similarly, the gap between global life expectancy and life expectancy for low-income Sub-Saharan countries grew from 8 years in 1950 to 9 in 1960, 11 in 1970 to 12 in 1979 and for middle-income Sub-Saharan countries from 6 to 7 to 8 to 8 years, respectively.

While averages are appropriate to demonstrate the special problems of the Sub-Saharan region — which includes most of the least developed and most severely affected countries, it is important to recognize that the 45 independent states diverge widely in GDP per capita (Chad US $110 in 1981 to Gabon US $3800), in export levels and prospects relative to imports, in economic policy, in social cohesion

and in both scope and nature of basic health, education and water services. These differences are not, in fact, systematically correlated. There is also an apparent regional difference with Eastern and Southern Africa having higher life expectancies and lower IMRs and CDRs than West and Central Africa and placing greater emphasis on pure water provision. While these differences appear to relate substantially to climate, there are exceptions (e.g. Ghana in West Africa and Cameroon in Central have better than average life expectancies, IMRs and CDRs, Malawi in Southern and Rwanda in Eastern, substantially poorer) which suggest that policy and resource allocation are also factors. Further, statistics for Sub-Saharan Africa are notoriously weak, making intercountry and even intertemporal comparisons in one country subject to significant margins of doubt.

For this reason a substantial portion of this study will concentrate on three selected countries — Nigeria, Tanzania and Zambia — for which somewhat more complete and, perhaps, comparable data is available from the Jobs and Skills Programme for Africa Basic Needs studies.[5]

However, the vast majority of Sub-Saharan economies and societies share a number of characteristics arising out of their poverty and late independence which both hamper development and limit resilience in the face of external shocks:

(a) Not only are numbers of middle and high level personpower very low relative to population but so is their average experience and that of the institutions in which they work.

(b) Foreign exchange earnings are in almost all cases dominated by a handful of primary products. While in a few cases sustained rapid growth of exports has been possible, all are subject to volume and price setbacks — as the recent record of diamonds, uranium oxide and petroleum demonstrates. Further, several key agricultural exports (e.g. coffee, tea, cocoa, sugar, tobacco, sisal) are estimated to have poor medium-term price prospects.[6]

(c) The industrial sectors — with the partial exception of Zimbabwe — are relatively small, unintegrated and import-dependent, leading to forced multiplier contraction when import capacity declines rather than to increased import substitution.

(d) While petroleum consumption is low, it is dominated by transport of goods and electricity generation and is therefore remarkably hard to compress without severe economic damage.

(e) Food production growth in the 1970s at 1.7% was barely over half the nearly 3% population growth, reducing average calories produced well below adequate levels. Given increasing pressure on land and much fewer tested innovations than in Asia, prospects for a sharp reversal of this sluggish trend are unlikely.

(f) A high proportion of the population — over 70% for Sub-Saharan Africa as a whole — is rural, increasing problems and costs both of emergency food movements and of providing rural services.

(g) Because of high birth and population growth rates, Sub-Saharan Africa has a virtually 1 to 1 child dependency ratio (90 aged 0—15 for every 100 aged 14—64). This places growing pressure on health, education and water services and renders children particularly vulnerable to falls in family real income and access to food. There is little evidence to suggest early substantial falls in birth rates.

African economies have not only been relatively weak in respect to ability to weather shocks, since the early 1970s they have suffered from such shocks more severely than most LDCs. The 1972—74 oil and food import price crisis was accompanied both by stagnant or falling export prices and by widespread drought. While a majority of African economies adjusted relatively effectively and 1977—79 growth rates were high historically and relative to all LDCs, this recovery in several cases rested on abnormally favourable export prices. The 1979—80 oil price increase was paralleled by world recession-induced collapses in export prices and, in some cases, volume. And by 1983, drought conditions were the worst of the century in substantial parts of Western and Southern Africa.[7] Further, armed conflicts have placed severe strains on several economies — notably the Southern African ones who bore the cost of Rhodesia's destabilization and aggression against its neighbours and who now face similar actions by South Africa.

In many cases deferred maintenance from 1974—75 was never fully made good and arrears increased rapidly after 1979. As a result many infrastructural and directly productive assets cannot be utilized at capacity or are available only intermittently (e.g. in Tanzania up to 50% of rural water systems have been out of operation for significant periods each year since 1980).

The loss of import capacity has had a dramatic negative effect on government revenue — directly in respect to taxes on imports and indirectly through curtailment of domestic manufacturing (and thus sales tax) and general employment and profit levels (and thus income tax). The result has been a combination of cutbacks on services and of longer use of currency and domestic bank borrowing to cover increased deficits, often leading to 25% cost of living index inflation rates, with food prices rising more rapidly than others. Social services have, in general, fallen both in real terms and as a proportion of government expenditure since 1979. Imports for them — e.g. drugs, paper and texts, water pipes and pumps, fuel to ensure delivery of rural services — have fallen even more (apparently over 50% in some cases). Economic services may have been cut somewhat less but the main increases have been in debt service and — in a significant number of cases — defence.

The external balance position is increasingly unviable.[8] In 1981—82 little over 50% of Sub-Saharan Africa's imports — already at below minimum levels for sustaining and operating existing capacity in many countries — were financeable from exports. External debt service payable[9] has risen to over 30% for many African countries. For a majority, short-term payment arrears — to commercial houses and manufacturers as well as financial institutions — are significant. In extreme cases (e.g. Tanzania, Zambia) they exceed a full year's export earnings.

In a majority of African countries the problem is no longer one of living with slow growth in per capita production or adjusting to relatively speedily reversed external shocks. Rather it is one of distributing very severe declines in per capita output (over 50% in the case of Zambia) which have continued for several years and show no signs of early reversal. In this context, protection — as to maintenance and use — of existing productive, infrastructural and service capacity becomes more important than generalized expansion. This is especially true in countries which have made significant progress toward building up broad provision of basic services and have trained personnel to operate them but now find their quality and even operationality threatened by import strangulation.

The emergency (or crisis) character of the situation imposes a shortened time horizon. Consolidation is necessary to avert disaster. Rescue, damage limitation, protection of capacity and of groups most at risk — including children — are more relevant than generalized high levels of investment or 20-year perspectives which operate as if 1980–83 was a transient aberration and the starting point could be 1977.

However, consolidation by itself is not enough. The structure of production requires changing both to reduce the ratio of necessary imports to production (especially in respect to food, energy, construction materials and basic consumer goods) and to raise exports (in whatever products can be produced and which afford the least bad medium-term prospects). Similar considerations apply to basic services and human investment — in water, health and education. Safeguarding the chance of a better future requires safeguarding children and averting a reversal of the slow, but significant, falls in IMRs and CDRs and rise in life expectancy.

Neither the will nor the incentive for consolidation *and* structural change is lacking. The problems turn on lack of adequate data and analysis to formulate courses of action and of resources to implement them. In respect to inputs — financial, conceptual and personnel — into consolidation and structural change related to safeguarding and strengthening the state of African children, a heavy burden falls on WHO and UNICEF, both in respect to their own resources and to mobilizing broader governmental and voluntary agency support.

In the context of falling real resource availability, the rural poor have tended to be the most vulnerable group even where the basic policy is both egalitarian and rural biased (e.g. Tanzania). Poorer transport leads to disproportionate cuts in the availability of services and goods in rural areas — especially the most distant or inaccessible, which are often the poorest. This is very noticeable in large, sparsely populated countries, e.g. Sudan, Zaire, Zambia. A vicious circle is created in which decline in rural incentives (services to use, goods to buy) leads to population shifts and/or falls in production which exacerbate national problems. Services critical to children — e.g. vaccination and immunization — seem particularly at risk. These difficulties are superimposed on the already severe physical and financial difficulties associated with providing basic services to largely rural populations with low average density.

The situation in respect to food is more complex. Malnutrition has probably grown at least as rapidly overall in urban as in rural areas — as has absolute poverty. Wages have risen less rapidly than food prices or rents and in Sub-Saharan Africa most peasant households produce the bulk of their own food and shelter. However, the most severely affected groups are in rural areas hit by natural disasters. Those living where emergency food provision is inadequate for financial, physical or other reasons — as in much of the Sahel and Horn — are most at risk of malnutrition-related deaths.

The rise in food prices may marginally improve rural/urban terms of trade (a welcome reversal of 1960s and 1970s experience were it in a context of rising rather than falling overall per capita consumption); how much is in doubt, because actual prices received and paid by growers are exceedingly hard to ascertain. Similarly, while peasants whose chief cash income is from food — on average — have lower than average rural household incomes, this is not necessarily true of those able to respond by increased output, especially in a context of severe shortages and delays in receiving agricultural inputs. Further, the rise in food prices harms food deficit, overcrowded area households (e.g. much of Rwanda and Burundi and the Kano Plain and Owerri Plateau in Nigeria) and accelerates the flow to urban areas which — given the position of new informal sector entrants — is now probably more of a push than a pull phenomenon in many countries.

The rise in food prices clearly has negative

effects on dietary patterns, perhaps most markedly in poor urban households. The explosive increases in the cost of fish, meat, milk, eggs, beans and pulses and cooking oil in a majority of Sub-Saharan countries worsen the already marked protein and fat deficiencies. Similarly, the increase in the cost of staples worsens the existing widespread calorie deficiencies, with especially negative impact on children directly and through their mothers' ante- and postnatal dietary deficiencies. The shift is both to less balanced diets and less food. While some of the cheaper staples substituted for wheat flour, rice and fine ground maizemeal may be more nutritious, e.g. 'roller meal' in Zambia, millet and sorghum in a significant number of countries — the same cannot be said of the commonest shift which is to cassava.

Other availability and price increase problems particularly adverse to children affect soap, infant diet supplements (although, this may be a mixed curse, given their widespread unhygienic and low quantity use), shoes and sandals, baby clothes and (in the cooler areas) blankets. Similarly the cost and lack of construction and maintenance materials are leading to worsening of housing standards, especially in urban low-income areas and most of all in respect to the new arrivals in squatter, shanty town and other slum areas. The last group is also very ill-provided with ⋅basic services, introduced in the 1970s, because of the constraints over the past four years in expanding them. As a result environmental risks to children's health are rising.

The combination of less and poorer food, worsening shelter, cleansing and clothing and reduced access to pure water and health care — especially in respect to vaccination and basic drug supply — can hardly fail to have severe adverse affects on children's morbidity and mortality rates as well as on their physical and intellectual development. This is not easy to demonstrate by quantitative data   partly because of the poor quality and long lags in statistics for Sub-Saharan Africa and partly because the positive trend in IMRs, CDRs and life expectancy apparently was initially resistant to reversal by the crisis. However, the first reason concerns appearances not reality and one cannot be sanguine about how long the second can survive.

In respect to services, purely quantitative data are, in any event, misleading. Resource cuts reduce quality even when quantity is sustained or increased. Enrolments in education are, by and large, still rising. However, so are class sizes, absenteeism and lack of the most basic texts and teaching materials. Similarly, medical personnel and patient data can show rises when lack of drugs, vaccines and adequate hospital diets suggests that the total volume of both curative and preventive care is declining if quality of treatment is taken into account. Likewise, numbers in principle served by rural (and urban) water systems hide the number of days of non-availability of water because of breakdowns, fuel shortages or demand in excess of capacity.

A related point is that financial stringency — and increasingly forcefully pressed advice from, particularly but not only, the World Bank[10] and IMF — is leading to the raising or reintroducing of school fees, standpipe and rural water user charges and medical treatment fees. This is true even in strongly egalitarian societies like Tanzania where primary school fees (abolished in the late 1960s) have been reintroduced. Such costs clearly hit the poorest families most and — especially in respect to education — have a disproportionate impact against children.

The recent past, present and short-term future evolution of the state of Africa's children cannot be described as other than grim. External events — often but not always exacerbated by imprudent domestic policies, including delayed response, have swamped a majority of Sub-Saharan African economies. Nutrition, shelter, clothing, education, health care and pure water quantities and qualities are declining for a majority of Africans, especially the rural and urban poor, many of whom had very little margin above ill health and destitution even before 1980.

2. NIGERIA: A MIDDLE-INCOME OIL EXPORTING ECONOMY

Nigeria has grown rapidly with 1981 GDP reaching US $870. This has been based on petroleum with output rising rapidly from the late 1960s through 1981 plus the 1973–74 and 1979–80 price increases. The results have been extremely mixed both in terms of immediate social impact and of long-term development.

As in the immediate pre- and post-independence commodity-based boom, the two sharp rises in oil exports have created a situation in which foreign exchange and finance constraints were perceived to be irrelevant. Big investment projects — based on no clear strategy — were initiated. While dominantly urban, these did include a number of large-scale, high-cost rural

projects which (as in the first boom) proved
to have similar problems of cost overruns,
doubtful viability and negative impact on
income distribution, including raising the
numbers of absolutely poor urban and rural
Nigerian households. The 'trickle down' model
— despite massive financial injections — has not
worked. The ILO Basic Needs report concluded[11] — before the present retrenchment —
that many Nigerians were worse off in terms of
quantitative measures such as diet and also
in quality of services and of life (e.g. rising
crime and accident rates).

Nigeria has achieved near universal primary
education and rates of secondary and tertiary
education well above the average for Sub-
Saharan Africa (though far below the global
lower middle-income average)[12] albeit adult
literacy is still only 34%. But in life expectancy,
IMR and CDR, it is worse than the average for
Sub-Saharan Africa. Its provision of medical personnel is above the Sub-Saharan and low-income
averages but significantly worse than that for
lower middle-income economies and, indeed
for several poorer African economies. Average
food availability at 91% of required caloric
levels[13] was only marginally above the general
Sub-Saharan picture and probably worse than
that for West Africa as a whole even before
1982–83 restrictions on food imports. This
is a rather dispiriting record for an economy
which during much of the period since 1970
had much greater room for manoeuvre in respect
to foreign exchange and fiscal contraints than
all but one or two others in Sub-Saharan
Africa.

Inequality is not new in Nigeria. Many
historic (pre-colonial) Nigerian states were
characterized by very marked inequality as
was the colonial period and the years of independence before the oil booms. However, the
nature of inequality has shifted away from
traditional mutual obligation and patron
systems toward much more individualistic
wealth acquisition and very high levels of
open corruption. Especially given the combination of great wealth, substantial state (and
private) resources available for meeting basic
needs and combating mass poverty, the new
forms of inequality have corroded social
cohesion and raised levels of cynicism. Whether
the ILO Report's attempt to draw an analogy
with Iran of the 1970s is fully apt is a different
question. Experience with a military revolution,
military coups, the civil war and the relatively
small Islamic messianic uprising has meant that
violent change is also regarded with some
cynicism and more suspicion as to its results.

Since 1960, growth of GDP — excluding
oil and sectors directly financed by it (such as
government and much of construction) — has
been relatively slow and distinctly unbalanced
against agriculture. This pattern predates the
oil boom. Over 1960–71, GDP grew 0.6%
per capita per annum (3.1% a year gross),
above the average for Sub-Saharan Africa SSA
but well below the 2.6% per capita (5% gross)
average of all middle-income countries. Further,
absolute agricultural output declined 0.4% a
year. Admittedly the civil war contributed to
both the overall and the agricultural record but
neither was much higher even in the first half
of the decade.

In the 1970s, the 0.4% a year decline in
agricultural output continued, in part as a result
of price distortions (including a buoyant
exchange rate) resulting from the oil export
boom. From under 200,000 tonnes in most
of the 1960s, grain imports rose to 399,000
in 1974 and 2,441,000 in 1981. Despite this,
food availability per capita declined 9% in the
1970s. Food production probably rose slightly
— especially if the shift of oil seeds and palm
oil from export to local consumption (bolstered
by imports) is so classified. However, despite
very rapidly rising prices (which have now made
wheat flour the cheapest staple), staple root
crop output has stagnated and that of rice has
fluctuated. Agricultural exports — except
cocoa — have virtually vanished, partly because
of lower production and partly (e.g. palm oil,
cotton, groundnuts) by shifts to domestic use.
As a result, Nigeria is now a mono-export
economy. The cost of this has been two draconic
cutbacks to growth and development — in the
late 1970s and from 1982 — when oil sales
volume fell. While Nigeria's long-term debt is
low (under 10% debt service ratio), short-term
credit is high with up to US $1.8 billion bank
credits and US $2–3 billion commercial firm,
manufacturer and contractor arrears at the peak
after the early 1983 squeeze on payments.

In addition to inequality, an exchange rate
providing negative protection to agriculture
and industry and high wages, oil revenue has
fuelled inflation quite as effectively as import
constraints have in other Sub-Saharan economies. In the 1960s, Nigeria had an average
annual inflation rate of 4% and in the 1970s of
14.2%, slightly above the middle-income
averages of 3 and 13.1%, respectively.

Perhaps more serious, oil resources to date
do not seem to have been employed effectively
toward building an integrated economy either
to weather fluctuations in oil sector fortunes,
to provide broad employment opportunities

(and self employment opportunities at decent income levels), to create – except in education – human capital, or to build a foundation for a post-oil economy. Agriculture is stagnant at best, manufacturing seems less diversified and more import-dependent not only than in Zimbabwe but also by comparison with Kenya and Tanzania, health and water services are not notably above general Sub-Saharan standards; urban infrastructure is massively overloaded and deteriorating, many state governments are bankrupt.

Oil revenue did not cause these results but it did allow emphasis on scale and modernization and absence of attention to managerial efficiency, setting of priorities or development of the non-oil tax base (which is both weak and – according to the ILO Report's findings – regressive even in respect to direct taxation). Social programmes and direct action to reduce poverty have not had high priority nor has child development (except education). Rural poverty has remained constant – largely because of a sustained urban population growth of nearly 5% a year over two decades, about half from rural to urban migration. Over 1974–79, the number of urban households below the poverty line increased sharply, perhaps by as much as 100%, implying an increase in the proportion in absolute poverty nationally.

Rural services – especially in the poorer states – are very thin except for primary education. Rural investment has – throughout the period since independence – been concentrated on settlement schemes, plantations and similar large-scale, modern approaches which exclude poor rural households while internal migration associated with opening up previously sparsely populated areas has often been at the expense of the original – usually below average rural income level – resident households.

Urban services have not expanded fast enough to cope with urban expansion. Low investment allocations have tended to be underspent. Both public (e.g. water and sewage) and private (e.g. low-income area housing) infrastructure quality has declined. The impact on the environment in which children live and the supporting services available to them when they fall ill seem clear. The decline in average food availability and the rise in absolute poverty point in the same unsatisfactory direction.

Nigeria, however, is not a typical Sub-Saharan economy. It is very large, its foreign exchange resources and public revenues (even at 1983 levels) are substantial. Further, relative to other African states, it has very large numbers of middle and high-level personpower and of entrepreneurs. Thus the constraints on achieving consolidation, devising structural change toward better balance (notably in respect to resumed rural output growth) and financing basic services – including child protection and development – if these come to be seen as priorities, are far less rigid than in most of the region.

This is not to say that Nigeria's position is comparable to that of Saudi Arabia, Libya or even Gabon. Nigeria is a lower-middle-income oil exporter with a large population and high (if perhaps not always effective) absorptive capacity. But it does have the resources to develop a more coherent economy and to finance basic services adequately (as the example of the Cameroon which has substantially lower oil revenues per capita may suggest). The success – in restoring macro-economic balance even if at high cost – of the 1960s and 1970s cutbacks (and the likely 1982–84 parallel) do indicate that consolidation (even if sometimes little more selective or prioritized than boomtime spending) is achievable. Priorities and management seem to pose the most urgent challenges.

3. ZAMBIA: A LOWER-MIDDLE-INCOME MINERAL EXPORTER IN DEPRESSION

Zambia – with a 1981 GDP per capita of US $600 – is a lower-middle-income economy ranking seventh among the 30 Sub-Saharan economies with populations over one million. Its IMR and, especially, CDR rates and life expectancy are below the average for such economies (and above those of Tanzania) but significantly better than those of Nigeria despite its one-third higher per capita GDP.[14]

Zambia has historically been a mono-export economy (copper plus its by-product cobalt) and in boom years that sector has contributed over 50% of GDP. Its rural economy has tended to be neglected – except on the southern 'line of rail' (a large farmer enclave, formerly expatriate but now mixed expatriate and Zambian) – which has interacted with the copper and government employment centred economy to produce an urbanization rate of 23% in 1960 and 44% in 1981 (approximately tied with the Congo Peoples Republic for first place in Sub-Saharan Africa and – by 1981 – well above the lower-middle-income average). The combination of relatively high copper and government wages and salaries, recurrent (at least until 1975) copper booms, a large farm enclave and little concentration on development of peasant production has also given rise to large and growing inequality nationally, in the rural sector and in the urban sector. In this last sector, high- and middle-income urban cores are surrounded by slum areas inhabited by informal sector and semi-unemployed low-income households. However, Zambia, both in terms of policy and of resource allocation, has placed substantial priority on basic services (primary education, health, water) and, to a degree, on safeguarding the condition of children albeit with a distinct urban bias.

Zambia's real income per capita has declined by almost 60% since 1974 — indeed it is now lower than at independence in 1964. Real copper prices, after fluctuating around a constant trend over 1945—74, have in the 1980s fallen to their lowest levels in the century. The terms of trade — also affected by rising import prices and increased transport costs initially imposed by the Rhodesian Rebellion and sustained by South African-incited and organized sabotage of Angolan and Mozambique routes since 1980 — have fallen by two-thirds since 1974.

The results of this long squeeze have been severe. Shortages of almost all basic goods are either endemic or episodic. Deferred maintenance has been building up for a decade. Public services are starved of inputs to complement personnel — notably in health and education where personpower development has been impressive. Further, any relaxation of the import or government revenue constraint leads to explosive rises in both imports and public spending — e.g. 47 and 50% respectively in 1979. These increases would, in fact, have been unsustainable without a sustained boom. Instead, real import capacity and revenue have resumed their decline. The result has been periodic debt reschedulings and a build-up of financial and commercial arrears by 1983 probably exceeding US $1000 million, equivalent to a year's exports and over a third of annual GDP.

Over 1965—74, real GDP per capita oscillated sharply but fell 0.5% annually on average. This fall accelerated to 3.7% a year over 1974—78 with a further fall of over 35% in 1978—80, 5% in 1981 and perhaps 3% in 1982. The dominant cause — directly and by multiplier effects — has been the terms of trade. Had these remained at 1970 levels — even excluding multiplier effects (e.g. operating industry at 60% not 30% of capacity) — then real GDP in 1981 would have been 63% higher than it actually was. Over 1970—81, the cumulative

losses were over three times annual GDP. The length and severity of the external pressure has repeatedly overwhelmed efforts at stabilization and consolidation.

Attempts to limit scarcities by concentrating imports and production on mass consumed goods and to limit the impact of inflation by price controls on essential goods plus subsidies on maize meal (the main urban and — except for the north — rural staple food) were moderately successful until the late 1970s. Since then the scarcities have overwhelmed the allocations and price controls and revenue constraints plus IMF pressures have forced abandonment of subsidies. In 1983, attempts to hold relatively long deferred wage increases below 10% against a 25—30% expected cost of living increase were also abandoned.

Food production per capita declined 8% between 1969—71 and 1979—81. Agricultural output grew 1.8% a year but population grew 3.1% so that even a shift to food from industrial crops (e.g. cotton, tobacco) could not sustain per capita food production. Grain imports rose from 93,000 tonnes in 1974 to 295,000 in 1981. In both 1982 and 1983, Zambia has been significantly affected by the Southern African drought with further declines in production per capita and average calorie availability.

There have been significant internal weaknesses — especially the relatively low, episodic and modernization-oriented agricultural resource allocations. However, since the Rhodesian Rebellion in 1965 and, especially, the onset of the secular terms of trade/import capacity crisis in 1974 these have often been because external shocks used all Zambia's limited personpower, analytical and institutional capacity and imposed a short-term crisis alleviation time and priority frame. The ILO Report[15] stresses this negative interaction with external shocks exacerbating the results of national weaknesses while reducing capacity either to adjust to the shocks or restructure national policies. Given the dramatic and sustained fall in resources available, the record is by no means discreditable in maintaining social objectives and basic services (albeit with qualitative deterioration and increasing rural area breakdowns especially since 1979).

Over the 1975—79 period, government expenditure per capita declined 75 and 35% in capital and recurrent, respectively. While the latter was largely reversed in 1980, that attempt proved unsustainable and 1983 levels are probably another 15% per capita below 1979 in respect of recurrent spending. Over

1975–79, private consumption fell 21% – massively increasing poverty (including inadequacies of nutrition, clothing, shelter and cleansing). With over 50% of the population consisting of children under age 15, deterioration in their conditions of life cannot but have been significant. Again the decline has continued both for urban residents because rapid inflation (7.6% in the 1960s, 8.4% in the 1970s, but since then probably in excess of 20% a year) has outstripped wages and informal sector income and for the rural population because poor weather has decreased availability of food for both consumption and sale by peasant households.

Social service expenditure – within a shrinking total – has fallen from 29.5% in 1972 to 26.8% in 1974 and 20.5% in 1980. This may be more apparent than real because of the higher share of wages (which have risen less rapidly than other costs) in social service spending. The main cuts have been in education; health spending has been better sustained. The main increases in expenditure have been those imposed by rising debt service and increasingly aggressive neighbours (i.e. defence). However, the share of economic services has held up better than that for social services. In the face of a production crisis there is a tendency to seek to concentrate on speedy production gains rather than on long-term investment in children and in poverty reduction. Basic needs – judging from Zambian (and Tanzanian) experience – seem to be more closely linked to at least modest real growth than much of the debate might suggest. Redistribution out of growing resources may be difficult; actually raising the incomes and access to services of the poor – and especially of children – in the fact of steadily falling per capita resource availability is virtually impossible.

In education, primary enrolment has reached 95% but class size at 47.1 is high even by African standards. Further severe constraints have impeded expansion of secondary and tertiary education despite acute middle- and high-level personpower shortages and the evidence of high returns in Sub-Saharan Africa on investment in educational expenditure.[16]

The ratio of doctors and, especially, nurses and paramedical personnel to population has improved significantly over 1960–81 albeit most of the increase came by 1970. However, lack of drugs, equipment, maintenance and fuel are eroding the quality of health services and – in some rural areas – even their operationality. Access to pure drinking water at 42% is high by African standards. However it is concentrated in urban areas (about 80% versus under 20% in rural) and represents in part the high degree of urbanization.

The ILO Mission found substantial evidence of worsening of the condition of children in the 1970s.[17] The situation in the below average income, rural Northern and Luapula Provinces showed incidence of child malnutrition and anaemia two to three times those in the Southern and Central Provinces (the latter including Lusaka). This gap has apparently increased. Compared to national survey data of 1969–70, there was a clear decline in height for age, with a more mixed picture in weight but with declines (including for infants) outnumbering improvements.

In Northern Province, children's clinics fell from 122 in 1973 to 86 in 1977 against a national rise from 928 to 1004.[18] In Luapula Province, the health services seem to lack virtually all resources except personnel.[19] While relatively low-cost vitamin provision programmes could radically reduce 'Luapula blindness', the absence of funds has resulted in a growing incidence, with over three quarters of adults and many children in some communities suffering from impaired vision or total blindness.[20]

In Zambia, unlike Nigeria, the most urgent requirement is additional resources and, in particular, foreign exchange. Substantial infrastructure, growing numbers of trained personnel and reasonably well-articulated priorities and policies exist especially in the basic services sector. But nearly a decade of falling resource availability has reduced their effectiveness drastically. The worsening plight of Zambia's children and its declining ability to combat that deterioration create a strong case for external assistance in respect to child protection and development, especially because the basic causes of the decline lie abroad in copper markets and Pretorian aggression taking up the role of the Rhodesian rebels.

4. TANZANIA: A LOW-INCOME RURAL ECONOMY

Tanzania is a low-income economy with a 1981 GDP per capita of US $280.[21] While its population at 20 million is large in African terms, it is not dense and the more productive rural areas are scattered, leading to high transport and service provision costs. Over 1960–78, the rate of growth of GDP was 2.7% per capita and of agricultural output per capita 1–1.5%.[22]

In respect to most health and education indicators, Tanzania is among the top four or five Sub-Saharan countries and above the low-income country average, excluding China and India. Its adult literacy rate of 79% is the highest in Sub-Saharan Africa and above the upper-middle-income country average. Over 1960–78, rapid progress was made in respect to health, education and water supply in both urban and rural areas while average calorie availability rose from 87% of requirement in 1960 to 117% in 1977–78.[23]

However, since 1977–78 Tanzania has been confronted with a series of external shocks to which initial adjustment was unduly delayed. As a result, Tanzania is today in the middle of a debilitating economic crisis, one which threatens the living standards and the basic needs fulfillment of much of the Tanzanian nation. Unless some way is found of restoring economic activity to its previous levels and/or resuming economic growth, improvements in health, education, sanitation and nutrition will not be possible and even present achievements in these fields may come under severe threat.[24]

Until 1974 Tanzania had achieved relatively stable – although never dramatic – growth in production albeit slow export growth after 1965–67 already posed a potential external balance problem. The 1973–74 shock was very severe because it coincided with two successive years of severe drought and the 1972–74 world grain price increases. However, rapid curtailment of growth in resource use and mobilization of external finance restored growth and by the end of 1977 the economy appeared to be booming with inflation under 10% (against a 4.5% average in the 1960s and 12.6% over 1970–81) and external reserves at over four months of imports. However, this was partly fortuitous, 1975–78 were all good weather years (indeed in 1977–78 food exports exceeded imports in tonnage and calorie, albeit not value, terms) and the 1976–77 external accounts had been bolstered by the beverage boom following Brazil's severe 1975 frost.

In 1977 Tanzania succumbed to pressure from the IMF and World Bank to liberalize imports precisely as the underlying trade balance began to worsen with falling coffee prices. In 1978 Idi Amin invaded Tanzania, setting off a war which cost Tanzania about US $700 million. The year 1979 began a series of bad weather years continuing through 1983. The terms of trade continued to decline – by more than 50% over 1977–81 – with export price declines and oil price increases.

Export cover of imports (themselves cut to levels inadequate to maintain and operate basic production and services capacity by mid-1980) fell from 70% in 1977 to about 40% in 1980 with subsequent recoveries related to cuts of critical imports leading to strangulation of industry, transport and, to a lesser extent, agriculture and basic services, not to an increase in real export earnings. When the 9% 1977–80 volume fall in exports was more than reversed in 1981, terms of trade falls (basically the coffee price) wiped out the potential gain. By 1983, arrears in payments approached US $500 million, i.e. one year's exports and 8% of GDP.

GDP growth declined in 1978, was negative in 1979 and temporarily recovered in 1980 with the first adjustment programme. However, GDP collapsed to negative rates again in 1981–83 as inability to import forced capacity utilization in manufacturing from 65–70% in 1977 to 25–30% in 1982, weakened transport and hampered procurement of agricultural and basic services inputs. Because the ratio of imports to GDP is fairly low (about 20%) and easy compression was used up over 1973–74, all cuts since 1979 have had a high negative multiplier effect on domestic production. The industrial decline has radically reduced real government revenue with the recurrent budget going into deficit for the first time in 1978–79 and the domestic bank borrowing requirement rising to nearly 10% of GDP over 1981–83. The rate of inflation rose to 25–30% a year over 1980–83. In 1982, it was necessary to abandon attempts to defend the real minimum wage (which had never made good its 1973–76 fall) and, to a lesser extent, real grower prices from the ravages of terms of trade deterioration and import strangulation.

Tanzania has been opposed to consumption subsidies on goods as opposed to free or low-cost access to basic services. Wrong cost information led to heavy *de facto* subsidies on grain over 1978–80 which were then eliminated except for maizemeal. In that case the subsidy was cut and partly financed by a higher sugar price, leaving consumer subsidies at 1.5% of the budget. Producer (or excess transport and handling cost) subsidies – especially for export crops – are much higher, totalling over 10% of the recurrent budget.

Basic needs services (including agriculture, water supply and rural development as well as social services) have received priority in allocation amounting to 25–30% of government expenditure. Including the producer subsidies, the share has changed little, excluding them, the decline has been from 26% in 1977–78 to 18.5% in 1981–82.[25] Social service expenditure fell over the same period from 21 to 15.7%. The increased shares were debt service and defence (the latter reversed beginning in 1981–82) plus producer subsidies and reconstruction of capital of badly managed agricultural marketing corporations and other parastatals hit by the 1979–82 deterioration of the economic climate.

The volume of social and basic needs services has not in fact declined. Indeed primary enrolment (now about 100%) and access to health services (about three visits a person a year in rural and 10 in urban areas for an average of four) and to pure water systems have risen. Part of the explanation is the high wage/salary component in these sectors – real government wages have declined over 6% a year since 1977. However, much relates to cuts in supporting inputs – probably over 50% for texts and paper, drugs, water spares, maintenance and vehicles and fuel – cuts which severely impair the quality of services (and, in the case of water supply, the sustained functioning of many systems).

Tanzania's political economic priorities – especially since 1967 – have been oriented to basic human needs, egalitarianism and protection of low-income groups, socialism, rural bias and attainment of adequate growth rates to achieve the other aims.[26] These aims have not deterred it from operating a stringent austerity programme over 1974–76 and attempting tough structural adjustment programmes in 1980, 1981 (in that year termed National Survival Programme) and 1982. However, it has prejudiced negotiations with some external sources of funds including the IMF and World Bank because the patterns of cuts and allocations were non-standard as well as because Tanzania did not have an articulated export development strategy until 1981. Further, as in the case of Zambia, increased demands and reduced resources resulting from external shocks have decreased the effectiveness of management and shortened its time horizon (in the private as well as the public sector).

Tanzania's priorities are perhaps clearest within the social sectors. For example, the share of rural health services has risen sharply as has the ratio of paramedical personnel to doctors. By 1978–79 there was one dispensary per 6700 rural population and one health service worker per 1600 rural people. However, 'there are wide gaps between what has been provided and what is functioning and actually available to people'.[27] Trained personnel are increasingly

available but drugs, vaccines, equipment, kerosene for refrigerators and fuel for transport increasingly are not. Thus the level of immunization per 1000 children, after rising from 50 per 1000 in 1970 to 600 in 1978–79, has fallen back to perhaps one-third its peak level. By 1982–83 drug imports were one-third optimal levels on the national 300 basic drug list versus about two-thirds in 1979–80. Attainment of the 1983–84 target level equal to 1979–80 can be achieved only if substantial specific concessional finance for drugs (and possibly fridges and fuel) can be secured. Ideally such aid would be in the form of intermediate and semi-finished products to allow utilization of the substantial (but nearly idle) domestic tabletting and manufacturing capacity but even at its 1980 peak of about US $6 million, grant drug aid has almost entirely been in the form of branded finished products.

A comparable situation exists in education. Adult education (continuing as well as literacy) and primary education have been priorities as have been tertiary and decentralized (usually employer-related) middle-level personpower development. Again, quantity has continued to rise – here with greater strains on personnel supply (e.g. the primary class size rose from 47 to 50 in the 1970s) with the introduction of universal primary education. But paper and text supplies – as well as other teaching materials – are well below half the 1977 levels. Again, printing capacity for texts is available but not foreign exchange to import paper and ink.

Rural bias has resulted in peasant average household consuming power exceeding that of the minimum wage. Nearly equal at the time of the ILO Mission, the shift has now happened with food values and grower prices continuing to rise much more rapidly than wages. Unfortunately, this has happened in a context of falling real incomes for both urban and rural households. Egalitarianism has been enhanced but only on a 'weaker boats sink less rapidly' not an 'all boats float higher' basis. Thus the probably greater shortage of food in urban than in most rural areas (excluding districts particularly hard hit by natural disasters in that year) reflects a decline in urban diet rather than an improvement in rural diet.

Direct evidence of the impact of recession on children is hard to secure. However, indicative facts are available. Average calorie availability fell from about 117% of requirements in 1977–78 to 93% in 1982–83.[28] Drug availability fell 50% over 1979–80 to 1982–83. Soap has been extremely scarce and expensive since 1981 as have baby clothes and blankets since 1980. Materials for maintenance of dwellings are often unavailable or prohibitively costly. Real wages fell about 50% over 1977–82 and real rural household consuming power perhaps 15%. School fees were reintroduced (albeit with waiver provisions for poor families) and medical charges increased. A further indication can be gained from a 1978–79 study of under-5 mortality by income class. The rate was only 10% as high for Group IV (high-level professionals and managers — under 1% of the population) as for Group I (minimum wage earners and below — about 70% of urban residents), a ratio very close to the inverse of that for pre-tax household incomes. The income difference between Group II (artisan/trader)

and III (mechanic/clerk) was 1 to 2 and that of child mortality 1 to 1.7.[29] While other factors apply, these findings strongly suggest that continued falls in household real incomes will reverse the decline in IMR and CDR and the rise in life expectancy.

In the case of Tanzania, as in that of Zambia, additional foreign exchange is the most critical condition for restoring production and social service growth. Because the crisis was largely caused by external shocks and has by the strains it imposed lowered efficiency, further demand reduction (as opposed to supply enhancement) or seeking to improve efficiency other than in a context of reduced resources constraints seem likely to be counter-productive — most of all for Tanzania's children.

NOTES

1. *World Development Reports (WDR)* (1981, 1982, 1983).

2. *WDR 1983*, p. 38.

3. *WDR 1983*.

4. UNICEF data.

5. ILO/JASPA, *Nigeria* (1981); *Zambia* (1981); *Tanzania* (1982).

6. *WDR 1983*, pp. 31–32.

7. See G. Lean (1983); SADCC (1983).

8. Based on papers of the African Centre for Monetary Studies Conference, 'Debt Problems of African Economies in the 1980s' (Tunis: September 1983).

9. Most published balance-of-payments accounts only show debt service actually paid which is substantially lower in the economies under severe pressure.

10. See World Bank (1981); Allison and Green (1983).

11. ILO/JASPA, *Nigeria* (1981).

12. *WDR 1982, 1983*.

13. In general, African diet and calorie data are very weak.

14. ILO/JASPA, *Zambia* (1981), p. 8; *WDR 1982, 1983*.

15. ILO/JASPA, *Zambia* (1981), p. XXV.

16. The figures are 29% on primary, 17% on secondary and 12% on higher education. See Timothy King *et al.* (1980).

17. ILO Mission Technical Paper No. 4, Vol. 2, Tables A.46–47, pp. 64–65.

18. *Ibid.*, p. 62.

19. ILO Mission Technical Paper, No. 9.

20. *Ibid.*

21. ILO/JASPA, *Tanzania* (1982); *WDR 1983*.

22. There are serious problems with all Tanzania agricultural series. The best study — by an FAD team studying food and nutrition — estimated the trend rate of growth of food production at 3.5–4% over 1960–80.

23. Tanzanian Food and Nutrition Centre data summarized in Technical Paper 10, pp. 367–369.

24. ILO/JASPA, *Tanzania* (1982), p. 15.

25. *Ibid.*, Table 3.3, p. 18.

26. See Green (1983).

27. ILO/JASPA, *Tanzania* (1982), p. 62.

28. Estimated from data cited in note 23 and from subsequent production data.

29. ILO/JASPA, *Tanzania* (1982), pp. 306–308.

REFERENCES

Allison, C. and R. H. Green (eds.), *Accelerated Development in Sub-Saharan Africa: What Agendas for Action?*, *IDS Bulletin* (Institute of Development Studies, University of Sussex, UK, January 1983).

Green, R. H., 'Political economic adjustment and IMF conditionality: the case of Tanzania 1974–81', in J. Williamson (ed.), *IMF Conditionality* (Washington, D.C.: Institute for International Economics, 1983).

ILO Mission Technical Paper No. 4, 'Better nutrition for Zambia's children'.

ILO Mission Technical Paper No. 9, 'Luapula: a regional comparison, 1975 and 1980'.

ILO/JASPA, *First Things First: Meeting the Basic Needs of the People of Nigeria* (Addis Ababa: 1981).

ILO/JASPA, *Zambia: Basic Needs in an Economy under Pressure* (Addis Ababa: 1981).

ILO/JASPA, *Basic Needs in Danger: A Basic-Needs Oriented Development Strategy for Tanzania* (Addis Ababa: 1982).

King, Timothy *et al.*, 'Education and income', World Bank Staff Working Paper, No. 402 (Washington, D.C.: 1980), cited in World Bank (1981), Table 6.1.

Lean, G., 'Sahel faces its worst famine', *Observer* (9 October 1983).

Southern African Development Coordination Conference (SADCC), 'Drought', Working Paper prepared for SADCC–Lusaka (January 1984) (Gaborone: 1983).

World Bank, *Accelerated Development in Sub-Saharan Africa: An Agenda for Action* (Washington, D.C.: 1981).

World Bank, *World Development Reports, 1981, 1982, 1983* (Washington, D.C.: 1981, 1982, 1983).

Recent Trends in the Condition of Children in India: A Statistical Profile

SUDIPTO MUNDLE*

Centre for Development Studies, Trivandrum, Kerala, India

Summary. – Global recession has not affected the status of Indian children directly, thanks to the basic insularity of the country's economy, but it has constrained the government's ability to maintain/expand child-related programmes in real terms. This paper analyses recent trends in a large set of quality of life indicators for children in India. While labour market data and nutrition statistics appear ambiguous, other measures such as anthropometric measures, e.g. infant mortality, life expectancy and literacy rates, do not show generalized deterioration and occasionally provide evidence of improvements. The latter, however, show important inter-state variations, with conditions actually deteriorating in some states. Moreover, the improvements observed have been registered under very low absolute conditions of living.

1. INTRODUCTION

At last count (Census 1981), India's population was 685 million and growing at an average rate of about 2.5% per annum. Of this, approximately 260 million were children under age 15.[1] Roughly 70% of this total population depends on agriculture. Hence, the bulk of the population, both children and adults, are exposed directly to world recession only to the extent that India's agriculture depends on external markets. As exports account for only about 3% of the value-added in agriculture, the agriculture-dependent population is even less susceptible to the recessionary impulses of world trade than would appear from the overall export/GNP ratio of 6% in recent years (Government of India, 1983).

There are, however, other less direct but nevertheless real mechanisms through which the recession may significantly affect the status of children in India. World recession – more specifically the oil shock which probably set it off – has pushed India into a serious balance-of-payments problem. The low level of exports, which appears to be an advantage in insulating India from the recession's direct impact, turns out to be a major problem when compared to the higher level of imports. India's trade deficit of around Rs. 10 billion in 1977–78 had grown to a deficit of nearly Rs. 60 billion by 1980–81. This is reflected in the current account deficit which had reached a level of well over Rs. 20 billion by the early 1980s. After taking account of capital transactions, the total deficit which had to be met through external assistance in 1980–81 was over Rs. 31 billion, including drawings from the IMF of over Rs. 8 billion.

This deteriorating balance-of-payments situation must be seen along with an equally serious problem of deficits in the government's own budget. A growing gap exists between the government's total outlay and the sum of its current revenue and capital receipts. This gap, which has to be met through either external assistance or domestic deficit finance, had grown to over Rs. 50 billion by 1980–81 from Rs. 13 billion in 1978–79 and Rs. 35 billion in 1979–80 (Government of India, 1983). Final estimates for the last two financial years are not yet available, but in all probability this gap has grown even larger. External assistance has increased from Rs. 7 billion in 1978–79 to Rs. 8.9 billion in 1979–80 and Rs. 16.7 billion in 1980, with the overall deficit for those periods growing from Rs. 6.3 billion to Rs. 26.6 billion to Rs. 34.6 billion. In view of India's serious balance-of-payments problem, the government obviously cannot resort to indefinitely growing volumes of external assistance or deficit finance to meet the increasing gap between its total outlays and total receipts on current and capital account.

Under these conditions, there has been strong pressure on the government to curtail various

---

* The views expressed in this paper are those of the author and not necessarily those of UNICEF.

development programmes, welfare schemes and subsidies, including those relating specifically to children. Even if outlays in money terms are not actually cut, the scope of these programmes may be reduced in real terms or their rate of expansion at least brought down. The effectiveness of such programmes is studied in the last section of this paper, following an examination of available data on recent trends in the quality of life for Indian children.

2. CHILDREN IN THE WORK FORCE

Although there are a number of micro-studies which document the pitiable working conditions, long hours and shockingly low wages for children in urban areas (ICCW, 1977; NIPCCD, 1978; George, 1977; Seal, 1980; etc.), child labour in India is essentially an agrarian problem. Data on the sectoral distribution of child labour from the 1981 Census is not yet available, but the 1971 Census and the 1978 Survey of Infant and Child Mortality, both conducted by the Registrar General of India,[2] revealed that around 80% or more of all child labourers as well as male and female child labourers taken separately, were engaged in agriculture and allied activities.

From the rural labour enquiries conducted in 1964–65 and again in 1974–75, three features in the condition of child labour stand out most sharply: (a) the extremely rapid growth of child labourers (an increase of 64% for all India from 1964–65 to 1974–75) as well as of total labourers (a 51% increase over the same period); (b) the miserably low wages of both child and adult male labourers; and (c) the predominant fact of a decline in real wage rates in both cases (children's wages decreased by 7% from 1964–65 to 1974–75 while male labourers' wages went down by 10%). A question now arises regarding the possible relationship between the rapid growth of child labour and the low and declining real wage rate. Both child and adult agricultural labour increased while real wages declined, apparently representing a perverse phenomenon of larger numbers of children and adults being forced to enter the rural labour market despite declining wages. This increase in child labour might therefore be interpreted as reflecting general deterioration in the condition of rural children.

However, no clear relationship emerges between the fall in real wage rates and the growth of child labour across the 14 states surveyed: Andhra Pradesh, Assam, Bihar, Gujarat, Karnataka, Kerala, Madhya Pradesh, Maharashtra, Orissa, Punjab and Haryana, Rajasthan, Tamil Nadu, Uttar Pradesh, West Bengal.[3] For example, child labour increased by 75% in Punjab–Haryana, while real wages rose by 36%. In Rajasthan, child labour did not increase at all, whereas real wages increased by 8%. In Kerala, male wage rates declined by 29% and child labour remained the same. In 10 states where real wages declined along with increases in child labour, there is no clear inverse correlation between the proportionate increase in child labour and the proportionate decrease in real wage rates. Furthermore, in nine cases, the growth of child labour was higher than that of all labour including adult male labour. However, in only four of these nine states do we find a greater fall in the real wage rates of child labour as compared to the fall in male real wage rates. We cannot therefore offer any simple explanation that child labour was being forced into the labour market by impoverishment consequent upon a fall in real wages any more than we can attribute falling real wages to the growth of child labour.[4]

To interpret the rapid growth of child labour, we must therefore examine it in relation to the total child population growth. The data on labour force participation rates of children reveals that the aggregate participation for all children appears to have declined from about 8% in 1961 to just under 5% in 1971. This decline is borne out by the 1978 survey (Office of Registrar General, 1980), both the 1961 and 1971 Censuses and a completely independent set of participation rate estimates, based on the 16th round (1960–61) and 27th round (1972–73) of the National Sample Survey.[5] Finally, a brief reference to literacy trends serves as a useful cross check against our inference regarding participation rates. We would normally expect child work force participation rates to decline as child literacy rates rise. As discussed in Section 6, child literacy rates were indeed rising during the 1960s and 1970s for both boys and girls in both rural and urban areas. The combined evidence establishes that participation of children in the work force is actually declining over time. The rise in the absolute number of child labourers reflects the increase in the child population from 180 million in 1961 to 230 million in 1971 and further to around 260 million in 1981.

Although the absolute number of child labourers has grown phenomenally and their real wages have fallen, we have seen why these may not be good indicators of the changing status of children, particularly in view of the declining *incidence* of child labour. Furthermore, real wage rates are by no means a good indicator of trends in the level of living, even among agricultural labour households. Studies have shown that at the same time as real wage rates or annual wage incomes per labourer are falling, the real per capita income in agricultural labour households may be rising because of increasing non-wage income, rising earning strength of the family and other similar factors (see Mundle, 1982a,b). We must therefore move beyond labour market statistics to more direct indicators of the physical quality of life, starting with estimates of poverty and nutrition.

3. POVERTY AND NUTRITION

It is now increasingly believed that because food is not equitably distributed within the poor family, poverty–nutrition trends for the aggregate population may conceal trends specific to the child population (Sen, 1982).

Accordingly, we present here data from the National Institute of Nutrition which shows the age-specific nutritional status of children belonging to age groups 1–4 years and 5–10 years in 10 states: Andhra Pradesh, Gujarat, Karnataka, Kerala, Madhya Pradesh, Maharashtra, Orissa, Tamil Nadu, Uttar Pradesh, West Bengal. The estimates are based on surveys conducted by the National Nutrition Monitoring Board (NNMB) which cumulatively sampled 28,055 households (19,632 rural and 8423 urban) in the 10 states, examining a total of 162,837 individuals up to December 1979. Estimates for the year January–December 1979, during which a total of 4809 households were surveyed (31,566 individuals examined), are compared with estimates based on the pooled data for the period 1975–79. Children of both age groups have been classified into four nutritional status groups: Protein Inadequate–Calorie Inadequate (p c), Protein Inadequate–Calorie Adequate (p C), Protein Adequate–Calorie Inadequate (P c) and Protein Adequate–Calorie Adequate (P C). The minimal concept of Mean-2 Standard Deviation of the recommended daily allowance is treated as the criterion of adequacy.

The data show that the category of children with adequate calorie intake but inadequate protein intake is practically a null set in all states for both age groups during the period 1975–79 as well as the year 1979. In other words, whenever calorie intake is adequate, protein intake is also adequate, such that the latter can be ignored as a separate nutrient requirement in the present case. Except in a few extreme cases, children with adequate intake of both calorie and protein accounted

for about 30–50% of all children in both age groups. The proportion of children deficient in calorie intake but having adequate protein intake again ranges from between 30 to 50% in most states although it is higher in a couple of extreme cases.

Thus the general nutritional status of children in India is extremely depressing, with between 50% to over 70% of all children across different states suffering from inadequate calorie intake and around 10–20% of children suffering from protein deficiency as well. However, the picture regarding changes over time is ambiguous. In the case of 1–4-year-olds, the share of best category (P C) has declined in only three states (Karnataka, Kerala and West Bengal). The share of the worst category (p c), although accounting for less than 20% of all children in most states, has increased in seven states: Gujarat, Karnataka, Kerala, Madhya Pradesh, Maharashtra, Uttar Pradesh and West Bengal. In the case of 5–13-year-olds, the share of the best category (P C) has declined in these same seven states while the share of the worst category has increased in four: Kerala, Madhya Pradesh, Uttar Pradesh and West Bengal.

4. ANTHROPOMETRIC MEASURES

Gopalan (1983) has recently emphasized the difficulty of getting accurate estimates of child nutrition from diet surveys using the household as the basic unit of observation, even though data may be collected separately for different age–sex groups within the household. He has also pointed out that the minimal adequacy criterion employed by the NNMB, i.e. Mean-2 Standard Deviation applied to the recommended daily allowance, may seriously underestimate malnutrition from a biological view. Children surviving at this minimum level of calorie intake would most probably suffer from other nutrient deficiencies as well (although not protein, as we have seen), and would in the long run experience the development of various biological deficiencies/ailments not reflected in the diet surveys. Gopalan has suggested the use of nutrition surveys along with data on morbidity, clinical symptoms of undernutrition, biochemical counts and anthropometric measures such as the distribution of heights, weights, arm circumference, fat fold at triceps, etc. We therefore examine here two standard anthropometric measures: the height and weight of children, based on the NNMB survey data discussed earlier.

Data available from the National Institute of

Nutrition compares, separately for boys and girls, the average heights recorded during 1979 with the average for the period 1974–79 at different ages in the 10 states covered by the NNMB survey. The 1979 height turns out to be neither uniformly higher nor uniformly lower than the 1974–79 average height at ages 2, 5 and 9 in most of the states. However, the comparison at age 13 is more meaningful as it represents the cumulative result of childhood growth. At age 13, the average height recorded for boys in 1979 is lower than the average for 1974–79 in only one state: Karnataka. For girls at this age, the average height recorded in 1979 turns out to be lower than the 1974–79 average in four states: Andhra Pradesh, Gujarat, Madhya Pradesh and Uttar Pradesh. In all other states, the 1979 average was greater than or equal to the 1974–79 average. In general, therefore, the heights of children in 1979 appear an improvement compared to the average for the late 1970s as a whole. This conclusion must be treated cautiously since the differences between the 1979 and 1974–79 averages are quite small — much less, for instance, than one standard deviation. However, this is not unexpected since average heights of children are not expected to change dramatically from year to year and the available data restricts comparison to a period of only five years.

The data on the distribution of children according to weights yields a much sharper picture of anthropometric changes during the 1970s. Data available from the National Institute of Nutrition compares the percentage share of each category in the Gomez classification (per cent of standard weight) in 1979 with the average share of that category during the period 1975–78 for pre-school children (age 1–5 years) in the 10 states surveyed by the NNMB. Barring extreme cases, the proportion of children severely underweight (less than 60% of standard weight) has generally ranged between 5 to 10% of pre-school children in most states. At the other end, children of normal weight (90% of standard) have accounted for between 10 to 20% of the total. The large majority of pre-school children in most states belong to the middle categories of mildly underweight children (75–90% of standard), who generally account for 35 to 50% of the total, and moderately underweight children (60–75% of standard), who account for about 30–40% of the total.

The comparison over time shows that the proportion of normal weight or mildly underweight children declined in only three states — Tamil Nadu, Madhya Pradesh and Orissa — which accordingly were the only states where the

proportion of children severely or moderately underweight increased. The proportion of severely underweight children increased only in Madhya Pradesh and Orissa. The share of normal weight children increased in six states, remained unchanged in Orissa and West Bengal and declined only in Tamil Nadu and Karnataka. Whichever way we look at the statistics, therefore, the disaggregated state-level picture confirms that the weight status of children in India has shown distinct improvement in recent years. This positive trend is reinforced by data from UNICEF New Delhi which suggests a substantial improvement by the end of the 1970s in the physical status of children aged 1–5 years as measured by the Gomez classification. We must, however, remember that there are a number of states in which the situation is either not improving or actually deteriorating and that the absolute level of living at which the improvements have been registered remains abysmal.

5. INFANT MORTALITY AND LIFE EXPECTANCY

Can the inferences made so far as to the changing status of children in India be tested on the basis of some independent source of data? The trends in real income or standards of child care and nutrition, which are reflected in anthropometric measures, should also be reflected in demographic indicators of the physical quality of life such as infant mortality, age-specific child death rates or life expectancy. This section examines trends in such demographic variables starting with estimates of infant mortality rates reproduced in Table IX.1. Actuarial reports based on the decennial censuses show that the infant mortality rate during the 1960s, while still high in absolute terms, had distinctly improved compared to that of the 1950s, which in turn was significantly lower than the rates prevailing during the first half of the century (barring the estimate for 1946–50 which appears to be exceptionally low and needs to be examined more carefully).

It is not possible to judge on the basis of any comparable set of estimates whether this declining trend of infant mortality was maintained during the 1970s until the actuarial report for 1971–81 based on the 1981 Census becomes available.[6] However, an independent set of annual estimates for the 1970s (based on the Sample Registration Scheme and the 1979 Survey of Infant and Child Mortality, Office of Registrar General, 1980), shows that the infant mortality rates, after rising around the middle

Table IX.1. *Infant mortality rates*, 1911–78

Period	Deaths per 1000 live births	Period	Deaths per 1000 live births
1911–15	204*	1970	129†
1916–20	219*	1971	129†
1921–25	174*	1972	139†
1926–30	178*	1973	134†
1931–35	174*	1974	126†
1936–40	161*	1975	140†
1941–45	161*	1976	129†
1946–50	134*	1977	129‡
1951–61	146§	1978	125‡
1961–71	129§		

Source: Office of Registrar General (1980).
*Five year average.
†Sample Registration Scheme.
‡Survey.
§Actuarial Report.

of the 1970s, declined toward the end of that decade to a level lower than that observed at the beginning of the decade. The 3-year moving average of deaths per 1000 live births rose from 132 in 1971 to 133 in 1974 and then declined to 128 in 1977. For the decade as a whole, therefore, the decline in infant mortality rates observed for the 1960s appears to have been maintained.

A closely related demographic variable is the life expectancy at birth, which is estimated on the basis of life tables computed from infant mortality rates along with age-specific death rates. Trends in life expectancy at birth estimated from different sources (Table IX.2) confirm the inferences tentatively suggested so far, i.e. that the living standard of the broad mass of India's child population was improving during the 1970s but that the improvement was registered at absolute levels of living which continued to be abysmally low.

Table IX.3 presents age-specific death rates in 1972 and 1978 for children of three different age groups, differentiating between males and females in rural and urban areas. While both male and female death rates decline between 1972 and 1978, the decline was faster in the case of females in both rural and urban areas, thus reducing the difference between male and female death rates. In the two older groups the male–female difference has virtually disappeared. But against this positive change there has been no narrowing of the rural–urban differential in death rates. This applies to all children and across age groups, but is especially disturbing in the youngest age group, 0–4 years, which shows an extremely high death rate compared to the two other groups. These inter-age group differences in child mortality have not narrowed and the youngest children continue to be the most vulnerable.

A sharper focus on this vulnerability of the youngest children is necessary in order to better judge the remedial action required. Table IX.4 summarizes the relevant information on the sources of infant and child mortality. Note that

Table IX.2. *Life expectancy at birth*

Source (0)	Period (1)	Male (2)	Female (3)
Census life tables	1951–61	41.9	40.6
Census life tables	1961–71	46.4	44.7
Expert Committee on	1971–76	50.1	48.8
Population Projection	1976–78	52.6	51.6
SRS life tables	1970–75	50.5	49.0
SRS life tables	1976–77	50.8	50.0

Source: Sample Registration Bulletin, various issues.

Table IX.3. *Age-specific death rates*

Control group	0–4 years		5–9 years		10–14 years	
	1972	1978	1972	1978	1972	1978
Rural						
Male	58.5	48.9	5.6	4.2	2.1	2.1
Female	67.2	57.9	6.2	5.5	2.9	2.2
All persons	62.7	53.2	5.9	4.8	2.5	2.2
Urban						
Male	29.1	25.5	2.5	1.5	1.0	0.9
Female	35.7	27.2	2.7	1.5	1.4	1.1
All persons	32.2	26.3	2.6	1.5	1.2	1.0
Combined						
Male	53.2	44.7	5.0	3.7	1.9	2.0
Female	61.7	52.1	5.6	4.7	2.6	2.0
All persons	57.3	48.3	5.3	4.2	2.2	2.0

Source: Sample Registration Bulletin, various issues.

Table IX.4. *Sources of infant and child mortality*

	Rural				Urban			
	Infant mortality	Neonatal	Postnatal	Death rate 0–4 years	Infant mortality	Neonatal	Postnatal	Death rate 0–4 years
(0)	(1)	(2)	(3)	(4)	(5)	(6)	(7)	(8)
1970	136	80	56	58.1	90	49	41	32.3
1971	138	85	53	56.2	82	47	35	32.3
1976	139	83	56	55.2	80	49	31	29.7
1978	136	76	60	53.2	70	42	28	26.3

Source: Office of Registrar General (1980).

in both rural and urban areas the mortality rate for infants (age 0–1 year) is more than double the average death rate for children age 0–4 years. This implies that the special vulnerability of children below 4 years is really concentrated among infants less than 1 year old. Furthermore, the neonatal mortality (that occurring in the period immediately following birth) is much higher than the postnatal mortality.

This evidence suggests that the special vulnerability of infants has much to do with the condition of birth itself, the condition of the mother during pregnancy and the nourishment available to mother and child during the neonatal period. This is confirmed by 1981 data from UNICEF New Delhi which shows that respiratory disorders, fevers, digestive disorders and other clear symptoms account for about 80% of deaths among children age 1–4 years. They are also important causes of death among infants, but account for only 35% of infant deaths as compared to about 60% of infant deaths attributed to factors peculiar to infancy such as childbirth, condition of pregnant mothers and neonatal nutrition status of nursing mothers and babies. Infant mortality, we have seen, is a key element in the status of children. It is now clear that childbirth facilities, the condition of expectant and nursing mothers and neonatal or postnatal child care will play a key role in reducing infant mortality rates.

The second important feature about infant and child mortality to be emphasized is the persistent difference between rural and urban rates, as already noted in the context of age-specific death rates of children (Table IX.3) and sources of infant and child mortality (Table IX.4). The glaring difference between rural and urban infant mortality rates is highlighted in Table IX.5. Especially disturbing is the fact

Table IX.5. *Infant mortality by sex in rural and urban areas*

1970 (0)	Rural			Urban		
	Males (1)	Females (2)	Total (3)	Males (4)	Females (5)	Total (6)
1970	–	–	136	–	–	90
1971	–	–	138	–	–	82
1972	141	161	150	85	85	85
1973	141	144	143	88	90	89
1974	–	–	136	–	–	74
1975	–	–	151	–	–	84
1976	133	146	139	78	82	80
1977	134	149	142	69	65	67
1978	130	142	136	69	71	70

Source: Office of Registrar General (1980).

that not only are the rural rates much higher, they did not decline during the 1970s, as did the urban rates. Thus, by 1978 the rural infant mortality rate was nearly double the urban.

Using infant mortality as a key indicator of the status of children, we now begin to have the broad features of a hypothesis as to the causes of higher or lower mortality rates. One aspect is the complex of factors involving the access of mothers to trained personnel and other facilities for child delivery, the nutritional status of pregnant and nursing mothers and the quality of health care and nourishment which babies receive. The other aspect, indicated by rural–urban differentials, is the possible importance of human settlement patterns in relation to the availability of health-care and related facilities such as potable water, excreta disposal systems, etc. Thus, in a spatial sense it is much easier and cheaper to make health and other basic services available to a community when it is densely settled rather than widely dispersed.

It is possible to argue, however, that both these sets of factors are closely related to a third one, namely, income levels. Poorer mothers and babies have less access to health care facilities and nourishment than those who are better off; urban communities are on average much better off than rural communities. That economic conditions play a crucial role in determining the status of both mother and child is beyond dispute. But the question really is whether this is the only decisive factor or whether factors such as the availability of medical facilities, health care programmes and nutritional programmes have an independent role. If so, then the settlement patterns which affect service delivery to the mother and child target groups become a relevant consideration.

These are clearly issues of some importance for policy and programme planning.

A comparison of infant mortality rates for different maternal control groups taken from a recent survey (Office of Registrar General, 1980) shows there is a strong inverse relationship between infant mortality and the level of education of mothers as well as their age of marriage. The infant mortality rate for the illiterate rural maternal control group was 132 in 1980, more than double the rate of 64 for rural mothers with primary schooling and above. In urban areas, the figures were 81 and 49 for these respective groups. The maternal control group of rural mothers younger than age 18 showed an infant mortality rate of 141. The figure for rural mothers aged 18–20 was 112 and dropped to 85 for those 21 years and over. For the urban control groups, the infant mortality rate was 78 for mothers below 18 years, 66 for those 18–20 years and 46 for those 21 years and over. Age of marriage and literacy are associated since marriages may be delayed for mothers who enjoy a longer education. Thus, the relevant consideration here is really the level of education and experience of women when they get married or bear children. But once again the question arises, are these independent factors making for lower infant mortality or are they themselves purely a function of the economic status of households?

A partial answer is provided by a comparison of rural and urban infant mortality rates for children of mothers belonging to more or less the same economic groups, again based on data from the same survey. This shows that even when the economic group is controlled, infant mortality rates are much higher within the rural group. There seems a clear case for arguing that economic conditions apart, access to various mother and child-care facilities in a purely spatial sense and the availability of basic services such as water and sanitation do play an important role in determining the physical quality of life for children. However, these questions are far too important to be easily resolved through such simple control group comparisons and we shall return to this question after reviewing literacy trends.

6. TRENDS IN LITERACY

We have seen that literacy of mothers may be one of the crucial factors affecting infant mortality. In addition, increasing literacy is in itself a desirable goal which is relevant in judging trends in the physical quality of life for children. Aggregate literacy rates for the past 80 years as estimated from the decennial censuses show that improvements during the 1950s and 1960s were maintained in the 1970s. However, the absolute level of literacy, at barely 36% in 1981 (47% for males and 25% for females), remains extremely low. Female literacy rates are still well below those for males yet have improved at a faster rate, greatly narrowing the male—female literacy gap. At the beginning of this century, only one in every 15 literate persons was a woman. By 1961, every fourth literate person was a woman. In 1981, one out of every three literate persons was a woman.

Literacy rates as they specifically apply to school-age children (5—14 years) bear out the same trends observed in the aggregate. Literacy rates for this group continued to improve during the 1970s with female literacy rates rising more rapidly, although remaining well below male rates in rural areas. In 1978, rural literacy rates for the 5—14 year group were 59 for males compared to 39 for females, a rise from the 1971 rate of 37 and 21 respectively. In urban areas, the male—female difference is quite small: 79 for males and 72 for females in 1978. As expected, the literacy rate specific to school-age children is higher than the average literacy rate, but in 1978 was still barely 50% in rural areas compared to nearly 80% in urban areas.

The proportion of children attending school in various school-age groups, as estimated in the 1979 Infant and Child Mortality Survey, show the rural proportions to be as usual, much lower than the urban and the female proportions lower than the male. In the 5—9 year age group, for example, 52% of boys and 37% of girls in rural areas attended school, compared to 76% of boys and 71% of girls in urban areas. The

male—female difference is now relatively narrow in urban areas. It is, however, important to point out that the relative stability of the enrolment ratio across age groups, as revealed by the 1979 survey, contrasts sharply with the figures for 1980—81 recently released by the Department of Education (1982). The survey estimates an enrolment ratio of 50% for the 5—9 age group which *rises* to 56% for the 10—14 age group. Against this, the Department of Education figures show an extremely high enrolment ratio of 83% for children in the 6—11 age group which declines to a mere 40% for the 11—14 age group. It is not possible to reconcile these wide differences in estimates and school enrolment statistics must be treated with caution. However, the Department of Education statistics are consistent with prevailing notions about the rapid drop-out rate of rural children as soon as they are old enough to do some useful work.

A pattern of inter-state variations in general literacy rates, female literacy rates and the rates of change in literacy can be derived from the 1971 and 1981 censuses. A ranking of states by female literacy closely resembles their ranking by overall literacy. Also, as noted in the all-India statistics, female literacy has grown faster than male (hence overall) literacy rates in all states. A further heartening feature is that the literacy rate and the rate of change of literacy seem to be inversely related such that inter-regional disparities have narrowed. But it must be remembered once again that all these positive changes are registered under conditions where the absolute level of literacy remains low, registering only 69% overall and 64% for females in 1981 for the highest-ranked state: Kerala.

7. PUBLIC PROGRAMMES AND THE QUALITY OF LIFE FOR CHILDREN

Our fairly detailed review of recent trends in a large set of indicators has indicated that the quality of life for children in India has improved in recent years. These improvements, however, have been registered in the context of absolute levels of living which remain abysmally low. Furthermore, these general trends show important inter-state variations with conditions actually deteriorating in a number of states. The important question now arises concerning the impact of public programmes on the status of children. If some of the programmes undertaken by the government, along with international agencies, have played a significant role in bringing about such improvements as have been recorded, then the ability of the government and these agencies to maintain and expand these programmes becomes a crucial factor.

The relevance of public programmes for the status of children has already been partly addressed in Section 5 which examined the various factors affecting infant mortality. The main issue which emerged was whether factors which obviously played an important role in reducing child mortality, such as female literacy, access to childbirth facilities and the nutritional status of expectant or nursing mothers and infants, could be treated as basically a function of economic conditions or not. Apart from economic conditions, were these variables also affected by factors such as access to the relevant government programmes and the settlement patterns influencing delivery of services?

The question is examined here with reference to the observed inter-state variations in infant mortality rates — which we are using as the basic indicator of the quality of life for children.[7] In Table IX.6, 15 major states for which Sample Registration Survey infant mortality estimates are available have been arranged in ascending order of infant mortality. The first group of six states are those with relatively low (below 110) and declining infant mortality rates. The next four states have a medium range of infant mortality rates (110–130) which are also rising over time except in Assam.[8] Finally, we have

five states ranged at the bottom which have high infant mortality rates (over 140) which are also rising over time. It is interesting to note a regional pattern in the distribution of these states. The best states in terms of child status arranged at the top are mainly states from the northern and southern regions. The worst states at the bottom comprise a central belt stretching from Gujarat in the West to Orissa in the East. Bihar and West Bengal are two major states in the region which are excluded since Sample Registration Survey data is not available for them.

Along with infant mortality rates for these three sets of states, Table IX.6 also gives data on female literacy rates, the hospital bed : population ratio, the doctor : population ratio, the proportion of large villages (over 5000 population) to all villages in the state, and the per capita State Domestic Product. While the picture for the middle category of states is somewhat ambiguous, a comparison of the values of these different variables between the six top states and the five lowest states reveals some interesting associations. The states with relatively high per capita State Domestic Product are clearly bunched in the top category, whereas those with low per capita State Domestic Product are bunched in the lowest category. There is therefore a clear inverse relationship between this variable and the infant mortality rate. As

Table IX.6. *Inter-state variations in infant mortality and related variables*

States	Average IMR 1975–77	1981 Female literacy	Hospital beds per 1000 pop.	Doctors per 1000 pop.	Villages over 5000 pop. (%)	SDP per capita (Rs.)*
Kerala	52	64	0.90	0.38	97.3	1000
Jammu and Kashmir	66	–	1.58	0.27	1.6	825
Karnataka	81	28	0.81	0.21	7.9	1038
Maharashtra	94	35	0.74	0.56	12.2	1455
Punjab	104	34	0.60	0.49	4.9	1688
Tamil Nadu	108	34	0.55	0.29	26.6	997
Haryana	113	22	0.54	0.17	12.7	1514
Himachal Pradesh	114	31	0.95	0.14	0.3	1165
Andhra Pradesh	123	21	0.65	0.36	16.1	897
Assam	128	–	0.47	0.40	1.3	848
Orissa	141	21	0.41	0.27	0.8	834
Gujarat	146	32	0.56	0.38	9.5	1236
Rajasthan	146	11	0.53	0.23	5.6	973
Madhya Pradesh	146	16	0.33	0.15	1.9	790
Uttar Pradesh	181	14	0.40	0.20	5.5	727

Sources: (i) Sample Registration Bulletin, various issues; (ii) Census of India (1981); (iii) Pocket Book of Health Statistics; (iv) Census of India (1971); and (v) UNICEF, New Delhi (1980).
*Current 1975–76 prices.

we would expect, the quality of life for children is better in the states where the average household is economically better off.

We also find, as suggested earlier, that infant mortality is inversely related to the female literacy rate which is generally higher for states in the top category compared to those in the lowest. But the question persists: is higher female literacy itself due to the better economic condition of people in the better-off states or is it more a function of public policy? To resolve this we must go beyond the literacy variable to others such as the hospital bed:population ratio or doctor:population ratio which in India are clearly dependent on public programmes rather than on the level of individual income. Table IX.6 shows these variables also tend to attain higher values in the top category states as compared to the bottom category — the contrast in the case of hospital bed:population ratio being sharper than in that of doctor:population. The inverse relationship between these variables and the infant mortality rate clearly indicates that, economic factors apart, public sector intervention such as government health programmes have an important impact on the status of children.

To test the proposition that access to public programmes may depend partly on the settlement pattern of rural communities which account for the bulk of India's population, Table IX.6 includes a measure of the size distribution of villages in different states. In general, villages in most states are clustered in the range of between 500 to 5000 population. We have therefore taken the ratio of large villages with more than 5000 population to the total number of villages in a state. If Jammu and Kashmir and Punjab in the top category and Gujarat from the lowest category are set aside, the proportion of large villages tends to be higher in the top category states as compared to the lowest category. Interestingly, in Kerala, which is now widely known as a classic case where all components of the physical quality of

life index are exceptionally high in relation to the level of per capita income, over 97% of the villages happen to be such exceptionally large villages with over 5000 population per village.

Enough has been said to establish the relevance of public programmes of health, education and welfare — including nutrition, sanitation, drinking water delivery — in improving quality of life for children. We must now examine whether the government has been able to maintain and expand the scope of these programmes in recent years or whether the world recession — via balance-of-payments and budgetary constraints — has forced the Indian government to curtail such expansion in real terms. A comparison of the proportionate and absolute share of actual government expenditure on child-related programmes during the past 10–15 years, i.e. the period from the Fourth Five-Year Plan (1969–74) onwards, can be made from Economic Survey 1982–83 data which includes actual plan expenditure of the Central Government, State Governments and Union Territories. The programmes covered are education, health, family planning, water supply and sanitation, social welfare and other programmes, including nutrition. During the Fourth Plan period, child-related programmes accounted for an annual average of 15% of total plan expenditure. In the Fifth Plan (1974–79), this fell to 11.5% and further to 9.8% in 1979–80, the first two years of the Sixth Plan. This declining share notwithstanding, the absolute expenditure on these programmes has increased in both nominal terms and real terms since the overall size of the plans has also increased. The real expenditure on child-related programmes during the Fifth Plan period amounted to a massive increase of over 44% compared to the Fourth Plan. Subsequently the rate of real increase fell to only 4% in 1979–80. However, it appears to have picked up in the last two or three years, recording a real increase of 11% in 1980–81 and 22% in 1981–82.

NOTES

1. The exact age composition of the 1981 population is not yet available. However children of age less than 15 years accounted for 42% of total population in 1971, 42% in 1973, 41% in 1976 and 39% in 1978 (Office of Registrar General, 1980). It seems reasonable to assume therefore that they accounted for roughly 38% of the total population in 1981.

2. Note that the survey had a much smaller coverage than the census and that there are also differences in

definitions. Although the two sets of estimates are not fully comparable, the distribution of both observations are close enough to reveal general patterns.

3. Some of the recently formed states and union territories have been excluded since data is not available separately for these regions in the 1964–65 enquiry.

4. In addition, the decline in agricultural real wage rates cannot be easily related to the world recession.

Apart from the insularity of Indian agriculture discussed earlier, we must also remember that we are here discussing a decade which precedes the major onset of world recession. However, it should be noted that in India itself industrial recession set in from about the mid-1960s.

5. Participation rates for females of both age groups in both rural and urban areas have declined according to the NSS estimates. Since the NSS observations are exactly comparable, this estimate should be accepted in preference over the estimated rise in female child participation rates shown by the comparison between 1971 Census and the 1978 survey.

6. In particular, the reader should be warned against comparing the 1961–71 census actuarial report estimates with the annual figures or average for the 1970s based on estimates from the Sample Registration Scheme and 1979 survey. The coverage and the methods employed in the SRS and the survey are different from those of the census, such that the two sets of estimates are not commensurate.

7. We have already seen above that trends in the status of children as reflected by this indicator are consistent with those reflected by other indicators, e.g. life expectancy, anthropometric measures, literacy rates etc. Infant mortality is therefore used as the proxy index for this whole set of indicators.

8. The demographic data for Assam must be treated cautiously since trends have been blurred by the high level of unrecorded immigration from across the border etc. The 1981 census could not be conducted in this state where demographic questions have become a sensitive political issue.

REFERENCES

Census of India, *Census of India 1971*, Series I (India: 1971), Part II-A (i) General Population Totals.

Census of India, *Paper I of 1981* (1981), Provisional Population Tables.

Central Bureau of Health, *Health Statistics in India, 1978* (1978).

Dasgupta, R., 'Estimation of nutritional intakes', *Centre for Development Studies Working Paper* No. 139 (Trivandrum: 1981).

Department of Education, *Selected Educational Statistics, 1980–81* (1982).

Department of Social Welfare, *Handbook of Social Welfare Statistics, 1976* (1976).

George, K. N., 'Child labour in Madras city', paper presented to National Seminar on Employment of Children, New Delhi: NIPCCD, 1977).

Gopalan, C., 'Measurement of undernutrition: biological considerations', *Economic and Political Weekly* (9 April 1983).

Government of India, *Economic Survey 1982–83* (1983).

ICCW, *Working Children in Urban Delhi* (New Delhi: Indian Council of Child Welfare, 1977).

Labour Bureau, *Rural Labour Enquiry 1974–75, Final Report on Wages and Earnings of Rural Labour Households* (1979).

Mukhberjee, M., 'Physical Quality of Life Index' (Bombay: Centre for Monitoring Indian Economy, 1979).

Mundle, S., 'Land, labour and the level of living in rural Bihar', mimeo (Bangkok: ILO/ARTEP, 1982a).

Mundle, S., 'Land, labour and the level of living in rural Punjab', mimeo (Bangkok: ILO/ARTEP, 1982b).

Mundle, S., 'The effect of agricultural prices and production on the incidence of rural poverty: a tentative analysis of inter-state variations', *Centre for Development Studies Working Paper* No. 169 (Trivandrum: 1983).

National Institute of Nutrition, *National Nutrition Monitoring Bureau Report, 1980* (Indian Council of Medical Research, 1980).

NIPCCD, *Working Children in Bombay* (New Delhi: National Institute of Public Cooperation and Child Development, 1978).

Office of Registrar General, *Survey of Infant and Child Mortality 1979 – A Preliminary Report* (1980).

Office of Registrar General, *Sample Registration Bulletin* (various issues, 1980).

Seal, K. C., 'Child labour in India', reprinted in A. P. Barnabas *et al., Profile of the Child in India* (Ministry of Social Welfare, 1980).

Sen, A. K., 'How is India doing?', *New York Review of Books* (Christmas Number, 1982); reprinted in *Mainstream* (Republic Day Issue, January 1983).

UNICEF, *An Analysis of the Situation of Children in India* (New Delhi: 1981).

The Global Economic Crisis and the Impact on Children in Sri Lanka

GODFREY GUNATILLEKE and G. I. O. M. KURUKULASURIA*

Marga Institute, Colombo, Sri Lanka

Summary. – By the 1970s, Sri Lanka had already achieved a high level of mass well-being, literacy and labour force skills, making it possible to mount a massive investment programme in the late 1970s. Measures taken in 1977 to open the economy emphasized foreign investment and expansion of production, export promotion and employment. Because structures and levels of outlays on essential social welfare were maintained and external resource flows increased, Sri Lanka's economic and health indicators over the 1970s show on balance an improvement in living conditions although pockets of disadvantaged households exist.

1. THE BASIC SITUATION

Sri Lanka is a small developing island which throughout the post-war period has contributed heavily towards social and human development. Public policy and the pattern of government expenditure continuously safeguarded the lower-income groups' access to essential foods and to health, educational and other infrastructural supports that helped eliminate acute deprivation. When the period of stress came with the two energy crises of 1974 and 1979, the country possessed a socio-economic viability not present in most developing countries. By 1971 the country had already achieved a mass level of well-being far greater than that of other countries with a comparable level of per capita income. In 1980, despite a per capita GNP of only US $270, the social indicators portray a level of well-being associated with middle-income countries. Life expectancy at birth was 65 years, adult literacy was at 78.5%, the infant mortality rate had dropped to 44.8, the crude birth rate was at 30.4 and the crude death rate at 7.7% (*World Development Report*, 1982). Over and above the earned money incomes of the poor, support was provided by free health services, free educational services, subsidized food and subsidized transport facilities in a relatively well-roaded country.

Sri Lanka's progress over the period 1977–82 was achieved despite its considerable external dependency. As late as 1975, food and drink constituted 48% of the total value of imports. By 1982, this had been reduced to only 8.4%, exclusive of the import of whole wheat amounting to about 5%. Sri Lanka was also heavily dependent on the export of tea, rubber and coconut products. In 1975, these amounted to 76% of total exports, compared to 47.4% in 1982. The Colombo Town Consumer Cost of Living Index reveals that the weightage given to imported items in the working class index amounted to 35%. Given the nature and extent of this external dependency, it is obvious that the pattern of events in the global economy would have a serious impact on conditions of life for the masses.

Pragmatic policies protecting the weak have prevented external price fluctuations from seriously harming either urban or rural low-income households and their children. The policy of all governments has been both to protect the general body of consumers by subsidies/price control of essential food items and to protect the rural community of food growers by ensuring a floor price for specified items of food crops. The guaranteed price for paddy, for example, which was Rs. 33–40 per bushel in 1978 went through four price changes before it reached Rs. 70 in 1983. The open market price of rice kept a little ahead of the guaranteed prices, improving farmers' incomes when non-farm items were rising in price.

Sri Lanka suffered a relatively continuous drop in dollar terms of export prices and a steady growth in price levels of imported intermediate and investment goods. The 1982

* The views expressed in this paper are those of the authors and not necessarily those of UNICEF.

World Development Report points out that the increase in the value of per capita GNP between 1960 and 1980 was reduced from 2.6% a year in real terms to 1.1% after changes in the terms of trade are taken into account. These also affected the purchasing power of foreign loans and aid. However, it should be noted that the terms of trade figures over a long period may not be strictly comparable because of the changing pattern of the composition of imports and because recent imports (such as high priced textiles) get re-exported after value added in local manufacturing.

2. TRENDS IN THE 1960s AND 1970s

The 1960s were a decade of steady economic growth in the industrialized world. However, monetary and financial difficulties of the developed world led to a devaluation of the pound sterling by 14% in 1967 followed by a compensatory devaluation of the Sri Lanka rupee by 20%. The devaluation strengthened the export trades but, in order to cushion its impact on the cost of living, the rice ration at the subsidized price was reduced in December 1967 from two measures (4 lb) to one measure per person per week *and one measure per person per week was given free*. The minimum *real* wage rate actually rose in 1968. In the 1960s, Sri Lanka's population growth rate ranged from 2.2–2.6%, compared to 1.6–1.7% in the 1970s. The growth rate of real GNP averaged 3.7% in the eight years 1960–67. After devaluation and the controlled liberalization of imports under a dual exchange rate from 1968 onwards, the average annual growth rate of GNP in the three years 1968–70 was 6%.

The Cost of Living Index of the Colombo Town Workers (despite its defects) serves as an indicator of the real income situation of the low-income groups. Over the eight years 1960–67, it grew at an annual average of only 1.11%. In the three years 1968–70, a period of increased economic activity and of some protective measures for low-income households, the annual average rate of increase of the Cost of Living Index was 6.38%. For the sub-index for food items alone, the average annual rise in 1960–67 was only 0.9% compared to 6.62% in the years 1968–70. The 1960s, however, saw the imposition of import controls and the formulation of a Foreign Exchange Budget which by 1966 covered all merchandise imports. By 1965–67, as much as 60% in value terms of the island's merchandise imports were

handled directly by the government or government-controlled corporations. All other importers were subject to licensing and quotas. However, up to 1967 the change in the Cost of Living Index was negligible although many middle-class consumption items and development goods were expensive and/or scarce. Thereafter, the rise in the cost of living was accompanied by favourable GNP growth rates. The rate of growth of employment nevertheless continued to be unsatisfactory.

The first half of the 1970s were difficult years, marked by unsatisfactory harvests, high prices for imported foods and the crop failure of 1975. In 1971, the year of an insurgency engineered largely by unemployed youth, the GNP growth rate fell to an all-time low of 0.9%, but rose to 2.6% in 1972. Although the world food crisis of 1972–74 affected food import prices, the low-income classes were protected by subsidies, price control and rationing of essential foods.

3. CHANGE OF DIRECTION

A change of government in 1977 introduced new policies leading to a stage-by-stage disengagement from economic controls, subsidies and administered prices. ('infant milk food', however, continued to be a protected item.) To soften the impact of higher prices, wages were increased across-the-board by 25% subject to a ceiling of Rs. 50 per month. The people were to be protected by an increase in economic growth and in the volume, intensity and diversity of employment with an emphasis on production and productivity. The dual exchange rate was abolished in November 1977 and the US dollar which had an official rate of Rs. 9.15 was put at Rs. 15.97 and allowed to float. The IMF provided a stand-by credit of SDR 93 million to meet the stress of the immediate removal of controls and the new openness to imports. By 1972 the income criterion had already been introduced to the food subsidy system. No free rice was allowed to families paying income tax. At the beginning of 1978, the ration books were validated in terms of income classes earning up to Rs. 3600 per annum and their dependents.

In September 1979, the government introduced the Food Stamps Scheme which gave a flexibility to the use of subsidy benefits for food items and enabled the government to determine in advance the financial cost of the subsidy in terms of rupee cash. The food stamps were available for members of households of five to six persons with a combined monthly income of less than Rs. 300. The monthly amounts payable were Rs. 25 for those under 8 years of age, Rs. 20 for those between 8 and 12 and Rs. 15 for those over age 12. Only children under the age of 12 of eligible families qualified for the sugar ration at the government-controlled price.

The value of the food stamps covered the value of the prevailing ration of essential items. A separate series of stamps was issued exclusively for the purchase of kerosene at the subsidized price. About half the population of Sri Lanka came to enjoy the benefits of the scheme. Recipients were free to spend their stamps on items of their choice ranging over rice, flour and other cereals, sugar, milk foods, dried fish and pulses. Of the stamps issued for the 6-month period ending November 1981, as much as 18.6% was for children under 8 years. The scheme was liberally applied and because of an understatement of income more households than necessary qualified for stamps. There is also evidence that some households which were eligible under the income criterion had, for various procedural reasons, failed to get the stamps.

Exchange depreciation, domestic inflation and consequent price changes reduced the purchasing power of the stamps between 1979 and 1982. But over the years the rapid expansion of employment, wage rates and the intensity of economic activities (providing 'overtime' benefits and subsidiary employment) combined with decreases in household sizes and the dependency ratio softened the impact of price changes. The availability of a wide range of imported foodstuffs in the open market and their ready purchase by middle-class and affluent households reduced the pressure on the prices of cheaper food items purchased by the lower-income classes.

The change of economic policy was backed by a massive investment programme which included the Accelerated Mahaweli Multipurpose River Valley Project, a nationwide housing programme, the establishment of an Export Promotion Zone, an invitation to foreign investment with tax benefits and a liberal import policy. Raw materials and spare parts came in readily and much of the excess capacity of installed capital was eliminated. The construction trade expanded rapidly.

Under the new policy, the basic welfare services of free health and education remained intact. The government began to provide free textbooks to all school children up to Grade IX and to assist private non-fee levying schools

in meeting teachers' salaries. Three free universities were established in the North, East and South districts. The free midday meal for school children continued while the programme for the free supply of nutritional supplements to expectant and lactating mothers and to infants suffering from malnutrition was extended and strengthened until it catered to almost 500,000 beneficiaries.

Despite the recession in the developed countries, response from abroad to Sri Lanka's new policies was exceptional and very favourable, with foreign investment flowing in at an increasing volume. In the face of a relatively stagnant situation in regard to export volume and export price in SDR terms, Sri Lanka began the period of change with a standby credit of SDR 93 million from the IMF and an unprecedented expansion in the inflow of foreign resources. As a newcomer to the garment export trade, the country received relatively favourable quotas for export and protectionism abroad did not inhibit it. In 1973, the total of 'Foreign Loans and Grants' received by Sri Lanka was only Rs. 248.6 million (32.7 million SDR) compared to 101.8 million SDR in 1975. By 1980 it had risen to Rs. 6135.7 million (285.1 million SDR). The element of foreign grants by themselves, only 6.1 million SDR in 1973, had reached 121.7 million SDR by 1980. Total 'Official Transfers' consisting largely of grants (both project and commodity aid) from foreign governments and international organizations increased 8% between 1980 and 1981, from Rs. 3118 million (SDR 136 million) to Rs. 3379 million (SDR 147 million). Direct investment per year which was negative in 1975 was 36.36 million SDR in 1979 and 44.82 million in 1982. Other private long-term capital which was negligible in 1975 rose each year, reaching 175.89 million SDR in 1982. Central Government long-term inflow of capital items reflected in the balance-of-payments accounts which was 72.86 million SDR in 1975 rose to 217.1 million SDR in 1982. The foreign exchange situation was further strengthened by a rapid rise in annual net migrants' transfers which rose from 2 million SDR in 1975 to 225 million SDR in 1982. The annual net inflow from Travel (Tourism) rose from 11 million SDR in 1978 to 73 million SDR in 1982.

Certain other domestic developments assisted the country's import capacity. The country had set up an oil refinery in 1971 which now exports 40% of its production. The export of refined petroleum products (bunkers and naphtha) at the high going prices of these products eased the burden of high import prices for crude. When naphtha was used for domestic fertilizer production it stopped the import of urea and some urea was also exported. The export of petroleum products constituted 17.7% of the total value of exports in 1980 and in 1982 it was 15.3%.

The drive for domestic food production had also begun to bear fruit not only in terms of the volume of output but also in terms of domestic and regional food availability. The domestic production of paddy had increased from 43 million bushels in 1959–60 to 103.3 million bushels (1.5 million metric tons of rice) in 1981–82. The import substitution policies which began in the 1960s (which included government corporations in manufacturing) also supported the economy in the period of rising import prices.

Some characteristics of the changed pattern of resource utilization may be noted. In 1973 the import of goods and non-factor services was 20% of the total available resources. In 1977 it was 23% and by 1981 it was 32%. In resource utilization in 1973 consumption constituted 70% of the resources. By 1977 it was 63% and by 1981 it was 60%. The corresponding figures for 1982 for the import of goods and non-factor services are 31.8% and for consumption 60%. Gross domestic capital formation in 1973 was 11% of the available resources. By 1977 it was still at 11%. By 1981 it was 20% and in 1982, a little better at 20.7%.

Looking at the economy in its overall performance we see that after the setback in the year of insurgency 1971, there has been a steady annual growth in the real GNP. The average percentage growth in the three years 1974 to 1976 was 3.3%. In 1977 it was 4.4%. The impact of the liberalization of the economy in 1977 and the stepped up level of investment through foreign aid and foreign capital led to a growth rate of 8.2% in 1978, 6.2% in 1979, 5.6% in 1980, 4.1% in 1981 and 4.9% in 1982.

4. SOME INDICATORS OF SOCIO-ECONOMIC CHANGE, 1973–82

The well-being of children depends very much on the well-being realized within the household as a whole, the number of its income receivers, their level of income and their general health. The GNP growth must be taken together with the levels of real income and income distribution. From this point of view, a few general indicators for Sri Lanka are presented, relating to the decade of world economic recession.

The *Labour Force and Social Economic Survey of 1980/81* carried out by the Department of Census and Statistics revealed that the employment rate rose from 81.3% in 1971 to 84.7% in 1980–81. In 1971, the age-specific employment rate was as follows for the younger age groups: 63.2% for the 10–14 age group, 59.6% for the 15–19 age group and 71.4% for the 20–29 age group. In 1980–81, the rates for these groups were: 83.2, 60.1 and 72.9%. The unemployment rate showed a decline from 18.7% in 1971 to 15.3% in 1980–81.

According to the *Consumer Finances and Socio-economic Survey 1978/79*, carried out by the Central Bank of Ceylon, the average number of income receivers per household increased from 1.44 persons in 1973 to 1.64 persons in 1978–79. The average number of dependents per household had fallen from 4.18 persons in 1973 to 3.82 persons, indicating the improvement in employment.

With regard to housing, the percentage of rural housing units owned by a member of the household had risen from 66.9% in 1971 to 72.1% in 1981. The percentage of housing units with electricity rose from 9% in 1971 to 14.9% in 1981. During this period the average number of rooms per person also improved, rising in the urban sector from 0.36 in 1971 to 0.44 in 1981; from 0.40 to 0.49 in the rural sector and 0.29 to 0.39 in the estate sector.

Literacy also improved further as seen in a comparison of the 1971 literacy rate of 78.5 (85.6 for males, 70.9 for females) with the 1981 rate of 86.5 (90.5 for males, 82.4 for females). The primary school enrolment ratio, i.e. the number of children aged 5–10 years enrolled in Lower Kindergarten to Grade 5 per 100 children of the same age group, had risen from 68.77 in 1977 to 89.5 in 1980. The *Consumer Finances and Socio-economic Survey 1978/79* provides the 1978–79 age-specific literacy rates in terms of sectors. For the 5–9 age group, rates for urban, rural and estate sectors were 83.9, 84.5 and 62.5%. For the 10–13 age group, the rates for the same sectors were 94.6, 94.7 and 78.2%. Finally, for the 14–18 age group, the rates were 95, 95 and 72%.

Several recent surveys on the condition of mothers and children have provided data which, however, are not readily comparable because of differences in methodology and coverage. A nutrition status survey of rural pre-school children was conducted in 1975–76. Anthropometric and clinical assessments of children aged 6–72 months showed that for Sri Lanka as a whole an estimated 6.6% of the children suffered from acute (i.e. short-term inadequacy) malnutrition. Chronic malnutrition (stunting) rates, reflecting a long-term inadequacy, affected about one-third of all pre-school children (*vide* Cabinet Paper of 27 July 1980 on the *Nutritional Status in Sri Lanka*, published by the Ministry of Plan Implementation). During 1979–82, the Nutrition division of the Ministry of Plan Implementation in association with the Nutrition Division of the Medical Research Institute, Colombo, conducted an *ad hoc* survey which found that the rate of acute undernutrition among pre-schoolers was at around 5% for the island as a whole. The rate of chronic undernutrition was higher than 5% for all districts, ranging from 13% for Puttalam to 34.6% for Nuwara Eliya. The maternal mortality per thousand in 1980 remained negligible at 0.8. The crude death rate fell from 7.8 to 6.0 in 1981. The disturbing factor however was the increase in the infant mortality rate from 37.1 in 1978 to 37.7 in 1979. Whether this is a temporary setback or a recent trend cannot be established because of the absence of the rates for subsequent years. It appears that the infant mortality rate had risen somewhat in the urban sector but had shown a drop in the rural and estate sectors.

In 1983 the Ministry of Plan Implementation released a document entitled 'Socio-economic Indicators of Sri Lanka'. A few of the statistics relating to the human situation between 1977 and 1979 are shown in Table X.1.

The drop in the child death rate (1–4 years) was effected largely by a significant drop in death from enteritis and bowel disease from 0.62 in 1978 to 0.50 in 1979. Substantial amounts of foreign aid have been directed to the health sector. As coverage of immunization, family health and supplementary feeding campaigns was improved, the incidence of diphtheria declined from 216 cases in 1978 to 36 in 1981 and poliomyelitis from 153 cases to 84. Neonatal tetanus dropped from 874 to 185. Beneficiaries of the supplementary feeding campaign increased from approximately 293,000 in 1975–76 to 519,400 in 1981. The health services, however, have been affected by shortages of personnel at several levels due to the exodus of trained persons. In order to counter this, intensive training programmes have been initiated.

5. THE MOVEMENT OF REAL WAGES

An important indicator of the economic circumstances of low-income households and their children is the *Real Wage Rate Index* based on the legally enforced minimum (money) Wage Rate Index. This index frequently understates the real improvement in conditions because it does not cover income from subsidiary employment and payments for 'overtime' work and bonuses. Annual Reports of the Central Bank of Ceylon give the trend in the Real Wage Rate Indices for different categories of workers from 1960 to 1981, based on the legally enforced minimum money wage rates (1952 = 100). These show a gradual improvement which the energy crisis of 1974 did not halt. The index for agricultural workers had risen from 113 in 1974 to 121.6 in 1975, while that for workers in industry and commerce rose from 126.9 to 138.7. This increase continued to 1979 but dropped in 1980 and 1981. The index for agricultural workers, which

Table X.1. *Socio-economic indicators*

Item	1977	1979
1. Infant mortality per 1000 live births	42.4	37.7
2. Neonatal mortality	25.9	24.2
3. Postnatal mortality	16.5	13.5
4. Child death rate per 1000 population		
(i) 1–4 years	4.72	3.15
(ii) 5–9 years	1.78	1.15
(iii) 10–14 years	1.10	0.82
5. Age-specific child death rates per 1000 of		
population 1–4 years		
(i) All sectors	5.14	3.39
(ii) Urban	10.76	8.41
(iii) Rural including estates	3.94	2.31

Source: 'Socio-economic indicators of Sri Lanka', Ministry of Plan Implementation.

peaked at 225.3 in 1979, fell to 224.9 in 1980 and further to 190 in 1981. The index for workers in industry and commerce also showed a decline, from 170.9 in 1979 to 166 in 1980 and 157.9 in 1981. The particularly bad 1981 setback created by external prices and domestic inflation was, however, arrested in 1982.

The wage and employment situation improved in 1982 because of the decline in the rate of increase in prices. The real wages in both the organized as well as the unorganized sectors of the economy are estimated to have increased. From 1 January 1982, various allowances attached to the original salary levels were consolidated and then combined with the *continuation of the cost of living indexed allowances introduced in* 1981. This ensured that the nominal wages of government employees increased at a higher rate in 1982 than 1981. Their real wages as estimated by the Central Bank increased significantly by 19% in 1982 as against a decline in 3% in 1981. In the organized private sector as well, increases in real wages were experienced together with an increase in the volume of employment. The report of the Central Bank for 1982 observes that in the organized private sector the minimum wages of workers in tea, rubber and coconut sectors rose by 13% in 1982 compared to a marginal decrease of 0.2% in 1981. The minimum wages of workers in industry and commerce increased by 12% as against an increase of 13% in 1981. The real wages of workers in agriculture which, according to the Central Bank, had dropped by 16% in 1981 showed an increase of 2% in 1982. In the case of industrial and commercial sector employees, the real wage rate increased by 1.5% as against the decrease of 5% recorded in 1981. Thus, in 1982 there has been a tendency towards stabilization and improvement in the income-earning capacities of households.

The Annual Report of the Central Bank for 1982 indicates that a notable feature of the year's economic performance was a significant abatement in the inflation rate. After three successive years of high increases in the price level, the rate in the general level of prices dipped to a single digit figure in 1982. The average annual rate of increase in the Colombo Consumers' Price Index between 1981 and 1982 was 10.8%, while the increase registered by the Wholesale Price Index (WPI) was smaller at 5.5%, compared to the 1981 increases of 18 and 17% respectively. This success was achieved by the government's conscious and consistent policy of controlling

inflation by reducing the impact of budget deficits. The continued tight monetary policies of the Central Bank led to the success in demand management policies, while stability in prices of some of the imported goods due to lower inflation rates in the world also contributed to stabilization policies.

6. INCOME DISTRIBUTION

While the growth rate of the GNP was favourable after 1977, the more crucial factor for the welfare of poor households was income distribution. All deciles of households ranked in terms of household income had gained in money incomes, with the uppermost decile faring best. In regard to overall distribution, the 1977 Annual Report of the Central Bank showed an adverse trend in income distribution in terms of Income Receivers. This was to be expected because of the large numbers of young new entrants to the ranks of employed persons. The final report of the Survey of Consumer Finances of the Central Bank 1978—79 presented the data in terms of households ranked by household income. The data on income distribution among households in several recent surveys show that the distribution pattern has altered little since 1973. The cumulative share (of the increased overall incomes) had dropped for the lowest two deciles but thereafter the cumulative shares were similar to the position in 1973. Comparative data is presented in Table X.2.

A 1980 survey of the Nutrition Policy Planning Division of the Ministry of Plan Implementation evaluated the impact of the Food Stamp Scheme, examining household consumption levels on the lines of the 1973 Marga study, *An Analytical Description of Poverty in Sri Lanka.* The Marga study estimated the cut-off point for absolute poverty in 1973 at Rs. 36.50 per capita per month within a household regardless of which decile of 'Household Income' it fell into. The cut-off point for satisfying 'basic needs' was estimated at Rs. 47 per capita. The Food and Nutrition Policy Planning Division estimated the corresponding level of satisfying 'basic needs' in 1980 was between Rs. 75 and Rs. 80 per capita. At RS. 80 per capita, the level had risen over the years by 70.2%. If we compare this with the change in the Cost of Living (COL) Index for the Colombo working class we see that the COL Index moved from 165.4 to 318.2 in the same period (1973—80), a rise of 92.4%. These figures are strictly not comparable for a number

Table X.2. *Percentage income distribution of total incomes*

Decile (cumulative share)	Survey of Consumer Finances 1973	Survey of Consumer Finances 1978–79	Labour Force and Socio-economic Survey 1980–81
Lowest decile	2.79	2.12	2.0
First two deciles	7.17	5.73	6.6
First three deciles	12.77	10.38	12.3
First four deciles	19.29	16.06	19.0
First five deciles	26.74	22.65	26.7

Source: Survey of Consumer Finances 1978–79, Table 84.
The surveys of Consumer Finances of the Central Bank relate to Spending Units, i.e. a group that does its cooking and major expenditure as a group regardless of occupying a part of a house.

of reasons. The Policy Planning Division was going by an estimated five-person family whereas the lowest decile of households are constituted of smaller numbers. Again, between 1973 and 1978–79 the *average household size* had dropped further and the number of Income Receivers per household had also risen from an average of 1.44 in 1973 to 1.64 in 1978–79. The general conclusion which may be drawn is that the condition *in the poorest households* has not deteriorated but improved marginally. At other levels the improvement was appreciably better.

Another aspect of the situation of poor households and their children is relative movement of wages and prices that may be gathered from field surveys. The Country-Wide Data Collecting System of the Central Bank published data on price/wage movement for 1979 and June 1981 from field investigations. Taking 1979 as a base year (100%) these show the following average daily wage rate changes over the period 1979–June 1981: 152.8% for female tea-plucking workers and 141.3% for males; 158.6% for female harvesters and 147.3% for males; 148.7% for female rubber tappers and 141.4% for males; 169.1% for master carpenters, 164.1% for skilled helpers; and 169.5% for master masons and 158.8% for skilled helpers. The average retail prices of selected consumer items showed the following changes over the 1979–June 1981 period: 155.7% for parboiled rice, 187.7% for sweet potatoes, 131.8% for eggs, 155.3% for tuna fish, 160% for fresh milk, 189.5% for soap, 217.3% for kerosene oil and 166.3% for firewood.[1] These patterns have to be viewed in the light of the higher level of employment and intensity of economic activity after 1977. It should also be noted that both prices and wages continued to move up unevenly after 1981 and 1982. Although there were increases from 1974 onwards in the price

of rice, wheat flour, sugar, pulses and milk powder, there was a small drop in wheat flour and sugar prices in 1982 and the price of rice was fairly contained through liberal imports. The increases in domestically produced food prices were a gain for the rural population.

7. CONSIDERATIONS FOR THE FUTURE

Despite the global economic crisis, evidence shows that the economic condition within households and the welfare of children have not deteriorated in Sri Lanka but have improved in some respects. If the gains achieved are to be consolidated and improved, it will be necessary to sustain the level of economic growth and employment opportunities. The government forecast of trends is encouraging: the Ministry of Finance publication, *Public Investment: 1983–1987*, predicts an annual average growth rate of 5.6% in real GDP and a continued flow of external resources at a reasonably high level. The government has shown concern that there is room for improving the performance of both traditional and new exports. Import demand management is to be strengthened by controlling the budget deficit, which had risen to 23.1% of the GDP in 1980, was at 15.6% in 1981 and 17.7% in 1982. It is to be kept at around 14% in 1983. To control inflation and the balance-of-payments problem, quick-yielding projects and those leading to import substitution and the expansion of exports will be emphasized. Nevertheless, the volume of traditional exports is not likely to increase appreciably and export prices depend on factors beyond the country's control. Domestic paddy production is, however, expected to grow at an average of a little more than 5% per annum. In the case of imports, a continued high volume of intermediate and investment goods will need to be imported despite their rising prices; terms of trade remain an uncertain factor. While a good part of the higher level of imports in recent years were aid-financed, it is noted that imports grew in 1982 by 14% as compared with a 1% increase in 1981. In 1982 the exports had a growth rate of only 3.4% in SDR terms. The deteriorating rate of exchange of the Sri Lanka Rupee is another cause for concern: its continual depreciation is not a solution in the context of complex global interdependence. It is hoped that the decline in world fuel prices and in international interest rates combined with domestic demand management will help to contain the current account deficit in the balance of payments. It is in this context that the country looks forward to sustaining its level of employment, real income and well-being.

There are other dimensions in the life of the child which will draw our attention in the years ahead. At the National Symposium on the Changing Needs of Children held in September 1981 (by the Children's Secretariat of the Ministry of Plan Implementation in collaboration with UNICEF), it was pointed out that no special attention has been paid to the needs of the children of the 5–14 age group outside the school system.[2] These include the children who do not enter school at all, estimated to be approximately 11% of the children of the relevant age group in 1979, as well as another approximately 30% of the 5–14 age group who drop out of the system before they complete secondary education. These children prepare themselves for adult life through informal apprenticeship within the household, within the family farm and within other activities of an informal character. There is at present no systematic effort to reach these groups of children either for the special programmes available to school children, such as feeding programmes and school health programmes, or for any type of skill formation enhancing their capacity to participate in economic activities and social life.

It was also noted at the symposium that one of the major deficiencies of the system has been the failure to mobilize community participation in programmes concerned with improving the well-being of children. Although there has been some increase in the activities of voluntary agencies in work relating to children's needs, this type of participation has still been organized by well-intentioned urban groups. While some of these groups have been able to create a village base for their activities, there are as yet no clear signs that a self-reliant village infrastructure is emerging. The government programmes themselves have not been directed sufficiently at creating such an infrastructure and have continued to be essentially extensions of the centre-based government administration. Finally, there have been no visible efforts to enhance the quality of children's lives in regard to other important facets of their experience, namely, the world of play, recreation, cultural assimilation and the fulfillment of their creative personalities.

NOTES

1. Economic and social statistics of Sri Lanka — Statistical Department, Central Bank of Ceylon, Vol. IV No. 1.

2. See background paper on 'The needs of children' by Godfrey Gunatilleke.

The Plantation Sector in Sri Lanka:
Recent Changes in the Welfare of Children and Women

KUMARI JAYAWARDENA*

Colombo, Sri Lanka

Summary. – Although Sri Lanka has achieved high standards of mass well-being, physical quality of life indicators for the historically deprived plantation population fall well below the impressive national averages. This paper analyses the position of women and children on the plantations within the context of the global recession and national economic strategies. It highlights some of the programmes which, along with a legacy of concern for social welfare in Sri Lanka, have attempted to maintain and even improve the living conditions of plantation women and children.

1. THE SRI LANKAN ECONOMY

The recession in the world economy has caused severe difficulties for developing countries. The pressures on the Sri Lankan economy are evident from its terms of trade, taken as 100 in 1977, which have worsened considerably to 69.8 and from the balance-of-payments deficit of Rs. 11 billion in 1982. This period saw a fundamental change in the country's economic direction: in 1977 a programme of reforms was introduced to transform the inward-oriented, state-regulated economy to one in which the allocation of resources was determined by market forces. These reforms included devaluation and unification of exchange rates, import liberalization, removal of regulation on prices, freedom of capital movements and budgetary and interest rate reforms. These measures were intended to provide tax and other incentives for private capital – both local and foreign – to invest and produce. Another set of measures, including the removal of a significant portion of subsidies, the adoption of market prices for most of the goods and services supplied by the state and certain tax reforms, were designed to shift a larger proportion of domestic resources from consumption to public investment, mainly to provide the economic infrastructures on the basis of which economic growth over the longer run was to be maintained.

Economic growth quickened immediately with the 1977 reforms. During the period 1970–77, the rate of growth of real GDP had been 2.9% per annum; growth thereafter has averaged about 6%, being fairly evenly distributed among all sectors of activities. However,

this success has been achieved at a price; whether it can continue without some serious change also seems open to doubt. One of the major constituents of the 1977 reform package was the withdrawal of consumer subsidies to divert resources to productive investment. The cost of these subsidies had risen more quickly than revenues and had reached a point where such subsidies and current expenses consumed the whole of the revenue, leaving no resources for public investment. It was equally true that these same subsidies had helped Sri Lanka to achieve social conditions better than those in countries with higher income levels.

The first subsidy tackled was that on food, which in 1977 accounted for 24% of the state revenue. In February 1978, the rice ration was withdrawn from the upper half of the population; in September 1979, the rice ration was totally replaced by a system of food stamps which recipients with incomes below Rs. 300 per month could use for purchasing selected items of food. Since the prices of these food items were simultaneously increased to reflect full costs, the effect was to shift the uncertainties of subsidy costs onto consumers. Food stamps can be used (at the recipient's discretion) to buy a range of food items but because they have also become freely negotiable for cash, food stamps often are spent on other, non-food, requirements. The scheme when originally introduced covered approximately half the country's population; recent pronouncements indicate that in the new year of issue over

---

* The views expressed in this paper are those of the author and not necessarily those of UNICEF.

IWRC–K

800,000 persons will have to be added to the roll, indicating that the numbers of poor are increasing and that their levels of nutrition are on the decline.

Another major subsidy programme was on kerosene, used both as a lighting and cooking fuel by the poor. By 1981, kerosene was being priced at full-cost and kerosene stamps had to be issued to food stamp recipients. Full-cost pricing has also been adopted in all areas of services provided by the state of publicly owned enterprises, such as electricity, transport, post and telecommunications.

The net effect of these measures has been to reduce the outlay on the major subsidies from 35.7% of the revenue in 1977 to 15.9% of the revenue in 1982. However, there has been no discernible shift of local resources from consumption to savings. Public savings have remained at 13–14% of revenue, the savings on subsidies having been consumed by increases in other current expenditures. It therefore follows that the main component in the investment effort – about 30% of GDP – has been the use of foreign savings, which has risen from 4.5% of GDP in 1978 to a high 19.8% in 1980, coming down marginally to 15.1% in 1982.

Part of the foreign savings has come from aid and grants from various donors. Since, however, the proportion of concessional aid has been decreasing, Sri Lanka has been forced to draw down its international reserves and to resort to commercial borrowing to finance the balance. The use of international reserves has been such as to turn an inflow of 4.4% of GDP in 1975 into an outflow of 1.1% in 1982. Net commercial borrowings in 1982 were at 4.9% of GDP. Given the world economic recession and high interest rates, the continuation of development programmes at such high levels of foreign savings would appear very problematic. The need to rely on foreign savings has been caused in large part by a steady decline in the terms of trade due mainly to two factors: a sharp increase in import prices caused mainly by the rise of petroleum prices; and weak export prices, particularly for the island's plantation products. The combination of these two factors has been disastrous. Sri Lanka's effort to continue with its development plans and to preserve the 'open economy' in the face of this situation has led to serious balance-of-payment problems.

The position worsened in 1982 when the current account balance went into a deficit of Rs. 11,793 million, the equivalent of 575 SDR million. Given Sri Lanka's limited prospects for earnings from exports, the current account

deficit is far higher than can be managed over the long term. The deficit can only be brought down through reductions in expenditure and the further mobilization of domestic resources, processes which are likely to squeeze income further. One of the manifestations of the deteriorating financial situation is the increase in the size of the country's external debt and in the debt servicing ratios. At the end of 1982, the total foreign debt outstanding was Rs. 34,957 million, an increase of 19% over that at the end of 1981. The debt service ratio had been coming down during the late 1970s; amortization and interest payments in 1981 had been 8.7% of foreign earnings. This was mainly the result of repayments on short- and medium-term borrowing incurred in the mid-1970s following the first rise in oil prices. However, the level of government borrowings has increased significantly since then; more importantly, the proportion of commercial borrowings – short-term and at high interest rates – and of suppliers' credit in the composition of foreign debt has increased. Thus debt service payment over the next few years will rise sharply – the projected payment in 1982 being four times as high as that in 1981. A projection assuming a 3% growth of the economy indicates that by 1986 the debt service ratio will be in excess of 21% of foreign earnings. This indicates that the country's external position in the next few years will come under severe pressure from two sources: the imbalance on the trade account and the debt service requirements.

Another manifestation of the current financial situation with serious repercussions for the poor is the high inflation which, measured by all the available price indices, has risen very sharply since 1978. A fair part of this inflation has reflected international price increases; as approximately half of the goods comprised in the indices are imported, movements in international prices and exchange rates have a significant influence on prices in the domestic economy. Internally, administered prices rose, reflecting the elimination of consumer subsidies, and prices of domestically produced goods increased, reflecting the increased prices of imported inputs. The growth in the money supply is another factor; money supply (construed as currency plus demand deposits) increased annually at an average rate of 11.72% during 1967 to 1978. Subsequently it has expanded even faster; broad money supply including time and savings deposits grew by 23% in 1981 and by 15% in 1982.

However induced, the inflation has had

serious effects on the purchasing power of the poorer classes, particularly the earners of fixed incomes. Workers in the state sector and some parts of the organized sector have received wage increases, but their real incomes have declined over the past few years. In 1981, agricultural workers' real wages dropped by 16% and those of industrial workers fell by 5% but increased by 2 and 1.5% respectively in 1982. In the state sector, the real wages of technical and clerical employees fell by 5% and those of school teachers by 6% in 1981, but rose by 18 and 14% respectively in 1982. With some wage increases and a cost-of-living allowance tied to the index, the position has thus improved in 1982, but the fact that inflation has had an adverse impact on certain groups of wage-workers remains true.[1]

Another aspect of the impact of current economic policies becomes apparent when the income distribution figures are examined. The Central Bank of Ceylon's *Report on Consumer Finances and Socio-economic Survey 1978/79* shows the changes in the percentage of total income received by each 10% of ranked income receivers from 1973 to 1978–79 as follows: 1.80 to 1.20% for the lowest decile; 3.17 to 2.56% for the second decile; 4.38 to 3.60% for the third; 5.70 to 4.76% for the fourth; 7.10 to 5.93% for the fifth; 8.75 to 7.29% for the sixth; 10.65 to 9.12% for the seventh; 12.65 to 11.23% for the eighth; 15.91 to 15.26% for the ninth; and 29.98 to 39.01% for the highest decile.

2. THE PLANTATION SYSTEM

Strong traditions of social welfare in Sri Lanka have given the island very high indicators of physical well-being. Impressive national statistics, however, have tended to hide the existence of deprived pockets within the population. Perhaps the most deprived population group – economically, politically and socially – has been plantation labour, the descendants of Indian immigrants brought to work on Sri Lankan plantations in the mid-nineteenth century.

Based on the cultivation of tea, rubber and coconut, the plantation sector is even today dominant in the country's economy. It is the biggest contributor to the GNP, the biggest earner of foreign exchange and the largest employer. One of the essential ingredients of plantation agriculture is a cheap labour force. The original plantation crop, coffee, required a large input of labour during harvesting. Labour of the type required could not be obtained

from within the country but the British planters found a close source for the necessary labour in the famine-prone districts of South India. Tea replaced coffee as the leading plantation crop by the 1880s and the seasonal migrations of cheap labour gave way to a permanent settlement. Still a dependent labour force, the migrants were housed on the estates in what came to be known as 'coolie lines'.

The plantations were nationalized under the 1972 Land Reform Law and its 1975 amendment. As a result, 63% of tea, 50% of rubber and 10% of coconut lands became state-owned; the bulk are managed by two state organizations: the Sri Lanka State Plantations Corporation and the Janatha Estates Development Board. Attempts to run some estates on a co-operative basis or as labour collectives either failed or came into political disfavour after 1977 and were abandoned. While nationalization has not resulted in any basic change in the plantation system, it has forced the state to take a greater interest in the health, housing and general well-being of labour.

Two specific characteristics of the labour force need attention. First, it was composed primarily of immigrants who were deprived of citizenship rights for a long time and were thus bypassed by many of the country's social and economic developments. The first attempts to reform the work conditions of Indian labour in Sri Lanka date to 1920 when plantation managements were obliged to provide primary education for estate children. In 1921, workers were empowered to break the bonds of indebtedness tying them to estates. The Indian government also began to take interest and, as a result, the Minimum Wages Ordinance was extended to plantation labour in 1927, marginally raising wages that had not changed since the nineteenth century.[1a] Second, more than half the plantation labour force is female. The women have traditionally been assigned to the two most labour-intensive tasks – plucking tea and tapping rubber – which could profitably be assigned to the cheaper labour. Women workers are lower-paid than males and are restricted to unskilled tasks. Subjects of traditional male domination both economically and socially, women form a further deprived segment within the deprived plantation sector.

(a) *Women and children in the plantations*

If a separate Physical Quality of Life (PQL) Index were done for the world's women, Sri Lanka would rate very highly. It has a female literacy rate of 82% (compared to a national rate of 86.2%), a life expectancy of around 67 and a maternal mortality rate of 1.2. Particularly remarkable are the literacy figures which are among the highest in Asia. However, despite these PQL indicators, women in Sri Lanka's rigidly patriarchal society are exploited at work and in the home, where the father is legally the head of the family.[2] The low economic and social status of women is most evident in the plantation sector.

In the first 50 years of coffee cultivation in Sri Lanka, there were only 2.7 women workers to every 100 men. With the switch to tea cultivation, the numbers and proportion of women on the estates rapidly increased. By 1911, there were 84 women to every 100 men, rising to a 1 : 1 ratio in the next decade.[3] The proportionate numbers of children on estates also increased and, like the women, the children became a good source of cheap, docile labour. In 1981, the total resident plantation labour force numbered 922,000. The resident labour force of the estates taken over by the two government plantation agencies after nationalization was 792,000 in 1981: 208,700 males, 220,000 females and 363,900 children. Of these children, 26,300 were under age one, 98,600 were aged 1–5 years and 239,000 were aged 5–14. Women form 27% of the total resident estate population and over 50% of the work force; children form as much as 46% of the resident population, where the island figure of children under 14 is 36%.

Children between 14 and 16 years are legally part of the plantation labour force; they are used for weeding and receive a special children's rate of pay. However, even younger children work at jobs which are often invisible and unpaid. They help their mothers in plucking tea and in cash plucking and Sunday plucking. The increased output is registered as their mothers' work. Similarly, when a family gets a weeding contract for a fixed amount of money, all family members work, including small children. Children also perform other household tasks and it is their unpaid domestic labour that often enables the mothers to go out to work. The children affected (especially the girls) must drop out or forgo the opportunity of attending school, as borne out by the school statistics for girls. It should also be noted that many young estate children are employed as servants in other parts of the island, especially during periods of economic hardship.

In the nineteenth century, the proportional difference between men's and women's plantation wages was 25%. What is striking is that over a long period this proportion hardly changed although money wages rose. Even today, the estate women and children remain at the bottom rung in terms of quality of life. An estate woman works at her job from 7.30 a.m. until 4.30 p.m. On occasion, in the 'flush' season, she starts cash plucking work at 6 a.m. for the extra money bonus offered and plucks tea until 5.30 p.m. if there is a good crop. But it has been estimated that, with her labour in the home as well as her job outside the home, she works an 18-hour day.[4] The tasks of child bearing and child rearing fall heavily on these overburdened wage-workers. The estate women traditionally eat whatever remains after the men and children have been fed. This inevitably means that they are malnourished and anaemic. It is therefore not surprising that such overworked and undernourished mothers produce weak children and have inadequate breastmilk or that the rates of infant and maternal mortality on estates are higher than the rest of the country.

Apart from being underpaid and exploited at home and at work, estate women are the least literate group of women in the country. They come mainly from the socially deprived 'low' castes, and they also suffer all the usual disadvantages of belonging to an ethnic minority which feels politically and economically insecure and which has been in recent years subject to physical violence during communal rioting. Because of the high incidence of drunkenness on plantations, the women are also frequently victims of domestic violence.

(b) *Income and indebtedness*

The plantation wage structure is governed by minimum wage regulations. Periodically, the wage rates are officially declared for men, women and children separately. Plantations have always been a low-wage sector of the economy, paying subsistence wages and unequal wages for women. Daily wage rates for tea plantation workers increased steadily from 1973 to 1979 for men (Rs. 3.85–Rs. 14.00), women (Rs. 2.91–Rs. 11.69) and children (Rs. 2.59–Rs. 11.13). These rates held steady for women and children until 1982; male workers received a slight increase to Rs. 14.04 in 1981. In April 1983, daily wage rates for men, women and children on tea plantations were Rs. 16.87, Rs. 14.27 and Rs. 13.71, respectively. Wages for workers on the rubber plantations are slightly higher but followed the same trend. The injustice of wage differentials between the sexes, currently around 15.4%, has frequently been emphasized by women's organizations in Sri Lanka.

Although estate workers are drawing higher money wages than before, there has been increasing indebtedness and malnutrition among this sector as compared to the rural and urban sectors. Between 1973 and 1978–79, indebtedness in the island in general increased from 19.5 to 34.6%. The increases in the urban sector were from 26 to 31% and from 17 to 35% in the rural sector. The highest rates were in the plantation sector: from 17% in 1973 to nearly 40% in 1978–79, which has been attributed to 'increased short-term borrowings from boutiques (shops) brought about by the upward movement of prices'.

Indebtedness is a severe problem — especially for women and children who often suffer from the father's mismanagement of family income. It is sometimes customary on estates for the father to collect the pay of all working family members, including his wife although technically this is illegal. Money that should be spent on better food often goes for conspicuous or harmful consumption of drinks, clothing and, more recently, consumer goods — all items for which spending is increasing. Thus, malnutrition can increase even when money wages have risen.

(c) *Health*

The general health of the plantation workers has always been much below the national level. In the nineteenth century, the plantation death rates were so high that periodically a Mortality Commission would be appointed to investigate the problem. By 1920, the national death rate was 27 per 1000 whereas the plantation rate was 52. Even in 1969 when the island death rate was 8 per 1000, the plantation rate was 12. The *Socio-economic Survey* of 1978–79 introduced the recording of health status by various sectors which showed that sickness in urban areas was 7.5% of the sample population, compared to 8.6% for the rural sector and 9.7% for the plantations. Absence from work due to illness was also highest in the plantations where the number of absent days per person was 2.42 compared to 1.56 for the urban sector and 1.82 for the rural.

Commenting on the lower incidence and shorter duration of illness in the urban sector, the survey stated 'The urban sector's better health facilities, both preventive and curative, explain its better health conditions . . . its population enjoys better quality housing and amenities, such as sanitary facilities. Also its more educated population and the medical propaganda . . . have probably resulted in their being more aware of the health hazards, nutrition, etc. than their counterparts in the other sectors'. In contrast one may note that the estate sector lacked adequate supply of safe drinking water, proper housing and toilet facilities and was less educated and therefore less aware of minimum requirements for health.

The main reason for the higher incidence of diseases on estates has been the general malnutrition affecting plantation workers. Environment and climate are also factors. For example, respiratory illnesses were the main killers and were caused by exposure to cold and rain and by overcrowded housing. Intestinal complaints caused by impure water supplies and bad sanitation were also very frequent on the plantations. According to the 1978–79 data, the highest incidence of illness on the plantations is caused by various types of fever (28%), diarrhoea and abdominal problems (12%), breathing problems (18%) and 'maternal problems' (4.6%). In the case of maternal problems, the rural and urban rates were 0.74 and 0.56% respectively. The incidence of blindness was found to be greatest in the estate sector, perhaps due to Vitamin A deficiency.

The health deficiencies in the plantation sector are also reflected in the prevalence of stunting among infants, caused by protein energy malnutrition. While wasting is not a severe problem (village and estate figures showing no great difference), the incidence of stunting among plantation children is seen as a serious problem in the 1975–76 figures of the Centre for Disease Control's *Sri Lanka Nutrition Status Survey*. These show the percentage distribution of children aged 6–7 months by Waterlow categories as follows: 31.4% of the total rural population (weighted), 27.8% of the villages and 56.3% of the estate population fell into the stunting category. With regard to the wasting category, the figures for total rural, village and estate sectors were 3.3, 3.4 and 3.6%, respectively. For the wasting stunting category, figures for total rural, village and estate sectors were 3.4, 3.0 and 6.1%, respectively.

(d) *Infant and maternal mortality*

The differentials between the infant and

maternal mortality rates between the plantation sector and the rest of the country have frequently drawn comment. These differentials are not new. In 1920, for example, the infant mortality rate on plantations was 224 (per 1000 births) compared to the island rate of 182.[5] Table XI.1 presents some startling figures from the last 50 years, which show that *infant mortality,*

Table XI.1. *Infant mortality in estate and non-estate areas of Sri Lanka, selected years**

Year	Estate	Non-estate	Non-estate as per cent of estate
1930	194	172	89
1940	149	149	100
1950	108	79	73
1955	115	66	57
1960	100	52	52
1965	94	49	52
1971	93	41	44
1973	103	42	41
1974	163	43	26
1975	102	41	40
1976	110	n.a.	n.a.

Source: S. A. Meegama, *Socio-economic Determinants of Infant and Child Mortality in Sri Lanka*, Scientific Reports, No. 8 (April 1980), p. 16.
*Deaths per 1000 live births.

rather than declining, increased in the 1970s and that in 1974 it reached proportions comparable to the 1930s figures. Commenting on this table, Meegama writes, 'The extent of the differentials is not only surprising but shocking . . . the statistics indicate that *estate infant mortality has remained at a level between 95 and 115 per 1,000 live births during the last 25 years (excluding the famine year of 1974) and has shown a tendency to increase during the last few years'.[6]* It is ironic that this increase has coincided with international praise for Sri Lanka as a country with impressive PQL statistics.

Detailed statistics were collected in the late 1960s by the Ceylon Planters Association Estates Health Scheme, which covered the larger and better managed estates consisting of over 60% of the plantation population (Table XI.2). They reveal the high neonatal (death under 1 month) mortality rates of 60–70 per 1000 live births, in contrast to the national figure of 30, and the high post-neonatal rates (death between 1–12 months) which are reflected in the high infant mortality figures.

Samples taken in 1949 and 1966 show that

Table XI.2. *Infant, neonatal and postnatal mortality in member estates of Ceylon Planters Association Health Scheme**

Year	Infant	Neonatal	Postnatal
1960	90.6	62.0	28.6
1964	92.0	65.8	26.2
1969	100.7	67.4	33.3
1970	96.6	64.9	31.7
1971	92.6	66.7	25.9
1972	100.6	70.0	30.6
1973	103.8	70.6	33.2
1974	144.0	67.9	76.1

Source: Meegama (1980), p. 38.
*Deaths per 1000 live births.

the main cause for the high neonatal and infant mortality rates was immaturity and congenital debility which in 1949 accounted for 85% of neonatal mortality and in 1966 for 72% of infant deaths on estates (as opposed to 33% such deaths in the non-plantation areas). The other causes of infant deaths on plantations in 1966 were pneumonia and bronchitis (10%) and convulsions (6.8%).[7] The basic cause of the high mortality and debility of infants on estates is the severe and increasing malnutrition among mothers. Doctors working in the plantation sector have frequently commented on the gross anaemia among estate women. Other factors are the lack of hospital facilities, trained midwives and antenatal care and the low levels of education among estate workers as a whole and women in particular.

The mortality among older children and maternal mortality on plantations is also a cause for concern. The child death rates on plantations are higher than the rest of Sri Lanka, mainly due to malnutrition, the hazards of pneumonia and bronchitis in the colder climate and the lack of hospital facilities. Maternal mortality on plantations has always been around double the national rates. The rates for 1969 were 2.7% per 1000 live births on plantations and 1.5% in the island, the island rate falling to 1.2% in 1975.

Linking infant mortality to maternal health, the Medical Director of the Estate Health Scheme of the Planters' Association reported in 1969 that the infant mortality in estates under the scheme had increased from 84.9 (per 1000 live births) in 1968 to 100.7 in 1969. Almost 67% of the infant mortality on plantations was of infants under one month of age; in this connection, 'the high neonatal mortality is undoubtedly due to the poor condition of the infants at birth — the direct result of the *unsatisfactory state of health of most of the expectant mothers, brought on mainly by anaemia and under-nourishment'.* The Medical Director attributed the high incidence of maternal deaths to gross anaemia and deliveries in insanitary 'line' rooms, pointing out that the extreme anaemia of most estate mothers leads to a tendency to haemorrhage and that overcrowded, badly lit 'line' rooms are ill-suited environments for such an obstetric emergency.[8] The State Plantations Corporation's data on births in hospitals and estate 'line' rooms reveal that even today, half the births still take place in the latter. The figure rises to 81% in regions like Nuwara Eliya and is lower for the regions with easily accessible hospital facilities.

The gravity of the problem becomes most evident in exceptional famine situations when the first to be affected are the weakest, namely the infants, children and mothers. In 1974, as a result of sudden price rises linked with the oil crisis, the plantation areas — non-food-producing regions — suffered famine conditions. In that year, the national infant mortality rate was 51 (per 1000 live births) but the plantation rate was 163; whereas the previous year it was 46 and 103 respectively. The dramatic increase can be seen from detailed statistics of infant mortality rates for certain plantation regions. In Kandy, infant mortality rose from 62 in 1973 to 92 in 1974; the figures for those respective years were: 78 and 119 for Nuwara Eliya; 56 and 73 for Badulla and 46 and 51 for the national average (Department of Census and Statistics, *Bulletin of Vital Statistics*).

The statistics provided by the State Plantations Corporation for its estates in 1980 also show regional variations in infant mortality in plantation districts: areas near important urban centres with better facilities had lower rates. For example, Galle and Kalutara, with plantations near important urban centres, had IMR rates of 42.9 and 47.8 while Hatton with the largest concentration of plantation population and no large urban centres, had the highest rate (86.5) and other plantation areas like Nuwara Eliya and Haputale registering rates of 83.8 and 83.9 respectively.

(e) *Housing and health*

For over 150 years, plantation workers have lived in 'line rooms': barracks-type rows of single rooms built originally for a migratory labour force. This remains the most usual form of housing despite some effort to provide separate 'cottages'. In 1877, the typical lines consisted of a long building, partitioned into rooms 10 feet by 12 feet, with a long verandah 5–6 feet wide. Whole families of eight to nine people would live in a room. A recent survey has shown that five to six people on average live in old-style 'line' rooms;[9] and a 1973 survey of consumer finances showed that overcrowding in houses was 35% in urban and rural areas respectively, but was over double (75%) in the plantations.

A recent survey (1979) shows that 23% of estate households live in one room and 50% in two rooms, while the corresponding rural figure is 8.2% and 20.6%. Comparison with the urban and rural sectors also shows the poverty of the estate sector in terms of facilities and equipment. For example: 43% of estate households lack latrines, compared to 11% of urban and 26% of rural households; 1.7% of estate households have electricity compared with 38% of urban and 6.7% of rural households. With regard to pipe-borne water inside, 2.6% of estate households had this facility, slightly higher than the 2.4% of rural households but much less than the 20.4% of urban households in the same category. The percentages of households with kerosene cookers, the most prevalent type of cookers, were 26% for urban, 5.3% for rural and 0.9% for estates.

(f) *Creches*

Since the plantation sector had the highest number of working mothers, some rudimentary provisions were made to provide creches in the interest of seeing that the women came to work. The scandal of the creches was described in 1973 in the Agency House report: 'These creches are in the care of an old or crippled woman who cannot work. On the estates visited by the Commission, the creche was a small bare room, with not even a mat or chair, let alone equipment or toys to keep the children occupied'.[10] The children received no meals and the conditions were so deplorable that many mothers preferred to leave their children at home in the care of older siblings.

In a 1980 study of women plantation workers, Kurian investigated the difficulties women had in using creches. 'Non-attendance is normally due to . . . the question of distance . . . the condition of the creche (which) is often a determining factor, particularly when it rains'. She adds that apart from the creches upgraded with UNICEF assistance, the rest of the creches are totally unsatisfactory. 'Most of the old creches are badly maintained; they have leaking roofs, no running water, inadequate space and very rarely any other facilities. Even today the majority of creches are still in this condition'.[11]

(g) The lack of education on plantations

One of the biggest obstacles to social amelioration on the plantations is the continuing (and increasing) illiteracy of the workers. Schools have remained the least important sphere of reform and, ironically, after the government's take-over of estate schools (a long-standing demand by the trade unions and others), they have deteriorated further. A number of schools have actually closed down and the school-going population on estates has declined in recent years. It is particularly unfortunate that Sri Lanka, which claims to have the highest literacy and educational standards among Third World countries should be retrogressing in the case of estate education. The difference in educational standards between plantation and other sectors is shown clearly in Table XI.3 from the recent Socio-economic Survey.

The Socio-economic Survey report comments on the fact that of all ethnic groups the Indian Tamils, the majority of whom are plantation workers, recorded the worst educational profile. As many as 45% of the Tamils were found to have no schooling and only 7.4% of them had proceeded beyond primary education. A majority of the Indian Tamils live in estates where educational facilities are limited. Another factor is that employment opportunities in this sector are available for those of a relatively young age without minimum educational requirements. Finally, in 1977 there were 723 estate schools offering primary education up to Grade V. Children who then wish to proceed to a secondary education have to go to schools in the nearest town or village where they can be taught in Tamil. Moreover, there are only a very few government schools in the plantation areas teaching in Tamil and few can afford to go to a private fee-levying school.

Though the Socio-economic Survey of 1979 does not break down educational figures for the plantations by sex, the 1969 Socio-economic Survey does reveal the low levels of female education in the plantation sector: 56.8% of the women had no schooling, compared to 26.8% of the men. While 59.5% of the men and

Table XI.3. Percentage of population by educational status and by sectors, 1973, 1978–79

Educational status	1973				1978–79			
	Urban	Rural	Estate	All island	Urban	Rural	Estate	All island
No schooling (illiterate)	23.56	28.31	44.11	28.95	18.57	22.47	43.58	23.40
No schooling (literate)	3.05	2.66	7.60	3.21	1.09	0.92	1.08	0.97
Primary	33.73	38.69	40.55	37.93	33.89	39.55	47.39	38.92
Secondary	30.96	24.44	6.15	23.89	31.80	27.12	6.67	26.43
Passed SSC/ GCE (O.L.)	7.62	5.23	1.51	5.33	12.38	8.60	1.28	8.84
Passed HSC/ GCE (A.L.)	0.47	0.42	0.04	0.39	1.35	0.84	0.00	0.88
Undergraduate	–	–	–	–	0.18	0.14	0.00	0.14
Passed degree	0.26	0.13	0.00	0.14	0.60	0.29	0.00	0.08
Other	0.35	0.12	0.04	0.16	0.14	0.07	0.00	0.08
Total	100.0	100.0	100.0	100.0	100.0	100.0	100.0	100.0

Source: Socio-economic Survey.

42% of the women had a primary school education, only 11.7% of the men and 5.6% of the women had middle schooling. In terms of passing 'O' levels, 1.9% of the men had passed compared to 0.6% of the women. Only 0.1% of the men passed 'A' levels and over; there were no women in this category. The plantation schools were all taken over by the Ministry of Education by 1981 and are handled by a separate section of the Ministry.

Some recent data are available for 436 estate schools with a total of 60,891 children (35,925 boys and 24,966 girls). The total child population on these estates was 91,225, indicating that only 66% attended schools. The disadvantages the girls face is seen in the breakdown of figures: girls form 41% of the students between 5 to 10 years and 39% of those between 11 and 15.

From 1971 statistics of estate education, a similar pattern can be seen for the age groups from 5 to 19 years. It is interesting to note that 57.7% of girls aged 5–9 years attended school, compared to 55.8% of the boys in the same age group. However, a drastic decline in female education occurred after the age of 10: only 49.5% of girls aged 10–14 attended school compared to 69.2% of the boys. For the age group of 15–19 years, the rate had fallen to 6.7% for girls and 20.8% for boys.[12]

3. CONCLUSION

We have argued that low wages and oppressive living conditions (especially for women and children) are a structural ingredient of the plantation system and that the nationalization of the plantations did not materially affect its basic characteristics. However, nationalization created a situation in which the state was compelled to look more closely at the conditions of plantation labour.

This process has been materially assisted by the intervention of UNICEF and other agencies. In keeping with its concern for women and children, particularly of the most deprived segments of the population, UNICEF entered the picture with both material assistance and well-formulated programmes of action. This helped to stimulate the state agencies responsible for the management of the plantations to increase their own flow of resources into social welfare facilities for labour. The Sri Lanka State Plantation Corporation's expenditure on social welfare in five of its regions shows a rising trend. Schools have been taken over by the state and their capital and recurrent expenditures are now borne by the budgets of the Ministry of Education. However, expenditures on social welfare still amount to only around 4% of the total budget of the State Plantation Corporation.

The programmes now being implemented with UNICEF assistance relate to three main areas: (a) water-supply and environmental sanitation; (b) maternal and child health; and (c) child-care services. The water-supply and environmental sanitation programme concerns the provision of adequate supplies of safe water and sanitation facilities. The majority of estates obtain their water from sources — streams and springs — that are unprotected and polluted. Storage tanks and pipes have deteriorated due to insufficient maintenance funds, in some cases leading to their abandonment. The two state agencies have now begun to improve the situation with UNICEF assistance. The scheme will cover the construction of safe and protected sources — enclosed wells and pumps — and the laying out of gravity-fed piped water supplies to labour housing.

Plantations have always had some facilities for the delivery of health services to their resident labour. Small hospitals, dispensaries and maternity wards staffed by Estate Medical Assistants have been a general feature of plantation life. Statistics of health on the estates reveal, however, the general inadequacy of such facilities. The present efforts to improve these facilities, carried out with UNICEF assistance, are linked with an immunization and health education programme. The 117 key estates and 700 satellite estates have already been supplied with all equipment necessary for the programme. Training has been provided for 229 Estate Medical Assistants in the theory and practice of immunization. In addition, other estate staff such as midwives and creche attendants have also been trained to work with the Medical Assistants in immunization and other health programmes.

The plantation workers have long demanded adequately staffed creches where working mothers can leave their infants. There are an estimated 1600 creches on the estates, managed by the two state agencies. The improvement of the creches has been a key area in the social welfare activities of the two state agencies. Assisted by UNICEF, they have embarked on a programme of activities in this area involving considerable expenditures; the SLSPC has, for example, increased its expenditure on creches and related activities from a total of Rs. 4,322,000 in 1981 to Rs. 5,940,000 in 1982.

UNICEF programmes were initiated in 1977

and by 1980 the state agencies had begun to increase their expenditure on creches. The attention now paid to this area, under the stimulus of the UNICEF programme, is clearly seen when individual estates are considered. Data from the State Plantations Corporation showed expenditure on creches in Rayigama (Kalutara region) for example, to have been only Rs. 4,388,000 in 1979. This had increased to Rs. 8,050,000 in 1980, rising further to Rs. 13,988,000 in 1981 and Rs. 21,854,000 in 1982. Expenditures on creches in the Mahakanda Estate (Haputale region) rose from Rs. 20,729,000 in 1980 to Rs. 35,048,000 in 1981 and to Rs. 42,363,000 in 1982.

As a result of the UNICEF programme, 800 creches have been upgraded. A total of 1461 creche attendants have been appointed and provided with basic training in the care and nurture of infants. These creche attendants are now adequately equipped not only to look after the children, but also to advise the mothers coming to the creche on such matters as nutrition, hygiene and general health, and to make the creche a community centre.

Housing is another important area to which increasing attention is being paid. Only since nationalization has an attempt been made to provide labour with better housing. There are estimated to be 184,000 living units of the line-type on the plantations. These are to be replaced by cottage-type units with two living rooms, kitchen, latrine and verandahs in front and back. The two agencies have a budget provision of Rs. 40 million a year to improve housing. The present levels of investment on housing stock are being maintained only with assistance from agencies such as the World Bank, the Asian Development Bank and supportive governments like the Netherlands. In these circumstances, the provision of acceptable standards of housing to all plantation labour is likely to take a very long time.

(a) Social welfare infrastructure

Both state agencies have begun to establish the infrastructure needed to carry out and develop further these programmes, including: a technical unit staffed by qualified engineers and assistants to advise on and implement water supply and sanitation projects; staff and facilities at each of their 15 regional offices for the supervision and monitoring of health welfare programmes on plantations in their respective regions; the provision of two mobile units with audiovisual and training equipment to seven

Regional Training Centres. It should be noted that the impetus for creating this infrastructure derived from the UNICEF programme and the need to implement and monitor its various activities. There are social welfare divisions in the two agencies and co-ordinators at the regional level. Another step which should have important repercussions is the new appointment of family welfare supervisors on each estate.

(b) The impact of these programmes

We have described the plight of women and children on the plantation as manifested in areas like maternal and infant mortality. While there have been significant improvements in some areas on the plantations as a whole, others show cause for concern. The 1982 infant mortality rate for the total population is not available, but the figures for some regions of the State Plantations Corporation show increases in infant mortality since 1980. The infant mortality rate in Haputale decreased from 57.5 in 1979 to 50.7 in 1980 but rose to 71.2 in 1981. The 1982 figure is estimated to be 70.7. Data for Nuwara Eliya show a similar trend: the infant mortality rate decreased from 92.9 in 1979 to 83.8 in 1980 but rose to 94.7 in the following year and to 95 in 1982. This trend is reinforced by figures from 270 estates managed by the State Plantations Corporation and covering their eight plantation regions. The 1980 infant mortality rate for the estate sector was 68; the most recent statistics from these sectors give an infant mortality rate of 74, a prenatal mortality rate of 98.8 and a neonatal mortality rate of 45.6. The selected indicators for these estates shown in Table XI.4 would appear to indicate that general health conditions of mothers and children on the plantations still remain far from satisfactory. The success of the immunization programmes in rendering plantation labour immune to the common sicknesses that assail them will only become evident in time.

In this context it is important to measure the effect of the UNICEF-aided programmes in improving conditions. One indicator of maternal health is the haemoglobin test which reveals the extent of the mother's anaemia, a count below 50 showing acute anaemia. On three estates with UNICEF-aided maternal and child health programmes, the percentage of acute anaemia cases found in pregnant mothers tested was 58% for Kiribathgala Estate, 13% for Deniyaya and 4% for Culloden. This situation contrasts starkly with conditions on estates without such

Table XI.4. *Selected vital statistics for 1982*

	Infant mortality rate	Maternal mortality rate	Prenatal mortality rate	Neonatal mortality rate
Hatton	96.3	0.49	127.2	59.0
Matale	63.6	2.24	115.7	41.6
Nuwara Eliya	95.0	1.83	108.0	69.0
Haputale	70.7	0.62	93.2	45.6
Balangoda	52.8	3.20	63.0	27.1
Kalutara	53.3	0.94	74.0	29.6
Ratnapura	90.1	2.20	103.4	49.3
Galle/Matara	60.5	1.98	87.0	30.8
Total average	74.0	1.60	98.8	45.6

Source: Sri Lanka State Plantations Corporation.

programmes. To take one example, of 147 pregnant mothers on Pitakanda Estate in Matale, 123 or 84% had a haemoglobin content of less than 50%.[13]

The effectiveness — and acceptance — of the UNICEF-aided creche programmes are indicated by a comparison of creche attendance on four estates with such programmes and in two estates where creches exist, but without the facilities of the UNICEF programme. The percentage of children aged 1—4 years attending UNICEF-aided creches in January 1982 and December 1982 were: 56 and 94% for Culloden; 85 and 85% for Sunderland; 52 and 55% for Talangaha; and 59 and 87% for Deniyaya. In contrast, comparable figures for creche attendance by the same age group over the same period on two estates with non-UNICEF-aided creches were 50 and 37% for Nicola Oya and 16% at both periods for Selagama. It is quite clear that the total package of services in the UNICEF-aided programme has found favour with parents, as shown in the high and increasing percentages of creche use.

Recent surveys covering the 1975—76 and 1980—82 periods have shown a marked increase in wasting among infants and young children aged 6—23 months in the estate sector and an improvement in the 2—5 year age group. This unfortunate increase in the younger age group probably reflects the increasing malnutrition among mothers due to diet deficiencies (caused by inflation), their consequent lack of adequate breastmilk and the debility in small children that results from maternal anaemia. It is significant that the children (2—5 years) who tend to use the creches more frequently and are *also fed at the creche* showed less wasting in 1980 than in 1975. This highlights the importance of the creche as a centre where correct feeding

programmes can in a short time improve the general health of growing children.

However, more significant in the long term is the change of attitude towards the living conditions of plantation labour.[14] Nationalization and other factors have contributed, but it is obvious that the cooperation of UNICEF and, following their example, other agencies like the World Bank and the Asian Development Bank, have *been the immediate impetus for a growing concern with the social conditions of plantation labour.* While plantation managements have not always shown such a concern, new recognition that investment in social welfare improves both the quality of life and the productivity of estate workers has resulted in a budgetary provision of Rs. 8 million over three years from the funds of the two agencies for the programmes outlined above, excluding housing. The grants from UNICEF supplement this expenditure.

The individual planters too have changed their attitudes to labour. It is a hopeful sign that estate managers who earlier acted as seigneurs of feudal domains, showing little or no interest in the working and living conditions of their workers, are today interested in having creches, immunization programmes and maternal care services on their estates. Visits to estates and discussions with planters show that there is recognition that a healthy and contented labour force is an asset to a more efficient functioning of the system. Competition among estate superintendents to update creches and welfare facilities is a noticeable feature today. Another attitudinal change has been seen on visits to plantations where there is a UNICEF input into social welfare; namely that the earlier paternalistic handing down of benefits is being replaced by efforts to involve the labour force itself in the programmes and to obtain their active participation in implementation. This has borne fruit, as is evident from the creche programmes.

Yet these programmes are only a beginning. To extend them to cover the whole estate population is the prime task before the state. Whether the resources for this purpose can be generated entirely from within the plantation system in a period of economic difficulties is uncertain. Precisely herein lies the importance and significance of programmes like those of UNICEF which, while providing valuable assistance, also act as a catalyst to both the state agencies and others in a joint effort to assist the poorest of the poor, who in Sri Lanka are the women and children of the plantations.

NOTES

1. Central Bank of Ceylon, *Annual Report* (1982), pp. 73–74.

1a. For further details on the introduction of minimum wages to the plantation sector and the rise of trade unionism in this sector see, Kumari Jayawardena, *The Rise of the Labour Movement in Ceylon* (Duke University Press, North Carolina, 1972).

2. Women's organizations and feminist groups in Sri Lanka have persistently campaigned for equality for women. See *Report on the Status of Women*, (University of Colombo, 1979) and journals of the 'Voice of Women' (in English) and others in Sinhala and Tamil.

3. C. Kondapi, quoted in Shireen Samarasuriya, 'Oppression and exploitation of women workers in the tea plantations of Sri Lanka', thesis for Master's degree in Development Studies (The Hague: ISS, 1981), p. 61.

4. Rachel Kurian, *Women Workers in the Sri Lanka Plantation Sector* (Geneva: ILO, 1982).

5. Administration Report of the Controller of Indian Immigrant Labour for 1925.

6. S. A. Meegama, *Socio-economic Determinants of Infant and Child Mortality in Sri Lanka*, Scientific Reports, No. 8 (April 1980), p. 38. Emphasis added.

7. Quoted in Meegama (1980), p. 39.

8. Report of Agency House Commission, pp. 135–136.

9. Helen Abell, *Tea Master Plan Study*, p. 30.

10. Report of the Commission on the Agency Houses and Brokering Firms, p. 142.

11. Kurian (1982), p. 102.

12. Quoted in Samarasuriya (1981), p. 141.

13. Statistics from the Sri Lanka State Plantations Corporation.

14. See Marga Institute, *Report on The Proceedings of the Mid-Term Pre-Review Workshop on UNICEF Projects* (April 1982).

Effects of the Current World Recession on the Welfare of Children: The Case of Korea

SANG MOK SUH*

Korea Development Institute, Seoul, Korea

Summary. — The remarkable growth of Korea's GNP during 1963–78 was achieved through export-led industrialization. The accelerating rate of growth in labour-intensive export industries provided job opportunities to the growing labour force. However, during the last years of the 1970s the Korean economy experienced bottlenecks and strong inflationary pressures which eroded its export competitiveness. As a response to these problems, the government implemented stabilization and restructuring programmes which did not affect the expansion of social welfare programmes for the poor and the vulnerable.

1. ECONOMIC GROWTH AND SOCIAL TRANSFORMATION: 1963–78

(a) *Korean miracle*

During 1963–78 the Korean economy grew at a rate of 9.9% per annum in real terms. In this period the annual growth of GNP in real terms never fell below 5.8%. This so-called 'Korean Miracle', a remarkable record by any standard, was achieved through export-led industrialization with exports and manufactured output increasing at a phenomenal 40.6 and 18.8% per annum, respectively. Within just 15 years, Korea became, by Third World standards, a highly industrialized economy. Value-added in manufacturing as a percentage of GNP increased from 14.6% in 1963 to 27.0% in 1978, while value-added in agriculture fell from 36.6 to 21.9%. Furthermore, employment in manufacturing as a percentage of the total employed population increased from 8.0% in 1963 to 22.4% in 1978, while employment in agriculture for the same period fell from 60.6 to 36.5%. High levels of investment were made possible during 1963–78 by a substantial increase in domestic savings from an average of 3.5% of GNP in 1960–62 to 24.9% in 1976–78. Total investment as a percent of GNP increased from an average of 12.8–28.0% in the same periods.

(b) *Economic policies and the role of government*

Underlying these quantitative increases in macro-aggregates were some significant policy and institutional changes during 1964–67 which reoriented the Korean economy away from import substitution toward export-led industrialization. In May 1964, the Won was devalued from 130 to 255 against the US dollar. In 1965, bank interest rates were approximately doubled for various types of loans. Other important reforms included a restructuring of the tariff system and a revision of the tax structure which, together with improvement in tax administration, ensured a substantial increase in government revenue, the ratio of tax receipts to GNP increasing dramatically from 7.1% in 1964 to 15.1% in 1970.

These policy changes — characterized as liberal — obviously contributed greatly to achieving the 'Korean Miracle'. However, they did not lead to a market-oriented economy because most decisions on industrialization and export expansion remained very much government-directed. For example, exporters were supported through the government-subsidized Korean Trade Promotion Corporation which was authorized to collect 1% of the value of imports for use as an export promotion fund. The government also set detailed export targets and monitored the performance of individual firms in meeting them.

Since 1962 the government has successfully formulated and implemented its Five-Year Plans. Although the first Plan was prepared in haste, planning techniques and procedures have

* The views expressed in this paper are those of the author and not necessarily those of UNICEF.

been greatly improved. The successful implementation of the Plans has been largely due to the seriousness accorded them. In 1962, the Economic Planning Board was established as a superministry in charge of plan formulation and implementation, headed by the Deputy Prime Minister, who also chairs the Council of Economic Ministers. Korea has used medium-term planning not only to chart a particular economic course, but to stimulate dialogue among divergent interests, to train government officials and to announce commitment to particular policies.

(c) Benefits of economic growth

Korea is often cited as an example of how growth can be achieved with equity. This was made possible through the country's export-oriented development strategy and its historically relatively even distribution of human and physical assets. When the Japanese withdrew from Korea in 1945, almost 90% of Korea's industrial assets and 27% of its cultivated land which had been owned by the Japanese, fell into the hands of the Korean government which disposed of these assets over a 10-year period. Shortly after two land reforms of 1947 and 1949, the percentage of absentee landlordship declined from 60 to 15%. In terms of human resources, educational opportunities were open to all after the liberation, thus increasing social mobility.

The accelerating rate of growth in labour-intensive export industries provided job opportunities to the growing labour force. Although the Korean labour force after 1960 grew at a rate of about 3% per annum, the unemployment rate fell from an average of 7.8% in 1960–62 to 3.6% in 1976–78. When human capital and national wealth are relatively well distributed, as in Korea's case, no distributive policy can be more effective than employment creation.

2. THE CURRENT CRISIS: 1979–83

(a) Economic trends and policies: 1979–81

Korea's rapid growth in the 1970s, particularly during the later years, created bottlenecks in the economy and led to strong inflationary pressures. A tightening labour market caused money wages in manufacturing to increase by 33% per annum during 1975–78 while real wages were growing at about 18%

per annum, clearly outstripping the 10% annual growth in productivity. Relatively rapid inflation, combined with exchange rate rigidity after 1974, eroded Korea's export competitiveness. By the end of 1978, export volume was showing signs of stagnation.

To tackle these problems, a far-reaching programme of stabilization-cum-restructuring was announced in April 1979. Tight monetary and fiscal policies were pursued while basic structural changes were initiated to steer the economy towards a market-oriented system further opened to international competition. However, this programme was overwhelmed by a series of unexpected events resulting in the most difficult period in Korea's recent history. The oil price increases in 1978 and 1980 raised the country's petroleum import bill from US $2.3 billion in 1978 to US $5.8 billion in 1980, with the price-induced increase equal to nearly 6% of GNP during 1979 and 1980. In October 1979, President Park Chung Hee, the chief architect of the Korean economic miracle, was assassinated. A period of severe political uncertainty and social unrest followed, with the situation returning to normal only after the ascendancy of the Fifth Republic under President Chun Doo Hwan in September 1980. Furthermore, unfavourable weather conditions caused a drop in agricultural output of about 22% in 1980, or over 4% of GNP.

As a result of these combined adversities, the Korean economy went into a recession in the second half of 1979, which further deepened during 1980. The real GNP growth rate was reduced to 6% in 1979, with the seasonally adjusted GNP declining during the last two quarters of 1979. GNP continued to decline during 1980, resulting in a negative 6.2% for the full year. In 1981, the Korean economy began to recover with a 6.4% growth of GNP. However, the increase in non-agriculture GNP was only 4%. Between 1979 and 1981, per capita real income declined by about 10%.

A rise in oil prices and devaluation of the Won accelerated the rate of increase in wholesale prices from 12% in 1978 to 39% in 1980. However, in 1981, inflation was substantially reduced mainly as a result of favourable external developments and a decline in agricultural prices due to good harvests. In 1981, wholesale prices increased by 20% on a period average basis but by only 12% on a year-end basis. The balance of payments in 1979–81 was heavily influenced by the sharp increase in oil prices and the slow-down in export growth. The current account deficit increased from US $1.1 billion in 1978 to US $5.3 billion in 1980, accounting for 9.4% of GNP in 1980. In 1981, the current account deficit declined to US $4.6 billion, despite a further increase in international interest rates.

The pattern of the Korean economy's adjustment to the second oil price increase contrasts in some important aspects with its response to the first. During the first oil crisis, Korea was able to reduce the current account deficit within three years to 1.1% of GNP in 1976 from the peak of 11.0% in 1974. This was achieved mainly through an extraordinarily rapid growth in export volume at an annual average rate of 29% during 1975—76. In contrast, the potential for export growth during the second crisis had been reduced by an erosion of Korea's external competitiveness and higher protective barriers in important external markets. The average rate of growth in export volume was only 15% in 1980—81 and the current account deficit declined to only 6.5% in 1981 from 9.4% in 1980. Economic growth suffered much more from the second oil shock which occurred during a slow-down in the Korean economy resulting from strong domestic demand pressures of earlier years. Finally, the sharp increase in world interest rates during the second oil crisis not only prolonged world economic recession but also intensified the pressure on Korea's balance of payments.

(b) Recent policy objectives

The Fifth Five-Year Plan (1982—86), launched amidst economic uncertainty in 1982, reflects a philosophy markedly different from the detailed quantitative targets and government controls of earlier Plans. Its basic objectives are to promote price stability, productivity efficiency and social development. During Korea's period of rapid growth, high inflation rates distorted resources allocation and contributed to worsening income distribution. Price stability, to be achieved primarily through monetary and fiscal discipline and wage restraint, has therefore been greatly emphasized in the current economic policy as necessary for efficiency and equity.

Productivity efficiency is to be enhanced through increasing internal and external competition. The government has implemented an Anti-Monopoly Act, taken measures to increase efficiency of the banking system and will change the current industrial incentive system to provide equal support and incentives for all viable projects. Social development is to be promoted in such a way that both equity and efficiency objectives can be met. The government's efforts to improve income distribution centre around the expansion of employment opportunities through rapid growth with minimum inflation. These efforts are combined with programmes designed to increase access to education for all groups in society. As the experience of many industrially advanced nations has clearly shown, enlarging educational opportunities is the surest way of guaranteeing an equitable income distribution in the long run, while increasing the supply of skilled and technical manpower in the short run.

(c) Recent economic performance

Korea's economic performance in 1982 was impressive, marked most satisfactorily by a sharp drop in inflation. During the year, the rise in wholesale prices was limited to 2.4% and the rise in consumer prices to 4.8%, due largely to a decline in commodities prices abroad. However, the government's efforts to finance budget deficits with minimum effect on the money supply and its active public campaign on wage restraint were contributing factors.

Korea's 1982 growth rate of 5.4% was achieved largely by a sharp rise in domestic construction activity, particularly in housing. Unlike other years, growth of exports was not a major contributor to the overall economic growth, amounting to only 5% real growth — a very poor performance by Korean standards. Reflecting the rise in savings and price stability, Korea's balance of payments improved substantially. The current account deficit, which was projected at US $4.4 billion early in 1982, shrank to US $2.5 billion.

(d) Short-term prospects

Overall growth for 1983 is projected by the Korea Development Institute (KDI) at about 8% on the assumption that the world economy, led by the US economy, will begin picking up substantially during the second half of 1983. In view of the Korean economy's growth rate of 9.3% during the first quarter of 1983, the momentum of high growth is sure to be sustained in the foreseeable future. Inflation should slow down further with an increase in consumer prices in the range of 4% and in wholesale prices in a 1—2% range. Expected stability in wage increase and oil price decline should more than offset any rises in the prices of imported raw materials.

3. POVERTY AND THE WELFARE OF CHILDREN

(a) Trends in key child welfare indicators

Lack of appropriate statistics makes it very difficult to measure trends in the welfare of children. However, the limited information we have indicates that the welfare of children in Korea has improved during the last decade or so. The infant mortality rate, still somewhat high compared to most developed nations, declined gradually from 53.0 per 1000 births in 1970 to 41.4 in 1975, 38.5 in 1978, 37.6 in 1979, 36.8 in 1980 and 35.8 in 1981. Similarly, morbidity rates of class 1 communicable diseases declined drastically except for bacterial dysentery, which appeared in the 1970s. The morbidity rate for typhoid, for example, declined from 13.1 in 1965 to 0.4 in 1981. Diphtheria fell from 3.8 to 0.1 over the same period.[1] The average height and weight of children of all ages also improved during the period 1970—81, as summarized in Table XII.1.

are employed; and, in some cases, children also must work.

In rural areas, child development problems are most severe in the remote island and mountainous areas which are characterized by a lack of access to proper facilities for meeting basic nutritional, health and educational needs. In general, the income level in these areas is far less than the national average level of rural households.

Several recent studies indicate the poor diet of pre-school children in urban squatter areas, whose intake of calories and all major nutrients was lower than the recommended dietary allowance.[2] The observed heights and weights of the children in these areas were generally lower than the national average. Similar conditions are found among pre-school children in remote island and mountainous areas. It can therefore be concluded that as the general health condition of children improves with economic growth, the policymaker's attention must focus more on low-income families, particularly in urban squatter and remote rural areas.

(b) Trends in poverty

Statistics indicate that during the last 15

Table XII.1. *Physical status by age, 1970–81*

Year	Age 6				Age 9				Age 12			
	Height (cm)		Weight (kg)		Height (cm)		Weight (kg)		Height (cm)		Weight (kg)	
	Male	Female	Male	Female	Male	Female	Male	Female	Male	Female	Male	Female
1970	111.9	111.9	19.3	18.8	126.3	124.8	24.8	24.3	143.7	144.2	36.7	37.5
1977	114.2	112.9	19.4	18.7	128.8	129.7	25.9	25.8	143.8	145.1	35.1	37.0
1978	114.2	113.1	19.7	19.7	129.1	129.4	25.9	25.8	143.8	144.6	35.1	37.4
1979	114.6	113.8	19.8	19.2	129.4	128.6	26.6	25.9	143.9	146.1	35.7	37.8
1980	115.0	113.7	20.1	19.2	129.9	129.4	26.8	26.3	144.2	146.5	35.6	38.1
1981	115.4	114.5	20.3	19.4	130.8	130.1	27.2	26.4	145.3	147.4	36.4	38.3

Source: Ministry of Education, *Statistical Yearbook of Education* (1971, 1978–82).

Despite this overall improvement in child welfare throughout the 1960s and 1970s, indicators in terms of health care, nutritional status and educational opportunities tend to show that low-income children fared less well than those from higher-income groups. Low-income urban households are mostly found in squatter areas where the cost of living is higher and the physical living environment often worse than in rural areas. The low family income influences child development in many ways: expenditure for nutrition is small, most mothers from low-income families

years absolute poverty has declined significantly as employment opportunities have increased rapidly, a result of high economic growth (Table XII.2). The incidence of absolute poverty (defined as 121,000 Won or less per month in 1981 prices for a five-member family) declined from 40.9% in 1965 to 9.8% in 1980.[3] However, the 1960s showed a higher rate of decline in the incidence of absolute poverty than the 1970s. This perhaps implies that the effectiveness of the high-growth strategy in this regard tends to diminish as the hard-core poor, who do not benefit directly from economic growth,

Table XII.2. *Trends in the incidence of poverty**

	Absolute† poverty	Relative‡ poverty
1965	40.9	12.2
Urban	54.9	17.9
Rural	35.8	10.0
1970	23.4	4.8
Urban	16.2	7.0
Rural	27.9	3.4
1976	14.8	12.4
Urban	18.1	16.0
Rural	11.7	9.2
1980	9.8	13.3
Urban	10.4	15.1
Rural	9.0	11.2

Source: Sang Mok Suh *et al.*, *Patterns of Poverty and the Anti-Poverty Programme for Korea* (Korea Development Institute, 1981).
*As a per cent of total population.
†Absolute poverty line defined as 121,000 Won in 1981 prices per month for a five-member family.
‡Relative poverty line defined as one-third of the average household income in a given year.

constitute a relatively larger proportion of the poor.

The regional composition of poverty in Korea changed markedly during the 1965–80 period. In 1965, only 36.1% of the poor were in urban areas compared to 61.7% in 1980. There are several implications as poverty increasingly becomes an essentially urban problem. First, as the price of land is much higher in urban areas, physical living conditions are likely to be worse for the urban poor than the rural poor. Second, as contacts among different socio-economic groups are more frequent in urban areas, the urban poor are more likely to be aware of their relative economic position in society. While for some, this awareness may serve as a psychological motivation to work harder, it may become a source of deep frustration for others.

The KDI study indicates that rural poverty in Korea resulted largely from the following two factors: the absence or small size of cropland, accounting for about 70% of the rural poor, and inability to work due to health reasons. While the relative proportion of poverty attributed to the latter cause is expected to increase, poverty caused by absence or small size of cropland is expected to decline as migration continues to urban areas. The same study shows that urban poverty stems mostly from four factors: inability to work due to health reasons (20%), migration from poor rural areas (60%), flight from North Korea during the

Korean War (10%) and descent from the middle class due to bankruptcy, dismissal or accident (10%).

(c) *Characteristics of the poor*

Determining the socio-economic characteristics of the poor is necessary for a deeper analysis of causes of poverty and for the formulation of an appropriate policy of response. Several characteristics of the poor in terms of household composition in 1974 are evident from the National Bureau of Statistics' *Special Labour Force Survey*. The following observations can be made:

(i) The average size of low-income households in urban areas was 4.8 persons, slightly higher than that of non-poor households (4.7). The average size of low-income households in rural areas was 5.0 persons, slightly lower than that of the non-poor (5.3). The proportion of those under 14 years of age was greater among the poor both in urban areas (2.0 in poor households, 1.6 in non-poor) and rural areas (2.2 and 2), respectively.

(ii) The proportion of households headed by a female or by a person over 60 was greater for the poor: in urban areas, 21.6% of poor households were headed by females compared to 12.6% for non-poor. In rural areas, the figures were 18.4 and 9.1%, respectively. The proportion headed by a widow or widower followed the same trend: for urban areas 16% of heads of poor households were widowed, compared to 8% for non-poor. The figures for rural areas were 16.7% for poor and 8.5% for non-poor.

From the same survey, the following observations can be made:

(i) In terms of the percentage of unemployed household heads, urban households in general show a higher rate than the non-poor. In 1974, the head of household did not work in 35% of poor urban households, compared with 14% for the urban non-poor, 20% for the rural poor and 8% for the rural non-poor group.

(ii) Among the urban poor with a non-working head of household, unemployment was the most common reason for not working, accounting for 36%, followed by 'too old' (26%), 'housekeeping' (19%) and disabled (11%). Among the rural poor, 'too old' comprised 45% of the non-working group, followed by unemployed (19%), disabled (17%) and 'housekeeping' (15%).

(iii) The working poor constituted a majority of the poor: 65% in urban and 87% in rural areas. This implies that low wages and low productivity are important causes of poverty, although the proportion of the working poor is likely to have declined since 1974.

(iv) The incidence of poverty was relatively higher among daily and temporary workers. In 1974, these two categories comprised 46% of the urban poor and 31% of the rural poor, compared with 18% for the urban non-poor and 12% for the rural non-poor. The incidence of poverty was relatively lower among employers and permanent employees: 19.5% of urban poor and 6.2% of rural poor compared with 49.9% of urban non-poor and 17.1% of rural non-poor.

(v) The incidence of poverty was somewhat higher among production and agriculture-related workers. In 1974, these two categories comprised 68% of the urban poor and 90% of the rural poor, compared with 48% for the urban non-poor and 84% for the rural non-poor. The incidence of poverty was relatively lower among professional, technical, administrative, managerial and clerical workers: 5.5% of urban poor and 1.6% of rural poor compared with 22.6% of urban non-poor and 8.3% of rural non-poor.

The employment status of the urban poor can be analysed using recent data from the 1981 KDI *Survey of Low-income Households in Seoul*. In 1981, 32% of the heads of poor households in Seoul were not employed. The reasons given were mostly lack of employment opportunities and inability to work due to old age, illness or housekeeping. The majority of those employed were unskilled labourers (36%) or street vendors (13%).

Schooling is often an important determinant of labour productivity and wages. According to the 1981 Survey of Social Indicators undertaken by the National Bureau of Statistics, 17% of the urban poor and 37% of the rural poor had no schooling, compared to 6% for the urban non-poor and 22% for the rural non-poor. Furthermore, 28% of the urban poor and 39% of the rural poor had only an elementary school education, as compared to 22% for the urban non-poor and 43% for the rural non-poor.

The vicious circle of ill health, malnutrition and poverty is well known. The Seoul Municipal Government's 1981 *Survey of Low-income Families* indicates that 8% of the poor in Seoul were physically or mentally handicapped and 12% were suffering from serious illness in 1981. Very often, the person who was not healthy was the household head. Although overall nutrition levels have improved with the rising level of real income in Korea, malnutrition still exists, particularly among the urban poor. Malnutrition often has a particularly serious impact on young children and expectant mothers. The heights and weights of urban squatter children are generally found to be much lower than the national averages.

The housing situation, generally inadequate in Korea, is especially bad for poor urban households. A Ministry of Health and Social Affairs survey of Livelihood Protection Programme (LPP) Beneficiaries showed that in 1981 about 83% of the poor households in large cities relied on rental housing and 79% of the poor households in large cities were living in one room. Furthermore, many of the urban poor were residing in illegal housing units. It is estimated that there were about 154,000 illegal housing units in Seoul in 1981. Assuming eight occupants per each illegal housing unit, about 15% of the population in Seoul resided in illegal housing.

4. EVALUATION OF SOCIAL POLICIES CONCERNING CHILDREN, THE POOR, AND THE VULNERABLE

(a) *Trends in social policies and expenditures*

During the 1962–78 period, Korea's economic policies emphasized growth rather than social welfare. The proportion of government expenditures in the social welfare field (excluding education) during 1976–78 was only 7%, well below the level for other countries with similar per capita incomes. Despite this low priority, the economic welfare of the general public improved significantly as a result of rapid growth, a clear example that promotion of economic growth is often the best welfare policy for a developing country.

In recent years, government social welfare expenditures have increased not only in absolute terms but also in relative terms with respect to other government expenditures (see Table XII. 3). During 1978–82, government expenditures in social welfare showed a nominal growth rate of 35% per annum and its share in total government expenditures increased from 22.4% in 1978 to 26.9% in 1982. The categories that

showed relatively higher growth rates during this period were social security and housing, as the government initiated several social welfare programmes, including medical insurance and aid programmes.

(b) Anti-poverty measures

Public assistance is the most direct means of helping the poor in Korea. Total government expenditures for various public assistance programmes amounted to 154 billion Won in 1982, reflecting a rapid increase in recent years (see Table XII.4). The Livelihood Protection Act of 1961 is the legal basis for the present income maintenance programme for the poor. Under the Act, the poor are classified into two categories: those unable to work (over 65 or under 18 years old); and those

Table XII.3. *Trends in government social welfare expenditures*

	1974	1978	1979	1980	1981	1982	Growth rate during 1978–82 (%)
Expenditures (trillion Won)	0.1840	0.7864	1.1746	1.5791	1.9250	2.5734	32.9
Education	0.1590	0.6426	0.9252	1.1961	1.5092	2.0386	31.7
Health	0.0087	0.0510	0.0856	0.0803	0.1005	0.1261	20.9
Social security	0.0150	0.0701	0.1310	0.1734	0.1948	0.2648	38.3
Housing	0.0013	0.0227	0.0328	0.1293	0.1205	0.1439	53.8
As a per cent of							
Govt expd.	17.7	22.4	22.5	24.4	23.9	26.9	
Education	15.3	18.3	17.7	18.5	18.8	21.3	
Health	0.8	1.5	1.6	1.2	1.3	1.3	
Social security	1.4	2.0	2.5	2.7	2.4	2.8	
Housing	0.1	0.6	0.6	2.0	1.5	1.5	

Source: Economic Planning Board.

Table XII.4. *Trends in public assistance expenditures**

	1965	1970	1975	1980	1981	1982
Livelihood Protection Programme	1.45	1.79	6.20	39.41	49.37	59.84
	(64.4)	(38.3)	(17.2)	(38.8)	(42.2)	(38.8)
Public works	0.30	29.21	31.90	18.04	13.00	13.00
	(13.3)	(42.8)	(81.2)	(31.4)	(15.4)	(8.4)
Medical assistance	—	—	—	10.71	22.47	32.47
	(0.0)	(0.0)	(0.0)	(10.5)	(19.2)	(21.1)
Emergency relief	0.49	0.88	0.57	19.52	27.10	48.93
	(21.8)	(18.8)	(1.6)	(19.2)	(23.2)	(31.7)
Total	2.25	4.67	35.97	101.54	116.98	154.24
	(100.0)	(100.0)	(100.0)	(100.0)	(100.0)	(100.0)

Source: Ministry of Health and Social Affairs.
*Billion Won; percentage in parentheses.

able to work but deemed absolutely poor. In 1982, about two million persons or about 5.4% of the population, received benefits from the Livelihood Protection Programme. In-kind assistance in the form of cereals is given to those unable to work. Cash assistance for fuel expenses and tuition exemption are available for both categories of the poor. Although it may be too early for an evaluation, the initiation of these tuition exemptions at middle schools and vocational training centres should enable children of low-income families to better compete in job markets. In 1982, a total of close to 43 billion Won was spent for the Livelihood Protection Programme.

The public work programme is an important means of helping the poor who can work. In 1974, 15.1 billion Won was spent on the programme, generating 15.5 million man-days of employment, an average of 34 work days per year for eligible households. After a rise to 19.6 billion Won in 1976, expenditure fell back to 15 billion in 1978, generating 6 million man-days or an average of 12.3 per eligible household per year. Public expenditures reached 34 billion Won in 1979 but have steadily declined, as the economic recovery has progressed, to 13 billion Won in 1982. The employment creation effect of the programme was estimated at 9.4 million man-days in 1980 (8 per household per year), compared to 2.3 million in 1982 (6 per household per year). The wage rates under the public work programme in 1982 were 3500 Won per day for a male worker and 3000 Won per day for a female worker. Typical work under this programme consists of road construction or improvement, cleaning of small rivers and streams, construction of rural irrigation facilities and miscellaneous urban construction.

When the new government took office in early 1981, liberation from poverty was singled out as a major objective of economic policy. At that time, the target population for anti-poverty measures was estimated at about 10% of the total population. Government asked KDI to undertake a comprehensive study on poverty and to make policy recommendations. The KDI study[4] played a pivotal role in charting the future course for anti-poverty policies in Korea. Its major recommendations, accepted by the government were the following:

(i) Top priority should be given to creating employment opportunities for the poor. The majority of the poor have the ability to work but remain poor because they cannot find suitable employment opportunities. Anti-poverty programmes should therefore focus on creating more jobs and improving the marketability of these people through job training and better placement services. Jobs are normally created through economic growth but when there is an economic slow-down, public work programmes should be increased as a counter-cyclical measure for the poor. Furthermore, job training programmes and placement services need to be strengthened, particularly in urban squatter areas. For those unsuitable for job training, business loans to small shop-keepers and street peddlers need to be expanded.

(ii) Special emphasis must be laid on preventing the transfer of poverty from parents to children. For this purpose, middle schooling and vocational training should be available free for low-income families and scholarship opportunities in higher education need to be expanded.

(iii) For those who cannot work for physical or mental reasons, various services available under the public assistance programme need to be improved. The government must protect these people by providing essential consumption goods or cash to buy these goods.

(iv) Family counselling by professional social workers and day-care centres for pre-school children are urgently needed, particularly in urban squatter areas. In developing a suitable delivery system for social services, private sector participation must be strongly encouraged to complement the government's leading role at the initial stage.

(v) The physical environment of urban slums must be ameliorated. Priority should be given to projects which will give high rates of return in terms of community welfare. In this respect, slum upgrading would be a more attractive project than construction of multistorey apartments and row houses. Once the government ensures security of land tenure, it can assist the residents' self-help efforts by supplying construction materials and tools at low cost.

(c) *Health policy*

Although the general health conditions have improved considerably in recent years, poor households do not yet have enough access to health care services. The government's health policies for the poor are thus extremely important, affecting the urban poor in particular. The government has recently made long-term plans for the promotion of mother and child health.

In the 1981 budget, expenditures for mother and child health care were increased to 5.24 billion Won from 0.99 billion Won in 1980, rising further to 11.74 billion Won in 1982. This was a drastic change, amounting to increases of 430 and 224%, respectively. In regard to both efficiency and effectiveness, mother and child health must be promoted in line with primary health care rather than independently.

As already discussed, economic and geographic factors exclude many rural residents from the health care system. Primary health care is considered a practical approach to making essential health care universally accessible to individuals and families in an acceptable, affordable way and with their full participation. Primary health care in Korea was first promoted by the Community Primary Health Care Demonstration project initiated by a loan agreement between the Governments of the Republic of Korea and the United States in September 1975. The project had two major purposes: first, to establish the capability within the government to plan, implement and evaluate low-cost integrated health delivery projects directed primarily toward low-income rural families; and second, to demonstrate successfully a multi-Gun (county), low-cost integrated health care delivery system that is replicable in other parts of Korea. The loan agreement created the Korea Health Development Institute (KHDI) which was charged with the actual implementation of the demonstration project.

At present, rural health care in Korea is made available through a dual system consisting of the public preventive health programme administered by the government and the treatment services provided mainly by the private sector. With strong support from the Ministry of Health and Social Affairs and with assistance from the United States Agency for International Development, KHDI asked that every effort be made to increase the support of private and public organizations in meeting the health needs of the rural poor.

In 1977 and 1979, medical insurance and assistance schemes were introduced which marked a turning point in the history of health care in Korea. In 1977, Korea embarked on a medical insurance programme designed to 'improve national health and enhance social security by facilitating access to medical care in the event of illness, childbirth or death'. (Article 1 of the Medical Insurance Law of 1976). In its first year, this programme provided compulsory coverage for both categories of LPP beneficiaries, a total of 3.2 million people or 8.8% of the population.

In January 1979, under complementary legislation, government officials, teachers and ancillary staff of private schools became compulsorily insured. This insurance programme has covered dependents of military personnel since January 1980 and pensioners and their dependents since July 1981. In 1979, the programme covered 7.9 million people, 21% of the total population. By 1982, coverage had reached 12 million people or 30.7% of the population.

In 1979, the medical assistance programme was initiated, which provided all medical services free to the first category of the LPP beneficiaries (those unable to work). The second category of LPP beneficiaries (those able to work) pay 50% of hospital expenses and have access to free out-patient services. The medical assistance programme, a turning point in improving health conditions for low-income families, currently covers about 10% of the population: all LPP beneficiaries and some additional low-income families. Total government expenditures for the medical assistance programme amounted to 33 billion Won in 1982 for a total of 3.7 million beneficiaries, compared to 1981 expenditures of 22 billion Won, again for 3.7 million beneficiaries.

5. CONCLUSIONS

In today's complex and interdependent world economy, the recent recession in developed economies has greatly affected developing economies such as Korea. The Korean experience has shown that the adverse impact of the worldwide recession can be reduced through some deliberate policy measures taken by the country concerned. In particular, the country can stimulate domestic demand so as not to seriously jeopardize its balance-of-payments position. Furthermore, the country can expand social welfare programmes for the poor and the vulnerable as the macroeconomic situation deteriorates. Obviously, the Korean experience may be unique to the Korean situation and may not be applicable elsewhere. Korea has been able to boost domestic demand through construction activity because of a large domestic demand and a very efficient construction industry. The fact that Korea also has a viable export sector and can actively resume its export activity with world economic recovery has enabled the Korean policymakers to rely on the domestic market as a 'second engine' of growth until the 'first engine' of growth (i.e. exports) regains its vigour.

NOTES

1. Ministry of Health and Social Affairs, *Yearbook of Public Health and Social Statistics*, 1982.

2. See Hee Kyung Kim and Sumi Mo, 1979; and Young Sun Choi and Sumi Mo, 1977.

3. Sang Mok Suh *et al.*, 1981.

4. *Ibid.*

REFERENCES

Chang, Soo Kyung, Michael Myungyun Park and Seoung Ho Oh, 'A survey of nutritional status of inhabitant and pre-school children in Korea Isle Area', *Journal of Korea Medical Art College*, Vol. 7, No. 1 (1976), pp. 13–22 (in Korean).

Choi, Young Sun and Sumi Mo, 'Studies on nutrition of pre-school children of low socio-economic group in Seoul', *Journal of Korea Public Health Association*, Vol. 3, No. 1 (1977), pp. 61–70 (in Korean).

Economic Planning Board, *Economic Management Plan*, 1980–83.

Government of the Republic of Korea, *The Fifth Five-Year Economic and Social Development Plan*, 1982–86.

Kim, Hee Kyung and Sumi Mo, 'Child nutrition survey in redeveloping area of suburbs of Seoul', *Home Economics Journal*, Vol. 4 (Seoul National University, 1979), pp. 33–49 (in Korean).

Mason, Edward E., Mahn Je Kim, Dwight H. Perkins, Kwang Suk Kim and David C. Cole, *The Economic and Social Modernization of the Republic of Korea*, Studies in the Modernization of the Republic of Korea: 1945–1975 (Cambridge, Mass.: Council of East Asian Studies, Harvard University, 1980).

Oh, Seoung Ho, Soo Kyung Chang and Michael Myungyun Park, 'Nutrition survey in Koje Island', *The Korean Journal of Nutrition*, Vol. 10, No. 4 (1977), pp. 231–246 (in Korean).

Park, Chong Kee and Kyu Uck Lee (eds.), *National Budget and Policy Objectives* (Korea Development Institute, 1981, 1982; in Korean).

Park, Chong Kee and Ha Cheong Yeon, 'Recent development in the health care system of Korea', *International Social Security Review*, Vol. 2/81 (1981), pp. 151–167.

Suh, Sang Mok, 'Patterns of poverty', in Chong Kee Park (ed.), *Human Resources and Social Development in Korea* (Korea Development Institute, 1980), pp. 336–371.

Suh, Sang Mok, 'Economic growth and urban poverty in Korea', *Social Science Journal*, Vol. IX (1982), pp. 37–48.

Suh, Sang Mok *et al.*, *Patterns of Poverty and Anti-Poverty Programme for Korea* (Korea Development Institute, 1981; in Korean).

Yeon, Ha Cheong, 'Medical insurance programme and its future development in Korea', *The Review of International Social Security*, No. 30 (1982), pp. 73–78.

The World Economic Crisis and the Children: A United States Case Study

C. ARDEN MILLER and ELIZABETH J. COULTER*

University of North Carolina, Chapel Hill

Summary. – This is a review of the United States experience with issues of child health and services, as they relate to changes in economic trends. No existing data systems are entirely adequate for reporting on the current health status of children, an important consideration for the monitoring of children's health in the United States is the focus on subgroups such as those who are disadvantaged for reasons of poverty, discrimination or geographic isolation. Ample evidence exists that children living in poverty suffer adverse health consequences and that the proportion of children living in poverty in the United States has increased steadily since 1975 and dramatically since 1981. Most measures of health status and health risks for children show steady improvements throughout the 1970s. The exercise of public responsibility for financing and providing essential services and supports held constant or improved during this recession period, especially during the recession of 1974–75. The health status and risks for children since 1981 appear to be adversely affected which must be attributed to a combination of circumstances that include serious recession, increased poverty rates for households with children and diminished health benefits and social support services. These findings suggest that when either local or widespread economic reversals are anticipated, health services and social supports for children need to be expanded rather than contracted.

1. THE POPULATION

With the post-war baby boom, the percentage of children under 18 years of age stood at a high of 35.7% in 1960, out of a total population of 180.7 million. As the baby boom children reached adulthood and the birth rate declined after the boom, the percentage of the population under 18 dropped to 34% in 1970 and under 30% out of a total population of 220 million in 1980. Reflecting the combined effect of the baby boom and the subsequent decline in the birth rate, the proportion, as well as the actual number, of children under age 5 showed a considerable drop in the 1960s, with a continuing decline in 1978, the proportion and number of children aged 5–13 years declined in the 1970s. As the baby boom children advanced in years, increased numbers of persons appeared in the job-seeking years and subsequently the early employment years.

The percentage of blacks in the population rose slowly from 10.5% in 1960 to close to 12% by 1979. With lower life expectancy and higher birth rates, the blacks constituted, however, higher percentages of the population of younger than of older persons; 12.5% in 1960 and 15% by 1979 for ages under 18 years.

2. TRENDS IN VITAL STATISTICS

Trends in natality, marriage/divorce and mortality provide additional information about

* Prepared by C. Arden Miller, Professor and Chairman, Department of Maternal and Child Health, School of Public Health, University of North Carolina at Chapel Hill, with the collaboration of Elizabeth J. Coulter, Professor, Department of Biostatistics, School of Public Health, University of North Carolina at Chapel Hill; and assisted by: Lisbeth B. Schorr, Adjunct Professor, Department of Maternal and Child Health, School of Public Health, University of North Carolina at Chapel Hill; Edward Brooks, Associate Director, Health Services Research Center, University of North Carolina at Chapel Hill; Amy Fine, Project Director, Child Health Outcomes Project, Department of Maternal and Child Health, School of Public Health, University of North Carolina at Chapel Hill. The views expressed in this paper are those of the authors and not necessarily those of UNICEF.

children and factors affecting their lives.

Birth rates per 1000 population declined from 23.7 in 1960 to 14.8 in 1976. A small increase in the birth rate occurred in 1977, followed by a slight decline again in 1978. Over the period of the 1960s and 1970s, declines in birth rates occurred especially among higher order births, above the second birth.

A sharp rise occurred from 1960 to 1978 in the proportion of births to unmarried women — from 2.3 to 8.7% among white women and from 21.6 to 47.6% among non-white women (*Natality*, 1978, pp. 1–5). It can be noted in this connection that the percentage of children under 18 years living with a single, never-married mother rose over the period 1970–79 from 0.2 to 0.8 among whites, from 4.4 to 11.9 among non-whites.

(a) *Divorces*

The estimated number of divorces and annulments showed a marked rise from 393,000 in 1960 to a little over a million in each of the years 1975–78, with an increase in the estimated rate per 1000 population from 2.2 in 1960 to 5.2 in 1978. The estimated number of children involved rose from 463,000 in 1960 to slightly over a million in each year from 1972 to 1978 — with an annual average of children involved per divorce (or annulment) of less than 1.4 throughout the period and of only about one from 1976–78 (*Marriage and Divorce*, 1978, pp. 2–9). Over the period 1970–79, the percentage of children under 18 living with a mother only who was divorced, rose sharply: from 3.1 to 6.4 among whites and 4.6 to 9.5 among non-whites.

(b) *Mortality*

Infant mortality rates have been of special interest, partly because in the past they have been used as important indicators of health status of a population. Over the period of the 1960s and 1970s infant mortality rates were considerably higher among non-whites than among whites. The rates showed, however, a marked and consistently steady drop over these decades. Specifically, the infant death rate per 1000 white live births dropped from 22.9 in 1960 to 17.8 in 1970 and 12.0 by 1978. The rate for 'black and other' births declined from 43.2 in 1960 to 30.9 in 1970 and 21.1 in 1978 (*Mortality*, 1978, pp. 2–3).

Death rates for children 1–4 years of age dropped slowly over the period 1960–78, going from 1.2 to 0.8 per 1000 males and from 1.0 to 0.6 per 1000 females.

Death rates for children 5–14 years of age showed a decline from 1965 to 1977, but the mortality rate for persons 15–19 years of age increased over this period. External causes of death — accidents, homicide and suicide — accounted for 80% of all deaths among young adults in 1979, up from 51% in 1950 (*Health United States*, 1982). In 1979 death rates for males were three times higher than for females and mortality among non-whites was 20% higher than among whites.

Rises in death rates due to homicides and suicides among the 15–19 year olds during the period 1965–77 merit special concern. For example, the homicide rate per 100,000 population in this age group rose from 4.3 in 1965 to 9.6 in 1975 (a year at the end of a recession period), followed by a small decline by 1977. The suicide rate per 100,000 persons in the 15–19 year age group rose from 4.0 in 1965 to 7.6 in 1975 and 8.9 in 1977 (Bureau of the Census, 1980, p. 98).

3. THE ECONOMY

(a) 1960–69

The decade of the 1960s was generally marked by economic growth except for some economic difficulties at its beginning and end. Gross national product in constant (1972) dollars rose irregularly each year throughout the decade, with increases in excess of 5% in 1962 and in each of the years 1964–66 (Table XIII.1). Output per person per hour (in 1972 dollars) for the private business sector rose by 1968 to 131.4 compared to 1960 as a base of 100 — a higher relative increase than for comparable periods of the 1950s and 1970s (Bureau of the Census, 1980, p. 410). Per capita income in constant 1977 dollars rose each year of the decade, from US $3620 in 1960 to US $4971 in 1969 (with a small subsequent decline to US $4958 in 1970).

There was little change over the decade in the overall civilian labour force participation rate, which remained close to 59% in most of the years of the decade. The rate dropped, however, among males from 83% in 1960 to 80% in 1969. On the other hand, it rose among females from 37.7% in 1960 to 42.7% in 1969 — a trend that continued into the beginning of the 1980s (Table XIII.2).

The unemployment rate for the civilian labour force was in a range of 5–7% for the years 1960–64. Throughout the remaining

Table XIII.1. *Gross national product, unemployment rate and Consumer Price Index, 1960–82*

| | Gross national product* | | | Consumer Price Index[†] | |
| | | | Unemployment rate as per cent of civilian labour force[‡] | 1967 = 100 | |
Year	Billions of 1972 dollars	Per cent change from prior year		Index	Per cent change from prior year
1960	737.2	2.2	5.5	88.7	1.6
1961	756.6	2.6	6.7	89.6	1.0
1962	800.3	5.8	5.5	90.6	1.1
1963	832.5	4.0	5.7	91.7	1.2
1964	876.4	5.3	5.2	92.9	1.3
1965	929.3	6.0	4.5	94.5	1.7
1966	984.8	6.0	3.8	97.2	2.9
1967	1011.4	2.7	3.8	100.0	2.9
1968	1058.1	4.6	3.6	104.2	4.2
1969	1087.6	2.8	3.5	109.8	5.4
1970	1085.6	−0.2	4.9	116.3	5.9
1971	1122.4	3.4	5.9	121.3	4.3
1972	1185.9	5.7	5.6	125.3	3.3
1973	1254.3	5.8	4.9	133.1	6.2
1974	1246.3	−0.6	5.6	147.7	11.0
1975	1231.6	−1.2	8.5	161.2	9.1
1976	1298.2	5.4	7.7	170.5	5.8
1977	1369.7	5.5	7.1	181.5	6.5
1978	1438.6	5.0	6.1	195.3	7.6
1979	1479.4	2.8	5.8	217.7	11.5
1980	1474.0	−0.4	7.1	247.0	13.5
1981	1502.6	1.9	7.6	272.3	10.2
1982	1476.9	−1.7	9.7	288.6	6.0

Economic Report of the President and Annual Report of the Council of Economic Advisers, 1983, pp. 164–165, based on data from the US Department of Commerce, Bureau of Economic Analysis; and US Department of Commerce, Bureau of Economic Analysis, 'The US National Income and Product Accounts: 1980–1982, First Quarter 1983', *Survey of Current Business*, 63, No. 7 : 7 (July 1983).

[†]For urban wage earners and clerical workers. *Economic Report of the President and Annual Report of the Council of Economic Advisers*, 1983, p. 221, based on data from the US Department of Labor, Bureau of Labor Statistics; and US Department of Labor, Bureau of Labor Statistics, *Monthly Labor Review*, 106, No. 8 : 64 (August 1983).

[‡]Relates to those 16 years of age and over. *Economic Report of the President and Annual Report of the Council of Economic Advisers*, 1983, p. 196, based on data from US Department of Labor, Bureau of Labor Statistics, with small adjustments introduced in the basic data in 1962, 1972, 1973, and 1978, and use of labour force data obtained from interviews in sample households.

years of the decade it stayed around 4% – low for the period 1960–83 (Table XIII.1).

Prices were relatively stable in the first half of the 1960s, with an average rise in the consumer price index of less than 2% for each year from 1960 to 1965. The price rises then began to accelerate, with an increase of approximately 4% in 1968 and 6% in 1970 (Table XIII.1).

The total sum (in 1972 dollars) for government purchase of goods and services, as part of the gross national product, increased from US $173 billion in 1960 to US $210 billion in 1965 and to US $250 billion in 1970. The sum for federal purchases accounted for US $90.4 billion of the total in 1960 and US $110.6 billion of the total in 1970 (*Economic Report of the President*, 1983, p. 165).

As in other times, special economic problems existed for selected groups in the population. For example, unemployment was relatively high for persons 16–19 years of age, for non-whites and for the less educated. Income was relatively low for some persons and families, such as those living in Appalachia.

Data on poverty in the 1960s are of special interest in view, partly, of attention that President Lyndon Johnson gave to the problems of the poor. In 1960, 22.2% of the persons in the United States were below the poverty level; by 1969 the percentage was 12.1. The propor-

Table XIII.2. *Civilian labour force participation rate, by sex, 1960–82*

Year	Civilian labour force as per cent of civilian noninstitutional population*		
	Total	Male	Female
1960	59.4	83.3	37.7
1961	59.3	82.9	38.1
1962	58.8	82.0	37.9
1963	58.7	81.4	38.3
1964	58.7	81.0	38.7
1965	58.9	80.7	39.3
1966	59.2	80.4	40.3
1967	59.6	80.4	41.1
1968	59.6	80.1	41.6
1969	60.1	79.8	42.7
1970	60.4	79.7	43.3
1971	60.2	79.1	43.4
1972	60.4	78.9	43.9
1973	60.8	78.8	44.7
1974	61.3	78.7	45.7
1975	61.2	77.9	46.3
1976	61.6	77.5	47.3
1977	62.3	77.7	48.4
1978	63.2	77.9	50.0
1979	63.7	77.8	50.9
1980	63.8	77.4	51.5
1981	63.9	77.0	52.1
1982	64.0	76.6	52.6

Source: *Economic Report of the President and Annual Report of the Council of Economic Advisers*, 1983, p. 196, based on data obtained from the US Department of Labor, Bureau of Labor Statistics, with use of labour force data obtained from interviews in sample households.
*16 years of age and over.

Table XIII.3. *Per cent of persons below the poverty level, by family status, selected years, 1960–81*

Year	Per cent* below poverty level†		
	All persons ‡	Persons in families	Related children under 18 years in families
1960	22.2	20.7	26.5
1965	17.3	15.8	20.7
1966	15.7	14.2	18.4
1966r	14.7	13.1	17.4
1967	14.2	12.5	16.3
1968	12.8	11.3	15.3
1969	12.1	10.4	13.8
1970	12.6	10.9	14.9
1971	12.5	10.8	15.1
1972	11.9	10.3	14.9
1973	11.1	9.7	14.2
1974	11.6	10.2	15.5
1974r	11.2	9.9	15.1
1975	12.3	10.9	16.8
1976	11.8	10.3	15.8
1977	11.6	10.2	16.0
1978	11.4	10.0	15.7
1979	11.6	10.1	16.0
1979r	11.7	10.2	16.0
1980	13.0	11.5	17.9
1981r	14.0	12.5	19.5

Source: Bureau of the Census, US Department of Commerce, 'Characteristics of the population below the poverty level: 1981', *Current Population Reports, Consumer Income*, Series P-60, No. 138, p. 7.
*Per cents are based on information obtained from population samples, with some limitation in comparability over time due to such factors as changes in sample design, census-based population controls, procedures for data collection, and definitions.
†Poverty levels were determined by definitions taking into account family or person income requirements in relation to food costs, with adjustments for family size and composition as well as price changes and without consideration of non-monetary transfers such as food stamps.
‡Beginning with 1979, includes members of unrelated subfamilies not shown separately. For earlier years, unrelated subfamily members are included as part of the family groupings.
r = Revised.

tion below the poverty level for related children under age 18 in families was 26.5% in 1960 and 13.8% in 1969 (Table XIII.3).

(b) 1970–78

The period 1970–78 brought changes and fluctuations in economic indicators that were in some cases disturbing, such as high unemployment in the worst recession that had occurred since World War II, slowing of the rate of productivity growth, and periods of considerable inflation. In interpreting these changes it is important to watch the indicators for some of the interrelated factors which contributed to the changes.

Gross national product (in 1972 dollars) declined slightly in the opening year of the decade (1970), then rose in the years 1971–73, declined in 1974 and 1975, and rose annually

by 5% or more for the remainder of the period 1970–78 (Table XIII.1).

A slowing of productivity growth occurred, with a variety of possible factors contributing to this: shifts away from some of the energy uses, relatively large proportions of new entrants into the labour force as the baby boom children reached adulthood and labour participation by women increased, and inadequate capital forma-

Table XIII.4. *Per cent of married women (husband present) who were in the labour force by presence and age of children, selected years, 1960–79**

Year	Total	No children under 18 years	Children 6–17 years only	Children under 6 years†	Children under 6 and 6–17 years
1960	30.5	34.7	39.0	18.6	18.9
1965	34.7	38.3	42.7	23.3	22.8
1970	40.8	42.2	49.2	30.3	30.5
1975	44.4	43.9	52.3	36.6	34.2
1978	47.6	44.7	57.2	41.6	40.9
1979	49.4	46.7	59.1	43.2	41.6

Source: Bureau of the Census, US Department of Commerce, *Statistical Abstract of the United States*, 1980, p. 403, as taken from Bureau of Labor Statistics, US Department of Labor, *Special Labor Force Reports*.
*Data are based on information obtained in surveys with some lack of comparability over time due to such factors as changes in sample design, census-based population controls, and procedures for data collection.
†With or without older children.

tion. The output per hour in the private business sector increased to only 113.9 when compared to the 1970 output as a base of 100 — considerably less than comparable increases for the periods 1950–58 and 1970–78. Increases in total hours worked by all persons along with a declining growth rate for the population helped, however, to offset some of the impact of the declining productivity on total output and output per capita for the 1970–78 period.

Following a decline in 1970, per capita income (in constant 1977 dollars) rose annually from 1971 to 1973, dropped to US $5462 in 1974 and to US $5425 in 1975, and rose in each' of the later years in the period, to reach US $5999 in 1978. Family income in constant 1977 dollars rose only 4% over the period 1970–77. A standardization for family composition brought the increase, however, to 7% (Bureau of the Census, 1980, p. 415).

Labour force participation rates increased somewhat in all but two years (1971 and 1975) of the period – from 60.4% in 1970 to 63.2% in 1978 (Table XIII.2). Following the trend of the 1960s a relatively large increase occurred in the participation rate for white females — from 42.6% in 1970 to 49.4% in 1978.

From 1960 to 1979 increases in labour force participation occurred among married women (husband present) with and without children under 18 years of age. For example, the percentage participation for the group with no children rose from 34.7% in 1960 to 42.2% in 1970, and to 44.7% in 1978. The percentages for the group with children under 6 years were 18.6 in 1960, 30.3% in 1970 and 41.6% in 1978 (Table XIII.4). Such increased labour force participation of women with children brought needs for changing types of services for

children, such as day care. It also potentially increased opportunities for the mothers to participate in work-related social benefit plans helpful for them and their families.

The unemployment rate for the civilian labour force increased from 4.9% in 1970 to 5.9% in 1971; then it dropped somewhat in 1972–73; rose again to 5.6% in 1974 and rose sharply to a peak of 8.5% in 1975; it remained above 7% in 1976 and 1977 (Table XIII.1). The rate was above average for such groups as women who maintain families, blue-collar workers, non-whites and especially for persons in the 16–19 year age group, reaching a level of 10% or more for each of these groups in 1975.

Another way of looking at unemployment is through the employment–population ratio, which looks at job holders in relation to the working-age population, rather than a labour force subject to considerable change in participation rates of the type seen in the past two decades. Data for the period 1970–78 bring out a different pattern of such ratios for adult males and females (20 years of age and over) in the non-institutional population. Civilian employment as a percentage of the population dropped, for example, from 76.3% in 1973 to 75.7% in 1974 and 72.9% in 1975 for males, while the corresponding percentages for females were 42.2, 42.7 and 42.3%.

Two types of cushions for the economic burden of unemployment should be noted:
(1) Presence of another employed wage earner in the family of the unemployed person. The entrance of increased numbers of women into employment as second earners helped provide such a cushion in the 1970s.
(2) Unemployment insurance. The year with

a peak unemployment rate for the 1970—78 period — 1975 — also saw peaks for this period for the state unemployment insurance programmes in the weekly average of initial claims for unemployment insurance of 478,000 and in the average weeks of benefits — 15.7.

The Consumer Price Index rose sharply in 1974, by 11% over the previous year, and by 9.1% in the following year. The percentage increase was, however, only 5.8% in 1976, followed by a rise to 7.6% in 1978 (Table XIII.1). The index for food and beverages rose especially sharply, by over 13%, in each of the years 1973 and 1974. The transportation index showed a sharp rise of 11.2% in 1974, with increases of over 9% in each of the next two years. In studying these price changes it is important to note that wage and price controls were in effect in the early part of the 1970s. A world oil price shock and worldwide crop failures which drove up food prices also occurred in the early 1970s.

Both federal and state/local government expenditures increased over the period 1970—78. The annual percentage increase in the expenditures was relatively great in 1975, especially for the federal government. The federal deficit also reached a marked peak in 1975. These increases have an importance for child health in ways that will later be emphasized.

The percentage of persons below the poverty level showed some increase in 1975. The percentage below the poverty level for related children under 18 years who were in families rose in both 1974 and 1975 and remained higher for the balance of the period 1970—78 than it had been from 1970 to 1974 (Table XIII.3).

(c) 1979—83

The period 1979—83 saw two recessions almost back to back, one in 1980, the other in 1981—82. The second recession brought considerable unemployment at a time when inflation started to drop. Important monetary controls and reduced federal support for some of the social programmes appeared during the time of the second recession.

Gross national product in 1972 dollars fluctuated over the years 1979—82, with a small percentage decline in 1980 and a larger one, approaching 2%, in 1982 (Table XIII.1). The annual index of output per hour for all persons in the business sector dropped in 1980 and then rose.

The civilian labour force participation rate rose slightly from 63.7 to 64% in the years 1979—82 (Table XIII.2). A relatively larger increase for white females, from 50.5 to 52.4%, continued the trend of the past two decades.

The unemployment rate for persons in the civilian labour force rose from 5.8% in 1979 to 9.7% in 1982 (Table XIII.1). With a rising seasonally adjusted monthly trend over the year 1982 it reached over 10% in each of the last months of the year.

An important change in the sex pattern of unemployment occurred in 1982. A particularly heavy impact of 1982 unemployment among adult men (ages 20 years and over) pushed their rate above that for adult women for all of the year. From July 1981 to December 1982 the unemployment rate for men rose almost 4.5 percentage points to 10.1%, while the rate for women went up about 2.5 points to 9.2%. 'This contrasts sharply with the 1973—75 recession, when increases were about the same for men and women (4.4 and 4.0 points) and the rate for men remained well below that for women' (Urquhart and Hewson, 1983, p. 7).

Age differences in unemployment in 1981 and 1982 are particularly important because of the impact both in the teenage group and on an age group in the population (20—24 years) in which a relatively high proportion first become parents.

'The employment situation for teenagers continued to worsen in 1982; their unemployment rate has shown a step-like pattern of deterioration since mid-1979. The teenage jobless rate levelled off in the final months of 1982, but was still a record 24.5% in December, more than 3 points above the rate reached during the 1973—75 recession' (Urquhart and Hewson, 1983, p. 8). Non-white teenagers had a particularly serious problem with an unemployment rate close to 50% during most of 1982.

The unemployment rate was considerably higher at ages 20—24 than at older ages, for each sex, in the third quarter of 1981 (at the outset of the downturn) and in the fourth quarter of 1982, as shown by the seasonally adjusted quarterly unemployment rates in Table XIII.5.

The extent of unemployment also differed considerably by state. In the first quarter of 1982 it was, for example, over 12% in Michigan (16.4%), Alabama (14.3%), Indiana (13.3%), Washington, Oregon, West Virginia, Ohio and Tennessee. On the other hand, it was under 5% in Oklahoma and Wyoming (Hewson and Urquhart, 1982).

Efforts have been made to determine the

Table XIII.5. *Adult unemployment rates, by age, selected quarters in* 1981, 1982, *seasonally adjusted*

Age group	Unemployment rate Third quarter 1981		Unemployment rate Fourth quarter 1982	
	Male	Female	Male	Female
Adults, age				
20 and over	6.1	6.8	10.0	9.0
20–24	12.6	11.3	17.7	14.1
25–54	5.3	6.2	9.2	8.5
55 and over	3.5	3.9	6.2	4.9

effects of unemployment on income. Survey data for 1980 showed 'the median income of families with one unemployed member or more during 1980 was 21% below the median for families not affected by unemployment ($19,076 compared with $24,020). Primarily because of lower earnings, 15% of the families affected by unemployment were in poverty in 1980. By contrast, among families where no working members experience unemployment, only 6% had incomes which fell below the poverty level' (Terry, 1982). Detailed information showed that the income effect varied considerably with the characteristics and family situation of the unemployed person. Changes in duration of unemployment, which may occur with economic fluctuations, could also influence the results.

The Consumer Price Index for urban wage earners and clerical workers rose by 11.5% in 1979 and 13.5% in 1980. The percentage rise was then only 10.2% in 1981 and 6.0% in 1982 (Table XIII.1). Favourable developments affecting food and energy contributed to the decline for 1981 (Howell and Thomas, 1982). Monetary policies aimed at decreasing consumer spending through increased interest rates contributed to the drop in 1982.

Federal government expenditures increased from US $509.7 billion in 1979 to an estimated US $762.6 billion in 1982, with a very large deficit for 1982. State and local government expenditures rose more slowly – from US $321.5 billion in 1979 to US $405.4 billion in 1982. Federal grants-in-aid to the state and local governments rose considerably in 1980 but subsequently decreased.

The percentage of persons below the poverty level rose from 11.7% in 1979 to 13.0% in 1980 and 14% (under a revised definition of poverty) in 1981. The percentage for related children under age 18 in families rose also in this period

– from 16.0% in 1979 to 17.9% in 1980, and to 19.5% in 1981 (Table XIII.3). The 1980 percentage for related children under age 18 in families reached 42 for the non-whites, 50.8% in families of all races with a female householder and no husband present, and 64.8% for the black group of families with a female householder and no husband present (Bureau of the Census, 1981, p. 7).

From 1979 to 1981 the percentage of families below the poverty level rose in both metropolitan areas from 8.3 to 10.1% and non-metropolitan areas from 10.9 to 13.5%. Particularly high percentages below the poverty level were found for black families in central cities of metropolitan areas and in non-metropolitan areas – 31.8 and 37.5% respectively in 1981.

4. THE MEANING OF POVERTY

The preceding analysis of economic indicators relates importantly to the health of children. Understanding the status and trends for the health of children in the United States requires appreciation of the country's great diversity. Important ethnic and cultural differences pertain from one area to another; the economic bases differ sharply in different parts of the country, and they are not all affected in the same way by such important determinants as national unemployment rates, and programmes for health services and social supports. The 50 states exercise extensive autonomy for the scope and quality of public services in education, health care, social support and family income supplementation. For example, in Mississippi a destitute mother with two children and no other source of income receives US $96.00 a month in welfare payment, whereas in 11 other states the same family would receive more than US $400.00 per month (Greenstein, 1983). This range of benefits is permissible within AFDC, a federally authorized programme (Aid for Families of Dependent Children, Social Security Act, 1935) that is dependent in part on financing from federal allocations to the states. The degree of freedom accorded the different states for the definition of many health and social benefits has increased profoundly by national policies implemented since 1981.

Special attention focuses on the subpopulation of children living in poverty. In the United States a level of family income is officially and periodically designated as the poverty threshold.

The determination is made based on the proportion of family income, adjusted for family size, required to purchase a standard amount of food. The designation is imperfect, criticized by some people as too meagre, providing sufficient food for short intervals of crisis but not enough for healthful nutrition over an extended period. Other people claim that the definition does not allow sufficiently for consideration of non-cash benefits that are also provided to some poor people.

High poverty levels among minority households are thought to reflect a long and — it is to be hoped — declining tradition of discrimination in educational and employment opportunities. Because vital records do not include designations for socio-economic status, many reports disaggregate data according to census tracts or according to racial or ethnic groups, and attempt to make comparisons suggestive of differences among socio-economic levels. It is important to bear in mind that even though minority populations are disproportionately affected by poverty, the entire poor population is predominantly white.

The United States may have the most unequal income distribution of any western industrialized nation. Only France had a more unequal distribution prior to changes that were effected in 1981; in the Federal Republic of Germany the spread between high and low incomes was 36% smaller, and in Japan 50% smaller than in the United States (Thurow, 1981). Budget cuts and changes in the tax structure enacted by the US Congress in 1981 had the effect of making the rich richer and the poor poorer (Havemann, 1982). '. . . The poorest fifth of the [US] population is now left with only 4.2% of the national income after federal taxes, while the richest fifth's share . . . has now edged up to 43% — or more than 10 times as much' (Greenstein, 1983).

Different age groups are not equally involved in poverty. Children are disproportionately affected. More than 50% of the occupants of poverty level households are under 21 years of age; a higher proportion of children than any other age group lives in poverty. The proportion of children living in poverty has increased markedly since 1980 (Figure XIII.1).

The affluence of the United States is so great when compared with many parts of the world that relative impoverishment in the midst of great abundance may seem a minor hardship. Note should be taken that government in the United States provides fewer social welfare, health insurance, child care, educational and unemployment benefits than most other industrialized nations. In 1980 expenditures by government at all levels as a proportion of gross domestic product was less in the United States than in Austria, Belgium, Canada, Denmark, France, Italy, Netherlands, Norway, Sweden, United Kingdom and the Federal Republic of Germany (Greenstein, 1983). These comparisons are all the more dramatic in view of the high military expenditures in the United States. Families in the United States must pay out of pocket for many benefits that are financed from tax revenues in other countries. Even so, an annual income in excess of US $8000, which is within the poverty level for

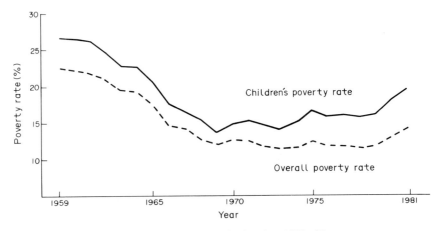

Figure XIII.1. *Poverty in America*, 1959–81

Source: Bureau of the Census, US Department of Commerce, cited in Children's Defense Fund (1983).
*Does not include children not living in families or married individuals under age 18.

a family of four people, would represent undreamed of opulence to most families in the world. What does it mean in the United States? For a high proportion of poor children it means increased risk of death, preventable disease and disability, and blighted opportunity.

The proportion of children living in poverty follows general economic trends. During the 1970s some additional influences accentuated the movement of children into poverty. These trends include an increase in teenage childbearing and a sharp rise in the proportion of single-parent families and female-headed households. The same years saw a sharp increase in the employment of both parents outside the home, a circumstance intended to stave off impoverishment for many families but which brought inadequately resolved issues of child care and supervision. These problems are serious for infants and preschool children, and no less disturbing for the latch-key children — those school-age children who are unsupervised during the after-school hours and before return of parents from work. These conditions all contributed to the distressing phenomenon of small children who were made responsible without supervision for the care of yet smaller children. Full exploration of these issues is beyond the scope of this paper except to point out that neither community care for children nor family subsidy for private day care has ever been adequately provided (Kamerman and Kahn, 1979).

A proposal passed Congress in 1971 for establishing and expanding comprehensive community based child development programmes including day care, but the programme was vetoed by the President. Ever since that time, arguments that the intactness of families in the United States is more threatened by neglect than by publicly sponsored supports have not been politically persuasive. The Alan Guttmacher Institute in 1981 surveyed 125 cities with populations in excess of 100,000 in order to determine the availability of various services for teenage mothers and their babies. Day care was by far the most deficient service, as reported by 71% of the cities (Alan Guttmacher Institute, 1981).

Single-parent families, and female-headed households which are in special need of outside supports and services are rapidly increasing. The proportion of children living with less than two parents steadily increased from 9% in 1960, to 13% in 1970, to 21% in 1981 and is expected to continue increasing. Glick projects that in 1990 one-quarter of all children will be living with only one parent (cited by Select Panel,

Vol. III, 1981). About 90% of children in single-parent families live with their mothers and over half of these households were under poverty levels in 1981 (Rivlin, 1983).

On the average women earn less than men and female-headed households are more likely to have low income. In 1978 children in families headed by women were about six times as likely as children in families headed by men to be living below the poverty level (Select Panel, Vol. III, 1981) (Figure XIII.2).

The teenage birthrate in the United States is among the world's highest and it contributes substantially to the proportion of infants and children who are raised in poverty (Alan Guttmacher Institute, 1981). One in five births is to women 18 years of age or younger (Reycroft and Kessler, 1980). The combination of early childbearing and households headed by women is especially predisposing to impoverishment.

About half of the money allocated by Aid for Families with Dependent Children (AFDC) in 1975 went to families in which the woman had given birth as a teenager, but only about one-quarter of teenage mothers receive AFDC payments (Alan Guttmacher Institute, 1981).

The prevention of much unwanted and high-risk childbearing had a beneficial effect on these circumstances. During the 1970s access to contraceptive and abortion services increased substantially (Torres et al., 1981; Henshaw et al., 1981). Figure XIII.3 and Table XIII.6 document the extent of the increases in the availability and use of family planning and abortion services.

These programmes improved infant health and mortality by means of preventing much high-risk childbearing. Between 1973 and 1978 there was a 13% increase in teenage pregnancies, but a decline in teenage childbearing. For the youngest group of teenagers the number of pregnancies increased by 5%, abortions increased by 31% and births decreased by 17% (Alan Guttmacher Institute, 1981).

5. SUPPORTS AND SERVICES

A close linkage relates health status to socio-economic levels (Edwards and Grossman, 1979; Starfield, 1982). This relationship may be especially pronounced in the United States because of the nation's relatively weak commitment to ensure participation of all people in essential and appropriate health services, independent of either broad societal or individual fluctuations in economic well-being.

The usual medical care provider system for

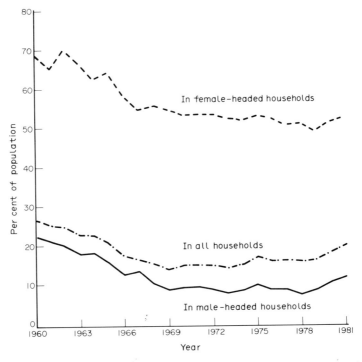

Figure XIII.2. *Per cent of US population under 18 living in families below the poverty line by type of house-hold, 1960–81.*

Source: Rivlin (1983).

most people in the United States is a privately practising physician, with financing of fees through Medicaid, private health insurance or out-of-pocket payments. Health benefits are available through some union groups or employers. Children are less well covered by private health insurance than any other age group. Children, or their parents, pay a higher proportion of medical costs out of pocket than any other age group (Budetti *et al.*, 1982).

The major mechanism for removing financial barriers to health services for the poor is Medicaid, a welfare benefit that pays medical fees for eligible poor people. Little assurance is provided that poor people actually have access to appropriate services. In fact, about 50% of practising physicians decline to see Medicaid patients (Davidson, 1982) and in many counties no practitioners are available for Medicaid clients. Both eligibility and benefits vary greatly from state to state (Davidson, 1978). Only about one-third of the poor are covered by Medicaid (McManus and Davidson, 1982).

Other problems are associated with Medicaid. An increasing proportion of Medicaid funds have gone to finance domiciliary care for the elderly. The remaining funds for children have

not always served the most cost-effective priorities. The programme ensures payment of medical bills without specifying service priorities or outcome standards, contributing both to medical inflation that exceeds the general inflation rate, and to the extensive utilization of expensive technologies. A balance has not been achieved ensuring that poor people participate appropriately in specialized care and receive, as well, the routine preventive health services.

Some paradoxical situations emerge from these circumstances. Survival rates for low birth weight babies are better in the United States than in most other countries, but a higher proportion of babies are born at low birth weight than in most other industrial nations. The *laissez-faire* approach to medical care enables and stimulates a sophisticated technological approach to medical problems, but does not serve well a broadly based preventive approach that would diminish both the problems and the need for some of the expensive technology.

Even though no national commitment exists to ensure participation of all people in essential health services, many cities, counties and states

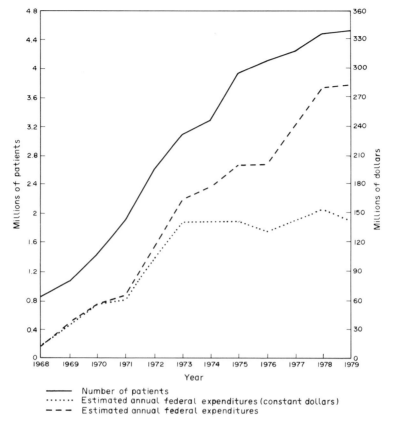

Figure XIII.3. *Number of patients served annually by family planning clinics in the United States, estimated annual federal expenditures for medical family planning services and estimated annual federal expenditures in constant* (1970) *dollars, 1968–79.*

Source: Torres *et al.* (1981).

have undertaken such a commitment by means of expanding personal health services available through public clinics of local health departments (Miller and Moos, 1981). These clinics have progressively expanded over the past two decades. Many people make use of the clinics for limited services such as family planning, prenatal care, immunizations, venereal disease control and well child supervision. The public health agencies identify many people with health problems through such organized screening programmes as those for diabetes, hypertension, sickle cell disease or lead poisoning. Public health clinics sometimes provide appropriate diagnosis and treatment subsequent to the screening programme and in other instances arrange for follow-up care by other providers.

A number of locales provide through local health departments a programme of comprehensive neighbourhood-based primary care for

a substantial number of poor or near poor people (Miller and Moos, 1981). The extent and quality of these programmes grew extensively during the 1960s and 1970s. The development of services and benefits through health departments of local government is unevenly developed from one area to another. No consistent infrastructure for publicly sponsored maternal and child health or other essential services exists in the United States.

Many US health service initiatives have featured small area demonstration projects that, even when successful, have not been extended to all underserved populations who would benefit from similar interventions. Special projects to provide care for underserved pregnant women, infants, children and youth were started in the mid-1960s. These projects were federally sponsored and successfully demonstrated both economical operation and favour-

Table XIII.6. *Number of reported abortions; number of providers; rate of abortions per 1000 women aged 15—44; and ratio of abortions per 1000 abortions plus live births; by metropolitan status, 1973—79*

Measure and metropolitan status	1973	1974	1975	1976	1977	1978	1979*
(1) No. of abortions (000s)							
Total	744.6	898.6	1034.2	1179.3	1216.7	1409.6	1540.0
Metro	720.2	860.7	985.7	1123.3	1258.0	1345.2	1469.0
Non-metro	24.4	37.9	48.5	56.0	56.7	64.4	71.0
(2) No. of providers							
Total	1627	2028	2398	2567	2688	2753	n.p.
Metro	1302	1615	1903	2037	2139	2198	n.p.
Non-metro	325	413	495	531	549	555	n.p.
(3) Abortion rate							
Total	16.6	19.6	22.1	24.5	26.9	28.2	30.2
Metro	22.7	26.7	30.2	31.6	34.7	36.4	39.1
Non-metro	1.9	2.8	3.4	4.4	4.6	4.9	5.3
(4) Abortions per 1000 abortions plus live births†							
Total	193	220	249	265	286	294	303
Metro	255	288	249	265	286	294	303
Non-metro	23	35	45	49	50	54	56

Source: Henshaw *et al.* (1981).
*Projected.
†Births 6 months later.
n.p. = Not projected.

able health outcomes. These projects were turned over to the administrative discretion of the separate states in the early 1970s.

The combined effect of these provider systems has not been impressive for ensuring full participation of all people in appropriate services. For example, during the late 1970s attention focused on the disparity in immunization rates between poor and non-poor children. A national immunization programme, implemented through the official health agencies of state and local governments, finally achieved acceptably high immunization levels for most groups of children. On the other hand, no major national effort has been mounted to ensure participation of pregnant women in early and continuous prenatal care.

These and other circumstances led a congressionally authorized Select Panel for the Promotion of Child Health to recommend in 1980 that a major national programme be instituted to ensure at public expense the participation of all appropriate people in a cluster of well· defined essential basic services that included prenatal, delivery and postnatal care; comprehensive health care for children from birth to age 5; and family planning services (Select Panel, Vol. 1, 1981). The report had been authorized by Congress during the Carter administration but the recommendations did not become available until soon after the election of President Reagan.

Few of the Select Panel's recommendations were implemented and in fact a pronounced ideologic shift took place in government that diminished the recognized responsibility of government to provide or ensure participation in essential health services. The ideology, a resurgence of New Federalism, holds that services whenever possible should be made available through the private market rather than through government, and that in so far as a government responsibility may exist to provide services, that responsibility should be exercised at state and local levels.

Many national programmes for health services were discontinued in 1981 and their funds made available in Block Grants to the states. The total amount of public money made available for health services was dramatically reduced and few national guidelines, standards or priorities were provided to advise state discretion. These changes were defended in part with the hope of streamlining public programmes in order to enhance their efficiency.

Uneven implementation of programmes characterized not only efforts to ensure participation in health services, but to provide income supplementation and support for the poor. Aid to Families with Dependent Children (AFDC) is the federal programme intended to protect poor children from the worst effects of poverty by means of income supports to their families. About two-thirds of AFDC recipients are children, the remainder being adult parents, about four-fifths of whom are single women. The turnover rate among AFDC families is high. Each year about one-third of them move off the rolls to be replaced by other families. Great variation in benefits among the states characterizes AFDC, but for the most part benefits are distressingly low and have not kept pace with inflation. Recipients lost about 20% of their purchasing power between 1976 and 1982 (*Children's Defense Fund*, 1983). Benefits have been redefined since 1980 resulting in an appreciable decline in potentially eligible families. In 1982 spending levels for AFDC fell by about 5% in real terms (Rivlin, 1983). Only about one-third of poverty level families are enrolled for AFDC benefits.

The national expenditure for food stamps is about the same as for AFDC. These are the two largest income supplementations that benefit eligible poverty households with children. Food stamps and other nutrition benefits will be considered in a subsequent section.

Health services and income supports in the United States are not limited to the poor. Non-means-tested benefits include Medicare (a federal health insurance programme for people over 65 years of age), subsidized school lunches, employer or union provided pension plans, and employer or union provided group health insurance. In 1981, nine out of 10 households received at least one non-cash benefit (Bureau of the Census, 1983). Even within the publicly financed programmes the benefits to the non-poor are appreciable. About 75% of the entire federal health care outlay went for benefits to the non-indigent in 1977 (Office of Management and the Budget, 1977).

6. HEALTH STATUS AND RISK MEASURE

(a) *Infant mortality rate*

Infant mortality rates for the United States, although declining, have persisted at higher levels than for other industrialized nations and higher even than for some nations of exceedingly modest national resources.

Brenner analysed relationships between economic growth and infant mortality for the United States and reported that fluctuations occur regularly, bearing an inverse relationship to environmental changes associated with economic swings (Brenner, 1973). Brenner's data were drawn largely from the years before the impact of the major social benefit and health service programmes that were initiated in the mid-1960s. Infant mortality rates for the United States had shown only the most meagre improve-

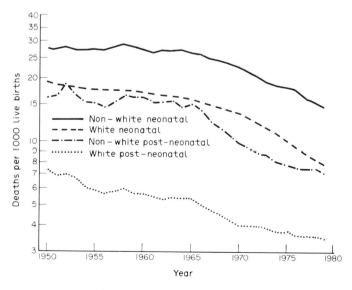

Figure XIII.4. *Neonatal and post-neonatal mortality rates, according to race, 1950–79.*
Source: National Center for Health Statistics: computed by the Division of Analysis from data compiled by the Division of Vital Statistics, cited in National Center for Health Statistics, *Health United States* (1982).

ments for the 25 years preceding these reforms. The pronounced downward trend after 1965 was well sustained through 1980, but was disappointing in that the gap between non-white and white rates was maintained (Figure XIII.4).

Grossman and Jacobowitz analysed a group of public policies and programmes initiated between 1964 and 1977 in order to measure their relative impact on infant mortality rates. The programmes included Medicaid, Maternal and Infant Care Projects, federally subsidized family planning services for low-income women, legalization of abortion and the widespread adoption of oral and intra-uterine contraceptive techniques. The increase in the legal abortion rate was the single most important determinant for the reduction of neonatal mortality rates (Grossman and Jacobowitz, 1982). The second greatest determinant was the use of organized family planning services by low-income women. Medicaid had no impact on white neonatal mortality rates, and an effect for non-whites that was less than either of the other two factors. Note should be made that in most states public funding of abortion has been discontinued and federal funding of family planning has not increased in real dollars since 1973. Support for both programmes has been reduced sharply since 1981 and the Reagan administration actively pursues a policy that attempts to criminalize abortion.

(b) Low birth weight

A high proportion of babies in the United States are born weighing less than 2500 grams. The rate for non-whites is nearly double that for whites, but even the latter rate does not compare favourably with the best records in industrialized nations such as Japan, New Zealand, Norway and Sweden (National Center for Health Statistics, 1981). (See Table XIII.7.)

Table XIII.7. *Per cent of live births with low birth weight*, 1973

Race and area	Low birth weight*
US: Total	7.55
Non-white	13.25
White	6.41
Japan	4.74
New Zealand	4.69
Norway	4.16
Sweden	3.56

Source: National Center for Health Statistics, *Health United States*, 1981.
*2500 grams or less.

Although survival rates for low birth weight babies have improved dramatically during the past decade, little if any progress has been made in reducing the proportion of babies who are born too small or too soon. (Office of Technology Assessment, 1981). In fact the record for non-white babies may have worsened in 1977–78 (National Center for Health Statistics, 1981).

Various efforts have addressed one or more

Table XIII.8. *Per capita expenditures on defence and on programmes for low-income families and children*, FY1981–FY1988

Fiscal year	National defence	Programmes for low-income families and children
	($)	($)
1981	695	416
1982	762	372
1983	825	379
1984	892	350
1985	983	342
1986	1054	334
1987	1097	327
1988	1133	325
Change		
(%)	+438	−91
in dollars	+ 63.0	−21.9

Source: From Children's Defense Fund (1983).

of the factors affecting low birth weight in the United States, especially nutrition and prenatal care, with promising results. But no national effort has ever been mounted specifically to achieve a national health outcome of improved birth weights. The most relevant national programme was enacted in 1972, the Special Supplemental Food Programme for Women, Infants and Children (WIC). The programme features nutrition education and food supplementation for pregnant women but these benefits have reached only about a quarter of those eligible. Evaluations suggest that birth weights among participating pregnant women have been improved (Kennedy et al., 1982). One report suggests that the inducement of food has brought increasing numbers of poor pregnant women into prenatal care (Kotch and Whiteman, 1982). A review of all the piecemeal and small area US interventions to achieve reductions in low birth weight points out their many disappointments and methodological deficiencies (Hemminki and Starfield, 1978). These findings allow the interpretation that what is known about prevention of low birth weight is being applied on an inadequate scale.

One interesting intervention is consistently overlooked by most reviews. An experiment with a negative income tax found substantially increased birth weights among the involved families (Salkind and Haskins, 1982). While this study was no better controlled than most social interventions, the results are clear enough to suggest that further policy and programme development along these lines is warranted.

(c) *Prenatal care*

During the decade of the 1970s, among white women the participation in prenatal care during the first trimester increased only from 72 to 79%. The increase among non-white women was greater but so also was the problem; by 1979 about 40% of pregnant non-white women received no care in the first trimester (Figure XIII.5). Note should be made that the upward trend for participation in prenatal care was not reversed during or after the recession of 1974—75.

(d) *Nutrition*

In 1968 a Citizens Board of Inquiry issued a startling report that documented the considerable extent of hunger and malnutrition among children in the United States (*Hunger USA*, 1968). People were dismayed that nutritional deprivations that are associated with the poorest parts of the world existed in this affluent society. Marasmus and Kwashiorkor were more than oddities in some parts of the United States (Schaefer, 1977). Subsequent surveys confirmed extensive dietary inadequacy (insufficient calories) and growth stunting among poor children (Carter, 1974). For example, among two year olds from low-income families 37—46% of the children fell below the 15th percentile of standard growth charts. Nutritional growth stunting was found among all age groups of poor children.

The nation's response was prompt (the following material from Kotz, 1979):

— Food stamps grew from a US $288 million programme serving 2.8 million people in 1968 to a US $5 billion annual effort serving 16 million today (1979).

— Free or reduced price lunches for poor children grew from a US $42 million pro-

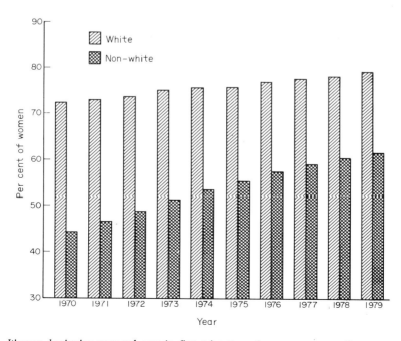

Figure XIII.5. *Women beginning prenatal care in first trimester of pregnancy, according to race,* 1970—79. Source: National Center for Health Statistics, Division of Vital Statistics, cited in National Center for Health Statistics, *Health United States* (1982).

gramme for 3 million children in 1968 to a US \$1.2 billion programme serving 12 million poor children today. The government spends another US \$500 million subsidizing in part the lunches of all 26 million participants (1979).

— Free school breakfasts have expanded from a US \$5.5 million programme serving 300,000 children in 1968 to a US \$200 million effort serving more than 3 million children today (1979).

— Child care and summer food service for children provide food for 3 million children today at a cost of US \$250 million in contrast to 1968 programmes serving 140,000 children at a cost of US \$3.2 million.

— Supplemental feeding for women, infants and children (WIC) has grown rapidly from a US \$14 million programme serving 206,000 people in 1974 to a US \$550 million programme serving nearly 1.5 million people today (1979).

Even with all these initiatives, the nutrition problems among US children were not eliminated. Ten years after the first survey of hunger in the United States, a new survey was undertaken and reported (Kotz, 1979). The report held that flagrant hunger and undernutrition no longer existed in the United States. The report cautioned that food supplementation programmes were not more than adequate and that continued vigilance and sustained effort to prevent malnutrition were required.

Following the policy and fiscal changes after 1981, the nutritional programmes, including school lunches, food stamps and WIC, were special targets for reduction. The administration reduced funding for these programmes and attempted to assign them for administration and for policy determination to the separate states rather than to maintain them as a matter of consistent national priority.

(e) Hazards from lead

Although recent expert opinion suggests that any blood lead level may be adverse, the Centers for Disease Control (CDC) have defined elevated blood lead as 30 micrograms or more of lead per tenth of a litre of blood (30 μg/dl), and recommends that at this level children should be referred for further observation and treatment. This standard has been revised downward over time and it is reasonable to project a further reduction in the future. Very high blood lead levels can result in severe anaemia, slowed or regressed mental development, mental

retardation, kidney and liver damage, convulsions, coma and death. There is growing evidence that even at slightly elevated levels excess blood lead can produce verbal, perceptual, motor and behavioural disabilities in children, including irritability, delayed development, inattentiveness, inability to follow instructions and lowered test scores for reading, spelling and I.Q. (Lin-Fu, 1979). Since lead can be stored in the bones, the blood lead level is an imperfect indicator of the total amount of lead in the body. In times of acute illness such as diarrhoea, large amounts of lead stored in the bones may move into the blood and cause symptoms of acute lead poisoning.

The National Center for Health Statistics estimates that 4% of pre-school children in the United States — 675,000 youngsters — have elevated blood lead levels of 30 μg/dl or greater. The proportion of non-white pre-school children with elevated blood lead levels is more than six times the proportion for white children of the same age: 12.2% as compared to 2.0%. Among non-white pre-school children from low-income families, nearly one in five (18.6%) have elevated blood lead levels.

Mean blood lead levels are significantly higher for low-income children than they are for children from wealthier families. For non-whites, the mean blood lead level among pre-school children whose family income is less than US \$6000 is 22.9 μg/dl, as compared to a mean of 17.2 μg/dl for children from families making US \$15,000 or more. Among white pre-schoolers, the mean blood lead levels are 18.1 and 13.7 μg/dl respectively for the two different family income groups. Children living in urban environments have a higher mean blood lead level than children living in rural environments. Among non-white pre-schoolers the mean blood lead levels of children living in large cities is 22.2 μg/dl, as compared to 18.3 μg/dl for children living in rural settings. Among whites, the comparable figures are 16.6 and 13.5 μg/dl (Annest et al., 1982).

The sources of lead are not entirely understood. They include paint on the walls of old housing, automobile exhaust and the soil, particularly along freeways. During the period 1976—80, the mean blood lead level for children 6 months—5 years old decreased 40%. This decline has been attributed in part to reduction in lead content of gasoline, which results in a reduction of lead in automobile emissions.

During the Reagan administration, regulations and standards for environmental protection have been substantially relaxed. For example the permissible level of lead in the air was doubled (Freedman and Weir, 1983).

Many other environmental toxins, some of them from industrial waste, are known to be especially hazardous for children (i.e. mercury, dioxin, formaldehyde and various pesticides). The full extent and nature of the associated health problems are not well documented, and understanding on these issues will not soon improve. A fifty per cent reduction in funds for research under The Environmental Protection Agency has occurred since President Reagan took office. Included in the funding cuts was a programme that was established under the Carter administration for research on the effects of environmental pollutants on children's health (Freedman and Weir, 1983).

(f) Findings from Early Period Screening Diagnosis and Treatment (EPSDT)

When Medicaid was enacted in 1966 the record was abundant that poor children experienced a disproportionate amount of impaired health. Hearing loss, growth stunting, and iron deficiency anaemia were especially prevalent (EPSDT, 1978).

Recognizing that many poor children had no regular source of medical care, Congress authorized an amendment to Medicaid that required all participating states to reach out to Medicaid eligible children and to involve them in screening for health problems, and to provide for diagnosis and treatment of any problems that were identified (EPSDT, 1978). The programme was slow getting implemented, and performance was quite uneven in the different states. By 1976 only about one-third of the eligible children were actually reached by EPSDT, but the findings about their health were impressive. Nearly half of all children who were screened required referral for diagnosis and treatment for an average of two conditions (EPSDT, 1978):
- 50% were found to be inadequately immunized
- 25% were found to have severe dental problems
- 10% had vision problems
- 12% had low haemoglobin levels
- 8% suffered from upper-respiratory problems
- 7% suffered from genito-urinary infections
- 9% in urban areas had elevated blood lead levels
- 3% had hearing problems.

Regrettably, only about half of the children who were found to have health problems received subsequent appropriate diagnosis and treatment. Through 1980 many reforms for EPSDT were formulated and implemented. The programme, so delayed and checkered, began to yield impressive results for involving increasing numbers of poor children in appropriate medical care (Davis et al., 1981).

(g) Health service utilization

Progress had been made over the past 15 years in improving access to medical care for poor children. In the mid-1960s non-poor children used 23% more physicians' services than poor children; and white children used 42% more than non-white (Davis et al., 1981). By the late 1970s poor children experienced more per capita physician visits each year than non-poor, but after adjusting for health status the situation was reversed. Poor children had fewer per capita visits than the non-poor (Kleinman et al., 1981). Important differences persisted in the characteristics of care for the two groups. Poor children:
- received fewer preventive visits;
- were less likely to see a privately practising physician and more likely to attend a public clinic;
- had greatly diminished access to telephone consultations for health problems.

The federal programmes that were intended to close the gap in health care between rich and poor children were enormously successful, but still not sufficient. Davis et al. (1981) identified some of the gaps in coverage. She analysed the proportion of children covered by Medicaid (34% of the poor), those covered by government-sponsored community health centre programmes (8% of the poor), and those who lived in medically underserved areas (36% of the poor). From this analysis Davis calculated that a substantial number of children (21% of the poor) live in medical 'triple jeopardy': not covered by Medicaid, not served by a community clinic and living in a medically underserved area. These were the circumstances immediately prior to the reductions in public financing of health care and services, and before the serious economic recession that came in 1981.

7. THE MEANING OF RECESSION FOR CHILDREN

During the country's serious economic recession of 1974–75, monthly unemployment rates reached 9.2% – at that time the steepest economic decline since the Great Depression

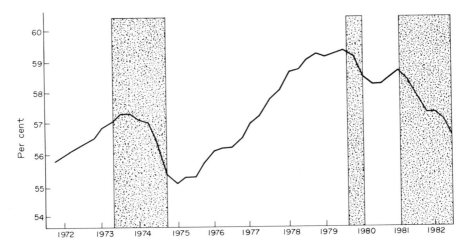

Figure XIII.6. *Employment–population ratio, seasonally adjusted quarterly averages, 1972–82.*
Source: Urquhart M. A. and M. A. Hewson, 'Unemployment continued to rise in 1982 as recession deepened',
Monthly Labor Review, 106 (February 1983), pp. 4 and 12.
Shaded areas denote a recession. Fourth quarter 1982 datum is an October–November average.

(Lee, 1979). The severity of the 1974–75 recession is illustrated in Figure XIII.6, which illustrates that the employment–population ratio was more depressed in 1975 than during mid-1982. The period 1974–75 also saw the rapid inflation of health-care prices following removal of price controls in April 1974 (Holahan, *et al.,* 1979). No increase in infant mortality rates, increase in the proportion of live-born babies with low birth weight, decrease in the participation of pregnant women in prenatal care, or decreased access of children to physician services are indicated by the trend graphs for the nation at large during those years or for the years immediately following.

The failure of these indicators to be adversely influenced by severe economic recession with high unemployment rates might be explained in several ways.

The effect of Medicaid and other social service benefits that had been initiated in the late 1960s may have mitigated against the adverse health impact of the recession. In adjusting to the 1974–75 recession, state governments generally attempted to maintain existing health and welfare programmes (Holahan, 1979). Federal spending on entitlement programmes for children and families, as measured in constant 1982 dollars, actually increased sharply during 1974–75 (Figure XIII.7).

The value of income transfers, such as Medicaid and other public assistance programmes, was essentially preserved in real terms, insulating persons on fixed incomes from

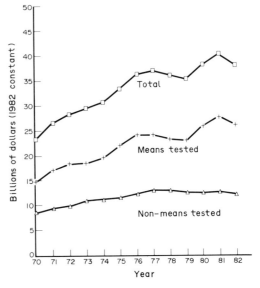

Figure XIII.7. *Federal spending on selected entitlement programmes for children and families, 1970–82.*
Source: Rivlin (1983).

erosion of purchasing power (Sloan and Bentkouer, 1979). Non-employment income available through public programmes and expansion of Medicaid enrolment partially offset income reductions attributable to job losses. These safeguards may have protected vulnerable populations from the worst effects of recession and enabled these groups to continue participation in essential health supports and services.

An alternative hypothesis holds that aggregate data for the entire country may conceal important adverse outcomes that might pertain for particularly disadvantaged sub-groups. In point of fact, the 1974—75 recession did not affect all states equally. Holahan (1979) identified, a group of eight states (California, Iowa, Kentucky, Louisiana, Maryland, Montana, Oklahoma and Texas) that experienced no fiscal strain. Another group of eight states (Georgia, Michigan, Missouri, Nebraska, New York, Ohio, South Carolina and Virginia) experienced severe fiscal strain. These two groups of states were compared through the years 1973—77 for differences in the general downward trend of neonatal mortality rates and for fluctuations in the generally stable rates of babies born weighing less than 2500 grams. No differences were found between the severely affected and the unaffected states either for total populations or for non-whites. (This analysis was completed by Martha Coulter to whom the author is most grateful.) Further careful analysis among especially high-risk populations (teenagers, unmarried mothers) might reveal significant adverse health effects from the 1974—75 recession, but they are not apparent to inspection of trend data.

A less optimistic appraisal of the impact of the 1974—75 recession is suggested by reports that post-neonatal infant mortality increased during those years (Hack et al., 1980; Zdeb, 1982). These reports suggest that neonatal intensive care makes possible the early survival of extreme low birth weight babies, but that for some of these babies mortality is delayed until the post-neonatal period. These circumstances suggest that the immediate survival of high-risk newborns may be technologically dependent but their continued survival is socio-economically dependent. The former supports are more readily available in the United States, even at times of recession, than the latter. This formulation has been extensively described for some developing countries (Bryant, 1969).

According to Sloan and Bentkouer, unemployment constitutes a greater threat to low-income families than inflation, provided that public assistance programmes keep pace in real terms, a condition that largely pertained in the economic recession of 1974—75, but not in the one after 1981 (Sloan and Bentkouer, 1979; Greenstein, 1983). Few people claim that supports and services for poor families in the United States have ever adequately addressed their need (Kenniston, 1977). But since 1981 two adverse influences came to bear simultaneously in ways that made previous neglects seem less egregious. After 1981, unemploy-

ment rates climbed to heights not seen in the past 50 years and many protective supports and services for children and poor families were withdrawn or sharply diminished (Greenstein, 1983). The impact of these circumstances on the health of children will be subsequently addressed.

Many reports confirm that during the 1970s there was a steady increase in the use of physicians' services by poor children (Starfield, 1982). Although no detailed analysis of this trend has been made with reference to the recession of 1974—75, no breaks in the trend of improved utilization are apparent from inspection of the published reports. This observation is consistent with the position that Medicaid and expanding public health services (Orr and Miller, 1981) offset the potential adverse effects of the recession as far as children's health is concerned.

8. HEALTH SUPPORTS AND SERVICES SINCE 1980

Under the Reagan Administration social support and health service programmes were substantially reduced, but paradoxically government spending has never been greater. The increases have been associated with military expansion (Table XIII.8).

The projected increase in defence spending at the expense of social programmes is confirmed by a recent analysis from the Congressional Budget Office (Congressional Budget Office, 1983a). Between 1982 and 1985 spending for national defence will increase from 25.7 to 29.9% of the federal outlay. During the same years income security programmes will decline from 11.1 to 9.4%; federal expenditures for higher education will decline from 1.1 to 0.9%; grants to state and local governments for education, employment and social services will decline from 2.3 to 1.9% of the total federal outlay.

The cuts in specific programmes are indicated in the following data taken from Greenstein (1983).

Food stamps — cut by US $2 billion per year. Nearly one million food stamp recipients terminated. About 8% of the cut has occurred in families below the poverty line. *AFDC (Aid to Families with Dependent Children)* — cut by US $1.5 billion per year, about half this amount from the states and the rest from federal cuts. About 365,000 families have been terminated, and an additional 260,000 have had benefits reduced. In about half the states, families who lose AFDC benefits also lose Medicaid coverage.

Medicaid — in 1981 federal Medicaid payments were reduced by US $1 billion. The reductions came about through a variety of changes in eligibility and benefits by the states. Forty states reduced Medicaid programmes in 1981 and 30 states made additional cuts in 1982. Working families within the poverty level but not receiving welfare payments tended also to lose Medicaid coverage. Those families who continued their Medicaid coverage tended to lose benefits such as eye-glasses, a restriction on the number of physician visits, or a deductible on co-payment requirement on fees.

School food programmes — the school health programme was cut by US $1 billion per year, or nearly 30%. Three million fewer children are participating. The school breakfast programme was cut by 20% and 200,000 fewer children are participating.

Maternal and child health programmes — the federal money granted the states for support of routine maternal and child health and crippled children's services was cut by 25%. Partial restoration of funds was made by the jobs bill passed by Congress in the spring of 1983. Those restorations are authorized for only one year.

Many other reductions were made in federal support of day-care, services for abused children, rat control, lead screening, support for community health centres in medically underserved areas, etc. The precise amount and nature of the cuts are difficult to document because programmes and budgetary allocations were merged in block grants to the states. The aggregate of merged programmes was consistently funded at lesser levels than previously.

Some programmes benefiting children were increased by congressional action. Examples include Head Start (pre-school health, education and day care) and WIC. The aggregate effect of all changes indicates that *nominal* funding for all children's health programmes changed relatively little between 1980 and 1982 (Rivlin, 1983). In terms of real dollars, reductions did in fact occur overall, and those reductions were substantial for many children's health programmes as indicated above. Circumstances are not apt to improve in the years immediately ahead according to present projections (Rivlin, 1983).

9. HEALTH STATUS AND RISKS SINCE 1980

When the newly elected President Reagan announced his economic and social policies he reported that anticipated long-range increases in economic productivity would in time benefit everyone, but that in the meantime poor people would suffer. No one emphasized sufficiently that poor people in the United States are predominantly children. No national survey or monitoring programme was initiated to measure the extent and nature of their hardship. This neglect is paradoxical in view of the meticulous reporting and measurement that were undertaken to record trends on the state of the nation's economy.

Assessment of changes in the health status of children since 1980 has been difficult because of the lag in analysing and reporting traditional sources of data. Provisional results are still being issued for 1980; very little on a national scale is available since then. Some data sources have in fact been lost since 1981 because reporting that was linked to categorical service programmes has been discontinued with merger of those programmes into block grants to the states (Green *et al.*, 1983). As a result of these circumstances, a review of the relationship between national economic reversals and the health of children since 1981 must rely in large part on small area data and on anecdotal reporting. Both approaches require validation but they cannot be disregarded altogether, for they carry a certain legitimacy of consistency.

In the absence of a concerted national governmental effort to monitor the health of children, a great many voluntary efforts, both local and nationwide in scope, have emerged. These efforts sometimes pursue the concern of specific disease categories, or the support and services of certain agencies or professional groups. These monitoring efforts, including their data sources and reporting systems, have been carefully reviewed, and a project is under way to synthesize their information and to make it widely available (Schorr *et al.*, 1983).

New emphasis has been given to the importance of health outcome measures. The new policies initiated since 1981 are largely based on the premise that resource inputs and service systems, at least in the public sector, should be reduced. Evaluating the impact of these changes on the health status of children constitutes the critical concern. In the following reports, emphasis will be directed toward health outcomes except for some services that represent processes of risk reduction that are of undisputed

significance, such as prenatal care and immunizations. These changes in risk carry the advantage
of showing trends sooner than can be expected
for most health outcomes. In so far as trends
can be identified, no attempt is made to attribute
their antecedents either to the impact of new
social policies or to general economic reversals.
These two phenomena have been so inextricably
bound together since 1981 that differentiating
their impact, at least on a short-term basis, is
all but impossible.

In so far as economic reversals by themselves
have an impact on children's health, no attempt
is made to measure possible trends that have
been reported suggesting improvement in the
economy during the spring of 1983. So far
those trends have not reflected favourably on
unemployment rates, probably the most critical
indicator for the economy's impact on children's
health (Holahan et al., 1979; Sloan and Bentkouer, 1979). The influences that link unemployment with children's health are multiple and
include the loss of health insurance by 80% of unemployed families (Health Advocate, 1983).
Thirty million people in the United States lack
health insurance; 10.2 million jobless workers
and their dependents lacked any form of health
insurance in early 1983 as a direct result of
unemployment (Congressional Budget Office,
1983b).

(a) *Infant mortality rates*

Provisional US data from the National Center
for Health Statistics indicate a continued decline
in infant mortality when comparing the years
1980, 1981 and 1982. The occasional reports
that infant mortality rates have increased in
some areas are dismissed by some analysts as
representing usual seasonal or small area idio-
syncratic fluctuations (Brandt, 1983). Some of
the small area data are difficult to dismiss on
this basis.

Michigan has experienced a 30-year trend of
declining infant mortality rate, reducing it by
50%, but between 1980 and 1981 the rate rose
3%. Michigan experienced double-digit unemployment for 37 consecutive months beginning in December of 1979 (Walker, 1983). In
December of 1982, the state's unemployment
rate was 17.3%, and the rates for some counties
were much higher (Flint, 26.5%; Pontiac, 32.9%).
The infant death rates in Flint and Pontiac
counties rose to levels that were double the
state average (Walker, 1983). For many years
Flint has been the subject of special demographic studies by the Harvard School of Public
Health. The increase in non-white infant

mortality for Flint is reported to be valid within
the 95th percentile of statistical accuracy
(Gortmaker, 1983).

Other reports on increases in infant mortality
rates have come from Alabama (12.9 in 1981 to
14.8 in 1983) and from 34 cities (Noble, 1983).
Alabama is another state with unemployment
rates that are among the nation's highest.
Between 1981 and 1982 the infant mortality
rates for Central and East Harlem in New York
City increased from 21.1 to 27.6 and from 12.8
to 17.4, respectively (Public Interest Health
Consortium, 1983). Perhaps not all of these
reports will be shown to be significant, but to
ignore them altogether suggests too much
willingness to conceal within aggregate data
some important clues about adverse effects on
especially hard hit people and locales.

(b) *Low birth weight*

Verbal reports from several areas including
the State of Michigan suggest a recent increase
in the proportion of babies born with low birth
weight. Precise figures are generally not available.* One rural southern county that has been
extensively studied has experienced a fairly
steady rate of low birth weight among whites
(between 5.8 and 5.4) but a different experience
for non-whites. A high rate of 12.3 in 1975–79
fell to 10.7 in 1980, then rose to 12.1 in 1981
(Brooks and Miller, 1983).

(c) *Prenatal care*

No doubt can attach to findings about
prenatal care. Since 1980 an increased number
of pregnant women enter labour with inadequate
or with no prenatal care (Walker, 1983; Gebbie
and Penn 1983; Massachusetts Advocacy Center,
1983; Public Interest Health Consortium, 1983).
The findings in Oregon are especially well

---

* Two important reports appeared too late for
inclusion in the body of this text. Careful analyses in
North Carolina and in Michigan confirm the statistical
significance of increases in infant mortality rates
between 1981 and 1982. All of the increased mortality
in both states occurred in minority populations, who
experienced a decline in the participation of pregnant
women in prenatal care (Michigan), and a decline in
the weight of newborns (both states). Buescher, P. A.,
'The impact of low birth weight on North Carolina
neonatal mortality', presented at N.C. Public Health
Association Annual Meeting, Raleigh, N.C., 22
September 1983; Taylor, J. R., 'Infant mortality in
Michigan 1981–1982', presented at American Public
Health Association Annual Meeting, Dallas, 15
November 1983.

documented (Gebbie and Penn, 1983; Oregon State Health Division, 1982). Between 1972 and 1980 there was a steady decline (8.2–6.0%) in the proportion of pregnant women with inadequate prenatal care. After 1980 this trend was reversed by a one-sixth increase in inadequate prenatal care involving 7% of all births. The increases are most striking in the highest-risk pregnancies, teenagers and women over 40 years of age (11–16.3%) and among unwed mothers (13.5–17.3%) (Oregon State Health Division, 1982). Careful documentation from New York City comparing 1976 and 1981 are equally persuasive in documenting a decline in prenatal care (Public Interest Health Consortium, 1983).

Striking changes have occurred in the provider systems for prenatal care. All during the 1970s an increasing number of pregnant women received prenatal care in the clinics of local health departments (5.4% in 1959 to 12.8% in 1976) (Miller and Moos, 1981). The proportion is substantially larger if data include women who received partial prenatal and maternity services from the nurses of local health departments (nationally, 20% of all deliveries, and for some states 33%) (Miller and Moos, 1981).

After 1980 a veritable flood of pregnant women has left care in the private sector and sought prenatal care in public clinics (Walker, 1983; Brooks and Miller, 1983; Massachusetts Advocacy Center, 1983). In Massachusetts the increased demand for prenatal care in public clinics is three-fold (Massachusetts Advocacy Center, 1983); in Multnomah County, Oregon, it is nine-fold (Brooks and Miller, 1983). Because of reduced Medicaid eligibility and benefits, loss of health insurance and rising medical costs with more stringent billing systems, many pregnant women are unable to find care from private physicians and hospitals. For example in one city the local medical school's teaching hospital restricted charitable services and imposed a US $500 fee to be paid in advance for prenatal care. As a result of these measures women are turning in increasing numbers to public clinics.

The demand for services in public clinics cannot always be met (Walker, 1983; Brooks and Miller, 1983). Many of the public clinics have experienced reductions in support and staff necessitating reduced clinic hours. At the time of a recent site visit to Portland, Oregon, there was a two-month waiting period before women seeking prenatal care could be seen. In another community, circumstances were even less accommodating. Practising physicians issued vouchers for charitable prenatal care but not in

sufficient numbers to meet the need. The health department was thwarted from providing prenatal care on threat of their clients being denied intra-partum care in the local hospital. Consequently many pregnant women received prenatal care in free store-front clinics staffed by partially trained women's health aides (Brooks and Miller, 1983).

(d) Out-of-hospital deliveries

In the United States nearly all deliveries take place in hospitals, excepting only precipitate and inadvertent deliveries and a few that are planned at home by those seeking low-intervention family-centred childbearing. The latter category of home deliveries is important for reasons of preserving personal choice, but they do not represent more than a few per cent of all deliveries. In Oregon the proportion of out-of-hospital deliveries declined in 1978, 1979 and 1980. However, in 1981 there were 300 more deliveries at home than expected and 500 more in 1982. These increases were not among women who were seeking a more personally rewarding maternity experience. Fifteen per cent of them had had no prenatal care (Gebbie and Penn, 1983). Similar, though less well-documented reports, come from other parts of the country. In the 10 Southeastern states many community hospitals have been acquired by profit-making corporations. Reports are frequent that women in labour are turned away from some of these hospitals if assurances cannot be given that all bills will be paid (MCH Reports, 1983).

(e) Child abuse and neglect

Reports from many quarters agree that child abuse has increased and that our capacity to document and cope with it has decreased. High unemployment with anxious and frustrated adults spending more time in the home is regarded as a contributing condition. Sexual abuse is especially noted. Documentation of child abuse has always been a problem, but it has become worse. Staffs for social case work have been reduced so that careful investigation of suggestive situations is often not possible. Even so, the Illinois Department of Children and Family Services reported the rate of allegedly abused and neglected children (per 1000 children under 18 years of age) to have increased from 11.6 in 1980 to 15.9 in 1981 and to 18.3 in 1982 (Illinois Department of Children and Family

Services, 1983). The recidivism rate among abusing families increased in Washington, D.C. between January 1981 and June 1982 (Engel, 1983).

Neglect and abandonment of children have increased (Children's Defense Fund, 1983; Brooks and Miller, 1983; *New York Times*, 3 June 1983). In one southern city, the social welfare director reported that for the first time since the 1960s street people are seen. The new street people are not the social protestors of the 1960s, but entire families with small children having no home except perhaps for an abandoned automobile. Some of these families left former homes and migrated to other parts of the country in search of employment (Brooks and Miller, 1983).

(f) *Crimes and death associated with violence*

Death rates in the United States have declined for everyone except 15—24 year olds. Deaths in that group increased sharply after 1950 with accidents, murders and suicides being responsible for three out of four deaths (National Center for Health Statistics, 1982). Homicides account for the largest number of deaths (39%) among young non-whites. In 1979 the mortality rate among young non-whites was 20% higher than among young whites. Young non-white males consistently have the highest unemployment rate of any group. Their anger and despair are related by many analysts to high rates of violent death and crime.

Interviews in several metropolitan areas confirmed that deaths and crimes of violence among young people have increased since 1981. In Denver the Community Mental Health Clinics were closed as an economy measure. Suit was brought against the city on behalf of former clients, arguing that they were increasingly involved in crime and their mental health problems were now being cared for in city jails (Brooks and Miller, 1983).

(g) *Hunger and malnutrition*

Inquiries about hunger and malnutrition yield many reports of increasing problems (Brooks and Miller, 1983). Free food distribution centres are overwhelmed by increasing numbers and by a different clientele. They no longer consist predominantly of the social derelicts. Entire families including young children are now found in the food lines. An increase in growth stunting among poor children

has been reported (Brown, 1983). A survey among 20 counties in Michigan revealed that food distribution programmes have expanded to capacity and are no longer able to meet the need (Walker, 1983).

(h) *Access to medical care*

The withdrawal of support from publicly sponsored health service programmes did not drive more clients to prviate providers. On the contrary, more clients were driven to the public providers, which had a diminished capacity to respond with appropriate services.

Many clinics report that children are appearing more often at the public clinics for serious illness rather than for preventive services (Brooks and Miller, 1983). Tuberculosis rates are reported to have increased among the poor (*Health Advocate*, 1983). The reported cases of congenital syphilis rose 164% in 1981, presumably as a result of less adequate prenatal screening and treatment (Centers for Disease Control, 1982).

New national data on immunization rates are not available since 1981, but one state (Colorado) has reported unofficially a 6% drop in the proportion of fully immunized two year olds between 1980 and 1982 (Brooks and Miller, 1983). Clinic visits for Early Periodic Screening, Diagnosis and Treatment have declined in a number of surveyed communities (Brooks and Miller, 1983).

Not all community providers are responding to these circumstances in a far-sighted way. In Mobile, Alabama, five of the six community hospitals closed their emergency rooms on weekends '. . . to keep out people who cannot pay their bills' (*New York Times*, 27 February 1983).

In 1978—79, 15 communities chosen for their exemplary community health services were carefully studied. When the same communities were studied again in 1982—83, the following changes were found with impressive consistency:

(1) reduced budgets and staff for health services;

(2) reduced capacity to monitor unmet health needs (some local exceptions);

(3) initiation of fee systems (sometimes with considerable flexibility of enforcement);

(4) greatly increased demand for services in the public clinics, by many people who previously obtained care in the private sector;

(5) reduced home health services;

(6) generally less favourable working relation-

ships among hospitals, public clinics and privately practising physicians, with diminished referral systems;
(7) reduced outreach, casefinding, follow-up and social support services.

Some of the specific changes with relation to child health status and services are identified elsewhere in this report (Brooks and Miller, 1983).

REFERENCES

Alan Guttmacher Institute, *Teenage Pregnancy, The Problem That Hasn't Gone Away* (New York: 1981).

Annest, J. L. *et al., Blood Lead Levels for Persons 6 Months – 74 Years of Age, US 1976 – 80*; Advance Data from Vital and Health Statistics, US DHHS Publication No. (PHS) 82-1250 (Washington, 1982).

Brandt, E. N., Testimony before the Subcommittee on Rural Development Oversight and Investigation Committee on Agriculture, Nutrition and Forestry, US Senate (14 March 1983).

Brenner, M. H., 'Foetal, infant, and maternal mortality during periods of economic instability', *International Journal of Health Services*, Vol. 3 (1973), pp. 145–159.

Brooks, E. F. and C. A. Miller, unpublished material collected in 1982 and 1983 from documents and interviews associated with a study of health services in 15 communities in 13 states. During 1978 and 1979 these communities were studied and reported as models of exemplary community health care (Miller and Moos, 1981). A restudy was completed on all of the communities and their state health agencies in May 1983. This material is being prepared for publication as a doctoral dissertation by E. F. Brooks.

Brown, L., Testimony before the Senate Nutrition Subcommittee (6 April 1983).

Bryant, J., *Health and the Developing World* (Ithaca: Cornell University Press, 1969).

Budetti, P. P., J. Butler and P. McManus, 'Federal health programme reforms: implications for child health care', *Milbank Memorial Fund Quarterly*, Vol. 60 (1982), pp. 155–181.

Bureau of the Census, US Department of Commerce. *Statistical Abstract of the United States*, 1980, 1982–83.

Bureau of the Census, US Department of Commerce, *Social Indicators III, Selected Data on Social Conditions and Trends in the United States* (1980).

Bureau of the Census, US Department of Commerce, *Consumer Income: Characteristics of Households and Persons Receiving Selected Noncash Benefits, 1981* (Washington, D.C.: 1983).

Bureau of the Census, US Department of Commerce, *Consumer Income: Characteristics of the Population Below the Poverty Level: 1981*, Current Population Reports, Series P-60, No. 138.

Carter, J., *The Ten State Nutritional Survey, An Analysis* (Atlanta: Southern Regional Council, 1974).

Centers for Disease Control, US Department of Health and Human Services, 'Congenital syphilis among newborns – Texas, 1981', *Morbidity and Mortality Weekly Reports*, Vol. 31, No. 28 (23 July 1982), pp. 382–383.

Children's Defense Fund, *A Children's Defense Budget: An Analysis of the President's FY 1984 Budget and Children* (Washington, D.C.: 1983).

Congressional Budget Office, *Major Legislative Changes in Human Resources Programmes Since January 1981* (Congress of the United States, 1983a).

Congressional Budget Office, *Providing Health Coverage for the Unemployed* (Congress of the United States, 1983b).

David, R. J. and E. Siegel, 'Decline in neonatal mortality, 1968 to 1977: better babies or better care?', *Pediatrics*, Vo. 71 (1983), pp. 531–540.

Davidson, S. M., 'Variations in state Medicaid programmes', *Journal of Health Politics, Policy and Law*, Vol. 3 (1978), pp. 45–69.

Davidson, S. M., 'Physician participation in Medicaid: background and issues', *Journal of Health Politics, Policy and Law*, Vol. 6 (1982), pp. 703–717.

Davis, K., M. Gold and D. Makuc, 'Access to health care for the poor: does the gap remain?', *Annual Review of Public Health*, Vol. 2 (1981), pp. 159–182.

Economic Report of the President and Annual Report of the Council of Economic Advisers (1983).

Edwards, L. N. and M. Grossman, 'Income and race differences in children's health', National Bureau of Economic Research, Working Paper, No. 308 (Cambridge, Mass: 1979).

Engel, M., 'Child abuse cases surge, hospital study shows', *Washington Post* (12 May 1983).

EPSDT, *The Possible Dream*, US-DHHS, Health Care Financing Administration, Publication No. 77-24973 (Washington, D.C.: 1978).

Freedman, T. and D. Weir, 'Polluting the most vulnerable', *The Nation* (14 May 1983), pp. 600–604.

Gebbie, K. M. and R. Penn, *Oregon State Health Division, Maternity Services Plan* 1983–1985 (Portland: Health Division State Department Human Resources, 1983).

Gortmaker, S., Presentation at Workshop on Indicators for Monitoring Child Health Outcomes (Cambridge, Mass.: 24 January 1983).

Green, L. W., R. W. Wilson and K. L. G. Bauer, 'Data requirement to measure progress in the objectives for the nation in health promotion and disease prevention', *American Journal of Public Health*, Vol. 73 (1983), pp. 18–25.

Greenstein, R., *The Effect of the Administration's Budget, Tax, and Military Policies on Low Income Americans* (Washington, D.C.: Interreligious Task Force on US Food Policy, 1983).

Grossman, M. and S. Jacobowitz, 'Variations in infant mortality rates among counties of the United States: the roles of public policies and programmes', in J. Vander Gaag, W. B. Neenan and T. Tsukahara, (eds.), *Economics of Health Care* (New York: Praeger Special Studies, 1982).

Hack, M., I. R. Merkatz, P. K. Jones and A. A. Fanaroff, 'Changing trends of neonatal and postneonatal deaths in very-low-birth-weight babies', *American Journal of Obstetrics and Gynecology*, Vol. 137 (1980), pp. 797–800.

Havemann, J. 'Sharing the wealth: the gap between rich and poor grows wider', *National Journal* (23 October, 1982), pp. 1788–1795.

Health Advocate, Newsletter of the National Health Law Programme, No. 136 (Spring 1983), p. 6.

Health Resources Administration, *Health of the Disadvantaged Chartbook*. US-DHEW Publication No. (HRA) 77-628 (Washington, D.C.: 1977).

Hemminki, E. and B. Starfield, 'Prevention of low birth weight and pre-term birth', *Milbank Memorial Fund Quarterly*, Vol. 56 (1978), pp. 339–361.

Henshaw, S., J. D. Forrest, E. Sullivan *et al.*, 'Abortion in the United States, 1978–1979', *Family Planning Perspectives*, Vol. 13 (1981), pp. 6–18.

Hewson, M. A. and M. A. Urquhart, 'The nation's employment situation worsens in the first half of 1982', *Monthly Labor Review*, Vol. 105, No. 8 (August 1982), pp. 3–12.

Holahan, J., W. Scanlon and B. Spitz, *Public Finance: Impact of National Economic Conditions on Health Care of the Poor. Effects of the 1974–75 Recession on Health Care for the Disadvantaged*, US-DHEW Publication No. (PHS) 79-3248 (Washington, D.C.: 1979).

Howell, C. and J. Thomas, 'Price changes in 1981: widespread slowing of inflation', *Monthly Labor Review*, Vol. 105, No. 4:3,4 (April 1982).

Hunger, USA. A Report of the Citizens Board of Inquiry into Hunger and Malnutrition in the United States (Washington, D.C: New Community Press, 1968).

Illinois Department of Children and Family Services, *Labor Review*, Vol. 105, No. 4 (April 1982), pp. 3–14.

'Child abuse and neglect', Annual Report – FY 1982 (April 1983).

Kamerman, S. B. and A. J. Kahn, 'The day-care debate; a wider view', *The Public Interest*, Vol. 54 (1979), pp. 76–93.

Kennedy, E. T., S. Gershoff, R. Reed and J. E. Austin, 'Evaluation of the effect of WIC supplemental feeding on birth weight', *Journal of the Dietetic Association*, Vol. 80 (1982), pp. 220–227.

Kenniston, K., *All Our Children, The American Family Under Pressure*, The Carnegie Council on Children (New York: Harcourt, Brace, Jovanovich, 1977).

Kleinman, J. C., M. Gold and D. Makuc, 'Use of ambulatory care by the poor: another look at equity', *Medical Care*, Vol. 19 (1981), pp. 1011–1029.

Kotch, J. B. and D. Whiteman, 'Effect of a WIC programme on childrens' clinic activity in a local health department', *Medical Care*, Vol. 20 (1982), pp. 691–698.

Kotz, N., *Hunger in America: The Federal Response* (New York: The Field Foundation, 1979).

Lee, A. J., *Health Insurance Loss due to Unemployment: Descriptive and Behavioral Analyses. Effects of the 1974–75 Recession on Health Care for the Disadvantaged*, US-DHEW Publication No. (PHS) 79-3248 (Washington, D.C.: 1979).

Lin-Fu, J. S., 'Children and lead: Editorial', *New England Journal of Medicine*, Vol. 300 (1979), pp. 731–732.

McManus, M. A. and S. M. Davidson, *Medicaid and Children, A Policy Analysis* (Evanston: American Academy of Pediatrics, 1982).

Marriage and Divorce, National Center for Health Statistics, US Department of Health and Human Services, *Vital Statistics of the United States*, 1978, Volume III.

Massachusetts Advocacy Center, *For Want of a Nail. The Impact of Federal Budget Cuts on Children in Massachusetts* (Boston: Child Watch, 1983).

MCH Reports, Verbal reports made by employees of local and state governments at a conference in Chapel Hill, N.C. (14 April 1983).

Miller, C. A. and M. K. Moos, *Local Health Departments, Fifteen Case Studies* (Washington, D.C.: American Public Health Association, 1981).

Mortality, National Center for Health Statistics, US Department of Health and Human Services: *Vital Statistics of the United States, 1978*, Volume II.

Natality, National Center for Health Statistics, US Department of Health and Human Services: *Vital Statistics of the United States, 1978*, Volume I.

National Center for Health Statistics, *Health United States 1981 and 1982* (US-DHHS, 1981, 1982).

Newland, K., *Infant Mortality and the Health of Society* (Washington, D.C.: Worldwatch Institute, 1981).

New York Times, 'Emergency rooms shut on weekends in Mobile' (27 February 1983).

New York Times, 'Shelters and streets drawing more throwaway kids' (3 June 1983).

Noble, K. A., 'Are programme cuts linked to increased infant deaths?', *New York Times* (18 February 1983).

Office of Management and Budget, *Special Analyses: Budget of the US Government FY 1977*, US Government Printing Office Publication No. 041-001-00108-5 (Washington, D.C.: 1977).

Office of Technology Assessment, US Congress, *Neonatal Intensive Care, Costs and Effectiveness* (Washington, D.C.: 1981).

Oregon State Health Division, *Prenatal Care, Oregon, 1972–June 1982* (Portland: October 1982).

Orr, S. T. and C. A. Miller, 'Utilization of health services by poor children since advent of Medicaid', *Medical Care*, Vol. 19 (1981), pp. 583–590.

Pifer, A., *President's Annual Report* (New York: Carnegie Corporation, 1978).

President's Commission for the Study of Ethical Problems in Medicine and Biomedical and Behavioral Research, *Securing Access to Health Care* (Washington D.C.: Government Printing Office, 1983).

Public Interest Health Consortium of New York City,

memorandum with attached reports from Bureau of Health Statistics, Department of Health, The City of New York (30 March 1983).

Reycroft, D. and A. K. Kessler, 'Teenage pregnancy: solutions are evolving', *New England Journal of Medicine*, Vol. 303 (1980), pp. 516–518.

Rivlin, A., Statement before the Select Committee on Children, Youth, and Families, US House of Representatives (28 April 1983).

Roghmann, K. J., 'The impact of Medicaid', in R. J. Haggerty, K. J. Roghmann and I. B. Pless (eds.), *Child Health and the Community* (New York: John Wiley, 1975).

Salkind, N. J. and R. Haskins, 'Negative income tax: the impact on children from low income families', *Journal of Family Issues*, Vol. 3 (1982), pp. 165–180.

Schaefer, A. E., 'Nutritional needs of special populations at risk', *Annals, N.Y. Academy of Science* (30 November 1977).

Schorr, L. B., C. A. Miller and A. Fine, 'Current child health monitoring efforts using outcome measures', Monitoring Child Health Outcomes (Cambridge, Mass.: 23 January 1983).

Select Panel for the Promotion of Child Health, *Better Health For Our Children, A National Strategy*, Vols. I and III, US-DHHS (PHS) Publication No. 79-55071 (1981).

Sloan, F. A. and J. D. Bentkouer, *Access to Ambulatory Care and the U.S. Economy. Effects of the 1974–75 Recession on Health Care for the Disadvantaged*, US-DHEW Publication No. (PHS) 79-3248 (Washington, D.C.: 1979).

Starfield, B., 'Family income, ill health, and medical care of U.S. children', *Journal of Public Health Policy*, Vol. 3 (1982), pp. 344–359.

Temple-West, P. F. E. and C. Mueller, 'Preliminary

evaluation of the contribution of Federal Food Assistance Programme to low-income households' (Nutritional Development Services Archdiocese of Philadelphia, 1978).

Terry, S. L., 'Unemployment and its effect on family income in 1980', *Monthly Labor Review*, Vol. 105, No. 4 (April 1982), pp. 35–43.

Thurow, L. C., *The Zero Sum Society* (New York: Penguin Books, 1981).

Torres, A., J. D. Forrest and S. Eisman, 'Family planning services in the United States, 1978–79', *Family Planning Perspectives*, Vol. 13 (1981), pp. 132–141.

Urquhart, M. A. and M. A. Hewson, 'Unemployment continued to rise in 1982 as recession deepened', *Monthly Labor Review*, Vol. 106 (February 1983).

US Congress, S.2007 (21 January 1981).

US Congress, Veto Message, Economic Opportunity Amendments of 1971, S.2007, Document 92-48 (10 December 1971).

Villar, J. and J. M. Belizan, 'The relative contribution of prematurity and foetal growth retardation to low birth weight in development and developed societies', *American Journal of Obstetrics and Gynecology*, Vol. 143 (1982), pp. 793–798.

Walker, B., *The Impact of Unemployment on the Health of Mothers and Children in Michigan. Recommendations for the Nation* (Lansing: Michigan Department of Public Health, January 1983).

Weikel, M. K. and N. A. Leamond, 'A decade of Medicaid', *Public Health Report*, Vol. 91 (1976).

Zdeb, M. S., 'Differences in trends of postneonatal mortality by birthweight in upstate New York, 1968–1979', *American Journal of Public Health*, Vol. 72 (1982), pp. 734–736.

An Econometric Investigation of the Condition of Children in Italy

UGO COLOMBINO*

Laboratorio di Economia Politica,
University of Turin, Italy

Summary. — This paper provides some analytical contributions in evaluating the impact of worsening economic conditions and the prospect of more restrictive social policies on children's status in Italy. It specifies a causal model linking child's status to a set of variables (including, for example, parent's education, parent's employment, etc.). The specific effect of those variables has been estimated on the basis of two sets of data. The first consists of pooled cross-sectional and time-series information for infant mortality and the other variables indicated above. The second consists of data drawn from a 1979 household survey for the city of Turin. The results indicate that mortality rates, particularly neonatal rates, are sensitive to economic conditions and fluctuations. The employment level of mothers is also found to have a strong effect on child psychosocial status.

1. INTRODUCTION

In principle, one could evaluate the impact of economic deterioration and social policies on children in two different ways:

(a) One could try to measure the effect, if any, of a specific *event* – e.g. a dated change in the level of public spending for perinatal care or an increase in unemployment – on a certain process, e.g. the dynamics of infant mortality rates (IMR).

(b) One could specify a causal model linking the aspects of interests of children's status to a set of variables judged relevant according to some theoretical framework (medicine, epidemiology, social economics, etc.) and given a suitable body of data one could estimate the specific effect of those variables. The impact of any specific events – to the extent that the event is representable as a configuration of values of the explicative variables – can then be measured by inference from the estimates.

The first approach is practically closed to us. The seriously adverse economic climate in Italy is too recent to provide sufficient evidence. More important an explicit and clear-cut reduction in social spending has not taken place in Italy to date, although the trend of the last five to six years shows stagnation or a slight decline for certain items, and a true drastic contraction has been frequently predicted and is indeed currently a matter of political debate.

By and large, we will follow the second approach. As a reference framework we will use the theoretical and empirical literature on 'household production'.[1]

Given preferences, attitudes, environmental characteristics and wealth (full income), a certain amount of resources will be allocated to the 'production' of child health (or, more generally, 'quality of life'); the amount produced will obviously depend also on the technology which links resources to output. The implementation of this line of research ideally requires detailed individual longitudinal data with a sufficiently rich variation in environmental, household and policy variables. Given the lack of this kind of data, we resort to a compromise. We will illustrate the main trends concerning the demographic and social environment, disposable resources and opportunities facing households, on the one hand, and, on the other, trends related to 'output', i.e. to various aspects of children's health and status. Then we will present some original empirical results

---

* I wish to thank Professor L. Benso (Centro di Auxologia, III Clinica Pediatrica, Università di Torino) and Professor A. Ferro-Luzzi (Istituto Nazionale della Nutrizione, Roma) for helpful suggestions and materials. Dr F. Ortalda helped with very skilful computer assistance. The views expressed in this paper are those of the author and not necessarily those of UNICEF.

illuminating the technological relationship linking resources to 'output'.

The materials presented in this paper may be seen as relevant to four questions:

(a) Has the Italian economic situation significantly worsened during the second half of the 1970s and the early 1980s?

(b) Has social policy, during the same period, become more restrictive?

(c) Has children's health and status worsened during this period because of either one or both of the above?

(d) Is there any evidence of a significant effect on children's health and status of temporary and/or permanent changes in the economic and social environment?

The answer to the first question is obviously positive. The second question is more difficult, not the least because of the aspecific nature of social policy in Italy. It is probably fair to say that the period is characterized by stagnation, relative in some cases, absolute in others. We have already anticipated that we are not in the position of directly answering question (c). Indicators related to children's status are heavily trended. Some of them show a continuous improvement; others show a slowdown or stagnation. Overall, the events are not sufficiently clear-cut and the data not sufficiently detailed to permit the direct identification of a causal linking between the economic situation and children's status. Question (d), however, can be answered. Two original econometric works show significant effects on various indexes of children's health of temporary and systematic changes in economic opportunities. If one can say that children's overall status — however defined — has improved, it is also fair to say that there is statistically significant evidence suggesting that it would have improved *more* had the economic outlook been better and had social policy been more incisive.

The results of econometric analysis are not offered as definitive answers, but as a methodological exercise, showing the advantages of an approach which consistently links microeconomic modelling, appropriate statistical analysis and welfare economics reasoning.

2. THE INPUTS: ECONOMIC, DEMOGRAPHIC, SOCIAL AND POLICY ENVIRONMENT

(a) *Macro-economic indicators and policies*

The favourable trends in social indicators illustrated below are basically the welfare reflection of a doubling of GDP and consump-tion between 1960 and 1980. However the unemployment rate which was 3.9 in 1963, grew to 5.4 in 1970, 7.6 in 1979 and is 9.9 in 1983 (first semester). Similarly, the growth rate of GDP, which averaged about 6% in the 1960s and 3.5% in the 1970s, has recorded an increase of 3.9% in 1980, while stagnating in 1981 and 1982. In 1983 a sharp decline of about 3.5% is expected. During the last 20 years the economy has, therefore, gradually fallen below its productive capacity, due to two main causes:

(a) The first is long-standing. As the economy approaches the full employment of resources (which happened for the first time at the beginning of the 1960s), the structure of the productive matrix and of household consumption is such to imply an unbearable deficit of the balance of payments. In the absence of planned structural interventions, the only role for monetary and fiscal authorities is one of 'cooling down' the economy.

(b) The second cause is associated with the oil shocks of the 1970s and has similar implications since the increasing oil price put a heavier burden on the balance of payments.

More recent tendencies work in the same direction. Tax revenue, because of massive evasion and probably also because of the declining use of productive resources, is insufficient to finance spending, and the deficit (increasing in real terms, although only in the last two years) contributes to inflation.

Currently, the basic structural reasons forcing the economy to work progressively below its full capacity are somewhat removed from the political and scientific debate. Public deficit and inflation-related problems, mainly approached within a 'financial engineering' framework, absorb almost total attention. Over the past three years, the government's intentions — which have been continuously frustrated due to governmental instability — have been as follows:

(a) reduction of the public deficit *via* cuts in social spending;

(b) consequent reduction of inflation (possibly with contributions from some form of income policy);

(c) consequent better competitiveness of Italian products;

(d) loosening of the balance-of-payments constraints.

(b) *Family and social policy*

As hardly any *explicit* family policy exists

in Italy, discussion must necessarily begin with *social policy*. The implementation of the National Health System (NHS) in 1978 was certainly the most significant event of the last decade,[2] representing the materialization of projects conceived since the early 1960s and, indeed, of ideas expressed by the Constitution of 1948. However, this process presents at least two paradoxical elements:

(a) First, the Italian welfare system (of which the NHS is the cornerstone) comes to maturity more or less at a time when the Welfare State philosophy is suffering from a serious cultural and financial crisis all over the world.

(b) Second, the critical argument typically expressed as 'the booming of expenditures' put, for example, against the British NHS (which served as the model of the Italian system), immediately becomes the focus of the scientific and political debate, despite the fact that the empirical evidence as to the 'excessive' dimensions of the public intervention is – to say the least – controversial.

We will return to the first point later. The 'booming' argument is simply inconsistent with data expressed in real terms. While growing by about 70% between 1970 and 1980, real per capita social public expenditure between 1979 and 1980 has increased by only 1%, and between 1980 and 1981 has not increased at all. Moreover, if one looks at its composition (Table XIV.1) one can see that the only expenditures which are actually increasing are those

more one of cost-effectiveness. Looking more analytically into the health component, we see that the only expenditures which have increased significantly are those relative to hospitals and to administration. Apparently, the confluence of the implementation of NHS with restrictive spending policies has left little space for the expansion of anything but administrative costs and ex-post care in hospitals, and little, or even less space in particular for those progressive interventions which the system was supposed to introduce, i.e. prevention and hygiene and outpatient health care (Table XIV.2).

We have already seen that social assistance has actually decreased since 1975. First it must be observed that there are significant delays in the implementation of the 1977 law which transferred social assistance interventions to local authorities (*Regioni* and *Comuni*): at the end of 1982 only three *Regioni* had approved the complete normative framework for the actual implementation. Second, the introduction in 1975 of the most innovative element of social policy of the 1970s, *Consultorio Familiare*,[3] did not live up to expectations. The novel ideas contained in the project were:

(a) The multi-area and multi-disciplinary character of the intervention, bridging traditional hospital care to social and psychological care, counselling, etc.

(b) The focus on the family, more than the individual, as the proper target of social policy.

Table XIV.1. *Expenditure for social protection as per cent of GDP*

	1975	1977	1979	1981	1982
Health	5.7	5.6	6.0	5.8	5.2
Social insurance	13.7	13.1	14.1	15.7	–
Social assistance	1.6	1.5	1.4	1.4	–

Source: CENSIS (1983).

related to social insurance (mainly old-age pensions and pensions for the disabled), while those related to health and to social assistance are in fact stagnating, if not declining. It must also be remembered that public social expenditure in Italy is still one of the lowest (as per cent of GDP) in Western Europe and one of those which has increased least.

A serious criticism of NHS, therefore, cannot be based on any excessive volume of expenditure in absolute terms. The problem is

Table XIV.2. *Composition of public health services expenditure* (%)

	1978	1980	1981
Prevention and hygiene	3.71	4.06	4.14
Drugs	16.86	15.82	15.39
Fees	16.18	13.85	12.97
Hospitals	54.53	56.86	59.87
Outpatient care	8.72	9.41	7.61

Source: CENSIS (1983).

(c) The very decentralized organization and the opportunity to tailor the interventions to the specific characteristics of the community.

The realization of these principles has been rather disappointing. Financial problems, policy uncertainties and cultural and scientific deficiencies conjure to keep the experiment within very narrow limits, as the intervention remains standardized, mainly medical and individual-based.[4]

To close this section, the relatively advanced maternity leave in Italy must be mentioned. A 1971 law established compulsory leave for pregnant working women two to three months before and three months after delivery (with 80% pay) and an optional leave of six months for mothers, to be taken within the first year (with 30% pay).

(c) Monetary transfers and family allowances

As the model of the Italian welfare system is one in which the state itself tends to provide goods and services to the maximum extent, it should come as no surprise that monetary transfers are relatively unimportant and do not reveal any careful design. First, the standard transfer for each dependent member of the family (assegni familiari) has constantly been losing real value, as is clear from Table XIV.3.

Table XIV.3. Cost of living and value of transfers for one dependent member (indexes)

	Cost of living	Transfers
1958	100	100
1965	150	140
1975	245	210
1979	450	210
1982	755	420

Source: Gorrieri (1979), updated to 1982.

Second, the total monetary aid (tranfers tied to dependent members and tax allowances) covers a rather small (and declining as the number of components increases) proportion of the additional need (Table XIV.4).

A proposal to cut transfers to families with total income above a certain level is currently under discussion within the government. The act could be beneficial if it enabled the expansion of transfers to families below the level. In fact the present situation is paradoxical, since the burden to the public finances is far from insignificant while the transfers represent minimal assistance except for the very poorest households.

As a result of the broad social policy outlined above, we can note the following more specific trends in the areas of demography, health and nutrition, housing and education.

(i) Demography

Fertility rates have dramatically decreased during the last 20 years. The aggregate rate follows a steady path, as does the specific rate for women over age 30. The total rate, which was 72.4 per 1000 women in 1971, dropped to 53 per 1000 in 1978. However, the rate for younger women increased during the first 10 years and then decreased again. The shape of this trend is also reflected in marriages and female participation. As explained elsewhere,[5] if analysed jointly with data on male and female wages, this suggests that a relatively large number of decisions related to family building, fertility and presumably child care respond to market opportunities and to the economic environment in general, a point to which we will return. We can also observe that in 1978 Italy had — together with Denmark — the lowest birth rate in Western Europe and the second lowest death rate — after the Netherlands. Italy is, therefore, undergoing a relatively rapid process of aging. This is reflected both in

Table XIV.4. Total monetary aid (transfers plus tax allowances) for dependent members, and additional financial need*

Dependent members	Aid (1 month)	Need (1 month)	Aid/need (%)
Wife	34.8	158.2	22.0
Wife + 1 child	58.5	395.2	14.8
Wife + 2 children	80.3	594.9	13.5
Wife + 3 children	102.0	774.4	13.2
Wife + 4 children	123.8	941.6	13.1

Source: Gorrieri-Guerzoni (1982).
*In thousands of lire.

public opinion and social policy which focuses more on the problems of the elderly than on children's problems.

(ii) *Health and nutrition*

The evolution of life expectancy and of mortality rates by cause show a dynamic pattern typical of developed countries. Life expectancy for men, which was 63.8 years in 1950, had almost reached 70 years in 1974–79, while for women the equivalent values were 67.2 and 76 years. As in other European countries, one notices a widening gap between female and male life expectancy. The main trends in mortality by causes (see Table XIV.5) are also similar to those of the other industrialized countries.

fat and 432 of carbohydrate, i.e. more than satisfactory levels. The 1979 data, furthermore, indicate a significant increase when compared with equivalent 1975 data.

However, a more detailed investigation of nutritional quality (micro-components balance, etc.) would suggest more controversial conclusions. Going back to children's nutrition in particular (again interpreted as an input), a national survey on pre-school children (3–5 years) is summarized in Table XIV.6. We must note that the sample, composed of six different local situations, is not representative at national level. In this respect the message conveyed pertains more to the so-called socio-economic *gradient*. Even accounting for this qualification, some of the results are indeed worrying. For

Table XIV.5. *Mortality rates by causes per 100,000 people*

	1961	1971	1981
Infectious diseases	3.8	1.6	0.6
Tumours	15.6	18.9	21.5
Circulatory system diseases	42.7	44.0	44.2
Respiratory system diseases	8.6	8.3	6.9
Digestive apparatus diseases	4.8	5.9	5.5
Accidents, poisonings and traumas	5.0	5.5	4.9

Sources: For 1961 and 1971: ISTAT, *Statistiche Sociali* (1980). For 1981: CENSIS (1983).

Overall, the health status of the Italian population seems to be satisfactory, as shown by the results of a national survey of 1980, which found that the overwhelming majority of the population, except for the age group of 70 and over, enjoyed good health conditions. Unfortunately, because this was the first survey providing such information, comparison with previous years is not possible.

A specific phenomenon related to health which is more worrying is the high percentage of smokers. This is relevant of course to parents' health, but it is also an important (negative) characteristic of the physical and social environment in which children live. A number of studies have found a significant effect of parents' smoking on children's respiratory diseases.

Nutrition levels of the population confirm a sustained modernization trend, common to other social indicators. In 1979, for instance, the per capita daily average apparent consumption was of 101 grams of protein, 118 of

example, even the most favourable sample strata (CHU, CLU) seem to suffer from an insufficient iron intake, and as to energy intake an analysis of quantitative results shows that CHU's intake is barely sufficient (all other strata being below the standard).

(iii) *Housing*

Data on housing characteristics (which are certainly relevant to the quality of inputs to children's health) indicate that if basic needs seem satisfied to a considerable degree, the subjective evaluation of various aspects of housing and of the environment is somewhat disappointing, mostly due to environmental problems. For instance, while in 1978 virtually all households had access to drinkable water and electricity, 3.9% of households were in houses without toilets and 13% did not have a proper bath. It might be worth while to note at this point that these problems are mainly associated with economic development and are

Table XIV.6. *Nutritional adequacy of six groups of pre-school children (3—5 years), 1979*

Adequacy degree (%)	Energy	Proteins	Calcium	Iron
75	SR			SR, SU
75–100	SU, CR, CLU		SR	CR, CLU, CHU
100–125	CHU	SR	SU, CR	
125–150		SU	CLU, CHU	
150		CR, CLU, CHU		

Source: Ferro-Luzzi *et al.* (1979).
SR: Southern Italy, rural.
SU: Southern Italy, urban.
CR: Central Italy, rural.
CLU: Central Italy, low-income, urban.
CHU: Central Italy, high-income, urban.
Adequacy levels are those set in: SINU (1977).

likely to be sensitive in the short run to economic fluctuation, and might, therefore, contribute to paradoxical results in connection with economic slowdowns.

(iv) *Education*

During the decade 1950–60 the most important changes in the area of education involved first-level secondary school (up to 8 years of education), which has been the compulsory level since 1960. By 1971 over 99% of the population in the relevant age bracket was enrolled in the first secondary level. During the same period, enrolments for second-level secondary school (up to 13 years of education) also doubled but remain at a rather low absolute level. During the second decade, however, secondary-level enrolments more than doubled, reaching a respectable absolute level. At the end of the third decade, the total age-relevant population was covered by the compulsory system (primary and first-level secondary) and more than 50% was covered by second-level secondary school. These changes are reflected — obviously with some delay — in the composition of the population by completed years of education (Table XIV.7).

Table XIV.8 provides additional information

Table XIV.7. *Composition of the population by completed years of education*

Years of education	1961		1971		1980	
	Men	Women	Men	Women	Men	Women
0–5	79.1	85.9	68.7	76.7	52.5	61.6
8	12.8	9.1	19.6	14.8	30.0	25.2
13	5.7	4.3	9.1	7.2	13.9	11.2
18	2.4	0.7	3.0	1.3	3.7	2.0
	100.0	100.0	100.0	100.0	100.0	100.0

Source: ISTAT, *Statistiche Sociali* (1980).

Table XIV.8. *Number of students per class* and expenditure per student (index)[†]*

	1970	1975	1980
Primary school	17.2*	17.2*	16.7*
	100.0[†]	107.0[†]	134.0[†]
Secondary school, 1st level	21.6*	22.2*	21.8*
	100.0[†]	105.0[†]	97.0[†]
Secondary school, 2nd level	25.4*	23.9*	23.4*
	100.0[†]	107.0[†]	95.0[†]

Source: Deaglio and DeRita (1983).

relevant to the evaluation of total quantity and quality of resources invested in education. The situation is somewhat parallel to health and social assistance expenditures. In the same period (second half of the 1970s) when lamenting the boom of social expenditure became common, we see that there was in fact, some contraction in real terms. In the case of schooling, real total expenditure certainly increased due to the increase in enrolments; however, the expenditure for each secondary school student actually decreased between 1975 and 1980.

Table XIV.9. *Percentage of households and of children living below the poverty line*

No. of components	1975	1981
1	24	17
2	18	3
3	7	4
4, 5	7	8
6 or more	17	19
% of children in poverty	12.9	13.2

Sources: 1975: Beckerman (1980). 1981: Estimates of the author based on Banca d'Italia (1982).

3. THE OUTCOME: TRENDS IN SOME INDICATORS OF CHILDREN'S HEALTH AND STATUS

(a) *Poverty*

The category of poverty is not used in Italy as an input to the policy design process. The first — and by now unique — empirical studies attempting to assess the extent of poverty in Italy are those by Beckerman (1980) and by Sarpellon (1980). However, they use different criteria and therefore reach different results. Beckerman uses the *international standard of poverty line* (according to which the poverty line for a childless couple is the average national per capita income level; additional members are adjusted for by a system of equivalence scales). Table XIV.9 shows Beckerman's estimates for 1975 and estimates we have produced for 1981 using the same (inflation-adjusted) standards used by Beckerman, of percentages of households living below the poverty line, broken down by number of components. The table also presents rought estimates of the proportion of *children* living in poverty, obtained by using the average ratios of children to number of components. Although these estimates should be viewed with caution, we note that the percentage of children in poverty

is very near to the percentage of malnourished and/or stunted children (11% = 3% + 8%), presented in the section of this paper dealing with growth deficiencies.

The results, therefore, suggest that children's economic status has slightly worsened from 1975 to 1980, although the reader should keep in mind that, given the approximate procedure used, this difference is unlikely to be significant from a statistical point of view. The result is the outcome of a relative improvement of small households (three components) and a relative worsening of larger households (four or more components); since the proportion of children is larger in larger households, the net effect is a worsened — or at least a non-improved — children's economic status.

(b) *Perinatal mortality and infant mortality rates*

Not surprisingly, all measures of perinatal and infant mortality show a regular trend of decline, at least in the aggregate. Nonetheless, Italy is still above the average values for Western Europe (Table XIV.10). When the data are disaggregated one can observe large systematic differences and even temporary departures

Table XIV.10. *Natal, perinatal and infant mortality rates**

	Natal	Perinatal (1st week)	IMR
1960	24.5	17.8	43.9
1970	15.4	16.1	29.6
1981	7.9	9.3	14.2
1982	7.6	8.4	12.6

Source: For 1960 and 1970: ISTAT, 1975. For 1981 and 1982: ISTAT, *Bollettini mensili di statistica*.
*Per 1000.

from the trend. However, the rationale behind this more complex information cannot be disentangled without a proper statistical analysis (which will be illustrated in one of the subsequent sections).

Table XIV.11 shows infant and child mortality rates by cause. The trend is typical in showing the emergence of causes connected to development and urbanization (tumours and accidents, traumas and poisonings both of which increase their relative weight among the causes). We note even an absolute increase in death rate by accidents, etc. for infants, between 1961 and 1978. This suggests that parents might lack the proper equipment (possibly informational and organizational rather than financial) to face an increasingly complex and risky urban environment.

(d) Growth deficiencies

In the second half of the 1970s a number of surveys — most of them local — began to check the anthropometric characteristics of the Italian population. The overall trends fit the European standards set by Tanner et al. (1966), but significant — local — problems remain.

In a national survey of 8077 children aged 3–5, two categories have been used: (a) wasted, if weight/age ratio is less than 90% of the standard set by WHO, 1978; and (b) stunted, if height/age ratio is less than 95% of the standard. According to these rather strict criteria, 8% of the sample has been judged wasted and 3% has been judged both wasted and stunted (Ferro-Luzzi et al., 1981). Signifi-

Table XIV.11. *Infant and child mortality rates by cause**

Age (years)	0–1			1–14		
	1961	1971	1978	1961	1971	1978
Infectious diseases	586.2	246.0	63.1	19.0	4.9	1.2
Tumours	14.9	8.9	4.7	9.8	8.6	7.6
Circulatory system diseases	11.7	4.6	2.5	4.6	1.5	1.6
Respiratory system diseases	785.1	510.1	144.0	17.0	6.4	3.0
Digestive diseases	83.8	47.9	19.2	5.3	1.6	0.8
Accidents, poisonings, traumas	11.6	19.6	18.0	19.9	16.1	12.6

Source: CENSIS (1983).
*100,000 individuals.

(c) Morbidity

The composition by type of disaese of the population aged 0–13 in poor health reveals the overwhelming (73.4%) prevalence of respiratory diseases, followed by infectious (6.9%) and nervous diseases (4.4%), and others. These indications are confirmed by data on the relative prevalence of various diseases. The results come from a national survey taken in 1980. Unfortunately, this is the first survey of this kind, and a comparison with previous years is, therefore, not feasible.

Although the percentage of people in poor health in this age group is rather low (slightly over 4%), the incidence of respiratory diseases seems alarming. One can compute that about 3% in this age group currently suffer from some form of respiratory disease (1% from chronic bronchitis).

cant differences exist between urban and rural areas and by income level, a result common to other surveys, for example Greco et al. (1983).

(e) Schooling

Table XIV.12 illustrates the trends in percentage of drop-outs and percentage of students repeating the year. These data are difficult to interpret because the mix of students, and, therefore, the distribution of abilities has changed so dramatically during the period, at least for secondary school. However, the different trend of students repeating in primary school and in secondary school is roughly parallel to the respective trends in real public expenditure per student. In this respect, the stagnation of expenditure at the secondary level probably did not help.

Table XIV.12. *Percentages of drop-outs* and of students repeating the year†*

	Primary school		Secondary school, 1st level		Secondary school, 2nd level	
	*	†	*	†	*	†
1960	–	8.2	–	12.5	–	6.4
1970	–	8.4	–	10.1	–	8.0
1975	–		4.0		8.1	
1980	–	1.3	4.3	8.1	10.1	7.3

Source: ISTAT, *Annuari di Statistiche dell'istruzione.*
– Information missing.

4. THE TECHNICAL RELATIONSHIP BETWEEN INPUTS AND OUTPUTS

The technical relationship between inputs and outputs is in our view the most crucial point to be illuminated in terms of designing and evaluating social policy. We have already said that the information at our disposal is far from adequate. A number of studies have investigated the relationship between socio-economic indicators and mortality, or socio-economic indicators, nutrition, anthropometric measures and physical performance of children. Conclusions reached are mixed and tentative. This is not surprising, given the complexity of the subject, but in our view these studies are not particularly satisfactory mainly because of:

(a) the statistical methodology used, which is inspired by the traditional univariate experimental setting, which is not appropriate to the intrinsic multivariate character of the subject;

(b) the largely non-parametric approach to modelling, which makes it difficult to extract the implications for policy analysis.

In the following sections we present the results of research which tries to specify empirical models along the lines suggested by micro-economic theory, which produces results in the format relevant to welfare economics, and which uses appropriate econometric methodologies. It will be evident that these results do not provide definitive answers; however, they do illustrate promising lines of research.

(a) *The elasticities of household technologies*

In this section we present some results related to the measurement of household responsiveness of allocation-of-time decisions to changes in economic opportunities. Households derive utility from ultimate commodities (health, shelter, etc.), which they 'produce' by combining time inputs with market goods, public goods and services, subject to a specific household technology. In particular, children are a relatively time-intensive commodity. For convenience, let us use the term 'child quality of life' to signify the set of various aspects of children's health and status which interest us. Two types of substitution are relevant: first, the degree to which the household is able to divert other commodities and time to child quality of life in response to some change in economic environment; and second, the degree to which the household is able to substitute among inputs to the production of child quality of life. Suppose the household suffers from the reduction in some sort of resource which is used as an input to child quality of life (e.g. a reduction in some sources of income, or a drop in the delivery of some public service, etc.). The effect on child quality of life will depend on the absolute and relative magnitudes of those two elasticities.

(b) *A nation-wide model of perinatal and infant mortality*

We have used pooled cross-section and time-series data to estimate short- and long-term effects of fluctuations in disposable economic resources (proxied by the unemployment rate) on natal mortality, mortality in the first year and mortality in the first month. The structure of data allows us to control both for factors which change between units of observation but are constant through time (such as permanent income) and for factors which change through time *and* between units of observation (such as birth rate). The model, the estimation methodology and the results are fully explained in the Appendix. Table XIV.13 presents the most relevant implications of the estimates, i.e. the percentage variation in the indexes of mortality due to a one-point increase (respec-

Table XIV.13. *Short- and long-run effects (% varia-*
tion) in index of mortality due to 1 percentage point
increase in unemployment rate

	Short run	Long run
Natal mortality	0.100	0.199
Perinatal mortality		
(1st month)	1.530	1.643
Infant mortality	1.480	0.000

Source: Author's calculations.

tively temporary or permanent) in the unemployment rate.[6]

For example, suppose we start from a situation with a natal mortality rate of 1% and an unemployment rate of 5%. Suppose that in a certain year the unemployment rate jumps to 10%, i.e. increases by 5 percentage points. Then, that year the expected natal mortality rate, other things being equal, will be: 1.005% = 1% + 1%(1 + (0.001)5) or 1005 out of 100,000 (instead of 1000 out of 100,000 as before). If the increase in unemployment is permanent, the long-run change in natal mortality will be roughly twice: in the example, 1010 out of 100,000. The effects on the infant mortality rate are much higher in the short run. The same five-point increase in unemployment rate would on average produce an increase in infant mortality rate from, say, 15 per 1000 live births to 16 per 1000. The long-run effect, however, is estimated to be not significantly different from zero. This means that in the long run, households would realize the permanent cut in resources and would successfully adjust (presumably reallocating resources) to push down the infant mortality rate towards previous levels. This makes sense if we admit that:

(a) in the long run, households are more responsive to exogenous shocks than social policy authorities or decision-makers;

(b) households have less control and/or less information on factors affecting natal mortality than on factors affecting mortality in the first year.

These conditions while not realized everywhere, might be true of Italy.

The effect on mortality in the first month in the short run is slightly larger than the effect on the infant mortality rate. The long-run effect is positive and larger than the short-term effect, but only marginally so. Both these results seem logical: the first month (in particular the first week) is a very delicate period, especially in presence of low natal mortality

rates (which *ceteris paribus* imply a larger proportion of fragile live individuals). It is, therefore, reasonable that the mortality in this period would be the most sensitive to economic fluctuations. In the long run the households are apparently not able to adjust, although the increment with respect to the short run is less than that observed for natal mortality.

In conclusion:

(a) Mortality rates seem indeed sensitive to economic fluctuations and to permanent changes in economic opportunities.

(b) Mortality rates in the first month are the most sensitive, while natal mortality rates are the least sensitive.

(c) In the long run, households seem to be able to adjust for permanent economic changes as far as infant mortality rate is concerned; this is not the case, however, of natal mortality and of mortality in the first month.

(c) *Child psycho-physical disturbances on the basis of a local survey*

In this section we apply the same kind of reasoning to a very different kind of phenomenon and to a very different set of data. Despite these differences we want to stress that models estimated are derived from the same theoretical approach.

The data used in this analysis come from a survey of 1000 households in Turin, interviewed in 1979. The survey covers a broad range of issues, in a 'quality of life' perspective. In the section concerning health status, parents are presented with a list of disturbances (e.g. eating difficulties, enuresis, difficulties at school or nursery and insomnia) and asked whether their children (in two age groups: under age 6 and age 6–13) are suffering from these disturbances.

Even if not particularly worrying in the short term, such disturbances can be symptoms of more serious problems emerging in the long run, and may themselves permanently affect children's social and educational performance. They are, therefore, relevant to social policy analysis and design.

(i) *An exploratory analysis*

Table XIV.14 presents the results of an exploratory analysis. As a dependent variable we use a dummy variable which takes value = 1 when at least one of the disturbances is recorded as present; it takes value = 0 otherwise. The analysis is limited to children aged 6–13. The

Table XIV.14. *Maximum likelihood estimates of equation* 1 – *exploratory analysis for children* 6–13

Variable	Coefficient	χ^2
Constant	1.840	2.14
Father underemployed	−0.240	0.72
Father's education	−0.340	0.74
Mother's education	−0.061	1.58
Mother unemployed	1.331	12.32
Mother underemployed	0.299	0.28
Mother's hours	0.478	9.84
No. of children	0.265	1.80
Income	−0.013	0.43
Noise	0.035	0.02
Air pollution	0.106	0.17
No green	0.216	0.70
Bad housing	0.744	4.50
$-2 \log(L^*/L^\circ)$	397.89	
No. of observations	352	

model specified is a logistic model. Probability (at least one disturbance is recorded) = $(1 + \exp(\mathbf{xb}))^{-1}$ (1) where $\mathbf{x}$ is a vector of personal and environmental characteristics and $\mathbf{b}$ is a vector of parameters. These parameters are estimated by maximum likelihood method.

The variables included in vector $\mathbf{x}$ are the following:

Constant: a constant term

Father's education: father's years of education

Mother's education: mother's years of education

No. children: number of children aged 6–13 in the family

Mother's hours: mother's annual hours of work (= 0 if she does not work)

Income: total annual family income (thousands of lire)

Mother unemployed: dummy = 1 if mother is unemployed

Mother underemployed: dummy = 1 if mother is underemployed

Father underemployed: dummy = 1 if father is underemployed[1]

Noise: dummy = 1 if parents lament noisy area

No green: dummy = 1 if parents lament absence of green areas within reach

Air pollution: dummy = 1 if parents lament air pollution

Bad housing: dummy = 1 if parents lament bad housing conditions (dampness etc.)

Parents' disturbances: dummy = 1 if at least one disturbance (gastric disturbances, health disturbances, insomnia, depression) is present among parents.

Only households which have at least one child in the age group 6–13 are included in the estimation sample. Therefore we are left with 352 cases, out of the original 1000 interviewed households.

When looking at results reported in Table XIV.14 and at the significance of coefficients, the effects of *mother unemployed* or *mother's hours* and of *bad housing* are most impressive. For example, the coefficient of *mother unemployed* would imply that if the mother is unemployed then the probability of disturbances for her children increases by 89%.[8]

The coefficient of *mother's hours* can be given an interesting interpretation. If time inputs to child care represent roughly a constant proportion of total time available in the year *minus* hours of work, then the coefficient of *mother's hours* is a measure of (−) the effect of mother's time input to child care (up to a multiplicative constant). This suggests the specification of a structural model where *mother's hours* is replaced by mother's *market wage* (interpreted as the opportunity cost of time). This should produce theoretically better estimates, since *mother's hours* is endogenous, while *mother's wage* is not.

(ii) *A structural model*

Details of the derivation of this model are given in Colombino (1981). As far as the empirical specification is concerned, the only differences with respect to the previous exploratory analysis are:

(a) *mother's hours* is replaced by the log of mother's market wage (actual or potential);[9]

(b) *income* is replaced by the log of 'full'

income (*full income*), i.e. maximum monetary income attainable by the household.

Results are given in Table XIV.15. As one would expect, the coefficient of *wage* is positive. A higher cost of time will make time-consuming activity (such as child care) more costly. As a consequence, less of these activities will be performed. In particular, time inputs to child care will be reduced and a lower level of children's health will be 'produced', *other things being equal*; probability of disturbances will then increase.

unemployment, since the sample does not include any unemployed fathers. Therefore mother's unemployment is to be interpreted as a general proxy for the household's disequilibrium on the labour market. Although this disequilibrium is taken into account by the introduction of a simple dummy, our model enables us to give a rather precise interpretation to the coefficient of this dummy, and to draw rather interesting implications. The coefficients of *mother unemployed* implies that if the mother is unemployed, children's

Table XIV.15. *Maximum likelihood estimates of equation* 1 – *structural model for children* 6–13

Variable	Coefficient	χ^2
Constant	1.857	2.14
Wage	0.787	2.04
Full-income	−0.440	0.41
Mother unemployment	0.714	3.95
Father's education	−0.037	0.86
Mother's education	−0.065	1.54
No. of children	0.289	2.16
Noise	0.009	0.00
No green	0.233	0.32
Air pollution	0.147	0.83
Bad housing	0.592	2.89
Adult's disturbance	0.276	0.92
$-2 \log(L^*/L^\circ)$	406.25	
No. of observations	352	

As to the main focus of this analysis, the coefficient of *mother unemployed* is still very large and significant. If mother is unemployed, the probability of disturbances increases by 47.34%. It is interesting to compare this result with the estimates of the previous section. There, the effect of 1 point increase in unemployment rate on mortality indexes ranges between 0.100 and 1.53. Here, a 1 percentage point increase in the probability of unemployment (which is the analogue of the unemployment rate for a 'representative' individual) means an increase in the probability of disturbances by 0.47%. Therefore, despite the differences in data, methodology and nature of phenomena, the orders of magnitude of the effects implied by the estimates are quite comparable and somewhat reassuring on the reliability of these results.

As we have seen, we are unable to measure the effect of a more comprehensive index of

health level is reduced by 80% with respect to its previous level. Reasoning as before, a 1 percentage point increase in the probability of unemployment means a reduction by 0.8% in health level relevant to those disturbances.[10]

Percentage variations in probability for a 1 point increase in selected variables have been computed. Another perspective could be obtained by the calculation of equivalence scales. For example, one more child implies that the cost of producing the same level of health for all children increases by 93%; thus there are very weak — if any at all — economies of scale in the production of children's health. This is in sharp contrast with equivalence scales computed on the basis of household consumption budgets, which suggest very strong scale effects. It is also in contrast with current policy indications for family allowances (or similar institutions), which usually assume large-scale effects.

NOTES

1. See Becker (1965) for a general presentation and survey; see Grossman (1972) and Rosenzweig and Shultz (1980) for some applications to children's health.

2. It must be noted that before 1978 almost all of the employed population was already covered by public or private (mainly firm-based) insurance. Therefore, the NHS is probably more correctly interpreted as a nationalization rather than as the introduction of a novel system. This qualification can help to understand the unsympathetic reactions to the NHS from significant proportions of the population. In fact, a massive financial redistribution is likely to have taken place.

3. District-based centre which supplies a wide and integrated range of services (counselling, health care, prevention, contraception, etc.) to the family.

4. See, for example, Donati (1982).

5. All the effects reported are based on estimates which are statistically significant at standard levels.

6. As Note 5.

7. No unemployed father is present in the sample.

8. As in the previous model, the proportional effect on the probability of a unit increase in a variable x is $b \, (1 - P)$ where b is the estimated coefficient of x, and P is a starting value of the probability of disturbances. Therefore, if we start from the average value of P over the sample (0.33), the percentage effect of *mother unemployed* going from 0 to 1 is $1.331 \, (1 - 0.33)^{100} = 89\%$.

9. Potential market wage for non-working women is estimated with a consistent procedure over the subsample of working women. Results of this estimation are not reported here. See Colombino and Zabalza (1982).

10. It can be shown that the attained level of health (h) can be approximated as:

$$\bar{h} = h \, (1 - \theta d), \; 0 < \theta < 1$$

where d = *mother unemployed* and h is the level that would be attained in equilibrium. The resulting coefficient of *mother unemployed* is equal to $- (1/s) \log \, (1-\theta)$, where $(1/s)$ is the coefficient of *full income*. Therefore

$$1 - \theta = \exp \, (-s\beta_d) \approx 0.20$$

where β_d is the coefficient of *mother unemployed*.

REFERENCES

Banca d'Italia, *I bilanci delle famiglie italiane nel 1981* (1982).

Becker, 'A theory of the allocation of time', *Economic Journal* (1965).

Beckerman, 'Povertà in Italia nel 1975', *Rivista internazionale di Scienze Sociali* (1980), pp. 220–249.

CENSIS, *Spesa pubblica e politica sociale* (F. Angeli, 1983).

Colombino, U., 'The economics of the disturbed child', *Micros*, Vol. 2 (1981), pp. 10–16.

Colombino, U., 'Un modello per la stima delle preferenze e delle technologie familiari', *Ricerche Economiche* (1983).

Colombino, U. and DeStavola, 'A model of female labour supply in Italy using cohort data', *Journal of Labor Economics* (forthcoming, 1984).

Colombino, U. and A. Zabalza, 'Labour supply and quantity constraints: Results on female participation and hours in Italy', Discussion Paper No. 125 (Centre for Labour Economics, London School of Economics, 1982).

Deaglio and DeRita, *Il punto sull'Italia* (Mondadori, 1983).

Donati, 'I servizi sociali in Italia', in Donati and Rossi, *Welfare State, problemi e prospettive* (F. Angeli, 1982).

Ferro-Luzzi *et al.*, 'Nutrition, environment and physical performance of preschool children in Italy', *Bibliotheca Nutritio e Dieta* (1979), pp. 85–106.

Ferro-Luzzi *et al.*, 'Nutritional deficiencies in preschool and prepubertal children', *Bibliotheca Nutritio e Dieta* (1981), pp. 30–42.

Gorrieri, *La giungla dei bilanci familiari* (Il Mulino, 1979).

Gorrieri and Guerzoni, *Il salario sociale* (Edizioni Lavoro, 1982).

Greco *et al.*, 'Factors affecting growth in Campania's school children', *Acta Medica Auxologica* (1983).

Grossman, 'On the concept of health capital and the demand for health', *Journal of Political Economy* (1972), pp. 223–255.

ISTAT, 'Tendenze evolutive della mortalità infantile in Italia', *Annali di Statistica*, VIII, 29 (1975).

ISTAT, 'Indagine statistica sulle condizioni di salute della popolazione e sul ricorso ai servizi sanitari', *Supplemento al Bollettino di Statistica*, No. 12 (1982).

Ministero del Lavoro, *Relazione della Commissione sui problemi della famiglia* (Rome: 1982).

Rosenzweig and Shultz, 'Birth weight, the production of child health, and input demand', Discussion Paper 352 (Yale Economic Growth Center, 1980).

Sarpellon, 'Definire e misurare la povertà nuovo tentative per il caso italiano', *Rivista Internazionale di Scienze Sociali* (1980), pp. 264–290.

SINU, *Livelli di assunzione raccomandati di nutrienti per gli italiani* (Rome: Istituto Nazionale della Nutrizione, 1977).

Tanner *et al.*, 'Standards from birth to maturity',

Archives of Diseases in Childhood (London: 1966).

WHO, 'Reference data for the weight and height of children', NUT 78/1 (Geneva: 1978).

APPENDIX

We will consider a model of the following type:

$$y_{it} = \alpha u_{it} + \delta u_{it-1} + \gamma y_{t-1} + \psi U_i + X_{it}\beta + v_{it}. \quad \text{(A.1)}$$

where $y_{it} = \log\left(\dfrac{\widetilde{P}_{it}}{1 - \widetilde{P}_{it}}\right)$

$\widetilde{P}_{it}$ = index of infant mortality in unit i at time t (alternatively, proportion of born dead over total births, or proportion of deaths in the first year or in the first month over total number of children born alive)

u_{it} = unemployment rate in unit i at time t

u_{it-1} = lagged value of u_{it}

y_{it-1} = lagged value of y_{it}

U_{it} = 'permanent' (average) unemployment rate in unit i

X_{it} = vector of relevant variables changing across units and/or throughout time.

The period is the year, the units of observation are the regions. Therefore we exploit the informational advantages of time-series and cross-section pooling. Unemployment u_{it} and u_{it-1} is assumed to unexpectedly *ration* the quantity of labour, and hence income, to which households have access. Variables which do not vary over time, such as U_i and others appearing in X_{it}, are meant to measure permanent differences between units, at any time, and are treated as exogenous. They tend to permanently shift the budget constraint faced by the households. U_i is a sort of 'permanent' unemployment rate. In contrast with what happens with u_{it}, households *know* about U_i and make plans conditional on its value. Uncertainty, frictions, unexpected constraints, etc. will force households to revise their plans, try to adjust, etc. All these processes are approximately taken into account by the introduction of the lagged dependent variable y_{it-1}.

Note that from this model we get two estimates of the long-run effect of unemployment. One is directly measured by the coefficient of U_i, ψ. The other is implied by the estimates of the time-series dynamics:

Long-run effect = $(\alpha + \delta)/(1 - \gamma)$.

It seem reasonable to impose the restriction

$$(\alpha + \delta)/(1 - \gamma) = \psi$$

which amounts to imposing that the long-run effect of unemployment estimated from cross-sectional variations (ψ) must be equal to the long-run effect estimated from time-series variations $(\alpha + \delta)/(1 - \gamma)$.

(a) *Data and variables*

We use annual data from 1959 to 1982 for the 20

Italian regions. We have therefore $20 \times 24 = 480$ observations. Since we use one-period lags, we must eliminate the 1959 observation for each region, and we are then left with 460 observations.

We estimate two models. In the first, $\widetilde{P}_{it}$ is the proportion of children who die in the first year. In the second, P_{it} is the proportion of children who are born dead. Variables included in vector X_{it} are the following:

A *constant* term

Birth$_{it}$: birth rate in Region i at time t

Beds$_i$: No. of hospital beds (per 1000 people) in Region i (measured in 1980)

Bad health$_i$: proportion of adults declaring themselves in a 'non-good' health status in Region i (measured in 1980)

Illiteracy$_i$: proportion of illiterates in Region i in 1971

Trend$_t$: a time trend (1, 2, . . . , 24).

Table A1 contains averages and standard deviations of variables for the whole sample. Statistical sources are as follows:

Mortality rates: Istat, *Annuario di Statistiche Demografiche* and *Annuario Statistico Italiano*, 1959–81; *Bollettino mensile di Statistica*, 1982.

Unemployment rates: *Annuario di Statistiche del Lavoro*, 1959–81; *Bollettino mensile di Statistica*, 1982.

Beds: *Annuario Statistico Italiano*, 1981.

Bad Health: Istat, *Indagine speciale sulle condizioni di salute della popolazione*, 1980.

Illiterates: Istat, *Statistiche Sociali*, 1980.

Table A1. *Means and standard deviations of variables used in Appendix**

Variable	Mean	S.D.
Natal mortality	15.06	7.59
1st year mortality	26.70	12.34
Birth rate	15.55	4.24
u	4.84	3.13
U	4.84	3.13
Beds	7.33	1.96
Bad health	14.80	2.61
Illiterates	7.38	5.65
Selection	0.04	0.02

*Whole sample.

(b) *Results*

Table A2 presents the results of the estimation of the model for the proportion of children who are born dead. As explained before, we impose the restriction:

$$(\alpha + \delta)/(1 - \gamma) = \psi.$$

Moreover, preliminary estimates suggests that parameter δ is not significantly different from zero. Our final specification used for the estimation is therefore:

$$y_{it} = \alpha u_{it} + \gamma y_{it-1} + \frac{\alpha}{\Lambda - \gamma} U_i + X_{it}\beta + v_{it}. \qquad (A.2)$$

Table A2. *Estimates of equation* (A2) – *probability of natal mortality*

Variable	Coefficient	t-statistic
Constant	−1.967	−13.93
u_{it}	0.001	2.54
y_{it-1}	0.551	17.32
U_i	0.002	–
Beds$_i$	−0.012	−6.28
Bad health	0.008	8.86
Illiterates	0.010	7.36
Birth	0.008	5.56
Trend	−0.019	−12.42
Coeff. of autocorrelation	0.33	
No. of observations	460	

As the equation is non-linear in parameters, we adopted an iterative procedure. We start from an initial 'guess' for γ, then we estimate α; from this we get a new estimate for γ, and so on until a reasonable stability in parameters is reached.

The first remarkable result to be noted is the significance of the current unemployment rate on mortality. The estimated coefficient implies that a temporary increase of 1 point in unemployment rate, other things being equal, induces an increase of 0.1% in natal mortality. (In the logistic specification used, the proportion and effect on probability of death of a 1 point increase in a variable x is $b(1 - P)$ where b is the estimated coefficient and P is the average probability of death.) For example, if unemployment rate goes from 5 to 10%, natal mortality will go from 1 (say) to 1.005% or from 1000 out of 100,000 to 1005 out of 100,000.

The long-run effect of unemployment is roughly twice: i.e. a permanent increase of 1 point in unemployment rate will imply an increase of 0.2% in natal mortality. Table A3 does not report an exact standard t-statistic for this effect because of the iterative technique adopted; however, the coefficient is surely significant (in fact its t-statistic must lie somewhere between the t-statistic for u_{it} and the t-statistic for y_{it-1}.

The coefficient of *birth* also appears with the right sign and with a good level of significance. One point less in birth rate implies a decrease in natal mortality of 0.8%. This probably captures the effects of less children per woman, younger age of mothers,

and a trade-off between quantity and quality of life of children.

Beds, bad health and *illiterates* are all significant with the correct sign. They account for permanent differences in health services supply conditions, social environment, educational family background, genetic inheritance. As such, these variables are just proxies. If we knew the technical relationship between these indexes and social expenditure, we would be able to estimate the marginal effect of social expenditure on birth mortality. We can infer that the effect must be rather large. For example, one more hospital bed per 1000 implies a decrease of 0.8% in birth mortality. Table A3 computes per cent variations in birth mortality rate due to a 1 point increase in selected variables.

Table A4 presents the results of the estimation of the model for the proportion of children dying during the first year. In addition to the restriction

$$(\alpha + \delta)/(1 - \gamma) = \psi$$

we found that we could not refute the hypothesis of the long-run effect of unemployment being zero. Therefore, our final specification is in this case:

$$y_{it} = \alpha(u_{it} - u_{it-1}) + \gamma y_{t-1} + X_{it}\beta + v_{it} \qquad (A.3)$$

In addition to the variables included in model

Table A3. *Percentage variation in probability of natal mortality for a 1 point increase in selected variables*

Variable	% variation in probability
u_{it}	0.100
U_i	0.199
Beds	−1.192
Bad health	0.794
Illiterates	0.993
Birth rate	0.794

Table A4. *Estimates of equation* (A.3) – *probability of death in the first year*

Variable	Coefficient	t-statistic
Constant	−1.921	−24.80
u_{it}	0.015	9.40
y_{it-1}	0.488	23.54
U_i	0.000	–
Beds	−0.017	−10.17
Bad health	−0.000	0.01
Illiterates	0.000	−1.90
Birth	0.014	13.67
Selection	3.910	13.91
Trend	−0.019	−22.70
Coeff. of autocorrelation	−0.15	
No. of observations	460	

(A.2), here we have a selection-bias-correction term (*selection*), which accounts for the fact that we are estimating our parameters over the subpopulation of survivors.

The unemployment coefficient is again very significant. The effect is larger than on birth mortality. A 1 point increase in unemployment implies an increase in the probability of death in the first year by 1.48%. So if we start with an unemployment rate of 5% and a mortality rate of 1.5%, if unemployment goes to 10%, then the mortality rate goes to 1.9%. The long-run effect of unemployment is estimated to be not significantly different from zero. Unexpected variations in the budget constraints do have their effects on mortality, but households appear to be able to completely adjust and compensate in the long run: if confronted with a permanent increase in unemployment, they would reallocate disposable resources to restore the previous level of child health. In contrast, they do not seem able to do the same as far as birth mortality is concerned. (This makes sense if we assume that households: (a) have less information on the 'technical' relation between resources and birth

mortality risks than they have on the relation between resources and mortality in the first year; and (b) have less control over birth mortality risks than over risk of mortality in the first year.)

The effect of birth rate is also significant and larger than in the first model.

Among environmental variables only *beds* is significant and has the correct sign.

The term for selection correction seems to be effective. Table A5 presents the implied percentage variations in the probability of death in the first year for a 1 point increase in selected variables.

Table A5. *Percentage variation in mortality in the first year for a 1 point increase in selected variables*

Variable	% variation in probability
u_{it}	1.48
Birth	1.38
Beds	−1.67

A Summary and Interpretation of the Evidence

GIOVANNI ANDREA CORNIA*
UNICEF, New York

1. THE PREMISE: SETTING THE RECENT EVENTS IN A LONG-TERM PERSPECTIVE

How can one summarize the ways children have been affected as falls in incomes and cutbacks have spread around the world? What kind of broad policies should be promoted to counterbalance the deteriorations illustrated in the 11 case studies presented here? Will the economic recovery automatically reintroduce steady improvements in child welfare? Is any action being taken to maintain or even improve the situation of children during the present adverse economic circumstances? Before addressing these questions, attention must be paid to the structural determinants of social and child welfare, some of which have been discussed in the survey of the literature (pp. 187–202). Besides preventing overemphasis on the short-term aspects of child welfare, these considerations are important for identifying appropriate policy measures.

According to the central theme of the development literature[1] of the late 1960s to the early 1980s, poverty, malnutrition and high infant and overall mortality primarily result from *structural* (as opposed to *cyclical*) causes, and progress in human welfare depends more on the *pattern* rather than the *rate* of economic growth. In many instances, domestic factors such as unequal land distribution, insecure and inequitable tenancy agreements, a skewed distribution of income, misuse of public finance and the socio-cultural marginalization of entire sections of the population on religious, class and ethnic grounds have a far greater influence on standards of living than the growth — or the decline — of the overall economy. Often, the constraints imposed upon human development by such domestic factors are rigidified even more by the overall dependence of many developing countries on the industrialized nations. Colonial inheritance, technical and financial dependence, structure and chronically deteriorating terms of trade and, more recently, heavy indebtedness have contributed and still do contribute very dis-tinctly and directly to the impoverishment of large sections of Third World populations.

The case for concentrating on structural factors rather than on economic fluctuations, however severe, is reinforced by the experience of several countries which — despite rapid growth in output and incomes — have witnessed stagnation, or even increases, in their numbers of absolute poor. Indeed, unless particularly severe, economic fluctuations may not have a very obvious impact in terms of child welfare. Conversely, their end — however welcome — might not be in itself a solution to the structural problems of children. For children, in other words, reflation is not enough.

While the structural context of child welfare problems is fundamental, the present crisis — unprecedented in terms of its length, depth and pervasiveness — has severely aggravated the situation of children of several social groups and has certainly slowed down improvements. The argument that 'poor people are so poor that they do not have access even to the world crisis' may have some validity in regions such as Latin America where the economic crisis has primarily affected the urban middle-lower classes engaged in the formal economic sector, or for India's rural poor masses who are largely insulated from the world economy. On the other hand, the sharp fall in incomes and severe cutbacks in social services caused or aggravated by the international recession are in many parts of the world swelling the army of the unemployed who have less access to social services and who tend to fall below a given poverty line. Clearly, the children of these new poor, as well as those of the 'old' poor,

---

* The perceptive comments of Richard Jolly on an earlier draft of this paper are gratefully acknowledged. My gratitude goes also to Sharon Meager who skilfully collaborated in the editing of this paper and to Josephine Rajasegera and Sarup Jha who patiently reproduced the various drafts. None of these persons bears any responsibility for any remaining error. The views expressed are those of the author and not necessarily those of UNICEF.

face weak prospects of overall welfare and often, in some cases, risk of death.

2. MEASURING CHANGES IN CHILD WELFARE

(a) *Factors influencing child welfare*

Measuring child welfare obviously implies agreement on its main determinants and their impact, as well as on the type of quantitative indicators used to assess its level and changes. Methodologically this poses a number of well-known problems which this paper will largely avoid by measuring social, and more particularly, child welfare through an array of economic and social indicators. These have been used jointly — and somewhat subjectively — to determine whether the situation of children has improved, deteriorated or remained constant.

Figure XV.1 presents a very simplified scheme of 'production' of child welfare which also highlights the mechanisms through which international economic events may contribute to changes in the situation of children. This framework has several obvious limitations. Highly simplified, it does not differentiate either the impact of the relevant factors or the manner in which the world economic crisis is transmitted to countries with different socio-economic characteristics. Moreover it does not clearly separate the influence of long-term, structural factors from that of short-term fluctuations.

As shown in Figure XV.1 and as illustrated in the survey of the literature included in this issue, there are three dominant types of influences on child welfare. The first is the set of *family and community circumstances* determining the child's physical, social, cultural and psychological environment. Parental education, for example (the mother's in particular), has a most important influence on child welfare,

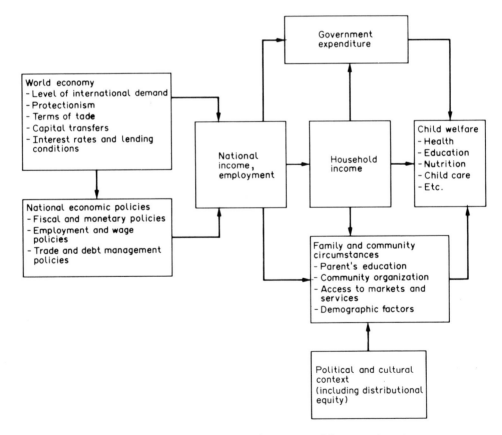

Figure XV.1. *Linkages between world economic recession and child welfare.*

mediated through means such as enhancing proper utilization of household and community economic resources through better knowledge of child-feeding and rearing practices. Short recessions are unlikely to profoundly alter this pool of family and community knowledge and awareness.

The second major influence on child well-being, overwhelmingly so for poor families, is *household income*. Household income (in cash or kind from wage labour or agricultural work) is obviously necessary for the satisfaction of a child's needs, particularly in the areas of nutrition, clothing and housing and, in some countries, health and education. A decline in employment, agricultural output or other changes will reduce such income, harming family and child welfare of low-income households, particularly when the fall is sharp and sudden, since possibilities for adjustment (shifting consumption patterns, migration, etc.) are greater when changes take place gradually.

A third influence is represented by *government expenditure* on social services. Resources for such services are generally raised through tax revenues, which can dip dramatically in the event of sharp falls in production, trade and consumption. Reductions in expenditure are then unavoidable, but the type of public expenditures cut (armaments, health, food subsidies, etc.) is a matter of choice. Clearly, the seriousness of the consequences for social equity and child welfare depends on the choices made.

(b) Classes of indicators

Household income, government expenditure on social services and other family or community resources (largely immaterial, such as parental education) can be considered *inputs* for the 'production' of child welfare. The higher (lower) these inputs, the higher (lower), the level of child welfare. Among these three inputs, family and community resources vary very slowly over time and it is unlikely that even a severe and prolonged recession such as a current one can substantially reduce their current level. In contrast, sharp declines in household income following economic recessions are bound to affect child welfare directly and immediately as poor families must cope with reduced purchasing power in the areas of nutrition, clothing and housing sanitation, as well as health care, in the case of private medicine. A minimum level of consumption can be maintained for some time when households dispose of some form of savings, even if current incomes fall below the value of a basic needs basket. But when financial savings, food stocks and other assets are depleted and in the absence of income transfer (from other members of the extended family or from lenders, etc.), households are forced to curtail their consumption levels. In the case of poor families — who routinely spend more than 80% of their household income on food and other necessary consumption — overall welfare and nutritional status obviously suffer.

The third main input to child welfare, government social expenditure, also varies closely with the overall economic situation. Even if expenditure can be maintained for a while thanks to inherent time-lags operating between approval of appropriations and actual expenditure of funds, government *real* expenditure will decline as revenue from taxation is reduced by a lower level of economic activity. The expansion of the monetary mass can temporarily finance the same level of services but at a cost of higher inflation reducing household purchasing power. Expenditure can also be maintained by internal or external borrowing, but this can only be a short-term solution.

A first, rather indirect, way to measure change in child welfare, therefore, is to measure the variation in the level of *inputs* for child welfare. However, when faced with economic retrenchment, both households and government might rationalize their expenditures, for instance, switching to equally nutritious but cheaper foods or to low-cost but equally effective social services. Although rare, another option would be to concentrate social expenditure on the most disadvantaged social groups.

The second, more appropriate method of determining child welfare relies on *process indicators* which measure the amount of goods and social services available to children, regardless of the level of input indicators. In this case, it is even safer to assume that a decline in process indicators (health care services actually made available, food actually acquired by the families, etc.) indicates a decline in child welfare.

The third and certainly most accurate class of child welfare indicators consists of *outcome indicators* which measure the actual modifications in child welfare in the areas of nutrition, health, education, etc. These indicators, which are unambiguous in pointing to a deterioration in child status, include the rates of malnutrition, morbidity, infant and child mortality, literacy, etc.

Behavioural indicators include child abandonment and abuse, child delinquency and such indicators as the suicide rate among children and young people. While deterioration of these indicators certainly reflects a loss of child welfare, it is difficult, and at times impossible, to establish a clear relation between such indicators and the economic conditions of the child's household or community, let alone global economic crisis. Indeed, in some cases changes in level reflect behaviour modifications of societal origin which are much more difficult to interpret.

(c) Data limitations in measuring the social effects of recession

Empirical evidence of the effects of recession on children cannot be any stronger than the data-gathering system which attempts to document changes in child welfare. Unfortunately, the work of investigation and policy formulation in this area is very seriously limited by the overall inadequacy of the information available and by the almost complete lack — even in the most advanced countries — of an information system capable of timely reporting on child health and welfare.

Information on input and process indicators is often incomplete. Long delays in availability diminish its value for timely policy-making. Outcome and behavioural indicators are almost universally derived from surveys, the coverage and frequency of which do not always allow prompt reporting on fluctuations in child status. Several of the case studies analysed here explicitly recommend the creation of an advanced warning system on child status, focusing on outcome indicators.

Analysis of the case studies indicates that situations are assessed, inferences made and policies developed on the basis of *fragile, incomplete* and *dated* information. The situation can become even paradoxical. Authorities often deny the aggravation of social conditions because of insufficient official evidence even when social tensions increase and the sporadic reporting that does exist gives ample reason to worry and to act. A major conclusion is therefore that the effects of the international recession or of any major crisis are likely to be *underestimated*, sometimes grossly as in the case of Sub-Saharan Africa, because of the sheer lack of adequate and timely information on the status of the poor, the children and the vulnerable.

3. SELECTIVE EVIDENCE OF THE EFFECTS OF THE RECESSION ON CHILDREN

Evidence about changes in child welfare derived from the case studies (and other sources) is presented here according to the four types of indicators discussed: input, process, outcome and behavioural indicators.

(a) Effects on income and resources for children (input indicators)

— As amply documented in several case studies, *unemployment has been rising*, particularly in the urban-based manufacturing and export-dependent sectors. For the first time since the early 1960s, employment in manufacturing has decreased in absolute terms in developing countries. Agricultural incomes and employment have been far less affected, with the exception of plantation labourers (as in Sri Lanka) and cultivators of cash-crop for export. Indeed, for the poor in most Third World rural areas, the effects of climatic changes seem to be far more important than those of the recession.

— *Real household incomes have been reduced*, often drastically, even in those countries with some type of transfer payment system, by a combination of falling or slowly rising money incomes and inflation. In certain cases (Costa Rica, Zambia) the fall in real incomes over the last few years has almost reached 40%. In Chile, the drop in income per capita over the 1982–83 period is in excess of 30%. Eight out of the 12 countries analysed experienced negative growth rates of income per capita in 1982, compared to only two, four and six in 1979, 1980 and 1981 respectively. More generally, figures provided by the United Nations[2] indicate that out of about 90 developing countries for which information is available, 15 showed negative per capita growth rates of GDP in 1979, 30 in 1980, 42 in 1981 and 51 in 1982. Preliminary estimates for 1983 show that GDP per capita for the developing countries is expected to drop by 3%. Only South and East Asia seem to be exempted from this general decline.

— Although firm evidence could not be collected systematically, there are indications that, in at least some of the case studies analysed (e.g. Chile, United States), the *fall in real incomes has been more severe for the poorer social groups*. Altimir's paper shows that in the case of Panama, Venezuela, Costa Rica, Chile and Colombia, the strata at the bottom of the social pyramid have been hit harshly whenever the recession has been severe. In these countries, however, a sizable proportion of lower-middle-class households has also been hit. As the poorer families tend to have larger numbers of children, falls in their income are particularly detrimental for children. Even in countries where overall poverty has declined (Colombia, Panama and the rural areas of Los Andes in Venezuela) due to modest but sustained economic growth, the situation among households with large numbers of children has worsened. This suggests that these households may constitute a particularly 'hard core' of poverty, whose situation may be more difficult to alleviate than other types of households.

– Fragmentary indications (United States and the Philippines) suggest a deterioration in income distribution. However, for the five Latin American countries mentioned above, the distribution of income appears to have remained stable through the recessionary period.

– However, even in the absence of income redistribution, the decline of total household incomes documented above implies an *increase in absolute poverty*. In Chile and Costa Rica, countries which have recently faced serious economic disruptions, the proportion of absolute poor has increased in only two years (1980–82) from 12 to 16% in the former and from 17 to 29% in the latter. Similar trends were observed in Caracas, while the number of people and children living below the poverty line shows an upward trend in the United States (beginning in 1975 but particularly since 1981) and in the Philippines (since 1981). Conversely, a stable income distribution and a modest but positive economic performance reduced the incidence of poverty in Colombia and Panama.

– Within a context of declining overall real government expenditure *the share of social expenditure out of the total is shrinking* in at least nine of the 12 cases analysed. Social expenditure in 1982 in Chile, for instance, was 8% less than in 1974 in real terms. The comparison is even less favourable if carried out in per capita terms (for Chile as well as Brazil). Even in some countries striving to protect the poor, social expenditure on basic needs declined (e.g. in Tanzania, from 26 to 18% of the total in only a few years). In certain cases (United States), there are indications that the recent

cuts are far deeper than those of the 1974–75 recession.

– Within the social sector, certain priorities seem to prevail in cutting expenditure, hitting first, new services (which very often are those directed to children); second, capital expenditure; third, current inputs (drugs, kerosene, teaching aids, etc.); and fourth, current salaries and other forms of remuneration. This results first in *stopping the expansion of new services* and then in a *drop in the quality of existing services*. Cutting current inputs (drugs, etc.) before salaries puts the burden of adjustment on the consumer rather than on the producer of the public service, often compounding inefficiencies and cost ineffectiveness.

– *Cuts in education* (Tanzania and others) *and food subsidies* (United States, Sri Lanka, Zambia) *seem to precede those in health services*. In general, since the mid-1970s, educational expenditures have shown a downward trend as a proportion of total public expenditure and GNP. As UNESCO has pointed out, between 1970 and 1977–78 the proportion of total public budgets allocated to education in the developing countries declined on average from 16 to 15%. Information for recent years is unavailable, but sample figures indicate a continuation of the downward trend.

In conclusion, judging on the basis of input indicators, the deterioration in child welfare appears widespread, unambiguous and, in some cases, extremely severe. The situation would have been worse but for increases in world food production and low international prices which prevented a recurrence of the 1974–75 situation when the slump in the world economy was accompanied by a world food shortage and high international food prices.

(b) *The impact on the availability of services (process indicators)*

– The picture is complex. Certain countries have been affected by an *absolute decline in the amount of services offered*. In the United States, the overall public health staff for child care, outreach and difficult follow-up cases has dropped while prenatal care services for women declined substantially over the last two years. In Northern Zambia, the number of child clinics declined in the second half of the 1970s; in Chile availability of housing, potable water, electricity, sanitation and sewerage services in low-income areas has rapidly diminished, while admission to primary education dropped by 11% and the number of school lunches for children aged 6–14 has been curtailed.

— In certain countries (Sri Lanka, Italy, United States, Chile) the availability of services has been implicitly reduced by the *introduction of fees* for previously free services (most frequently health services, but also schools) or by *cuts in subsidies on basic need items* (food and kerosene) to increase their market price and reduce their availability to poorer people.

— In a third group of countries, social expenditure cuts have•resulted in a *qualitative rather than quantitative decline in services*. Enrolment ratios have continued to go up (Tanzania) but so have teacher/pupil ratios. Deterioration in the quality of education is compounded by the dramatic fall in availability of books, paper, pencils and other teaching materials. Literacy and non-formal education programmes for women are negatively affected in most cases, except where a strong political commitment (Cuba, Tanzania) provides protection. The expansion of pre-school child care programmes, which do not command the political support enjoyed by primary education, has been squeezed by the recession. Where the number of primary health clinics has been maintained or even increased (Tanzania), the supply of drugs, vaccines and other necessary inputs has become extremely irregular, seriously hampering their normal functioning.

One may therefore conclude that a general and widespread *contraction* has occurred in the quality and quantity of child-related services. This is particularly serious for a large number of developing countries where, because of backlogs and high population growth rates, coverage was already only partial. Services which are essential for child survival and development have been cut back when they needed to be substantially accelerated.

(c) *Impact on child survival and welfare (outcome indicators)*

— There are clear indications that where the fall in earnings and/or government cuts has been particularly severe *IMR has shown a clear upward trend*. This was the case for the plantation sector in Sri Lanka between 1979 and 1982 and in the states of Michigan and Alabama, 34

cities and Central and East Harlem in the United States over the 1981–82 period. In all these areas, unemployment has been rising to double-digit figures (in Flint and Pontiac counties, Michigan, for instance, reaching 26 and 33%, respectively), real wages have been dropping sharply and government services have been severely curtailed. These data confirm the findings of Sri Lanka, Costa Rica, Brazil, Bangladesh, India, the United States, and others presented in the survey of literature as well as the results of a recent paper on the Kosi region in Bihar, where overall and infant mortality, high in any case — infant mortality among the children of labourers is estimated at over 300 per 1000 — seem to have risen between 1970 and 1980, particularly among girls.[3] Moreover, lack of recent reliable data prevents the substantiation of anticipated increases in infant mortality rates in several parts of Africa and Latin America (Bolivia and Peru).

— In spite of these setbacks, it appears that IMR (and some other child welfare indicators) continue to show signs of improvement in most cases analysed (even in the presence of moderate recession). In a number of these cases, however, the *decline in infant mortality rate seems to have been slower than it would have been in the absence of recession*. For Italy, a recent econometric study shows that although the infant mortality rate decline up to 1980 was quite respectable, the rapid rise in unemployment over the last two years may have produced a statistically significant slowdown in its rate of decline. Similar phenomena are observed in Brazil and Costa Rica, where it is feared that the downward infant mortality trend may be shortly reversed (and in rural India, where infant mortality rate has stagnated over the last 10 years).

— Even in countries where the infant mortality rate has continued to decline, there has been a *deterioration in nutrition indicators*. In Costa Rica, the number of children treated for severe malnutrition has doubled over the last three years, and in Brazil the decline in infant mortality rate has been accompanied by an increasing share of infant deaths due to malnutrition, possibly suggesting a deterioration in the children's nutritional status. In the United States and Brazil the incidence of low birth weight babies has increased. A marked increase in wasting is found in Sri Lanka between 1975–76 and 1980–82, perhaps as a result of the cuts in food subsidies. Stunting among poor children appears to be on the increase over the last few years in the United States while height for age declined for all four age groups of children in some of Zambia's poorer northern regions.

— *Stagnant or deteriorating health conditions* are also found in a number of countries despite sometimes notable declines in mortality. Situations as different as those of Brazil, Sri Lanka and Kerala State (India) continue to be characterized by a high incidence of morbidity in general or of infectious diseases in particular. In Chile, typhoid fever and hepatitis are on the increase, possibly because of cuts in government expenditure on drinking water and environmental sanitation. In the United States, the general deterioration in health status among low-income groups has been accompanied by a resurgence in tuberculosis (an illness associated with poor environment). Even in the area of education, one finds some forms of deterioration such as a decline in the rate of achievement recorded in the State of São Paulo.

In sum, the resulting picture shows that where the recession has been particularly severe, the deterioration in child welfare is reflected by such extreme indicators as infant and child mortality rates. This is all the more true for the very poor countries of Africa and Asia. In most of the other countries analysed, while infant mortality has continued to decline — although at reduced rates — indicators of health and nutritional status and school achievement have started to show consistent deteriorations. The latter should be seen as *warning signals* of a far deeper crisis which may well result — with some time-lags and unless countervailing measures are taken — in significant increases in infant and child mortality. Only in South Korea and Cuba — countries that have deliberately implemented policies to protect children and the poor even in times of relative economic adversity — have the broad trends towards improvement in child welfare continued almost unaffected. They have also been less affected by recession.

(d) *Other effects (behavioural indicators)*

— There are indications of *increasing child labour* in agriculture (India) and in various sectors of the economy (Philippines) with obvious negative effects on their health and education.

— Child abandonment and vagrancy has increased in Costa Rica, while in Brazil *the number of abandoned children has also increased*. In Chile the pressure on women of seeking remunerated employment has meant that young children have increasingly been left to themselves or in their siblings' care.

— *Youth delinquency* has increased sharply in Italy (in 1981 the index was 191 as compared to 100 in 1970), while in the United States the suicide and homicide rate among young nonwhites has increased in recent years.

— Lastly, *the number of female-headed families has increased*. In the United States one notices a sharp increase in the single female-headed families (which have a strikingly lower level of income per capita than two-parent or male-headed households). In São Paulo, the number of female-headed households increased between 1970 and 1977 by 80%.

(e) *A few general relations*

On the basis of the 11 case studies and of the literature reviewed, one can formulate some tentative working hypotheses on the nature of some of the mechanisms and responses operating when a country faces serious economic dislocations. These are essentially three: (i) linkages; (ii) multipliers; and (iii) time-lags.

(i) *Linkages — the nature of the economic mechanisms affecting the welfare of children*
     The main factors affecting children are: *(1) decline in employment, wages, or both, leading to reduced incomes; (2) inflation, particularly for food; (3) cuts in social expenditure; (4) overall deterioration of income distribution.*

With the exception of the non-monetized and non-wage-dependent sectors of the economy (which can be quite large), economic recessions generally provoke loss of employment, lower money or real wages and, as a result, *lower household incomes.* Contrary to the belief of many, household incomes have a very direct influence on child welfare. This is confirmed by several works quoted in the survey of the literature as well as by some of the 11 case studies. Obviously, the decline in household income is much more likely to jeopardize child welfare in poor countries and households where about 80% of the disposable income is spent on food. In these circumstances, a loss of employment or lower wages mean — in the absence of transfer payments or income maintenance programmes — lower food intake (possibly more so for children, the females in particular), self-exclusion from health, education and all services which charge a fee or demand the expenditure of some money (for transport, etc.) for their utilization.

Inflation, food inflation in particular, is a second major factor having extremely negative effects on child welfare and, in many cases, chances of survival. Indeed, sudden jumps in staple food prices have been observed during most major famines or in the Sri Lanka 1974–75 crisis, when post-neonatal mortality increased by almost 40% following a doubling in bread prices and the halving of rice rations. Increases in food prices can have endogenous origins or, as in the case of Sri Lanka, reflect the reduction of food subsidies. In other cases, this price inflation can be triggered by changes in external conditions. This was certainly the case in Companiganj thana (Bangladesh) in 1974–75 where, despite better than normal harvests, the price of rice and wheat more than doubled because of hoarding and smuggling to neighbouring India or to international markets in the region where higher prices were prevailing. High international prices were due to crop failures in some of the major producers or importers of grains such as the Soviet Union. High food inflation and the terrible ensuing loss of welfare cannot automatically be associated with a decline in food availability or a slowdown of the whole economy. Even in times of famine, decline in food availability has, except in one case, never occurred and is not the cause of high food prices and of the subsequent increase in mortality. Other mechanisms at work should, therefore, be the object of investigation.

Cuts in government expenditure are the third economic factor affecting child welfare during recessionary periods. In most cases analysed, social expenditure declines at a rate faster than overall government spending, reflecting diffused discrimination towards social spending, which is erroneously considered unproductive. The effects of such cuts on child welfare are, perhaps, less immediate than in the case of declines in incomes or food inflation. In many developing countries, because access to public social services is limited to a relatively small proportion of the population, their retrenchment may not affect masses of people. In addition, cuts are often translated first into a decline in the quality of services rather than in their absolute contraction. In particular, where the tradition of public health is long-established, even a poorly staffed and badly stocked health clinic can have the potential of maintaining the health status of children and of the population. Therefore, the short-term effects of cuts in social spending might be less evident than expected because of the play of stock variables. However, should this trend continue for some years, the long-term loss of welfare would be very large indeed and it would take many years to regain the previous level of well-being.

Deteriorations in income distribution have also been shown to have a negative effect on child welfare. No clear direction of the changes in the shape of income distribution by size in recessionary times can be identified, however. Some of the evidence reveals a certain stability in the income distribution by size in some Latin American countries variously affected by the recession. Fragmentary evidence from other studies appears less conclusive. Modifications in the relative income distribution are normally mediated by changes in income levels, internal terms of trade and prices. These effects have already been discussed and need not be taken up again. But it is worth mentioning that the literature on income distribution in relation to infant mortality[4] points to the enormous gains that can be obtained — even in recessionary periods — by a gradual improvement of the income distribution by size, or, conversely, to the huge losses of welfare ensuing from a highly skewed distribution of income.

(ii) *Multipliers*

Even a relatively modest drop in GNP or other economic changes in the industrialized countries can have forbidding consequences for large groups of poor people and their children in trade- and financially-dependent developing countries. This amplification of negative effects is a result of several 'multipliers'.

— A recent paper[5] suggests that a 1% decline in the rate of growth of GNP of industrialized countries is associated, on average, with a 1.5% decline in the rate of growth of GNP of the developing countries (that is, a multiplier ratio of 1:1.5). For developing countries producing primary commodities, the impact may often be greater. It has been estimated that a 0.3% drop in United States GNP between 1969 and 1970 may have produced a 12% decline in copper prices. For Zambia, a country highly dependent on copper exports, this could result in a decline in GNP of about 3% or a 1:10 multiplier *vis-à-vis* the drop in GNP in the United States.

The impact of the above multiplier becomes much larger after adjusting for: (a) the higher population growth rate in the developing world (2.2% annually, on average, in 1980) as compared to developed countries (0.8%), and (b) the fact that the population of the developing world group is at least three times larger than that of the developed.

At the local level, other multipliers may further amplify these negative effects. It is not uncommon for a 2—3% decline in national income in developing countries to result in a 10—15% decline in the incomes of the poorest classes. In this case, the multiplier ratio is around 1:5.

In terms of child welfare, the disproportionate decline in the income of the poorest families is aggravated by the fact that poorer families generally have a larger than average number of children. The child of a poor family may face, therefore, an additional negative multiplier of the magnitude of, say, 1:1.5. Lastly, within the family, a drop in available resources, including food, may be shared in a way which adversely affects children (particularly girls) because of skewed intra-family food distribution.

If we take into account the combined effect of these multipliers, it is easy to see that for a poor child of a large landless family in a low-income externally dependent country, even a drop of 2 or 3 points in the growth rate of GNP of the industrialized nations may easily result in a deterioration of income of 50% or more. Even this ratio conveys an incomplete picture of the actual impact, however, since the loss of welfare is far greater when a poor rather than a middle-income household loses half of its subsistence income.

Fortunately, not all of the rural or urban poor are in such a dependent situation. The multipliers are not inevitable consequences — nor do all of them operate with the same intensity and in the same direction. *Much depends on social policy priorities and choices.*

(iii) *Time-lags*

There are time-lags between the inception of the economic recession and the point at which deteriorations in child welfare and survival become apparent.

The reasons for these time lags have already been given. The length of the lags varies substantially, depending on the characteristics of the community or country involved. In societies which lack capacity to resist crisis, these lags can be very short. During the 1974—75 Bangladesh famine, the doubling of rice prices was followed by an increase in crude and infant death rates within a period of two to four months.[6,7] The obvious conclusion is that in poor societies with low saving, scarce food stocks and lack of institutional or traditional mechanisms for redistributing or transferring incomes at times of crisis, serious economic dislocations are almost immediately reflected in rising death rates, particularly for children, the oldest and the poorest.

In countries with wider resource margins, these time-lags are longer. For Costa Rica, these time-lags (between externally induced economic crisis and rises in infant mortality) have been estimated to be between one to two years.[8] For the United States, post-neonatal mortality rates have been found to lag three to five years behind economic downturns.[9]

One should note that appropriate policy measures can largely, or even totally, offset the negative impact of the recession, particularly for countries with some resources. The recent aggravation of child status in the United States is certainly policy-induced as much as economy-dependent. Similarly, the policy measures launched recently in Korea to reach the poorest 10% of the population and their children in a year of economic crisis, or the Cuban government's decision to maintain social spending despite a decline in overall budgetary resources, result from precise policy responses.

However, these macro-economic measures, while protecting levels of social expenditure, did not represent any change in the nature of interventions on behalf of children. Indeed, in Cuba this redirection of social expenditure dates from the 1960s, while in Korea efforts were concentrated on *extending* service coverage. More generally, there was no evidence in the countries examined of the restructuring of public spending towards cost-effective, high-priority action which can protect children even in times of recession and cutbacks. A partial exception is perhaps the case of Brazil where a massive immunization campaign launched by the government and carried out largely by volunteers has all but eradicated polio. In addition to immunization, other low-cost measures which can have a major impact on improving child welfare in a relatively short time include breast-feeding, food supplementation, female education, child growth monitoring and use of oral rehydration salts to control diarrhoeal disease. These measures, as clearly illustrated in UNICEF's *State of the World's Children* reports for 1983 and 1984, have been identified as capable of substantially accelerating child survival and development even in periods of declining resource availability.

4. AN OVERALL INTERPRETATION

The above summary clearly reveals that the decline in incomes and resources for children is general, unmistakable and, in certain cases, extremely severe. The decline in quality and quantity of available basic needs goods and social services also appears to be very general although less profound and — as in the case of education — of a more long-term nature. The impact on child survival and welfare seems, on the contrary, more composite. Risk of death for children has increased in those cases where declines in household incomes and cuts in social services have been particularly severe. One does not observe, however, a general worsening of infant and child mortality even in countries experiencing moderate recession. Rather, infant mortality rates and some social indicators have continued to improve — although at much reduced rates. In most countries one observes, however, a serious deterioration in indicators of nutrition, health status and school achievements, and it is quite evident that if this process is not reversed it will lead to more dramatic deteriorations which will then be reflected in a higher rate of infant and child mortality.

How can one explain then this apparent discrepancy between input and process indicators on the one hand, and outcome indicators on the other? Four explanations can be put forward.

— *First*, among the 15 countries[10] analysed in some depth here, six (India, Sri Lanka, South Korea, Cuba, Panama and Colombia) did not experience any major economic downturn during the 1979—82 period. Negative growth rates were experienced only in India in 1979, and Korea in 1980. One would not have expected, therefore, a deterioration in child welfare apart from the influence of structural forces.

— *Second*, as repeatedly mentioned throughout this paper, in most of the countries where economic recession has been — for external or internal reasons — most staggering, there simply is not enough recent information to substantiate widely anticipated losses of welfare and expected increases in child mortality. Zambia, Tanzania and Nigeria, for instance, face radical, prolonged and structural crisis, for which the most recent and limited infor-

mation about child welfare dates to the late 1970s or to 1980. In these — and other — cases, therefore, it is not possible to document the loss of welfare and lives which is very likely already taking place.

— *Third*, the countries analysed are very different in terms of level of income, openness of economy and types of social adjustment policies implemented during the economic crises. One should not, therefore, expect a totally uniform pattern to emerge. Middle- and higher-income economies, for instance, have an inherent higher capacity to resist crisis which should be reflected in their social indicators. In large, mostly rural and highly insulated economies like India, the effects of the world recession are bound to be felt only marginally if at all. In general, the majority of agricultural and rural populations in the Third World are more subject to changes in domestic policies and weather conditions than to fluctuations of the international economy.

— *Fourth and perhaps foremost*, the evidence strongly suggests the existence of time-lags between the deterioration of input indicators and that of process and outcome indicators. Among the latter, increases in child mortality seem to be normally preceded by changes in indicators of health status, nutrition, etc.

The existence and length of these time-lags can be explained as follows:

(a) by the willingness of families to draw down their savings and food reserves, and to liquidate their working capital or incur debts rather than reduce food and other essential consumption below critical levels. Similarly, governments typically try to delay cuts in social expenditures, particularly of a politically sensitive nature. Many public sector outlays already in the pipeline cannot easily be reduced.

(b) by the build-up and maintenance, in spite of recession, of centres of health knowledge and social organization and practice (e.g. levels of mothers' education, hygiene customs, traditional health practices, etc.) which help cushion the effects of economic misfortunes. The strength of positive aspects of these circumstances will partially determine the length of the time period during which families can avoid the most serious consequences of recession. Similarly, with regard to governmental institutions, the public sector's capacity to make appropriate adjustments to declining revenues will depend to some extent on past investment in the development of staff capacities and morale, as well as managerial competence and flexibility.

In conclusion, it is realistic to note that a very real deterioration has and is taking place in the lives of children around the world. While the initial worsening has been somewhat slowed — particularly in middle-income countries — by the existence of resources, experience and facilities accumulated in the past, there are strong reasons to believe that the present crisis could turn into a major setback — particularly for the very poor people and countries — in a matter of a few years. The evidence provided by this report should be considered not only indicative of the *deterioration which has already occurred*, but as a *warning signal*. The conditions of children's lives will suffer far greater deterioration within a relatively short time unless action is taken now.

NOTES

1. Among the vast literature on this subject, see Griffin (1977).

2. UN-DIESA unpublished data.

3. Rodgers (1983).

4. Rodgers (1979) and Flegg (1982).

5. Singer (1983).

6. McCord *et al.* (1980).

7. Langsten (1980).

8. Rosero Bixby (1983).

9. Brenner (1973).

10. Besides the 11 national case studies presented separately, information about Costa Rica, Panama, Colombia and Venezuela was contained in the paper by Altimir (pp. 261–282).

REFERENCES

Brenner, M., 'Foetal, infant and maternal mortality during periods of economic instability', *International Journal of Health Services*, Vol. 3, No. 2 (1973).

Flegg, A., 'Inequality of income, illiteracy and medical care as determinants of infant mortality in underdeveloped countries', *Population Studies*, Vol. 36, No. 3 (November 1982).

Griffin, K., 'Increasing poverty and changing ideas about development strategies', *Development and Change*, Vol. 8 (1977).

Langsten, R., 'Causes of changes in vital rates: the case of Bangladesh', Ph.D. dissertation (University of Michigan, 1980).

McCord, C. *et al.*, 'Death rate, land and the price of rice, 1975–78', Evaluation Unit Report No. 4, Companiganj Health Project, Noakhali (Christian Commission for Development in Bangladesh, March 1980).

Rogers, G., 'Income and inequality as determinants of mortality: an international cross-section analysis', *Population Studies*, Vol. 33, No. 2 (July 1979).

Rogers, G., 'Poverty ten years on: incomes and work among the poor of rural Bihar', *Population and Labour Policy Programme*, Working Paper No. 130 (Geneva: ILO, May 1983).

Rosero, Bixby, L., 'Social and economic policies and their effects on mortality: the Costa Rican case', (Paris: IUSSP-INED, 28 February–4 March 1983).